PHILOSOPHY, NEUROSCIENCE AND CONSCIOUSNESS

ALSO BY REX WELSHON AND PUBLISHED BY MQUP

The Philosophy of Nietzsche

PHILOSOPHY, NEUROSCIENCE AND CONSCIOUSNESS

REX WELSHON

McGill-Queen's University Press
Montreal & Kingston • Ithaca

© Rex Welshon 2011

ISBN 978-0-7735-3841-2 (cloth)
ISBN 978-0-7735-3842-9 (paper)

Legal deposit first quarter 2011
Bibliothèque nationale du Québec

Published simultaneously outside North America
by Acumen Publishing Limited

McGill-Queen's University Press acknowledges the financial support of the
Government of Canada through the Canada Book Fund for its activities.

Library and Archives Canada Cataloguing in Publication

Welshon, Rex, 1955-
      Philosophy, neuroscience and consciousness : an introduction / Rex
Welshon.

Includes bibliographical references and index.
ISBN 978-0-7735-3841-2 (bound).--ISBN 978-0-7735-3842-9 (pbk.)

      1. Consciousness. 2. Neurosciences. I. Title.

B105.C477W44 2010   126   C2010-906333-3

Printed in the UK by MPG Books Group.

CONTENTS

PREFACE

In this book, I neither solve the problems of consciousness, nor reduce consciousness to anything, nor discover consciousness in everything. Rather, I *introduce* some of the current neuroscientific proposals about consciousness and *discuss* them from a philosophical point of view.

As impressed as I am by the extraordinary advances made in the past twenty years in the scientific study of consciousness, I am even more impressed by the philosophical and empirical difficulties researchers continue to face trying to make consciousness tractable. It is a peculiar feature of this line of work that virtually every promising empirical and philosophical theory of consciousness faces devastating empirical and philosophical objections. Some other scientific debates also have this feature (one thinks, for example, of Freudian psychology and quantum mechanics), but in the case of consciousness, it is part of the weft and weave of the phenomenon being studied. Consciousness is a most peculiar phenomenon, and our thinking about it inevitably reveals that peculiarity.

Self-assured advocates for this or that view wince at such claims. They patiently point out that the peculiarities of consciousness arise only when this or that assumption is made and that we can live easily without this or that assumption, or that we are hoodwinked by language and are well advised to shed this or that semantic prejudice, or that some branch of science, working alone or in concert with other sciences, will, were we only to turn the job over to them, eliminate the mysteries. I admit that I have never been as confident as some that this approach will work, yet I will not deny that there was a time when I wished that I was. But simple and incontrovertible features of consciousness entail massive peculiarity. However, unlike those who agree that some features of consciousness are strange but who then insist that they should therefore be eliminated, I hold that their strangeness is no reason for elimination. And, unlike those who agree that consciousness is strange but who then insist that it should therefore be studied by disciplines other than scientific ones, I hold that strangeness is no excuse for abandoning the scientific study of consciousness. Rather, the strangeness must be accepted, and the best scientific theories of consciousness will respect it.

This book's argumentative stance is indirectly inspired by what is now probably an obscure source, the Sellars–Chisholm correspondence on intentionality, published fifty years ago in a collection of essays (Chisholm 1957b). In that exchange of letters between the philosophers Roderick Chisholm and Wilfrid Sellars, the reader is treated to a debate about intentionality, the phenomenon that our thoughts and sentences are *about* something else. Chisholm insists throughout, and contrary to Sellars, that intentionality is irreducible to language and is, rather, a symptomatic feature of the mind. I still vacillate about who wins the arguments in these letters, but allow me to report that reading it for the first time when I was a graduate student left an indelible impression. Over years of rereading the letters, what I have come increasingly to admire is the *way* Chisholm and Sellars debate the arguments for the different options: without viciousness but also without any attempt to soft-pedal differences. I hope to borrow the *spirit* (whatever "spirit" might mean) of that debate as I introduce and discuss certain views about consciousness here. I do not doubt that at some point in the future entire regions of current philosophical and empirical debate about consciousness will be assessed with bemusement by others whose knowledge exceeds our own. But I doubt, as does Chisholm, that we will *ever* be able to reduce all the curious features of consciousness to something else.

I would like to acknowledge Ernest Sosa and Jaegwon Kim, who with Chisholm are the most important influences on both the substance of my thoughts about many of the matters discussed in what follows and the manner in which I develop arguments. Although neither will probably agree with much of what is suggested herein, their views continue to inform my own in philosophy of mind, and their examples as philosophers confirm my conviction that, regardless of intellectual disagreement, a life of the mind can be a generous and convivial one. I also thank Steve Hales and Chris Shields for their friendship over the years and for their philosophical acumen. In addition, I thank my colleagues in the University of Colorado at Colorado Springs (UCCS) Departments of Philosophy and Psychology for discussion and the UCCS College of Letters, Arts, and Sciences Dean's Office for a congenial working environment. I thank Tunde Bewaji in the Philosophy Division of the Department of Language, Linguistics, and Philosophy at the University of the West Indies, Mona, for hosting me and my family during academic year 2008–9, where I completed the first draft of this book. I also thank the two Acumen reviewers for criticism of that draft. I thank Steven Gerrard, my editor at Acumen, for his patience. I thank Nancy Wells-Georgia for the appendix drawings and Leee Overmann for copyediting the manuscript. Finally, I thank my wife, Perrin, and our two children, Anna and Calvin, for putting up with me while I wrote this book.

INTRODUCTION

Every generation of scholars is prone to believing that it is the first to finally see things clearly. This is true also for the study of consciousness. However, Sigmund Freud and Gottfried Leibniz identified two of the fundamental problems posed by attempts to reduce consciousness to the goings-on inside the cranium, the first a hundred years ago, the second three hundred years ago. Freud states the first problem in his *Outline to Psychoanalysis*:

> We know two kinds of things about what we call our psyche (or mental life): firstly, its bodily organ and scene of action, the brain (or nervous system) and, on the other hand, our acts of consciousness, which are immediate data and cannot be further explained by any sort of description. Everything that lies in between is unknown to us, and the data do not include any direct relation between these two terminal points of our knowledge. If it existed, it would at the most afford an exact localization of the processes of consciousness and would give us no help towards understanding it.
>
> (Freud 1938: Preface)

This puts the *explanatory gap problem* of consciousness succinctly: we know we are conscious, but even if we were to know that conscious events occur in the brain, indeed in particular processes precisely localized within a region of the brain, we still would not understand *how* those processes generate those conscious features (Levine 1983). After all, what happens in cortical neural assemblies is electrochemical, but the qualitative richness, subjective perspectivity, and unified nature of conscious events appear on all counts not to be electrical or chemical but something else altogether.

Leibniz states another fundamental problem posed by any attempt to physically reduce consciousness, whether to the brain or to something else. In his *Monadology* Section 17, he entertains the following thought experiment. He asks us to imagine:

1

a machine whose construction would enable it to think, to sense, and to have perception, one could conceive it enlarged while retaining the same proportions, so that one could enter into it, just like into a windmill. Supposing this, one should, when visiting within it, find only parts pushing one another, and never anything by which to explain a perception. Thus it is in the simple substance, and not in the composite or in the machine, that one must look for perception.

(Leibniz [1714] 2005: §17)

This is a blueprint for the *hard problem* of consciousness: not only would localizing conscious events to the brain not close the explanatory gap, we do not have any idea how a collection of electrochemical processes *could possibly* generate consciousness (Chalmers 1995, 1996). Since electrochemical neural processes elsewhere in the body – in the peripheral nervous system, for instance – are not conscious, that the electrochemical neural processes in the brain are conscious appears to be a miracle.

The hard problem of consciousness and the explanatory gap problem present stark challenges to anyone who thinks that consciousness is easy to explain by identifying particular neural processes and correlating their activity with the instantiation of conscious properties, for both problems prompt worries about the apparent epistemological distance between the world of electricity, chemistry and physics and the world of conscious experience and about the apparent difference in kind between the two domains. The project of explaining conscious properties as natural and neural properties is committed to closing that distance and defusing that difference. The first step in this undertaking is to recognize that the hard problem of consciousness and the explanatory problem of consciousness are distinct. The explanatory gap problem asks: given that the brain's activity results in consciousness, how *does* it generate consciousness? The hard problem of consciousness poses a different question: since none of the brain's activity is any different from the workings of a windmill, how *can* it generate consciousness? Thus, the explanatory gap problem challenges anyone who looks in the brain for answers to questions about the nature of consciousness to be mindful of the apparent distance between what seems obvious to us in reflecting about consciousness and what neuroscience says goes on inside our cranium; the hard problem rejects the merits of any answer found by doing so.

To these two sceptical challenges, a third is often added. The *ontological problem* of consciousness is stated simply: just what *is* consciousness? On one end of the spectrum of answers are those that make consciousness a unique property of the soul and a gift from God. But that answer tells us how we *get* consciousness, not what it *is*. It would be better to say that consciousness is spirit. If so, what then is *spirit*? Presumably, it is a kind of non-physical element that humans, and perhaps other organisms as well, somehow possess. Without a healthy serving of miracles, this looks unpromising. On the opposite end of the spectrum are those who deny consciousness's existence outright and argue that it is, to borrow Ryle's phrase, nothing more than a ghost in the machine (Ryle 1949). Between spirits and ghosts there is a tangle of views – theories, proposals, hypotheses, research programmes, speculations, gut feelings and guesses – that neither pump consciousness up into a non-spatial emanation nor take all the air out of it. This is the territory explored in this book, those views of consciousness that acknowledge its existence yet reject its supernatural origins. According to this kind of naturalism about consciousness, it is a real, albeit peculiar, natural phenomenon.

Thus circumscribing investigation into consciousness to views consistent with naturalism (broadly conceived) still leaves a huge and motley assortment, ranging from those that attribute consciousness to molecular structures and their quantum mechanical properties (Hameroff 2006) to those that make of it a social or linguistic phenomenon (McCrone 1994). Again, we spend our time in theoretical territory lying between these two extremes. Not every puff of physical existence is conscious and not only language-competent organisms are conscious. Conscious events occur only given a fairly advanced brain structure, but language is not necessary for their occurrence. Thus, both panpsychism – the view that conscious events occur everywhere – and linguistic reductionism – the view that conscious events occur only in language-competent organisms – are, we shall assume, false. That still leaves a number of views all of roughly equal complexity, some of greater plausibility than others. In this conceptual region are views that provide neural correlates for conscious events and identify conscious events with those correlates, views that provide neural correlates but refrain from identifying conscious events with them, views that reject neural correlates but accept that conscious events are localized within the physical contours of a functioning organism, and views that reject neural correlates and reject localization but accept that conscious events occur in a functioning organism acting in an environment.

The view that has garnered the most attention in the past twenty years is, without question, that according to which there are *neural correlates* of consciousness (Crick & Koch 1990; Koch 2004). These "NCCs" are the focus of an impressive amount of scientific and philosophical work. We take this work seriously. Some of it is offered as direct evidence for straight-up identification of conscious events and properties with neural activity, either activity in individual neurons, networks of neurons, functional neural pathways in localized cortical regions, or pathways connecting cortical regions, or pathways connecting subcortical and cortical regions. Other research programmes, while allowing that one or more of these neural correlates exist, suggest instead that conscious events emerge from but are neither reducible to nor identical with any one or even all of them. A significant development in this area, known as externalism, claims that events and objects in the extracranial world are constitutive elements of at least some conscious events. Given that some conscious events are at least

3

in part constituted by events and objects in the extracranial world, it is a non-starter to think that they reduce to anything intracranial, and, hence, anything neural.

For all the work on neural correlates in the past twenty years, at least as much directly relevant neural correlate research does not even mention consciousness. Most cognitive scientists and neuroscientists still avoid the word "consciousness" like the plague. It is unusual to find any mention of it in the vast majority of neuroscience articles, and when mention is made, it is usually in the general discussion section, and then usually in the last paragraph of the article. This reticence has its roots in methodological scruples established for psychological research in the early twentieth century, scruples that are in turn an implication of sceptical arguments about the quality of data gleaned from introspection. The work that respects these strictures – from neurologists, neurophysiologists, neuropsychologists, biopsychologists and cognitive neuroscientists – directs its focus instead to studying particular processes that happen to be conscious. The most relevant of these processes are arousal and tonic alertness; perception (audition, vision, gustation, touch and olfaction); interoception (thirst, hunger, pain, air hunger and others); proprioception (sense of oneself as a being in space and time); affection (fear, disgust, love, depression and others); and cognition (attention, working memory, phasic alertness, executive functions, reasoning, control, metacognition and others).

Conducting controlled experiments to measure these processes and to identify their cortical locations, scientists have been able, in a manner of speaking, to sneak up on consciousness from behind protective camouflage. Since each of these perceptual, affective, interoceptive and cognitive processes are at the same time conscious processes, the imaging and lesion studies conducted on them also provide indirect and *prima facie* evidence that conscious events and properties have neural correlates. Still, the uneasiness that resulted in the ban on consciousness research for more than seventy years pervades the thinking of many of those who design imaging and lesion experiments. Most neuroscientific and cognitive scientific data and theories continue to rely on experiments whose designs are consistent with the methodological principles that in their initial formulation excluded studying consciousness. So, many of the neuroscientific experiments that focus on cognitive, perceptual, interoceptive and affective phenomena only serendipitously point to their uniquely conscious facets. This state of affairs is changing slowly. As neuroimaging and microlesion techniques improve and studies become more closely focused, and as the tasks measured in such studies become specified with greater care, resistance to talking about consciousness has begun to fade. There are now several hundred academic neuroscientists, neuropsychologists and cognitive scientists who talk directly about conscious events and properties and their neural bases.

If scientists have only recently started talking seriously about consciousness, philosophers have rarely *stopped* talking about it over the past two thousand years. Many philosophers in the Western tradition prior to the twentieth century had something to say about the vexing questions that the nature of the conscious mind provokes, and what they had to say exposes numerous difficulties with the topic. But, since it is philosophers who started and, by and large, then sustained the discussion of consciousness for most of the past two thousand years, the levels of abstractness and disagreement are high, for philosophers are by the argumentative nature of their discipline condemned to disagree. This disputatious precocity has its benefits, one of them being that anything that can withstand the onslaught of philosophical argumentation and remain standing is thereby strengthened. Such occurrences, while uncommon, are not unknown, and some of the most deeply entrenched philosophical claims cluster around the nature of consciousness. These claims – the result of centuries of refining argument and counterargument – cannot be easily dismissed by someone seriously interested in the nature of consciousness.

Of course, not every idiosyncratic hobbyhorse that a philosopher mounts is worthy of discussion. Any crank can announce that the rest of the scientific world labours under the delusions of a mistaken paradigm that only he is astute enough to see, and philosophy has more than its fair share of cranks. The history of the discipline is littered with private languages and idiosyncratic worldspinning, worth reading for occasional insights or a system's internal coherence but disconnected otherwise. *That* kind of philosophizing and *those* kinds of philosophers are not our concern. Our interest lies rather in the small number of philosophical issues that consciousness poses and that have found traction within the sciences of the mind. These issues are the topic of this book. We categorize them as follows. First, there are the unique features of conscious psychological events – intentionality, qualitative character and subjective perspectivity – and certain core philosophical concepts – identity, reduction, emergence and representation – that have to be introduced. These tasks make up the first part of the book. Next, there is the welter of neuroscientific evidence on behalf of reduction of conscious properties to neural properties of brain events. This task makes up the second part of the book. Finally, there are the philosophical issues that the neuroscientific evidence for reduction of conscious properties poses. This task makes up the third part of the book. As will be seen, the challenges to neuroscience of consciousness come from a variety of sources, some from past scientific practice, some from certain philosophical commitments, some from inside contemporary neuroscience itself, and some from outside contemporary neuroscience.

1. CONSCIOUSNESS AND CONSCIOUS PROPERTIES

Our topics are consciousness, its properties, what neuroscience has to say about them, and whether what neuroscience has to say about them is enough to warrant reducing conscious properties and events to neural assemblies, their activities and their properties. A psychological state, process, or event is conscious in the full sense of the term whenever it is intentionally structured, qualitatively endowed and subjectively perspectival or, more pedantically, whenever it has the properties of being intentionally structured, qualitatively endowed and subjectively perspectival. As so understood, a conscious event is complex, for it is a set of properties instantiated by a psychological event, state or process. Since it is a set of properties that are instantiated when a psychological event, state or process is conscious, any such event, state or process that has deficits to one or more of these properties is compromised. Neuroscience confirms the existence of compromised conscious events, states and processes.

In this first chapter, we begin the process of untangling the knots posed by consciousness and its properties by trying to appreciate why intentionality, qualitative character and subjective perspectivity are so confounding, to understand what these properties are, and to clarify some of the ways the terms "conscious", "unconscious" and "subconscious" are used in contemporary neuroscience and philosophy. In subsequent chapters, we discuss in a philosophical environment the nature of various candidate relations between conscious events and their properties, and neural processes and their properties. We then turn to evidence that there are neural correlates of conscious properties. In the final four chapters, that evidence is assessed from a philosophical perspective.

SPECIES OF CONSCIOUSNESS

Investigating scientific and philosophical work on consciousness immediately reveals that "consciousness" picks out not a single phenomenon but rather a whole family of phenomena. Philosophers, cognitive scientists and neuroscientists variously talk about each of the following: awakened arousal; tonic alertness; phenomenal consciousness; access consciousness; peripheral consciousness; higher-order consciousness; reflective consciousness; primary consciousness; monitoring consciousness; self-awareness; self-consciousness; state consciousness; creature consciousness; altered states of consciousness; unconsciousness; non-consciousness; subconsciousness. It is all a little bewildering. Moreover, this list does not even include the conscious processes of greatest interest to neuroscientists, states such as perception, interoception, proprioception, emotion, attention, working memory, cognition and metacognition. We take this opportunity to disentangle some of the kinds of consciousness frequently used and to describe in a little greater detail the kinds to which we will return again and again. We introduce perception, interoception, proprioception, emotion, attention, working memory, cognition and metacognition presently.

Arousal and *tonic alertness* refer to a state of an organism.[1] An organism is aroused when neurochemical activity in its central nervous system is activated to a sufficiently high level that the organism is responsive to stimuli. An organism that is not aroused is asleep or either in a stupor, a deeply unresponsive state interrupted only by applying repeated and forceful stimuli, or in a coma, a deeply unresponsive state that continues uninterrupted despite repeated and forceful stimuli. Coma and stupor are distinct from vegetative state, a superficially similar disorder characterized by preservation of the sleep–waking cycle and the absence of higher-order mental activity. Dream sleep is an interesting state, of course, because while we dream, arousal is dissociated from qualitatively endowed, intentional and perspectival experience: we are not responsive to stimuli but experience dream content. Tonic alertness is a level of neurochemical activation that obtains only if arousal has obtained, contains no specific content, and underwrites the sustenance of a coherent line of experience, thought or action (Filley 2001, 2002). Tonic alertness is intermediate between arousal and phasic attention, the latter of which is an isolable state of augmented alertness in which there is affective and cognitive orientation to, selection of, and concentration upon, some content in the field of experience.

Phenomenal consciousness and *access consciousness* are widely used terms associated with the work of Ned Block (2005, [1995] 2007), a contemporary philosopher. Informally, phenomenal consciousness is qualitatively endowed consciousness. *Qualitatively endowed consciousness* refers to the set of conscious events that have qualitative character, where *qualitative character* refers to any of the myriad ways conscious events are like for the subject. A psychological event, state or process is phenomenally conscious if there is something it is like to have that event. Phenomenal consciousness has been discussed by philosophers for centuries. In psychology, the situation is different. Having made a brief appearance in psychology with James, Wundt and Titchener, phenomenal consciousness quickly slipped into scientific disrepute and has only recently been rehabilitated in neuroscience with the emergence of sophisticated imaging techniques that can identify its neural correlates. *Access consciousness* is the set of conscious psychological events, states and processes that are poised for subsequent cognitive (thinking) and affective (emotional) activity. A psychological event, state or process is access conscious if it can be used for subsequent psychological activity. Block has recently (2007a) dropped both terms, replacing them with the less loaded "phenomenology" and "accessibility". We concur with this decision – in this book, neither "phenomenal consciousness" nor "access consciousness" is used. We instead assume that phenomenology and accessibility are conscious properties. We further assume that phenomenology and accessibility are properties of certain psychological states, events and processes (Burge [2006] 2007). These properties are introduced in greater detail in the next section.

Of the four kinds of states, processes and events described so far, arousal is arguably not properly a kind of consciousness at all, for while it may be required for consciousness, an organism can be, as is the case of someone in persistent vegetative state, aroused but unconscious. Tonic alertness, on the other hand, is arguably close to a baseline conscious state, if not actually a baseline conscious state. Phenomenology and accessibility are conscious properties. The relations between tonic alertness and phenomenology and accessibility are discussed in later chapters.

However one establishes a minimal conscious state, other species of conscious states that do not occur without more basic species also bear introduction. Phenomenally conscious states and the most basic of access conscious states are species of *object-level* or *primary* conscious states; that is, they are kinds of conscious states that occur without the occurrence of any more basic kinds of conscious states and whose occurrence is necessary for other less basic kinds of conscious states. Conscious states that cannot occur without primary conscious states and that are about primary conscious states are species of *secondary* or *reflexive* conscious states (Rees *et al.* 2002; Searle 2000). There are a number of related phenomena in this class, including reflection, monitoring, error detection, error correction, self-reflection and self-consciousness.

Perceptual, interoceptive, proprioceptive, affective and some cognitive events, states and processes that are phenomenally conscious are primary because they occur upon the foundation of subconscious sensory processing but prior to any reflexive conscious events, states or processes (Burge [2006] 2007). I may, for example, experience a rich and subtle palette of colours as the setting sun reflects off a mile-long escarpment of sandstone. That event is an example of a primary conscious event that has both phenomenal and access properties. I may of course direct attention to that event's phenomenological character. I may attend to the last colour seen as the sun sinks below the horizon. That subsequent event is reflexively conscious. In general, accessible events, states and processes are primary when they occur subsequent to subconscious processing but prior to conscious events, states or processes that are about them. Again, some access conscious events, states and processes – the reflexive ones – are about primary conscious events, states or processes. Included in the class of reflexive access conscious events are top-down attention, introspection, self-awareness and executive functions such as cognitive control, monitoring, error correction, metacognition, planning and decision-making. Each of these differs from the next either as to the nature of what it is about or represents or as to the nature of the cognitive or affective interest it brings to bear on what it is about. Thinking about our decision-making process in buying a car is, for instance, distinct from reflecting on our proclivity for being hostile to salesmen, and being angry that we were not chosen for the team is distinct from being angry at ourselves for being angry that we were not chosen for the team.

Creature consciousness and *state consciousness* refer to two distinct ways that "consciousness" functions in natural language. A creature is conscious if at least some of its psychological states are conscious, and if a creature is conscious then at least some of its psychological states are conscious. Any organism that does not have at least some conscious states is an unconscious creature. Some creatures are conscious creatures and some are not. Most people would include at least some mammals distinct from humans in the class of conscious creatures, but most would exclude at least some non-mammalian species from the class of conscious creatures. (A distinct use of the term "creature consciousness" is due to Rosenthal (2002), who uses it to describe a creature that is aroused or tonically alert. We do not follow Rosenthal's usage; see Chapter 4.) Finally, a psychological state, event or process is *sub*conscious whenever it is either unconscious or non-conscious. A psychological state, event or process is *un*conscious whenever it can be but occurrently is not conscious, and it is *non*-conscious whenever it cannot be conscious. The contrast between unconscious and non-conscious events is, thus, a distinction between those psychological states, events and processes that can be but do not happen to be conscious and those that are not, because they cannot be, conscious.

CONSCIOUS PROPERTIES

What makes a conscious event, state or process conscious in one of the above senses is, we shall assume, that the event, state or process instantiates one or more than one conscious property. Among all the properties that have been called conscious properties, a relatively small set has been recognized by philosophers, psychologists, cognitive scientists, neuroscientists and neuropsychologists as both worthy of scientific study and as persistently recalcitrant to such study. They are *subjective perspectivity* and *unity* at a time and over time, *intentionality* and *qualitative* or *phenomenal character*. We assume that any account of consciousness must provide a place for these properties or explain why they are not provided a place.[2]

Qualitative character and phenomenology

The way rum raisin ice cream tastes is something of which we are conscious. So too is the way a baby's head smells, the way Angus Young's guitar sounds in "Back in Black", the way sun-heated granite feels, the way the Caribbean sea looks on a sunny day. These qualitative elements of perceptual experience are what it feels like to perceive (Nagel 1974), and they constitute the *phenomenology* of perceptual experience. But it is not just perceptual experience that is qualitatively endowed. Interoceptive bodily events such as thirst, hunger, dizziness and headache all have qualitative character. So too do emotional events, such as shame, elation, amusement, delight, confusion, being turned on and being turned off. Each of these phenomenological features is a *quale*. A quale is a specific experiential character of a sensation, feeling, interoception or perception, and, perhaps, a cognition. "Qualia" is the plural of "quale".

It is often assumed that qualia are *private*. This is not the uncontroversial claim that my qualia are mine and yours are yours and mine are not yours and yours are not mine. It is, rather, the more provocative claim that no objective test of qualia can ever measure them. It is sometimes assumed that qualia are also *incommunicable* or *ineffable*. If so, large parts of our conversation with one another would make no sense. Moreover, compassion would make no sense. So we reject the ineffability of qualia. Even if there are ineffable features of qualia, their existence need not be an insuperable bar to a neuroscience of qualia (see, among others, Metzinger 2009a). But since qualia are not ineffable, they are not private in the contested sense either. Finally, it is often assumed that qualia reports are *incorrigible* (Dennett 1988, 1991). But there is again no reason to think that they are (see, among others, Block 2007a). Reports about qualia may be the obvious starting point, but it is possible to overrule them if compelling evidence requires it. That qualia are neither private, ineffable nor incorrigible eases many of the methodological concerns that have been thought to attach to them.

Humans are quite peculiarly infatuated with the qualitative dimension of experience. We are, to take but one example, the greatest novelty-seekers ever to walk the planet, a feature exemplified by our fetishized and aestheticized eating and drinking habits. We eat and drink things no mammal species other than rats would dream of putting in their mouths: durian fruit, haggis, mouldy cheese and tofu, giant grubs, scrapple, jelled blood, bug larvae, lamb eyeballs, retsina and seagull wine, to name a few. We uncouple the perceptual pleasures of taste and flavour from hunger and eat and drink things just because they are interesting. These qualitative features, and the higher-level pleasures we take in having such qualitatively rich and novel experience, must, if we are physicalists, also be explained as consequences of the activity of our unique brains.

A whole range of neurological disorders is directly pertinent to the study of qualitative character. Consider three (we discuss many more later). Phantom pain, in which a subject feels pain as if from a limb that has been amputated, is one such relevant disorder. Synaesthesia, in which neural dysfunction results in the phenomenological space for one perceptual modality bleeding into the phenomenological space of another modality, is another relevant disorder. So too is hemispheric neglect, in which an individual's attention to one side of the visual field is compromised due to neural dysfunction. For reasons that will become clear, qualia turn out not to pose as significant a philosophical challenge to neural reduction as has sometimes been thought. Indeed, I will argue that it is time to turn investigation of qualia over to science.

John Locke (1632–1704) introduced to the philosophical community the first description of one of the most persistent philosophical puzzles about qualia, a problem that has come to be known as the *inverted qualia* problem. Here is a statement of it, from his *Essay Concerning Human Understanding*:

> Neither would it carry any Imputation of *Falshood* to our simple *Ideas*, *if* by the different Structure of our Organs, it were so ordered, That *the same Object should produce in several Men's Minds different* Ideas at the same time; *v.g.* if the *Idea*, that a *Violet* produced in one Man's Mind by his Eyes, were the same that a *Marigold* produces in another Man's, and *vice versâ*. For since this could never be known: because one Man's Mind could not pass into another Man's Body, to perceive, what Appearances were produced by those Organs; neither the *Ideas* hereby, nor the Names, would be at all confounded, or any *Falshood* be in either. For all Things, that had the Texture of a *Violet*, producing constantly the *Idea*, which he called *Blue*, and those which had the Texture of a *Marigold*, producing constantly the *Idea*, which he as constantly called *Yellow*, whatever those Appearances were in his Mind; he would be able as regularly to distinguish Things for his Use by those Appearances, and understand, and signify those distinctions, marked by the Names *Blue* and *Yellow*, as if the Appearances, or *Ideas* in his Mind, received from those two Flowers, were exactly the same, with the *Ideas* in other Men's Minds.
> (Locke [1689] 1979: II, xxxii, 15)

So, were one person to experience violets as blue and marigolds as yellow (as most do) and another to experience violets as yellow and marigolds as blue, we would never be able to know that that was so, for both would call violets blue and both would call marigolds yellow. As will be seen, the inverted qualia problem has served as a kind of crucible for creating epistemological trouble for overly ambitious reductionist proposals for consciousness.

Intentionality and representation

Intentionality is the property of being *about* something else. As so described, intentionality characterizes a certain kind of relation between two entities: some something and what that something is about. Paradigmatic intentional events include perception, interoception, belief, knowing, hope, desire, memory and plans. For example, my thought that Utah is beautiful is *about* Utah, and my delight in Anna's accomplishments is *about* Anna and her accomplishments in some way. In comparison, a river flowing, a leaf rustling, a rock turning, or DNA replicating may be *caused* by certain events and may in turn *cause* other events but are not *about* anything else, so they are not intentional events.

The aboutness of intentionality is often unpacked by saying that intentionally structured events *represent* something other than themselves. If all conscious events are intentional events, and if all intentional events represent, then all conscious events represent. Both this conclusion and the arguments for it have proven controversial. First, it is not obvious that all intentional events represent, and, second, some conscious events may have qualitative character without representing anything. Examples of intentional but non-representational events include such behaviours as nest-building practices among birds, gorilla rock-thumping and preening displays found in many species. Examples of non-representational but qualitatively loaded events include some interoceptive events, such as feeling blue and sexual orgasm. Again, even if all conscious events are representational, it may yet be that not all representational events are conscious. But if all intentional events are conscious and all representational events are intentional, then all representational events are conscious. This conclusion is every bit as controversial as the conclusion that all conscious events are representational, for some representational events appear not to be conscious. We routinely attribute representational properties to events and things that are not conscious. Computer states represent the external world, thermostats know when the furnace has to turn on and robots believe that their surrounding environment contains chairs. The nature of intentionality and representation are thus wedge issues for a host of disagreements.

Representationalism has a long history in philosophy. A version of it is arguably already presupposed by the Scholastic category of intentional inexistence, and it is present in the work of Hobbes. But it was Locke again who set the terms of the representational theory of consciousness. Locke used the term "consciousness" to describe the inner perception of what passes in our minds: thoughts, passions, perceptions, hopes, willings, volitions, sensations and feelings. In fact, anything that passes before the mind can be the content of conscious acts. Following Descartes, Locke gave to these conscious contents the name *idea*, one of the most slippery terms in all of philosophy and psychology (Locke [1689] 1979). Shortly after introducing ideas in the *Essay*, he announces that an idea is *any* entity of which we are conscious, including objects of perception. But if what we are conscious of in perception is an idea, then either the objects of perception retreat entirely into the mind or we infer mind-external objects from conscious subjective ideas. The first view is idealism, and idealism is mistaken. The second view is *indirect realism*, and it does not work either. Thomas Reid's (1710–96) criticism of the view perhaps best captures the nub of the problem: if we cannot explain how consciousness is directed to mind-*independent* objects, it is equally inexplicable how consciousness is directed to mind-*dependent* objects. Inserting ideas simply moves the problem inside the head. On the other hand, if the directedness of consciousness on mind-dependent ideas can be explained, then ideas are superfluous, for whatever explanation they license may attach also to consciousness of mind-independent objects (Reid [1785] 2002).

If we want to hold on to the representational view of consciousness, another view is surely needed. Two candidates have been popular. The first, *representative realism*, claims that we are conscious of mind-independent objects by representing them in sensory perception, that these representations are mind-dependent, and that mind-independent objects are accessed by but neither inferred from nor identical to mind-dependent representations. The second, *direct realism*, rejects the claim that what we are conscious of in perception are representations of mind-external objects and affirms instead that what we are conscious of are mind-external objects themselves. Both representative and direct realism are very much alive in contemporary cognitive neuroscience and philosophy of consciousness.

One of the peculiarities of intentional events is that their occurrence does not entail the mind-independent existence of that which they are about. This peculiarity is a defining difference between intentionally structured consciousness and *everything* else in the world. People think of unicorns and of fountains of youth; hope for peace, love and understanding; yearn for some obscure object of desire; believe that the man they see on the beach is not the man with the blue windbreaker they saw earlier even though it is one and the same man; feel pain in a limb that no longer exists; and see things that never existed. Each such thought, hope, yearning, experience and perception can occur even when none of their objects exist outside of conscious experience. These are not just weird possibilities cooked up by perverse philosophers who think too much or the result of neural dysfunction. It is the stuff of everyday life, so much so that it is difficult to uncover it without effort. We take intentionality and its quirks more or less for granted, but finding some feature of *neural* activity that qualifies as the realizer of intentionally structured conscious events is not just hard but, if some arguments are sound, not even possible. According to these arguments, since intentional events are relational events and one of the relata of the event is sometimes external to the brain – as, for instance, when I look at the Henry Mountains – it is a non-starter to look for neural realizers of intentionally structured events. If so, intentionality cannot be reduced to anything in the brain.

Faced with the ineliminability of intentionality and its apparent recalcitrance to neural reduction, some have concluded that the study of consciousness is therefore not a scientific undertaking. Others think what is needed is a science of intentionality, development of which will resolve the problems.

Franz Brentano (1838–1917) is usually credited with reintroducing the thorny issues surrounding intentionality of conscious thought into psychology. The following passage has become canonical:

> Every mental phenomenon is characterized by what the Scholastics of the Middle Ages called the intentional (or mental) inexistence of an object, and what we might call, though not wholly unambiguously, reference to a content, direction towards an object (which is not to be understood here as meaning a thing), or immanent objectivity ... This intentional in-existence is characteristic exclusively of mental phenomena. No physical phenomenon exhibits anything like it. We could, therefore, define mental phenomena by saying that they are those phenomena which contain an object intentionally within themselves. (Brentano [1874] 1995: 88–9)

Brentano uses intentionality to distinguish the psychological from the physical: all psychological events are intentional and no physical events are intentional; so, no psychological events are physical events. Some of the philosophical problems introduced by Brentano's views on intentionality were analysed by Edmund Husserl (1859–1938) and Alexis Meinong (1853–1920). On the one hand, we can follow Husserl and bracket the ontological status of the intentional object altogether and enquire instead after its features *qua* intentional object. But if the intentional object is part of the mental act, then we are locked up inside our own heads and no two people ever think about the same thing. In thinking about Baffin Island, for example, I think of my Baffin Island intentional object and someone else thinks of his Baffin Island intentional object. On the other hand, we can follow Meinong's suggestion that, while conscious belief may by psychological, its intentional object is not psychological. But if I think about something fictional – that Billy Budd eats cereal, for example – then since Billy is the intentional object of my conscious thought and is not psychological, then we must allow for things that are but do not exist. That seems to bloat the world's population beyond credibility, for surely some of what we think *is* only inside our cranium. But if not everything we think of is intracranial and not everything we think of is extracranial, a univocal characterization of intentionality is threatened.

Subjective perspectivity and unity

Humans are conscious subjects; atoms, molecules and cells are not. Chimps, gorillas and orangutans are likewise obvious candidates for mammals that experience from a subjective perspective. What about dogs, cats, cows, lions, muskrats, gerbils, mice, rats and birds? What about salamanders, snakes, fish, frogs? Spiders, ants and beetles? Molluscs and slugs? Just as questions about how far down the phylogenetic ladder subjective perspectivity extends may be raised, so too are there questions about how far back in ontogenetic development it extends. Is conscious experience subjectively perspectival at birth? Before birth? Sometime after birth? If the latter, then how much later after birth does it become subjectively perspectival?

Typically, conscious experience is from the subject's perspective. In virtue of being so structured, conscious psychological events are typically perspectival, and the content of conscious experience is unified as owned by some subject. To say that conscious experience is subjective implies that the frame of reference for conscious experience as experienced is spatiotemporally *egocentric* rather than *allocentric*. An egocentric frame of reference locates entities in space and time as in relation to a particular subject; an allocentric frame of reference locates entities in space and time as in relation to one another. Conscious experience is from the perspective of the organism whose conscious experience that conscious experience is. There are, thus, no free-floating fields of conscious experience, nor does conscious experience exist entirely in the public domain.

Conscious experience is not only egocentrically perspectival, it is also unified across a number of dimensions. Of all conscious properties, this unity is arguably the most complex, the most multifaceted, and the most baffling. The simplest species of unity and integration are those that characterize perceptual experience. These species have been studied in neuroscience under the umbrella term *perceptual binding* (Singer 2001; Treisman 1996). For example, conscious perceptual experience of the world is spatially and temporally bound. The coherence of perceptual experience is an accomplishment achieved by ongoing neural activity that processes input from the senses, which senses in turn process input from the stimulus object. Indeed, the job of our sensory-perceptual apparatus is to reconstitute in unified and integrated conscious experience the world of unified and integrated stimulus objects.

Suppose you are cooking bacon in a frying pan one morning. The colour, shape, size and texture of the bacon are bound together to form an integrated experience of a curly, brown strip of bacon in the frying pan. Volume and pitch bind together to form an auditory experience of the bacon sizzling as it cooks. Odour intensity and odour character bind together to form an olfactory experience of the bacon's smell. Vision, sound and odour in turn bind together to form the multimodal perceptual experience of seeing, hearing and smelling bacon in the frying pan. Each of these accomplishments is a kind of perceptual *feature*

15

binding, the process of the separate sensory modalities feeding information forwards for increasingly sophisticated processing. Then, with a little neurological magic, the information from each of the sensory modalities is bound together to form an integrated multimodal perceptual experience.

Feature binding is only a kind of perceptual binding, and perceptual binding is only a kind of experiential binding, and experiential binding is only a kind of conscious unity. An example of non-feature-based perceptual binding is *part binding*, that facet of conscious experience that establishes various spatial groupings. There are individuals whose conscious experience is part *un*bound, who, for example, see the parts of composite objects as spatially independent of one another. They may visually experience a telephone as a scattered collection: the receiver here, the cord there, and the push buttons strewn around like candy. For someone with this disorder, a kind of *agnosia*, the world is visually experienced as composed of objects that have fallen apart all on their own.

An example of non-perceptual experiential binding is *temporal binding*, that facet of conscious experience that establishes sequentiality. Again, some individuals – amnesiacs and *Balint's syndrome* patients – have conscious experience that is temporally *un*bound, either short term or long term (Tonkonogy & Puente 2009). Balint's syndrome patients' visual experience is of a world presented in snapshots. They cannot drive because they experience cars as frozen at a location at a time that suddenly and discontinuously jump to a much closer location a moment later, without having moved through intervening space. More tragic cases of temporally unbound experience are presented by amnesiacs, some of whom live in sequential bubbles of a few minutes, each bubble disconnected from the past and future bubble by a lapse of memory across them. Since temporal binding does not yield easily to analysis in terms of perceptual binding, it is typically thought of as a non-perceptual but experiential species of binding.

Finally, conscious experience is subjectively bound or unified as *my* experiences and not someone else's experiences. There are neurological disorders that appear to compromise this synchronic subjective perspectivity. Individuals with *asomatognosia*, for example, deny that certain of their body parts are their body parts, and those with *somatoparaphrenia* go one step further: they not only deny that certain of their body parts are theirs, they also affirm that those body parts are someone else's (Feinberg *et al.* 2009). Although asomatognosia approaches subjective disunity of conscious experience, it falls short because denying that one of one's body parts is one's body part is consistent with affirming that one's perceptual experience of the body part is one's perceptual experience. Other neurological disorders – such as *autoscopy* (the experience of a duplicate of one's body in extrapersonal space), *heautoscopy* (the experience of two bodies, one real, one autoscopic from a perspective ambiguous between the two), and *out-of-body experience* (the experience of one's body from a distinct, autoscopic perspective) – are less clearly consistent with subjective unity

(Metzinger 2009b). Subjective unity may not be the result only of perceptual binding, and may not be the result of binding at all. There is surprisingly little neuroscientific work in this area, and what work exists is tentative. However, synchronic subjective unity must be explained, and if there are neural bases for every conscious property, there must be some neural basis for it.

Immanuel Kant (1724–1804) is generally conceded to be the philosopher who gave synchronic unity its paradigmatic treatment. It is hard to overemphasize the importance of Kant's influence on subsequent philosophy and psychology, for while his reflections on the mind and consciousness do not form the core of his philosophizing in his *Critique of Pure Reason* ([1797] 1958), they arguably do form the philosophical and methodological core of cognitive science (for defence, see Brook 1996, 2005, 2006; Hanna 2006).

One of the issues Kant takes up is familiar to anyone who has puzzled about the relation between logic and the world: can we be confident that logic maps to the world as we experience it, and if so, why are we justified in being confident? Kant's answer is that we can be confident that logic maps to our experience and our confidence is justified because the categories of logic *must* apply to our experience for us to have experience *at all*. The argument for this claim is contained in a notoriously dense stretch of the *Critique*, and the passages in which Kant discusses the mind and consciousness occur right in the middle of the most difficult part of this stretch, a section entitled "Transcendental Deduction of the Pure Concepts of Understanding". Kant wants to explain how our kind of experience and, in particular, our kind of perceptual experience, occurs. For our kind of perceptual experience, products of the perceptual modalities of sight, hearing, touch, taste and smell are bound (or as he puts it, synthesized) into a unified perceptual experience of a mind-external world of objects standing in various relations to one another. What are the prerequisites for such experience? Kant's explanation is quite contemporary: the mind supplies certain abilities that, when deployed, organize or bind the confusion of sensory input into a unified and coherent perceptual experience.

Kant's analysis of synthesis proceeds on three dimensions: the synthesis of apprehension in intuition, the synthesis of reproduction in the imagination, and the synthesis of recognition in a concept. The synthesis of intuition is affiliated with space and time. Following Aristotle, the Stoics and the Scholastics, the synthesis of reproduction in imagination refers to our ability to put sensory input into the form of images, not to the flights of fancy and desiring we now associate with the term. Sensory input becomes perceptual image *via* the synthesis of reproduction, the activity of bringing together sensory input into a cohesive, unified perceptual image of an object.

The synthesis of recognition in a concept is the third binding activity of the mind and the activity *via* which the unity of consciousness is revealed. Kant claims that while perceptual experience that synthesizes apprehension in intuition and synthesizes reproduction in imagination is a possible kind of perceptual experience, it is not *our* kind of perceptual experience. Our kind of perceptual experience is additionally nuanced. We *recognize* objects because those objects fall under concepts. Our experience is *categorized* along dimensions of quantity (there is one or more than one object), quality (objects are real and have various properties), relation (objects are causally related to one another), and modality (objects are possible, actual or necessary). These dimensions – quantity, quality, relation and modality – are the logical categories of perceptual experience. For example, when we see a red book on the smooth table, it is one item (quantity) that is actual and red (modality and quality), and it is lying on (relation) a smooth and actual table (quality and modality). Since these categories are prerequisite for the kind of perceptual experience we actually have, they are necessary for that experience. Hence, as claimed, we may be confident that logic maps to our experience because its categories are prerequisites of the kind of perceptual experience we enjoy.

All of this synthesizing activity would be of little interest to us were it not for the fact that Kant argued that the activity of the synthesis of recognition in a concept entails certain features of consciousness. This argument highlights a crucial difference between reproduction and recognition: recognition, unlike reproduction, entails memory. Memory in turn entails apperception (consciousness), and apperception in turn is unified at a time and over time. Recognition entails memory because in order for me to recognize some object x as falling under a concept F, I must remember that other objects y and z are similar to x and themselves also fall under the concept F. But memory of this kind is a species of apperception, where by "apperception" we mean with Kant judging according to a rule when applying a concept. So, recognition is an apperceptive act – a conscious act – of bringing objects under concepts.

Having introduced apperception to explain synthesis of recognition in a concept, Kant claimed that apperception must itself be unified. This is the *transcendental unity of apperception*. The argument Kant produces for this claim is monstrous; a simplified version must suffice. On this simplified version, the key claim is that our kind of experience is reliably bound together along two different dimensions: it is unified not just in that which it is about but also in that which has it. Our kind of experience is subject-centred, and subject-centred experience presupposes (entails, requires) for each person that his or her experiences are *his* or *her* experiences. That looks trivial, but it is not. As I look at the red book lying on the table, it is *my* perceptual experience and not someone else's, say Calvin's. Of course, Calvin too can look at the red book lying on the table, and his experience would be *his* experience. Generalizing, I can say that each of my experiences is unified at a time and over time (that is, unified synchronically and diachronically) as *my* experience and as no other's experience. The possibility of always being able to attach "I experience" to my experiences is the transcendental unity of apperception or, alternatively, the transcendental unity of consciousness.

Even if one balks at his transcendental handling of the matter, Kant's analysis of the synchronic unity of consciousness reveals at least three distinct sub-issues: first, synthesizing or binding the outputs of the sensory pathways into a unified perceptual experience of a mind-external world; second, synthesizing or binding the outputs of neural pathways into the unified experience (perceptual or not) of a single subject *at* a time; third, synthesizing or binding the products of neural pathways into the unified experience of a single subject *over* time.

EPISTEMOLOGY, ONTOLOGY, CAUSALITY

The difficulties conscious properties as thus described pose for neuroscience and philosophy can be categorized as follows. First, there are *epistemological* matters associated with our knowledge about these conscious properties and the methods and evidence thought appropriate for gaining such knowledge. Conscious properties also pose *ontological* issues, that is, issues with identifying the *kind* of properties they are or if they are real. Third, conscious properties pose *causal* issues, that is, issues with trying to fit them into the networks of causation that bind natural events.

Epistemological issues

Typically, third-person methods and the evidence resulting from their use are prerequisite for deriving scientific results. However, first-person methods and the evidence resulting from introspection's use have historically enjoyed greater respectability in the scientific study of consciousness than in any other science. Unfortunately this is not the case today, but dismissing first-person evidence with a wave of the hand is not as persuasive in the case of conscious phenomena as it is elsewhere (Nagel 1974).

First-person methods such as introspection were forthrightly accepted throughout the early period of scientific psychology, in the latter half of the nineteenth century. Wilhelm Wundt (1832–1920), the founder of experimental psychology, was a consistent advocate of introspection as a source of evidence about psychological phenomena. Although he acknowledged that conscious phenomena emerged from phenomena studied by other sciences, such as physiology (to which he made important contributions), because they have uniquely subjective features, he insisted that conscious phenomena could not be forced into the objective, third-person mould of those other sciences. Since the domain of psychology was unique, it required a unique method: introspection supplemented by experiment. Wundt was particularly interested in the qualitative features of sensory perception. Wundt and various of his students – among them Edwards Bradford Titchener (1867–1927) – published hundreds of papers on the qualitative features of perceptual experience. Results were meagre. Dimensions of qualitative character were discovered, but quantifying them failed because experiments were unreplicable. Titchener's elaborate attempt to use introspection as an evidentiary base for articulating the structures of consciousness was nothing short of a fiasco. Using the elemental method from chemistry to determine the atomic elements of consciousness and starting with atomic sensations and thoughts, Titchener hoped to identify the way they aggregated to form psychological compounds. But researchers could not agree on the number of basic elements: were there 154 elemental sensations and thoughts? 7,671? 7,672? 44,059? 319? 2? Since evidence was introspective, it was impossible to adjudicate between different proposals.

In trying to quantify qualitative character and isolate its psycho-physiological loci of interaction, the introspectionists inadvertently stumbled on to some of the most difficult epistemological problems posed by studying conscious properties. The experience of magenta, the taste of mint chocolate chip ice cream, the sound of Bach's Sonata for Cello in C Major, and the meaning of a word are paradigmatic conscious events. But at what point, if any, and how, if at all, do wavelength, retinal activity and intracerebral neural firing become the conscious experience of magenta? How does the visual experience of a set of mounds of ink of particular shapes on a page become the meaning of "clairvoyant"? At what point do the vibrations of a bowed cello string become part of the judgement that this particular cello sonata is one of the great achievements of humanity? Early psychology allowed these problems to appear only long enough to confirm that experimental introspectionism was a bad way to solve them.

The hard lessons learned from this episode cleared the ground for behaviourism and effectively postponed most scientific work on conscious properties for more than eighty years. In early stimulus–response (S-R) behaviourism, the domain of psychology shrinks to the set of an organism's observable responses to stimuli, and the science of psychology is restricted to the science of explaining and predicting publicly observable and experimentally confirmable behaviour. Eschewing consciousness was a point of pride for the movement, especially its chief spokesperson, J. B. Watson (1878–1958), for whom conscious thinking was no more than subaudible talking to oneself. Subsequent behaviourists, while remaining wary, at least acknowledged that a psychology that ignores everything that happens intracranially is odd, akin to trying to do physics without studying atoms. Insisting that only what is publicly observable is admissible as evidence made psychology more stringent than other sciences that were progressing by adding unobservable and theoretical postulates. Behaviourism eventually followed suit. Throughout the 1930s, intervening or so-called organismic variables that refer to internal stimuli were added, and S-R behaviourism became S-O-R behaviourism. S-O-R behaviourism postulated the existence of any number of different kinds of phenomena – perceptions, drives, habits, emotions, dispositions – as events which, when added to the stimulus, more accurately predicted responses.

Adding organismic variables did not smuggle anything mysterious or introspectionist back into behaviourism, for behaviourists were careful to *operationalize* them, namely, to define them in publicly observable terms. Thus made respectable, organismic variables permitted a vast increase in behaviourism's theoretical scope, for there was now no reason for excluding internal processes, events, mechanisms and structures, even cognitive and other essentially "psychological" ones. Significant stretches of scientific psychology from the mid-1930s until the mid-1960s were devoted to limning the operationalized limits of our psyches and to isolating the features that could not be operationalized. In the end, operationalized behaviourism simply melted without fanfare into cognitive science, the oddball conscious features left to be discussed at some later time and safely ignored until then.

Cognitive science picked up steam in concert with the computer revolution and functionalism. Both begin with Alan Turing (1912–54). Turing was the British mathematician who in 1937 demonstrated that if a mathematical problem could be solved in a finite number of steps, then it could be solved by a computing machine (Turing 1937). The machine Turing had in mind was one whose functions were specified logically as kinds of computational states and transformations between such states but implemented physically as kinds of machine states and transformations between such states. Although the functions Turing had in mind were mathematical functions, the framework applies to non-mathematical functions as well. Compare photosynthesis. Here too, there is an input (absorbed light) that is fed into a transformation function (the process of photosynthesis) to yield an output (a form of energy). In fact, the notion of a function is so completely general that in the early sixties cognitive scientists and philosophers extended functionalism to psychology and argued that psychological events such as belief, desire and all the rest can also be viewed along the lines of functional states: a conscious event too is the event it is because it has certain inputs, performs certain operations on those inputs and has certain outputs. The belief that snow is white is construed as an internal event that receives information from the environment circuited through the perceptual system; performs certain manipulations on that information; and yields certain outputs, either other psychological events or behaviour. The mind is a vast system of such internal events, each causally connected to others and to different systems of the body, in a coordinated communication and behavioural network (Putnam 1975).

Computational models of human psychological activity dazzled significant segments of scientific psychology and philosophy of mind for most of forty years. As these models became deposited into the bedrock of scientific assumptions about the nature of the mind, a few philosophers started to note deficiencies, in particular deficiencies clustered around the properties of intentionality, qualitative character and subjectivity. Note that the discussion reappeared as a philosophical topic, not as a topic in psychology. It is only in the past fifteen years or so that intentionality, qualitative character and subjectivity have become topics of significant interest again in scientific psychology. One reason above all accounts for their re-emergence: brain imaging. The development of brain imaging technologies, which provide a near-real time look into the brain's activities at a high level of resolution, provides the epistemological access into the workings of consciousness that eluded both introspectionists and behaviourists.

Three tools dominate brain imaging research: electroencephalography, functional magnetic resonance imaging and positron emission tomography. Each is a direct measurement of certain kinds of activity occurring in the brain. Electroencephalography (EEG) measures patterns of electrical currents generated by neural dendrites. EEG tests employ a scalp cap that contains electrodes for measuring and amplifying neural electrical activity, and that activity is then plotted on an electroencephalogram. EEG is particularly useful for measuring different levels of electrical activity, for these levels are reliably correlated with different states or levels of consciousness. Human brain waves range from 0.25 Hertz (Hz) to 70 Hz (where 1 Hz is 1 oscillation per second). *Delta* waves (less than 4 Hz) are characteristic of deep sleep and coma. *Theta* waves (4–8 Hz) are characteristic of emotions, memory and other limbic activity. *Alpha* waves (8–12 Hz) are characteristic of awakened states in occipital and frontal cortex when active processing is not occurring. *Beta* waves (13–30 Hz) are found in frontal and prefrontal cortex when one is alert and actively processing. Finally, *gamma* waves (greater than 30 Hz) are found in prefrontal and parietal association areas when the brain is working hard.

Functional magnetic resonance imaging (fMRI) measures blood flow in the brain. When a particular neuronal group activates, the capillaries surrounding that group dilate to bring more blood and oxygen to the group. Oxygen is carried by haemoglobin, which contains an iron atom. When haemoglobin releases its oxygen in capillaries surrounding active neurons, it becomes deoxyhaemoglobin and its iron atom causes a disturbance in the surrounding magnetic field. Functional MRI measures this disturbance. So, if an individual has an fMRI scan administered before doing something and then has another administered while he is engaged in that activity, the differences in pre- and post-task magnetic disturbances across brain regions identifies the regions with the highest blood flow and, hence, the most neuronal activity. Functional MRI has high spatial resolution, as fine as 1 millimetre, but its temporal resolution is quite low: at best, four scans per second, but more frequently, one scan per second or less.

Positron emission tomography (PET) also measures blood flow to active neural regions but uses a different technique. Positrons are elementary particles with the mass of an electron but opposing electrical charge. When positrons are turned loose in a person's bloodstream, they destroy electrons and release energy in gamma rays, which can in turn be measured. In a PET scan, individuals have a slightly radioactive material injected into their bloodstream or drink a slightly radioactive liquid that enters their bloodstream. Detectors around the skull then measure gamma ray activity in their brains. Those regions with increased blood flow will also be regions with increased gamma ray activity. PET scans have been particularly useful in learning about the behaviour of neurotransmitters, for a particular neurotransmitter can be one of the ingredients of the cocktail introduced to the bloodstream. Its neurochemical activity is then measured. In later chapters, we report on the welter of evidence from studies using these technologies and assess the significance of this evidence for adjudicating the claim that conscious events and properties reduce to properties of neural assemblies.

Ontological issues

Issues with identifying the *kind* of property conscious properties are, or if they are really properties at all, are also plentiful. Of all the phenomena science studies, conscious properties are the most ubiquitous phenomena to have so successfully resisted explanation in terms of something physical. Ambitious proposal after ambitious proposal for explaining consciousness has come to grief over ignoring one or another of these peculiar properties. Most of this book is devoted to detailing neuroscience's attempts to come to grips with these peculiarities, so introducing those attempts here is misplaced. However, it is appropriate to identify five general ways of confronting the ontological issues posed by consciousness: substance dualism, idealism, reductive physicalism, non-reductive physicalism and eliminativism.

Idealism claims that everything is an idea. When conjoined with certain other assumptions about the nature of ideas and the things that have them, idealism becomes *panpsychism*, the view that everything is conscious. I have to admit that I find idealism and panpsychism so incredible as not to be amenable to counterargument. We do not consider either any further.[3]

Substance dualism claims that consciousness exists, that it cannot be reduced to another kind of stuff, including physical stuff, and that it is a fundamental kind. This alternative is not discussed in any great detail herein, but we do take the opportunity now to argue against it. Despite being the most popular ontological position about consciousness over the past two thousand years of philosophizing, every argument proposed for substance dualism has been disappointing. Some of the best are those offered by René Descartes (1596–1650). Descartes was convinced that the human body and its behaviour can be explained as a complex physical reflex mechanism that is subject to external stimuli and produces overt behavioural responses. But as far as he may have been prepared to go with mechanistic explanation, he remained confident that human action cannot be so explained, because, unlike behaviour, it is a causal outcome of an act of conscious free will. Eye blinking caused by bright light is mere behaviour, but eye blinking caused by free choice is not. Such mental causes troubled Descartes, and in his *Meditations* ([1641] 1984–91), he ruminated on the will, thought and consciousness. He concluded that thought is a conscious phenomenon and that consciousness is distinct from the brain and all its activities.

In this way of carving up cognitive responsibilities, Descartes followed a long tradition in philosophy, exemplified by, among others, Avicenna (980–1037) and Thomas Aquinas (1225–74). Both also claimed that while the brain is the seat of a great many psychological abilities, such as perception, emotion and even some kinds of thinking, it is not the seat of rational thought and conscious experience. For example, Avicenna's account of perceptual and cognitive experience identifies a common sense that binds sensory information of different modalities into unified perceptions of objects. The common sense is physically located in the first, front, ventricle of the brain. Towards the rear of the front ventricle lies the imagination, where representational perceptual images are stored for short periods and combined by the common sense, sometimes in the absence of ongoing sensory input. These iconic perceptual images are retrieved when needed by the cogitative faculty. The cogitative faculty is located in the brain's middle ventricle and combines images in various ways. Avicenna claimed that animals and humans both have a cogitative faculty, although in humans alone is it connected to the rational soul. The estimative faculty, also located in the middle ventricle, enables animals to gauge the significance of perceptual images (birds and monkeys, for example, know that shadows of particular shape signal dangerous predators) and humans to engage in strategic planning. Long-term memory, populated by information originally composed by the cogitative and estimative faculties, is located in the third ventricle. Unlike the imagination's short-term store, memory houses information laden with significance and emotional saliency. Finally, the rational soul is composed of reasoning and logic and the will. It was thought by Avicenna to be immaterial but manages somehow to communicate with the middle ventricle's cogitative faculty.

Aquinas adopted a view similar to Avicenna's, and Descartes adopted a view similar to Aquinas's. But Descartes also introduced a number of influential philosophical arguments for the conclusion that mind and body are distinct. Two in particular have been influential. The first is the argument from doubt, a variant on Avicenna's *flying man argument*. Assume a person suspended in air and otherwise deprived of sensory input. Such a person, while unaware of her body, is nevertheless a conscious subject of thought. Hence, she may conclude that her conscious soul is distinct from her body. Similarly, Descartes argued that while I cannot doubt that I am a conscious thing, I can doubt that I am a physical thing. Since indubitability is a criterion of a property being essential, consciousness is essential to me and being physical is not essential to me. And since being conscious is a contrary essence to being physical and nothing can have contrary essences, it follows that I am a conscious thing and not a physical thing.

The argument fails. First, epistemological properties – properties about what one knows or does not know – are not essential properties. Second, assuming that being conscious is contrary to being physical begs the question. These are contrary properties only if no conscious things are physical things. But *that* claim, namely, that no conscious thing is a physical thing, is the argument's conclusion and cannot be assumed as one of its premises. Descartes's second argument is similar. He claimed that an entity cannot have a property and that property's contrary. But, he continued, my body is divisible and has parts and my consciousness is indivisible and has no parts. Being divisible and composed of parts is contrary to being indivisible and being composed of no parts. So, I am a conscious substance and not a physical substance. Again, this is not a compelling argument. The past three hundred years of psychology, philosophy and neuroscience suggest instead that the brain *is* a conscious physical substance.

Most philosophers and scientists concluded long ago that separating consciousness from the brain is a calamity, for having separated the two it is difficult to see how to put them back together. Descartes's own solution was unconvincing. Following the collapse of the ventricular theory of cognitive localization in the sixteenth century, a number of proposals were floated. The most prescient was Thomas Willis's (1621–75) cortical model, presented in his *Cerebri anatome*, wrong in most details but right in at least locating cognitive activity in cortex. The cortical model was not the only one on the market. Descartes also had a proposal, a hybrid hydraulic–ventricular theory according to which liquids in and between the nerves composing the brain implemented various cognitive and perceptual activities. He claimed that some of these very fine liquids in the pineal gland, a small structure in the midbrain, translate non-spatial conscious thoughts into tiny waves, which then propagate through the ventricles, cause muscular contractions, and thus eventuate in observable physical behaviour. The view was loopy and rejected while Descartes was still alive. One problem is that attributing unique translational capacities to the pineal gland reveals a bit too much. By Descartes's own admission, there has to be some organ in the brain that mediates between the non-spatial realm of conscious thought and the spatial realm of bodily movement. But introducing the pineal gland as that location invariably cultivates the suspicion that it does not translate the non-spatial into the physical but engages in the same kind of work common to other parts of the brain – it is just one more physical component doing physical things.

It is tempting to think that by rejecting the dottier elements of Cartesian dualism we avoid all of the problems Descartes got himself into when he thought about consciousness. Few academic philosophers or scientists actually argue for substance dualism these days; most contemporary substance dualist arguments come from religious and other "spiritual" thinkers who follow Descartes's lead by trying to isolate an essential property of consciousness and asserting that a physical substance cannot have it. The arguments rarely get more sophisticated than Descartes's arguments; most of them are considerably *less* sophisticated. We do not consider them. But even if Descartes was mistaken that the mind is different in kind from the brain, not all of the conscious features he discussed – such as unity – are chimerical or easily explained naturally. Moreover, the vapours from Descartes's arguments continue to infuse non-reductionist arguments.

With neither substance dualism nor substance idealism available as options, the ontological positions left are at least consistent with thinking that everything in our world at least is physical. These views are variants on *physicalism*, the claim that everything is physical. According to the most stringent of such views, *reductive physicalism*, everything is physical and all conscious properties are nothing more than some kind of physical property. Reductive physicalism thus purports both to explain conscious properties and to identify what kind of properties conscious properties are. A variety of reductive alternatives are currently being debated by neuroscientists, cognitive scientists and philosophers of mind, and we shall spend significant portions of later chapters following their trails of implications.

Part of the complexity of the current consciousness debates is a result of concerns raised about the relation of reduction itself. Are the reduced and reducing phenomena events, states, properties, theories, frameworks? Establishing the kinds of phenomena that get reduced and those that do the reducing only exposes other problems. It is, for example, clear that identity of one phenomenon with another is sufficient for reduction of the one to the other, but it is not clear if anything weaker than identity is sufficient for reduction. On the assumption that there *is* something weaker than identity but sufficiently strong for reduction, determining whether conscious properties reduce to a proposed base is still a vexed issue. In part this is because setting the bar for reduction thereby also sets the bar for non-reduction. Set that bar too low and the suspicion will remain that what is unique about conscious properties has been forgotten or ignored; set it too high and conscious properties threaten to remain forever immune from incorporation into a naturalistic framework. Finally, if some conscious properties do *not* reduce to any natural property, the burden of proof shifts to the non-reductionist to defend which of many candidates best characterizes the relation between the domains. As we shall see, that is a perplexing matter.

Reductive physicalism is really a child of the twentieth century. Precursors are few and far between, albeit not entirely absent. David Hartley (1705–57) and Julien Offray de la Mettrie (1709–51) may be the first reductionists about conscious properties in the Western intellectual tradition. Both were eighteenth-century physicians, Hartley in Great Britain, La Mettrie in France and later in

Holland and Berlin. Hartley's *Observations on Man, his Frame, his Duty, and his Expectations* was published in 1749; La Mettrie's *L'Homme machine* in 1750. Philosophical physicalists certainly predated Hartley and La Mettrie. Democritus, Epicurus and the Stoics are the most famous among them. However, Hartley's and La Mettrie's reductionism, unlike that of their predecessors, explicitly included consciousness. Even Pierre Gassendi (1592–1655), a seventeenth-century physicalist, refrained from extending his atomism to consciousness, and Willis, the seventeenth-century neuroanatomist already mentioned, did not explicitly discuss consciousness. Hartley and La Mettrie, however, both claimed that the soul was through and through physical.

What made Hartley's *Observations* remarkable was that it employed a single methodological approach to study the conscious mind: associationism. With John Locke, Hartley claimed that the mind is at birth a blank slate on to which experiences imprint themselves and associate with one another. Hartley also employed the then-recent advances in Newtonian physics in his explanation of association: just as gravity binds physical objects and keeps them from flying around space, so association binds ideas together in our minds. Hartley even extended Newtonian views to the nervous system, developing a theory of Newtonian vibrations to explain nerve and motor behaviour. But he also added something quite extraordinary:

> Since therefore sensations are conveyed to the mind, by the efficiency of corporeal causes ... it seems to me, that the powers of generating ideas, and raising them by association, must also arise from corporeal causes, and consequently admit of an explication from the subtle influences of the small parts of matter on each other, as soon as these are sufficiently understood. (Hartley [1749] 1970: Prop. 11)

This is one of the earliest statements of reductive physicalism about conscious properties. Hartley claims that even our subjective life starts with corporeal events that "generate" and "raise" ideas by the powers that somehow "arise" from these corporeal events.

In *L'Homme machine*, La Mettrie was, if anything, more explicit than Hartley. Here is a fascinating passage:

> To be a machine, to feel, to think, to know how to distinguish good from bad, as well as blue from yellow, in a word, to be born with an intelligence and a sure moral instinct, and to be but an animal, are therefore characters which are no more contradictory, than to be an ape or a parrot and to be able to give oneself pleasure ... I believe that thought is so little incompatible with organized matter, that it seems to be one of its properties on a par with electricity, the faculty of motion, impenetrability, extension, etc. (La Mettrie [1750] 1999)

What is most astonishing is La Mettrie's confidence that thought is on a par with electricity and impenetrability as a property attributable to organized matter. With this, he affirmed that conscious properties are a property of structured matter.[4]

Finally, we introduce *eliminativism*, the view that any conscious property that cannot be explained as a physical property is to be eliminated. Eliminativism purports to explain away such conscious properties as not real at all but outdated folk concepts that have no scientific future. Eliminativism is very much a twentieth-century phenomenon. Gilbert Ryle (1900–1976), a philosopher, went perhaps as far as one can go in debunking consciousness. Ryle claimed in *The Concept of Mind* (1949) that consciousness is a myth. Of course, he was not talking about every use of the word "consciousness", being sanguine about any use of "consciousness" that could be redefined as behaviour, and he ended up calling a fairly small set of conscious features mythical. But against these conscious features, Ryle was relentless. His famous *category mistake argument* against dualism makes the strongest case for their mythical nature. The argument is straightforward. Philosophers routinely infer from the existence of conscious events that there is a non-spatial conscious substance whose events they are. But this, Ryle claimed, is a mistake, on a par with saying that cars jump for joy when they see a gas station. Cars are not the *kind* of things that jump for joy; just so, minds are not the *kind* of things that are conscious. This seems utterly fantastic – how could minds be anything but the kind of things that are conscious? But Ryle was confident that there are no conscious minds: the term "mind" is not a subject of predication at all but a collective name for a set of observable behaviours and unobserved dispositions to behave. Just as there is nothing called "the university" over and above its buildings, students and faculty, so too there is no thing called "the mind" over and above the set of observable behaviours and dispositions to behave. The conscious mind is nothing but a ghost in the machine.[5]

Causal issues

Many of the problems with conscious causation devolve from the mess bequeathed by substance dualism. If substance dualism is true, then causal relations between consciousness and the rest of the body, including its supposed seat, the brain, become completely mysterious. There is nothing inherently wrong with mysteries, but they do cry out for explanation. Unfortunately, the only explanations available to the substance dualist are occasionalism, parallelism and epiphenomenalism, and each is false. Nicholas Malebranche (1638–1715), a contemporary of Descartes, opted for *occasionalism*, the view that God effects causal interaction between consciousness and brain. Each instance of causation between a conscious and a physical event is, on this view, an occasion for God to perform a miracle effecting linkage. Gottfried Leibniz (1646–1715) instead chose *parallelism*, the view that God acts not on each occasion of causation but acts instead to establish all causation in one fell swoop at the beginning of creation. Causation between the conscious and the physical is apparent only, the result of two parallel courses running independently since creation, perfectly mapped onto one another. There is, third, *epiphenomenalism*, according to which consciousness has no causal effects of any kind. The first two views are preposterous outside a theological context and bizarre even within one, and any view of consciousness that embraces epiphenomenalism must be discarded unless no other view is available.

Concerns about conscious causation are prevalent in contemporary discussions of consciousness. Indeed, it is not going too far out on a limb to say that the issues of conscious causation are among the most vexing in contemporary philosophy of neuroscience. We appear to be faced with a stark choice – either allow that conscious events are distinct from neural events or do not allow it. If we do not, then conscious causation folds into the network of causes studied by other sciences but the *prima facie* uniqueness of conscious properties appears threatened with elimination. If we do allow that conscious events are not reducible to physical events, then we can hold on to their uniqueness but must introduce new species of causation. Currently the most popular candidate for this unique kind of causation is *emergent causation*, in which conscious events are taken to emerge from the activity of the neural networks and, having thus emerged, are henceforth taken to downwardly cause events in the networks from which they arose. Unfortunately, downwards causation is rife with conundrums, the most obvious of which is that emergent causes appear to simply duplicate causal work already done by the physical events from which they emerge.

To these epistemological, ontological and causal issues may be added the two overarching issues introduced earlier, namely, the *explanatory gap problem*, most frequently associated with the philosopher Joseph Levine (see Levine 2001), and the *hard problem* of consciousness, regularly associated with the philosopher David Chalmers (see Chalmers 1996). These problems are eventually considered, but only after introducing and discussing other, allegedly easier issues. These allegations are, as will be shown, mistaken. In the next chapter, four crucial relations that philosophers have analysed in detail – identity, supervenience, reduction and emergence – are introduced. In Chapter 3, four standard philosophical arguments – two on behalf of reducing conscious events to neural events and two against reducing conscious events to neural events – are introduced and dismissed as unsound. In Chapter 4, representationalist theories of conscious properties are discussed in some detail. These three chapters supply a philosophical background needed for understanding recent neuroscientific accounts of conscious properties, introduced in Chapters 5–8. We then return to doing philosophy in Chapters 9–12, using these neuroscientific accounts as the trigger for discussing the prospects of reducing conscious properties to neural properties. In Chapter 9, certain methodological and epistemological issues surrounding neuroscientific evidence are discussed. In Chapter 10, the differences between correlates, substrates and realizers are outlined. Using the analysis from Chapter 10, microphysical reduction is rejected and emergent causation defended in Chapter 11. And, in Chapter 12, recent externalist views about neural reduction are assessed. These externalist views, according to which neural reduction (whether microphysical or not) of conscious properties is a non-starter, are among the most provocative criticisms facing neuroscience.

2. IDENTITY, SUPERVENIENCE, REDUCTION AND EMERGENCE

Since neither substance dualism nor idealism are viable, the only option left is some kind of *physicalism*, which claims that physical entities or parts thereof exhaust everything that is concrete, where a physical entity is an entity quantified over by physics (Hellman & Thompson 1975). Yet although every *thing* and every *part* of every thing is physical, disagreement whether every physical thing or part need have only physical *properties* remains. Those who claim that they must are *reductive* physicalists; those who think they need not are *non-reductive* physicalists. For reductive physicalists, conscious properties are reducible to some kind of physical, usually neural, property. For most non-reductive physicalists, conscious properties bear some other relation to physical properties that is weaker than identity but still substantial enough to warrant neuroscientific investigation. For other non-reductive physicalists, conscious properties do not bear any relation substantial enough to warrant neuroscientific investigation.

In this chapter, the ontologist's laboratory is opened, and the options for these relations between physical and other kinds of properties are examined. The ontological lab is an intangible place whose equipment is logic and concepts, a sterile environment largely uncluttered by specific considerations about conscious properties. Each of the relations – identity, reduction and non-reduction, supervenience and emergence – has a unique logico/ontological signature that remains invariant across applications. These signatures are the subject matter of this chapter. Some of the discussions are at a level of abstraction not typically encountered in neuroscience. That abstraction is a good thing, however, for it means that no questions will be begged when results are applied to neuroscience.

IDENTITY

When what appear to be two things are claimed to be one thing, it is not that two things are *similar* to each other or that they are *qualitatively the same* for a particular property. Such qualitative identities are profligate. Any two things – no matter how dissimilar otherwise – share *some* properties, if only the property that they are or are not ten miles from Mexico City. Moreover, sharing even a lot of properties does not yield identity. Roger and I may both be men, over six feet tall, love Bach, like Mozart and dislike Beethoven, eat the same kind of pizza, enjoy road trips and never have been to Tibet. But we are not for all that identical. When we identify two purportedly distinct things, we affirm that what appear to be two things are in fact *one and the same thing* and that they share *all* properties, not that they share some or even most properties.

The identity of indiscernibles and the indiscernibility of identicals

Identity is captured by two claims: (a) if one thing x shares all its properties with another thing y, then what appears to be two things is rather one thing, and (b) if x and y are one thing rather than two things, then they share all properties. This is the *principle of identity*, enunciated first by Leibniz. It can be stated as follows:

(PI)   Necessarily, for all x and for all y, x is identical to y if and only if, for all properties X, x has X if and only if y has X.

This is often translated into the language of logic as follows:

(PI) $\Box(\forall x)(\forall y)[x = y \leftrightarrow (\forall X)(Xx \leftrightarrow Xy)]$

If (PI)'s main biconditional is split up, there is, first, the half that states the *sufficiency* condition of identity:

$(\text{PI})_S$ $\Box(\forall x)(\forall y)[(\forall X)(Xx \leftrightarrow Xy) \rightarrow x = y]$

This is the *identity of indiscernibles*: necessarily, for any things x and y, if x and y share *all* properties, then they are the *same* thing. Second, there is the *necessary* condition of identity:

$(\text{PI})_N$ $\Box(\forall x)(\forall y)[x = y \rightarrow (\forall X)(Xx \leftrightarrow Xy)]$

This is the *indiscernibility of identicals* (often called *Leibniz's law*): necessarily, for any two things x and y, if they are the *same* thing, then they share *all* properties.

The identity of indiscernibles fixes what must be the case if what appear to be two things share all properties: if so, then there is only one thing. But more follows from the identity of indiscernibles, for by contraposition, "if x, then y" is equivalent to "if not-y, then not-x". So by fixing what is sufficient for identity, the identity of indiscernibles fixes what is necessary for distinctness. That is, $(\text{PI})_S$ is equivalent to:

(PI)$_S$* $\Box(\forall x)(\forall y)[\neg(x = y) \rightarrow \neg(\forall X)(Xx \leftrightarrow Xy)]$

(PI)$_S$* says that, necessarily, for any x and y you choose, if x and y are not identical, then they do not share all properties. That is, there is at least one property that x has that y lacks or that y has that x lacks. So, (PI)$_S$* is equivalent to:

(PI)$_S$** $\Box(\forall x)(\forall y)[\neg(x = y) \rightarrow (\exists X)((Xx \wedge \neg Xy) \vee (\neg Xx \wedge Xy)]$

(PI)$_S$** says that, necessarily, for all x and y, if x and y are not identical, then x has some property X that y does not have or y has some property X that x does not have. In English, two things are distinct because one is unlike the other in some way.

The indiscernibility of identicals (Leibniz's law) fixes what must be the case if the identity of two things is claimed. As with the identity of indiscernibles, more follows from Leibniz's law. Again by contraposition, "if not-x, then not-y" is equivalent to "if y, then x". So, by fixing what is necessary for identity, Leibniz's law fixes what is sufficient for distinctness. That is, (PI)$_N$ is equivalent to:

(PI)$_N$* $\Box(\forall x)(\forall y)[\neg(\forall X)(Xx \leftrightarrow Xy) \rightarrow \neg(x = y)]$

(PI)$_N$* says that, necessarily, for all x and y, if x and y do not share all properties, then x and y are not one thing. That is, if there is at least one property that x has but y lacks or one property that y has but x lacks, then x is not identical to y. So (PI)$_N$* is equivalent to:

(PI)$_N$** $\Box(\forall x)(\forall y)[(\exists X)((Xx \wedge \neg Xy) \vee (\neg Xx \wedge Xy)) \rightarrow \neg(x = y)]$

(PI)$_N$** says that, necessarily, for all x and y, if x has some property X that y does not or y has some property X that x does not, then x and y are not the same thing.

The word "necessarily" is a strengthening agent: without it, it is easy to conflate accidentally true generalizations with scientific or causal laws. Suppose someone says, "If the nail jar is in the garage, then it has two hundred and sixty-nine nails in it." That is superficially similar to, "If extrastriate visual cortex projects to superior temporal cortex, then superior temporal cortex is a constituent of the visual pathway." But the first is accidentally true, and from it little follows. On the basis of the second, on the other hand, hypotheses can be derived and predictions founded. Still, as important as it is to distinguish scientific laws from accidentally true generalizations, it is easy to get carried away with necessity. Some philosophers take it for granted that rejecting naturalistic views of consciousness requires showing only that there *might* be beings whose consciousness is subserved by some other completely bizarre physiology or by no physiology whatsoever. Such claims trade on what is and what is not necessary.

Let us be clear: we are interested in some, not all, strengths of necessity. There are at least four strengths of necessity: logical, metaphysical, nomological and physical. A proposition is *logically necessary* if rejecting it violates a law of logic: "$p \lor \neg p$" is logically necessary (in a bivalent system) because its rejection "$\neg(p \lor \neg p)$" is equivalent to "$p \land \neg p$" and "$p \land \neg p$" is always false. A proposition is *metaphysically necessary* whenever rejecting it violates the laws of metaphysical possibility: "carbon is an element" is metaphysically necessary because there is no possible world in which carbon is not an element. A proposition is *nomologically necessary* whenever rejecting it violates a scientific law ("*nomos*" means "law"). For example, "dopaminergic neurons cause excitatory effects" is arguably a nomological necessity. And, finally, a proposition is *physically necessary* whenever rejecting it violates a law of physics. For example, "no particle travels faster than the speed of light" is arguably a physical necessity.

Arguments concerning logical and metaphysical necessity are *not* discussed herein. Nomological and physical necessities are strong enough for our purposes. Hence, an empirical counterexample is sufficient to falsify a proposition claimed to be nomologically necessary. If "dopaminergic neurons have only excitatory effects" is claimed to be a scientific law, then showing that there are dopaminergic neurons that have inhibitory effects is sufficient to falsify the law. Just so, discovering a possible world where conscious events are identical with hydraulic events is not on-point for rejecting a claim that conscious events are identical in us with neural events as a matter of scientific law. There may well be some possible world in which conscious events occur in beings who are just like us except that their brains are made of plasmas rather than neurons. But that possible world is not our actual world.

Excluding logical and, especially, metaphysical necessity from the discussions of identity in this book admittedly runs counter to what many philosophers think they are entitled to include when determining whether two entities, events or properties are really identical. After all, if possible worlds in which plasmas, rocks or fish gills subserve conscious events are excluded from being potential counterexamples to identity claims, then it may appear that the standards of identity are unacceptably low, that is, that things or events or properties are counted identical on such a standard when they should be counted distinct. In short, too much potential philosophical lightning and thunder is lost when the standards of identity require only nomological necessity. However, it is hard enough to show that neural events are even nomologically coextensive with conscious events. Raising the bar to require that they be metaphysically or logically coextensive is just unnecessary overkill.

Property identity

In what follows, we will be investigating properties – conscious properties, bio-logical properties, functional properties, neural properties, computational prop-erties – and we will be investigating whether certain conscious properties are identical with or reducible to any of the others. Unpacking property identity is a matter of considerable disagreement among philosophers and scientists alike. Two approaches are available. First, the law of identity can be redeployed for properties; second, certain requirements can be set for the relations between predicates that express properties.

On the first approach, the principle of identity is adapted to the special case of properties. Recall:

(PI) $\Box(\forall x)(\forall y)[x = y \leftrightarrow (\forall X)(Xx \leftrightarrow Xy)]$

To adapt (PI) to properties, we add second-order properties, that is, properties of properties, symbolizing them by cursive capitals "$\mathcal{X}$" and "$\mathcal{Y}$". The principle of identity for properties thus is:

(PIP) $\Box(\forall X)(\forall Y)[X = Y \leftrightarrow (\forall \mathcal{X})((\mathcal{X})X \leftrightarrow (\mathcal{X})Y)]$

This too is composed of two components, the identity of indiscernible proper-ties and the indiscernibility of identical properties (Leibniz's law), respectively:

$(PIP)_S$ $\Box(\forall X)(\forall Y)[(\forall \mathcal{X})[(\mathcal{X})X \leftrightarrow (\mathcal{X})Y] \rightarrow (X = Y)]$

$(PIP)_N$ $\Box(\forall X)(\forall Y)[(X = Y) \rightarrow (\forall \mathcal{X})((\mathcal{X})X \leftrightarrow (\mathcal{X})Y)]$

So, by $(PIP)_N$ two properties X and Y are distinct if they do not share all second-order properties. That is:

$$\Box(\forall X)(\forall Y)[(\exists \mathcal{X})[((\mathcal{X})X \wedge \neg(\mathcal{X})Y) \vee (\neg(\mathcal{X})X \wedge (\mathcal{X})Y)] \rightarrow \neg(X = Y)]$$

That is, two properties are distinct when one is unlike the other in some way.

Applying Leibniz's law to properties is not as obvious as it is for particulars, for second-order properties, while abundant, are not as familiar as first-order properties. Luckily, we need not detour far into this abstract jungle. If a con-scious property C is claimed to be identical with some neural property N, then C and N must share all second-order properties and, if they do not, then they are not identical. If, for example, it is nomologically possible that a conscious property C is instantiated by entities other than a neural system n, whereas it is *not* nomologically possible that a correlated neural property N is instantiated by entities other than n, then $C \neq N$. Likewise, if it is *not* nomologically possible that C is instantiated by a neural system n and it is nomologically actual that N is instantiated by neural system n, then, again, $C \neq N$.

The other way of looking at property identity is historically more influential, but it is not credible. On this way of thinking about the matter, the expression of properties by predicates of a language serves as a guide to establish property identity. Two predicates "x is F" and "x is G" are *coextensive* whenever the sets of entities that "x is F" and "x is G" pick out have the same members. For example, the predicate "x is a bird that has the ability to fly over trees" and the predicate "x is a bird that has the ability to engage in self-initiating winged movement over trees" are coextensive since they pick out the same set – flying birds. In this case, the predicates are not merely coextensive, they are synonymous, and synonymy-based predicate coextensivity is *sufficient* for property identity, since in such cases there is only one property expressed by distinct but synonymous predicates.

Were it only so clear, property identity would be a snap – all and only those cases of synonymy-based predicate coextensivity would be cases of property identity. So, since the predicate "attending to the sound of the airplane" is not synonymous with "activity in neural pathway n", the conscious property of attending to the rule of *modus ponens* is distinct from the physical property of activity in neural pathway n. Generalizing, identity of conscious properties and any neural correlate is uniformly false, and we can go our separate ways, philosophers over *here*, physiologists and neuroscientists over *there*. But things are not that easy. When a neuroscientist proposes neural activity in a particular neural pathway as a correlate for attention, synonymy of "attending to the sound of the airplane" and "activity in neural pathway α" is not going to be near the top of her concerns. She claims to be making an empirical discovery, not making a comment on word meaning. So, even if predicate synonymy is sufficient for property identity, it is far from necessary. Language may have misled us for a long time and may no longer be trustworthy in some areas. Jettisoning parts of language inconsistent with empirical discoveries is a price that has to be paid.

Suppose instead that not just correlations between certain conscious events or properties and certain neural pathways or their properties can be established but that coextensions between *all* the predicates expressing the correlated conscious and physical events or properties can be set. Then, for example, a predicate expressing a conscious property – say the predicate "attending to the sound of the airplane" – will be coextensive with a predicate expressing a neural property of some pathway, say "activity in neural pathway n". Generalizing, there would be a function that maps *non*-synonymy-based predicate coextensions. But even a complete map of non-synonymy-based coextension would *not* be enough for property identity. If it were, then where the domain is again flying birds, since "having feathers" would be coextensive with "having nostrils" (both pick out the same birds), having feathers would be the same property as having nostrils. This kind of example can be generalized. Since synonymy-based predicate coextension is sufficient but not necessary for property identity and non-synonomy-based coextension is necessary but not sufficient for property identity, arguing from either coextension or synonymy directly to property identity is doomed. So, for purposes of arguments here, we rely on the first approach.

Behind all of the dialectically clever and logically complex philosophical arguments about relations between conscious and neural properties are two straightforward thoughts, respectively fuelled by the identity of indiscernibles $((PI)_S)$ and Leibniz's law $((PI)_N)$: if a conscious property is not a neural phenomenon, then whatever role neural assemblies play in subserving conscious properties, they *cannot* be identical with those assemblies; and if a conscious property is a neural phenomenon, then whatever peculiarities there may be to conscious properties *must* be accounted for as properties of those assemblies. If there is one monkey wrench that can stop an otherwise smoothly running reductionist programme instantly, it is Leibniz's law. A sceptic about neural reduction and neural identity need only identify some conscious property that enough others agree is not identical with or reducible to a property of a neural assembly for the proposal to be in trouble. Defenders of the proposed identity or reduction immediately dismiss the sceptic's challenge as irrelevant or as based on some confusion or false assumption. When that does not work, reductionists have to show either that the conscious property in question really is or is reducible to a property of the neural assembly or that the conscious property is not a real property after all. The same dialectic bedevils the non-reductionist side of the debate. When someone claims, for example, that consciousness emerges from electrochemical activity of neural assemblies but is not the same as or reducible to that activity, a sceptic needs only to raise the spectre of epiphenomenalism to slow emergentists down. Emergentists immediately dismiss the challenge as based on some confusion or false assumption. When that does not work, they have to show either how conscious properties are causally efficacious after all despite their emergence or – what comes to the same thing – that microphysical neural properties are not the only causal powers out there. This back-and-forth is not a waste of time: it is how scientific and philosophical work gets done. And since Socrates, one of the philosopher's roles has been to caution against pretensions to know more than is actually known.

Events, states, types and tokens

When a scientist affirms that endogenous attention is a top-down loop from prefrontal cortical processes to intraparietal cortical processes or when a philosopher affirms that all conscious events are neural events or that all conscious states are functional states, the claims are that certain conscious events, states and processes are identical with or reducible to certain other events, states and processes, or that certain conscious events, states and processes have certain properties. But a properly philosophical question then presents itself: what are these things we are calling *events*, *states* and *processes*? For example, what *is* a state? Put simply, a *state* is a way a thing or particular is: I am a particular, and if I am currently standing up, I am in the state of standing up; a neurotransmitter is a particular, and when a neurotransmitter is released from a synaptic vesicle, that neurotransmitter is in a particular state. More precisely, we may say that a state is the exemplification of a property by a particular at a time. As so conceived, states are the same kind of entity as *events*, which are likewise exemplifications of a property by a particular at a time. So, for example, if a neuron fires at some rate at some time, there is the event of that neuron firing at that rate at that time. *Processes* are organized sets of events or states.

Two other technical terms – "property" and "particular" – were just introduced as well. A *property* is a characteristic of a thing, such as being periwinkle blue, being rectangular, being composed of buttons and a screen, being a visual process, and on and on. (Similarly, a *relation* is a characteristic between two or more things, such as one thing being to the left of another, one thing causing another, one thing being between two other things, and on and on.) We assume that properties are instantiated by things of various sorts and are not *just* predicates satisfied by things of various sorts. That is, we accept realism about many properties and relations and we reject views according to which all properties and relations extend no further than linguistic predicates (such views are *epiphrastic* views of properties). Of course, some predicates and some concepts may not express a property, and some properties may not be expressed by any predicate or concept. Scientific and philosophical theories are not guaranteed to carve nature at its joints, there may be undiscovered properties and relations, and what looks now like a property may turn out to be nothing but a predicate. Finally, a *particular* is a species of the genus of individual, where an individual is an entity that can have properties but is not a property. Since there are *abstract* individuals (e.g. sets), something unique to particulars is still required – the obvious candidate is that a particular is a *concrete* individual having spatiotemporal location.

The most general way of thinking about a *type* is that it is an abstract repeatable; the most general way of thinking about a *token* is that it is a concrete non-repeatable. If types are abstract repeatables, they are non-spatiotemporal and have instances. If so, then a type is a kind of property, but one that is more like its instances – its tokens – than most properties are like their instances. Tokens are distinct *concrete duplicates* of the type. The number of periwinkle blue things is huge and of hugely varying kinds – the sky, eyes, pieces of paper, some flowers, and so on. Such properties are non-specific, and their instances are not duplicate instances. Tokens of the type "written-capital-A" on the other hand, are all recognizably capital As: A **A** 𝒜 A ᴀ **A** (of course, if the type is written capital-A-in-Times-New-Roman, matters are otherwise: none of ᴀ **A**

𝒜 A ʌ **A** is a token of *that* type). Likewise, the type "1982 Mercedes 240D" is tokened by red 1982 240Ds with cloth interiors and yellow 1982 240Ds with leather interiors, but the type "red 1982 Mercedes 204D with cloth interior" is tokened by a smaller set of cars. (We acknowledge, but henceforth ignore, the philosophical distinction between trope and non-trope views of tokens.) Distinguishing between conscious and physical types and tokens is less obvious than distinguishing between letter or 240D types and tokens. Since a conscious event type and a physical event type are both abstract repeatables and since a conscious token event and a physical token event are both concrete non-repeatables, what distinguishes conscious from physical event types is not that one but not the other is a property, and what distinguishes conscious from physical token events is not that one but not the other is a particular. What differentiates conscious event types from physical event types *and* conscious token events from physical token events is the nature of the property instantiated by an event's particular.

SUPERVENIENCE

One implication of identity is that if there is a property of some thing x that cannot be attributed to another thing y, then x and y cannot be the same thing. However, it does not follow from their distinctness that there are no interesting relations between x and y or their properties. Perhaps, then, there is some relation between x and y or their properties weaker than identity but still strong enough to be of neuroscientific interest. This ontological region has been the hunting ground for various reductionists and non-reductionists in philosophy of mind for the past fifty years, and the results of their forays inform contemporary philosophical work on consciousness.

Most parties to the contemporary debates about consciousness agree that to be scientifically respectable, a candidate view of consciousness must satisfy some version of what has come to be called the *isomorphism constraint*, according to which there must be a one-to-one function from conscious properties to neural properties if instantiation of those neural properties is to be a neural substrate of the conscious properties (Chalmers 2000; Haselager *et al.* 2003b; Noë & Thompson 2004a; Revonsuo 2000). A one-to-one function is simply a way to assign all the members of one set to members of another set so that every member of the first set gets assigned to a distinct member of the second set.[1] Several candidate functions are available. Philosophers and neuroscientists who advocate on behalf of one or another of them as a model for the relation between conscious and other properties agree that the isomorphism constraint is a minimum necessary condition for reduction. They may disagree on what kind of physical properties conscious properties map to and they may disagree about what kind of one-to-one function best captures the nature of the relation, but they do not disagree that there must at least be the one-to-one function between conscious properties and something else before much of interest can occur. We share this assumption.[2]

In philosophy, the typical way of putting the isomorphism constraint is to say that reduction requires at a minimum a *nomologically necessary coextension* between families of properties, the to-be-reduced conscious properties and the physical properties to which they are reduced. That is, the predicates expressing the properties from the to-be-reduced family of properties must be true of all and only those entities of which the predicates expressing the properties from the reducing family of properties are true. This way of putting the matter should kindle a memory of the just-rehearsed discussion of property identity. Recall that where properties are expressed by predicates of a language, two predicates are coextensive whenever the sets of entities those predicates pick out have the same members. For example, "being a bird that has the ability to fly over trees" and "being a bird that has the ability to engage in self-initiating winged movement over trees" are coextensive predicates since they pick out the same set – flying birds – and exclude the same set – non-flying birds. The predicates express the same property because they pick out the same set. But recall also that some coextensive predicates are coextensive only by accident. That is why the qualifier "nomologically necessary" is added – only predicates that are coextensive by scientific law are candidate relata of a reduction relation.

Supervenience has been a popular candidate for specifying the parameters of a nomologically necessary predicate coextension. Informally, when one family of properties supervenes on another, there can be no changes in the supervening family without changes in the subvening basal properties (Davidson 1980b). Alternatively, one family of properties supervenes on another family of properties when there can be no discernibility across supervening properties without discernibility across subvening properties. Less informally and more carefully, supervenience is the following: as a matter of nomological necessity, some member of a subvening property family is instantiated whenever some member of the supervening property family is instantiated, and, again by nomological necessity, when anything instantiates that member of the subvening property family, it instantiates that member of the supervening property family. Where "$X_S x$" represents supervening properties and "$Y_B x$" subvening or basal properties, we can state this in the following formula:

$$\Box_N(\forall x)[X_S x \rightarrow (\exists Y_B)(Y_B x \wedge \Box_N(\forall y)(Y_B y \rightarrow X_S y))]$$

This version of supervenience is *strong* supervenience (Kim 1993). Strong supervenience asserts that whenever there is a supervening property instantiated by some event, there will be a subvening basal property also instantiated by that event and that as a matter of scientific law, any other event that has that subvening basal property will also have the supervening property.

Supervenience is a kind of one-to-one covariation from one family of properties to another family of properties, the supervening family and the subvening family. Note that the one-to-one function from supervening to subvening does not imply that there is a one-to-one function from the subvening to the supervening families of properties. In fact members of a subvening family of properties do not map one-to-one to members of supervening families. That there is not a one-to-one function from subvening to supervening is one of the ways that supervenience is distinct from identity. Identity is, as it is put, one-to-one and onto, so it is bidirectional; supervenience is one-to-one but not onto, so it is unidirectional.

Supervenience's unidirectionality is one of the reasons it has been an attractive candidate covariation relation for underwriting reduction claims. After all, reduction too is unidirectional: if one family of properties reduces to another, the latter does not reduce to the former. Occasionally, someone flirts with the idea that merely establishing supervenience between one family of properties and another family is enough to establish that all supervening properties thus reduce to their subvening bases. However, this "thus" is too quick: supervenience is not enough for reduction. Those who think that supervenience is enough for reduction parallel those who think correlation is enough for causation, and, indeed, the similarities between correlation and supervenience are more than skin-deep (Bacon 1986). Both are, for example, reflexive: although property families mentioned in most claims of supervenience are of different orders, this need not be so (Humphreys 1997). Properties supervene on themselves and properties of the same order often supervene on one another. Unlike typical correlations and like causation and reduction, the covariation modelled by supervenience is asymmetric rather than symmetric: for properties X_S and Y_B, it is not the case that if X_S supervenes on Y_B, then Y_B supervenes on X_S; likewise, for events E and F, it is not the case that if E supervenes on F, then F supervenes on E.

All physicalist views of consciousness, except eliminativism, accept supervenience. But some views of consciousness are consistent with supervenience yet not consistent with physicalism. Among such views are occasionalism and parallelism, both of which may affirm that whenever a conscious property is instantiated there is some physical property that is also instantiated and that anything else that instantiates that physical property also instantiates that conscious property. For example, the parallelist admits that the conscious and the physical proceed along their parallel and disconnected tracks. But parallelism is anything but physicalist about consciousness, since it is, after all, a species of dualism. Since supervenience is thus consistent with rejecting physicalism, it is also consistent with rejecting the supervenient's reduction to the subvenient. So, something else is additionally necessary for supervenience to yield reduction.

Even philosophers generally sympathetic with supervenience and with physicalism have debated what that additional something might be (Horgan 1993).

One way of entering into this debate is to consider the following: one might agree that conscious properties supervene on *something* but deny that what conscious properties supervene on is the activity of the neural pathways of the brain. Perhaps some conscious properties supervene on observable behaviour, or on the behavioural interaction between organism and environment, or even on some part of the extracranial environment. Such positions have enjoyed a significant number of philosophical and neuroscientific converts recently. We discuss these views later. Suffice it to say, supervenience is consistent with a wide array of views about the relation between conscious properties and whatever they supervene on. Some of these views are pretty clearly not physicalist in either letter or spirit, and some, while physicalist in letter, lend no support to neuroscience research programmes.

This state of affairs – physicalism without reduction – is one of the attractions of supervenience: it is strong enough to model the covariation of the supervenient by the subvenient but weak enough to safeguard the former from reduction to the latter. Strictly speaking, supervenience is not sufficient for reduction. Here is why. Suppose there is a family of conscious properties C and a family of neural properties N. Then supervenience of C on N guarantees that any time something instantiates a conscious property, it is going to instantiate a neural property and anything else that instantiates that neural property will also instantiate that conscious property, but it does not guarantee that C is nothing but N. Supervenience models a nomological *covariation* between conscious and neural properties of attention, but that is *all* that it models (Burge [1986a] 2007; Kim 1997; however, Kim 2003 expresses an opposing view).

Supervenience models only nomological covariation because it is neutral on causation and determination. Supervenience does not imply that a supervening property *cannot* be a cause, does not imply that a subvening property is the *only* cause, and does not imply that the causal powers of a supervening property are *nothing other* than those of its subvening property pair. Whatever does *that* comes from somewhere else than from supervenience. One might think otherwise because one reads the conditionals in statements of supervenience as expressing causal relations. But the arrows in statements of supervenience are logical arrows of the truth-functional conditional. The right-facing arrow between two terms "p" and "q" ("$p \rightarrow q$") means that the sentence "$p \rightarrow q$" is true whenever both "p" and "q" are true or "p" is false, and it is false otherwise. The term "p" has an effect on the term "q" but only on q's *truth*, not on *whether*, *when*, *why*, or *how* q occurs. The absurdity of taking the arrows to represent causes is exposed by trying to read the statement of supervenience off as such: anything x that instantiates C causes x to instantiate some N and anything y that instantiates N causes y to instantiate C – it does not even make sense.

Moreover, supervenience is asymmetric and reflexive – if x supervenes on y, then it is not the case that y supervenes on x, and x supervenes on itself. Asymmetry makes supervenience look kind of like determination, but its reflexivity entails that it really cannot be. Determination is also asymmetric – if x is determined by y, then it is not the case that y determines x – but it is irreflexive – nothing determines itself. An example makes the point. Consider the determination relation of composition, as when a material object's shape is composed of the shapes of its parts standing in a particular set of structural relations. Composition is a supervenience relation since the properties of the composed object supervene on its composition base properties. But the asymmetric covariance that supervenience describes is not what establishes the ontological primacy that composition models for the subvenient composition base. Rather, determination of a supervenient property by its subvening property pair comes from the causal powers of the supervenient property being no other than those of its subvening property pair. In short, supervenience is necessary but insufficient for reduction: reductionism does not go through without supervenience, but since reduction requires determination and supervenience is not a kind of determination, supervenience does not alone yield reduction (Horgan 1993; Kim 1997). Jaegwon Kim puts the point as follows: supervenience *states* but does not *explain* the problem of the relation between conscious and physical properties (Kim 1999). While necessary for reduction, supervenience just does not get to the crunch issues of, and so is not sufficient for, reduction.

REALIZATION, REDUCTION AND NON-REDUCTION

The holes left by supervenience are patched by a second set of claims that coalesce around the causal powers of supervenient and subvenient properties. If the causal powers of a supervenient property or entity are the same as their subvenient basal property or entity, then the former are realized by and reduce to the latter.

Realization and reduction

If consciousness reduces to something natural – perhaps something biological, and maybe something neural – then it is incumbent to be clear about reduction. An informal statement serves as a jumping-off point: one something reduces to another something when the former is *nothing but* the latter. As stated informally, reduction is a relation between things of some category and things of another category, whether the categories be entities, properties, events, states or processes. Of course, there are other ways for "reduction" to be understood: as a relation between kinds of knowledge or kinds of explanation, or as a relation between kinds of theories (Bickle 1998; Hooker 1981; Nagel [1961] 1979). Of these, only the latter is relevant to us. Some extraordinarily sophisticated work has been accomplished on theoretical reduction, but, reluctantly, we mention it briefly and pass most of it by. For the most part, we limit discussion to reduction understood as a relation between events or properties of events discussed by the sentences that compose theories. (Of course, if all the events or all the properties of the events discussed by one theory T_H reduce to the events or the properties of the events discussed by another theory T_L, then the former theory reduces to the latter.) When it comes to the relations between consciousness and the brain, what is typically implicated in contemporary debates are features of conscious events and their reducibility or irreducibility to neural properties or events.

What, then, is necessary and what is sufficient for reduction? One generally conceded necessary condition is that reduction presupposes physicalism. Physicalism, recall, is the claim that physical entities or parts thereof exhaust everything that is concrete, where a physical entity is an entity quantified over by physics, and being concrete is being a spatiotemporal, non-repeatable particular. Events and objects are paradigmatic concrete entities. Another obvious necessary condition for reduction is that the to-be-reduced entities supervene upon the reducing entities. A third necessary condition is a particular logical profile. Logically, reduction is a one-to-one function from one set to another set that is irreflexive (nothing reduces to itself), asymmetrical (if A reduces to B, then B does not reduce to A) and transitive (if A reduces to B and B reduces to C, then A reduces to C).[3]

The general idea about reduction pursued here is that all the properties from a supervenient property family for which a causal description of that property yields a *realizer* from the subvenient property family causally reduce to that realizer (Kim 1998; Melnyk 2003; Shoemaker 2007). Realization is, in turn, the conjunction of two claims. According to the first, the *functionalization thesis*, an instantiation of a functionalized supervening property is instantiation of a subvening property that satisfies a certain causal profile. According to the second, the *causal inheritance thesis*, if a functionalized supervening property is instantiated at some time in virtue of one of its subvening properties being instantiated at that time, the causal powers of the former are identical to the causal powers of the latter. Where a property with that causal profile is discovered, it is that supervenient's *realizer*, and where a supervenient property has a realizer, the former's causal powers are identical to, and thus sufficient for, the latter's causal powers. The causal powers of a functionalized supervenient property thus reduce to those of its realizer(s) (Kim 1992a; Fodor 1987 offers an antireductionist argument premised on causal powers).

With realization added to the pot, a version of physicalism that captures much of what is at issue in current discussions of the reduction of conscious properties to properties of activity in neural pathways becomes visible. *Reductive physicalism* is the conjunction of physicalism, supervenience and realization to microphysical properties: properties of a particular kind are supervening realized properties, and microphysical properties are subvening realizing properties. To make the claim explicit:

(RP)   Physical events or parts thereof exhaust everything that is concrete and there is a supervenience relation between all families of properties and microphysical properties such that subvening microphysical properties are always the only realizers of supervening properties.

So understood, reductive physicalism provides a clear recipe for determining when a subvening property is the reduction base for a supervening property. A subvening property is a reduction base of a supervening property whenever the subvening microphysical property is the only realizer of the supervening property. A version of (RP) specific to conscious properties can also be readily formulated:

(RPC)   Physical events or parts thereof exhaust everything that is concrete and there is a supervenience relation between all families of conscious properties and microphysical properties such that subvening microphysical properties are always the only realizers of supervening conscious properties.

(RP) and (RPC) have the benefit of at least being recognizably relevant for what's going on in cognitive neuroscience. Moreover, since (RP) and (RPC) lay it down that what is relevant for reduction is only the causal powers of the to-be-reduced and the reducing families of properties, some philosophical objections to reduction – those that invoke other possible worlds or that derive conclusions on the basis of what can be imagined – are ruled irrelevant because they are not tied down causally. Our concerns are not with possible worlds that are not in our nomological neighbourhood or with what can be conceived if what is conceived is not in our nomological neighbourhood. That, no doubt, will rile some philosophers – and perhaps some neuroscientists – and their sense of what is fair game in the hunt for arguments against reduction. Those who routinely unleash objections to reduction that rely on conceivability considerations and nomologically distant possible worlds (two conditions ruled out by (RP) and (RPC)) will be especially irked. To those, we suggest that if a proposed reduction cannot even satisfy (RP) or (RPC), then metaphysical and conceivability objections to reduction are not needed anyway. Put otherwise, if (RPC) is not true of conscious properties in this actual world, who needs some distant possible world to make the point? And if (RPC) is true of conscious properties in this actual world, the conceivability and possible world objections can then be reintroduced.

Given (RPC), stating neural reduction of consciousness falls out directly. Consider a position that we will refer to as *neural reductionism*:

(NR)   Physical events or parts thereof exhaust everything that is concrete and there is a supervenience relation between all families of conscious properties and microphysical properties of neural assembly activity such that subvening microphysical properties of neural assembly activity are the only realizers of supervening conscious properties.

(NR) puts the claim of the neural microphysical reduction of consciousness bluntly. (NR) is not a claim about some of the properties of consciousness or about some of the properties of properties of consciousness – it is the claim that *every* conscious property reduces to some microphysical property of neural assemblies because they inherit every one of their causal powers from microphysical properties of neural assemblies.

Non-reduction

Non-reductive physicalism – more frequently called *non-reductionism* – is the view that reduction will never be complete. In the past thirty years, three strands of non-reductionism, all of which accept supervenience, have been influential. The first – *anomalous monism* – claims that conscious properties and events are not lawful and, as such, are not candidates for natural science. The second – *multiple realizability* functionalism – claims that since functionalized conscious properties are realized in a number of different physical ways, they cannot be identical to any one of the ways in which they are realized. The third – *emergentism* – claims that conscious properties and events emerge from, and therefore do not reduce to, the microphysical properties of neural assemblies that are their subvenient bases.

Although these alternative forms of non-reductionism are discussed in detail later, it is salient to understand non-reduction here in a general setting so that specific versions can be better grasped. Let us begin by stating non-reductionism as explicitly as possible. What follows is a series of claims that narrow down what non-reductionism amounts to, both in the general case and in the specific case of conscious properties. We start with the obvious – non-reductive physicalism rejects reductionism as expressed by (RP). If (RP) is:

(RP)   Physical events or parts thereof exhaust everything that is concrete and there is a supervenience relation between all families of properties and microphysical properties such that subvening microphysical properties are the only realizers of supervening properties.

non-reductive physicalism says, to the contrary:

¬(RP)   Physical events or parts thereof exhaust everything that is concrete and there is *not* a supervenience relation between all families of properties and subvening microphysical properties such that subvening microphysical properties are the only realizers of super-vening properties.

This is a compound claim, a conjunction of physicalism plus a complex claim about the supervenience between all properties and microphysical properties. The most drastic way to be a non-reductionist is, of course, to reject physicalism, that is, to reject the left conjunct. But that alternative is substance dualism, and we are not interested in defending substance dualism. We limit discussion to those kinds of non-reduction that accept physicalism.

The right conjunct concerning supervenience is true under any of the following three conditions:

- reject supervenience + reject causal realization; or
- reject supervenience + accept causal realization; or
- accept supervenience + reject causal realization.

The first option is characteristic of robust conscious property dualisms that affirm the distinctness and causal potency of conscious properties. Property dualisms consistent with the second option maintain the distinctness of conscious properties but concede that members of non-supervening property families do not cause anything; they are instead *epiphenomena*. The third option – physicalism plus supervenience plus the rejection of causal realization – is the most attractive kind of non-reduction. This version frequently flies under the banner of *supervenience non-reductive physicalism*. Putting the claim positively:

(SNP) Physical events or parts thereof exhaust everything that is concrete and some families of properties supervene on subvening microphysical properties such that some of the realizers of supervening properties are distinct from subvening microphysical properties.

Variants on (SNP) are probably the most frequently debated in the philosophical literature on non-reduction.

(SNP) is itself complex because causal realization is the conjunction of functionalization and causal inheritance. Since functionalization and causal inheritance are distinct, it is possible to reject either or both. Rejecting functionalization is captured by the following:

$(SNP)_F$ Physical events or parts thereof exhaust everything that is concrete and some families of properties supervene on subvening microphysical properties and their instantiation is *distinct* from the instantiation of those subvening properties satisfying a certain causal profile.

Rejecting causal inheritance is captured by the following:

(SNP)$_I$ Physical events or parts thereof exhaust everything that is concrete and some families of properties supervene on subvening microphysical properties and some of the causal powers of those supervening properties are *distinct* from the causal powers of those subvening microphysical properties.

(SNP)$_F$ says, in ordinary language, that reduction is blocked whenever a supervening property is not exhaustively characterized as a functional property, that is, a microphysical property that satisfies a causal profile. In ordinary language, (SNP)$_I$ says that reduction is blocked if some supervening properties do not inherit all their causal powers from their subvening microphysical properties. Reductionists think that (SNP)$_F$ and (SNP)$_I$ are non-starters (Kim 1992a, 1998; Melnyk 2003).

Exactly the same steps can be followed when specifying the conditions in which conscious properties do not reduce to microphysical properties of neural assemblies. Start with the statement of neural reductionism outlined on pages 45–6:

(NR) Physical events or parts thereof exhaust everything that is concrete and there is a supervenience relation between all families of conscious properties and microphysical properties of neural assembly activity such that subvening microphysical properties of neural assembly activity are the only realizers of supervening conscious properties.

Rejecting (NR) yields:

¬(NR) Physical events or parts thereof exhaust everything that is concrete and there is *not* a supervenience relation between all families of conscious properties and microphysical properties of neural assembly activity such that subvening microphysical properties of neural assembly activity are the only realizers of supervening conscious properties.

Taking the version that accepts physicalism and supervenience and putting the resulting claim positively, we have a statement of non-reductive physicalism about consciousness:

(NPC) Physical events or parts thereof exhaust everything that is concrete and some families of conscious properties supervene on microphysical properties of neural assembly activity such that some of the realizers of those supervening conscious properties are *distinct* from subvening microphysical properties of neural assembly activity.

As above, (NPC) is composed of a functionalization claim and a causal inheritance claim. Rejecting functionalization yields:

(NPC)$_F$ Physical events or parts thereof exhaust everything that is concrete and some families of conscious properties supervene on microphysical properties of neural assembly activity and the instantiation of members of those families of conscious properties is *distinct* from the instantiation of subvening microphysical properties of neural assembly activity that satisfy a certain causal profile.

Rejecting causal inheritance yields:

(NPC)$_I$ Physical events or parts thereof exhaust everything that is concrete and some families of conscious properties supervene on microphysical properties of neural assembly activity and some of the causal powers of those supervening conscious properties are *distinct* from the causal powers of those subvening microphysical properties of neural assembly activity.

In ordinary language, (NPC)$_F$ asserts that supervening conscious properties are something more than the instantiation of certain subvening microphysical properties of neural assemblies that satisfy a particular causal profile, and (NPC)$_I$ asserts that supervening conscious properties have some distinct causal powers not had by the subvening microphysical properties of neural assemblies. Both theses are defended in contemporary philosophical literature. Anomalous monism is one version of the former; multiple realizability is a version of the latter. These philosophical views are investigated in the next chapter.

EMERGENCE

Anomalous monism and multiple realizability are typically used as *negative* arguments against reduction, for both arguments purport to identify a second-order property of conscious properties that cannot be attributed to physical properties. As such, neither anomalous monism nor multiple realizability provide an ontological analysis of the relation between supervening non-reducible properties and subvening basal microphysical properties. Emergentism, on the other hand, is most frequently offered as just such an ontological analysis of the relation between supervening non-reducible properties and subvening basal microphysical properties. Emergentism is thus a *positive* ontological proposal of the relation between two families of properties, and as such is usefully introduced here in a general setting.

Emergentism is currently basking in the non-reductionist's spotlight. A lively philosophical debate about what emergence is and whether it is a plausible candidate for a non-reductive form of physicalism about conscious properties is ongoing. Since this is an area of active research, consensus has yet to develop. There are three areas of ongoing discussion. First, what emerges? Second, what is the logical signature of the emergence relation? Third, is emergent causation a viable model for the relationship between conscious and physical properties?

Even those who do not think much of emergence agree that systemic properties are the most likely candidates for what emerges, where a *systemic property* is a property of a system or mechanism, which property is related to yet distinct from the properties of the system's constituents. Advocates of emergence nonetheless insist that such a view is a kind of physicalism, since the systems that have emergent properties are held to be systems composed entirely of physical entities or parts thereof and emergent properties supervene on basal properties (some outliers affirm that emergentism is committed to entities that are related yet distinct from physical entities). According to *weak* synchronic emergentism, these systemic properties of systems of physical entities supervene at a time on the non-systemic properties of that system's parts. *Strong* synchronic emergentism adds to weak synchronic emergentism the claim that, again at a time, a system's systemic properties are causally irreducible to basal properties. According to *weak diachronic* emergentism, some reducible systemic properties are, while supervenient, nevertheless new over time. *Strong diachronic* emergentism adds the claim that some new systemic properties are causally irreducible to basal properties (Stephan 1999).

Weak emergentisms are nondescript versions of reductive physicalism, but strong emergentisms cause considerable disagreement, for according to them even if emergent properties supervene on some basal properties, they are causally irreducible to those subvening basal properties. If so, then (RP) is false, for emergent properties will not have microphysical neural properties as their only causal realizers. Emergence may thus provide the means necessary to avoid reduction of everything to microphysics and to protect thereby the explanatory autonomy of sciences other than physics, such as chemistry and biology, and, perhaps, psychology, and maybe even consciousness science.

Whether synchronic or diachronic, strong emergentism assumes that the world's phenomena are organized into various layers according to the systemic properties instantiated at a layer and that the job of the different sciences is to investigate the phenomena fixed by property layer. Following traditions in science, there are (among others) microphysical, atomic-physical, chemical, biological, biochemical, neurological, computational, psychological and sociological kinds of properties (Block 2003; Bontly 2002; Emmeche *et al.* 2000; Kim 2003; Oppenheim & Putnam 1958). If there are properties of various layers and strong emergentism is true, then there must also be causal relations *at* and *between* layers of events, that is, *intra-* and *interlayer* causation. So, strong emergentism also requires both that some systemic properties are new and that intralayer casual powers of some such properties are distinct from and irreducible to those of the subvenient properties of the system's components. A *basal* cause is a basal event (where, recall, an event is the instantiation of a property by an entity at a time) that causes another basal event. An *upwards* cause is a basal event that causes an emergent event. An *emergent* cause is an emergent event that causes another emergent event. A *downwards* cause is an emergent event that causes a basal event.

While strong emergentism can be stated in general outline quickly, making the position clear requires introducing little line drawings that illustrate the kinds of causation to which strong emergentism is committed. Suppose at some time, t_0, there are all of a physical system's intrinsic and extrinsic microphysical events. Call that set "TP_0". TP_0 is the total physical state of that system at t_0. Suppose a group of physical events at t_0 causes the instantiation of an emergent at t_1. Call that physical group "P_0" and the emergent event "E_1". E_1 is then an instantiation of an emergent property by P_1. Suppose E_1 causes nothing subsequent to its occurrence. Then, where "$\rightarrow$" represents causation and "$= = =$" represents supervenience, there is a putative instance of *upwards* causation, as shown in Figure 2.1. Here, E_1 is an effect of upwards causation from P_0 and supervenes on P_1. But E_1 is epiphenomenal. It causes nothing – it is a momentary blip on the screen upwardly caused by a basal event. Suppose next that an emergent, E_2, is again generated but again causes nothing. Then we have the situation in Figure 2.2.

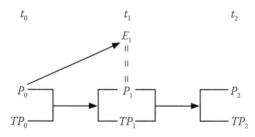

Figure 2.1 Upwards causation.

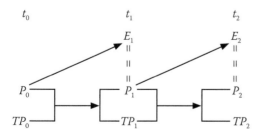

Figure 2.2 Iterated upwards causation.

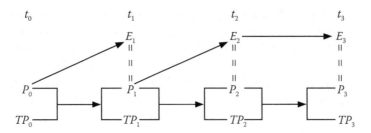

Figure 2.3 Emergent causation.

In Figure 2.2, two successive emergent events are represented as successive supervening epiphenomena upwardly caused by successive basal physical events. Suppose E_2 lays claim instead to cause an emergent event, E_3. Then there will be a putative case of *emergent* causation (Fig. 2.3). If Figure 2.3 represents a possibility, some emergent causes have emergent effects. Suppose finally that E_2 claims to cause a basal event, P_3. Then there will be a putative case of *downwards* causation (Fig. 2.4). If Figure 2.4 represents a possibility, some emergent causes have basal effects. So, if upwards causation is possible, then some basal events are upwards causes; if emergents are both emergent causes and downwards causes, then some emergent events are not epiphenomenal. Strong diachronic emergentism is committed to all three kinds of causal relations.

As will be seen later, downwards causation proves to be a particularly troublesome form of causation, for it appears on all counts to unjustifiably duplicate causes, adding to basal causes a layer of superfluous emergent causes. Since entire sectors of contemporary neuroscience of consciousness rely on emergence and downwards causation, entire sectors of contemporary neuroscience appear to commit themselves to this troublesome kind of causation. Unfortunately, the only other viable alternative to emergence and downwards causation – microphysical reductionism – is even less attractive than emergentism.

The four relations of identity, supervenience, reduction and emergence discussed in this chapter are central players in contemporary debates about the

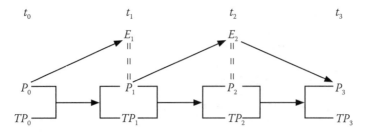

Figure 2.4 Downwards causation.

relation between conscious properties and properties of neural events in the brain. In the next chapter, four philosophical arguments about the prospects for reducing conscious properties to neural or microphysical properties that are premised upon these relations are considered and rejected. Following that, the numerous and impressive advances in neuroscience of consciousness and conscious properties are introduced. Only then will we be adequately prepared to return to more recent and more plausible philosophical arguments concerning reductionism and emergentism.

3. REDUCTIVE AND NON-REDUCTIVE PHYSICALISMS

Identity, supervenience-based reduction and non-reduction, and emergence are ontological options for conscious properties alive in the contemporary philosophical debates about consciousness. In this chapter, four substantive philosophical arguments for and against these options are entertained and rejected. These four argument types represent some of the most influential efforts by philosophers to fix the limits of debate about conscious properties. They use either considerations about the nature of the language used to talk about conscious properties or considerations about the logic of certain proposed relations between them and the brain's activity to buttress certain positions. Showing that these arguments are unsound clears the ground early and forestalls misleading appeals to them later. That in turn warrants a different kind of philosophizing about conscious properties, one informed as much by scientific discovery as by *a priori* argumentation.

The four arguments we consider fall into two classes: those about reductive physicalism and those about non-reductive physicalism. The first class includes arguments commonly made *for* reductive physicalism by old-fashioned type identity theorists on the strength of semantic considerations and those made *against* reductive physicalism by certain functionalists on the strength of an argument from the multiple realizability of conscious properties. The second class includes those made *against* non-reductive physicalism by certain other functionalists on the basis of the logical properties of supervenience and those made *for* non-reductive physicalism on the basis of the anomalous nature of conscious properties.

AN OLD-FASHIONED TYPE PHYSICALIST ARGUMENT FOR REDUCTION

In the past fifty years, the ontological alternatives on consciousness have become exhaustively articulated (see Fig. 3.1). Like most neuroscientists, philosophers and psychologists, we start from the assumption that conscious properties must

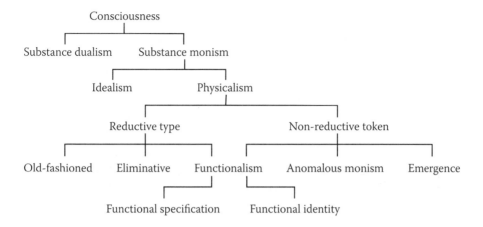

Figure 3.1 Ontological positions on consciousness.

somehow be properties of physical things. Everything rides on that "somehow" and what kinds of physical things we are talking about.

As noted, *physicalism* asserts that physical entities or parts thereof exhaust everything that is concrete, where a physical entity is an entity quantified over by physics. But physicalism so understood picks out a general view of which there are several species and subspecies. *Type physicalism* identifies conscious types with physical types instantiated by neural assemblies. Since types are a species of properties, type physicalism is equivalent to the following: any instantiated conscious property C is such that there is some neural property P with which C is identical. Type physicalism thus understood moves the debate away from the identity of conscious and physical substances to the identity of properties. So, in order for, say, some conscious event *c* to be identical to a neural event *n*, the conscious properties of the *c* event must be identical to the properties of the *n* event.

Old-fashioned type physicalists, such as J. J. C. Smart and U. T. Place, allowed that it was *prima facie* incredible to identify conscious properties with physical properties, but they offered a diagnosis of the situation that they hoped would defuse incredulity. First, kinds of "is" must be distinguished: there is the "is" of definition – a square is defined as an equilateral rectangle; the "is" of composition – a cloud is composed of a mass of water molecules; and the "is" of predication – a cloud is pretty. (One might wonder where the "is" of identity, introduced in Chapter 2, fits on this list. At the time that these arguments appeared (in the 1950s), positivism was just past its heyday, and positivism held that before any question concerning the "is" of identity could be answered, it must first be determined that what passes as an "is" of identity is not just camouflage for an "is" of definition.) According to old-fashioned type physicalism, claiming that conscious processes are not brain processes conflates the "is" of definition with the "is" of composition. Definitions are *analytically* true, where analysis is the procedure of providing necessary and sufficient conditions for the use of a term. As an example, "bachelor" just means "unmarried male" – that is, all and only bachelors are unmarried males. Analytic truths are thus true by definition of the terms contained, and asserting the negation of an analytic truth is a contradiction.

According to old-fashioned type physicalism, those who think that conscious processes are distinct from brain processes must think that since "how ice cream tastes to me" is analytically distinct from "insular cortex process 454 occurring", the way ice cream tastes is not identical to insular cortex process 454 occurring. But, they argued, this is confused: the *meaning* of "how ice cream tastes to me" may be distinct from that of "insular cortex process 454 occurring", but it does not follow that the way ice cream tastes to me is not – *compositional* "is" – insular cortex process 454 occurring. The meanings of terms may fall as they will without threatening the composition of conscious processes by brain processes.

Type physicalism's use of the distinction between meaning and composition is very much out of fashion these days. While it may be that the meaning of a conscious predicate is not that of a neural predicate, the disjunction between the "is" of meaning and the "is" of composition is hardly exhaustive, and when identity is analysed as a semantic relation between expressions rather than as an ontological relation, it leads to confusions concerning the necessity of identity. Kripke's efforts in this regard are instructive (Kripke 1980). He argues as follows:

P1: All identities are necessary and there are no contingent identities.
P2: If all identities are necessary, then the identity between conscious events and physical events is necessary.
P3: It is not the case that the identity between a conscious event such as pain and any physical event is necessary.
C: Conscious events are not identical to physical events.

The key premise is P3. Recall Leibniz's law: if two things are identical, then they share all properties. So, if conscious event C is identical to neural event N, then C and N share all properties. But now, suppose that C is the conscious event of pain and N is the neural event with which C is claimed to be identical, and consider the property of being painful instantiated by C and N. The conscious event of pain is necessarily painful, which is to say that it is not possible for a pain not to be painful. However, the neural event claimed to be identical to pain, say an event in insular or orbitofrontal cortex, is not *necessarily* painful, for, while it does in us have this property, it might not in a Martian's neurophysiology. So, the conscious event C is necessarily painful and the correlated neural event N is accidentally painful. Given Leibniz's law, it follows that the conscious event C is not N. Against old-fashioned type physicalism, this kind of argument is telling, since it moves discussion of identity away from definition and analysis. But since we limit ourselves to nomological necessity, possible worlds where neural events do not code for pain in our doppelgängers as they do in us are not our nomological neighbours. If perchance we discover otherwise, we can revisit the issue.[1]

Eliminativists are erstwhile heirs to old-fashioned type physicalists. Impressed by the tenacity of conscious predicates and properties to resist identification with anything physical but suspicious of the way such recalcitrance is used to reject physicalism, eliminativists defend the claim that physical properties are real and conscious properties are epiphrastic. An *epiphrastic view of properties* is one that takes properties to be entities that are not distinguished from a concept or predicate or description (Davidson 1993; the term "epiphrastic" is Quine's; cf. Quine 1981). With this distinction, eliminative physicalists sustain the primacy of physical properties and provide reasoned dismissal of conscious properties as colloquial backwaters of expression to be excised from science.

FUNCTIONALISM AND THE MULTIPLE REALIZABILITY ARGUMENT AGAINST REDUCTION

Most contemporary physicalists are neither old-fashioned nor eliminativist. They try instead to remain respectably scientific by emphasizing the need for views of conscious properties that place them in the framework of science, that is, views of conscious properties that preserve their causal efficacy. But they conjoin this with an open-minded willingness to refrain from inferring that conscious properties are also reducible to microphysical properties of neural events. Included in this class of generally agreeable types are functionalists. Functionalism is frequently thought of as a kind of token physicalism. *Type physicalism* requires that all conscious properties be identified with some physical property or properties. *Token physicalism* requires instead that all conscious events (or states or processes) be identified with some physical event (or state or process). If, as suggested above, an event is a particular instantiating a property at a time, it falls out neatly that type identity entails token identity but that token identity does not entail type identity. Since it is common ground across type and token physicalism that the particulars of all events are physical, the only difference there can be between them is the difference between the types instantiated by those particulars. If conscious types are physical types, then, since all particulars are physical, type identity entails token identity. The converse is not, however, true. Token physicalism requires that all events be physical; it does not require that all of an event's properties be physical. So, token physicalism is consistent with there being non-physical conscious properties instantiated by a particular. Hence, token physicalism is consistent with type distinctness and does not entail type physicalism.

Functionalism

One way of thinking about the relation between reductive and non-reductive physicalism is that reductive physicalism starts off as token physicalism but *acquiesces to* type physicalism because no viable non-reductive relation between conscious and physical properties can be found, whereas non-reductive physicalism *resists* type identity because at least one viable non-reductive relation between conscious and physical properties can be found. *Functionalism,* according to which conscious events have a certain causal input, perform a certain transformation on that input, and have a certain causal output, is supposed by many to resolve this issue. Most current debates about conscious properties arise in a functionalist setting. Conscious events are token identical with physical events because each particular conscious event is identical to a particular physical (usually neural) event; they are type distinct because there are many distinct physical structures in which a given functional conscious property can be implemented. Indeed, the most important feature of functionalism is that, if sound, it identifies a kind of description that makes physical implementation uninteresting. So long as there is some physical implementation or realization, androids and computers, humans, chimps and elephants, and Martians can all have the same type of conscious event despite those events being realized by silicon chips in androids and computers, by particular neural networks in humans and (perhaps) chimps, by different neural networks in elephants, and by who-knows-what in Martians. Since the conscious events each is in are functionally identical but realized by a variety of distinct physical events, no conscious event can be type identical to any one of its physical realizations. This is the enormously influential *multiple realizability argument* against type identity physicalism.

Multiple realizability arguments typically attach to claimed type identities *across* species or across biological organisms and non-biological entities. However, versions apply also *within* species across any two individuals at a time and in a single individual across times. Take any two people, Sid and Nancy for example. If Sid hopes that his next meal includes Ben and Jerry's ice cream and Nancy hopes that her next meal includes Ben and Jerry's ice cream, then for type physicalism to be true, the neural pathway through Sid's brain correlated with his hope must be the same neural pathway as that correlated with Nancy's hope in her brain. Sid and Nancy's distinctness notwithstanding, the likelihood of that being the case is astronomically small, for Sid's hope circuits through associative cortex and picks up memories with emotional valence of happiness from his childhood, while Nancy's hope picks up different emotional memories with different valence. Likewise, in a person at two times, one earlier, one later, the same hope is not realized by activity in the same neural pathway, for again, the later hope is embellished with that person's intervening psychological activity. If so, type physicalism is incapable of generalization across times for an individual or across individuals at a time (Block & Fodor 1972). We investigate these arguments in a later chapter.

Functionalism avoids the problems posed by multiple realizability by leaving implementation issues to others. Actually, that puts the point a little too strongly – this *brand* of functionalism avoids these problems by leaving implementation issues to others. Functionalism comes in a variety of brands, two of which are relevant. The functionalism discussed to this point is often known as *empirical* functionalism. According to this view, conscious events are functional events, so all the properties of a conscious event are identical with some functional property, and if there is a conscious property that has no causal powers, it is not a real property. Empirical functionalism is straightforwardly inconsistent with type physicalism, at least so long as all functional types are multiply realizable and no physical type is multiply realizable. But there is another brand of functionalism, according to which conscious events are *specified* as functional events without being identified with them. Specification functionalism – also known as *analytic* functionalism (Block [1978] 2007) – is used to argue for type physicalism.[2]

When functionalism first emerged in the 1960s, the use of "consciousness" was at its nadir – only a few oddballs dared to utter the word. Functionalism developed through the 1960s and 1970s in tandem with computer science from the ashes of behaviourism. The versions of functionalism introduced then often explicitly or implicitly used computers as their jumping-off point of comparison and carried more than a few behaviourist assumptions with them, notably the requirement for operationalizing inputs, transformations and outputs. Philosophers were not alone in helping themselves to those assumptions: vast stretches of cognitive psychology and neuroscience shared the assumption that the mind is like a computer in all but uninteresting ways.

The past twenty years of neuroscience, on the other hand, have been an ongoing exercise in analytic functionalism: functional properties attributed to theoretical entities from other psychological and computational theories are held constant while the hunt for the physical entities that implement those properties (or by which those properties are realized) is carried out. This is the milieu in which consciousness as a scientific topic has re-emerged. It is a curious twist that the process of looking for neural correlates of functionally described conscious properties has led to the realization that some functionalist programmes, notably computationalist functionalisms, are flawed because they cannot account for certain conscious properties. More on this later.

At its most general, functionalism is the injunction to find descriptions of phenomena that state their causal inputs, the manipulations those phenomena impose on their inputs, and the causal consequences of those manipulated inputs. Even if some formulations of functionalism carry a lot of baggage, refinements have allowed the problems of consciousness to emerge in a setting that should be common ground between scientists and philosophers.

It is difficult to see how scientific or philosophical thinking about conscious properties can disagree with the requirement that they be causally described (imagining otherwise is kind of like imagining theological thinking without God). Moreover, functionalism is better than old-fashioned type physicalism and eliminativism. Unlike old-fashioned type physicalism, it does not rule out scientific investigation into conscious properties on the grounds that all such investigations are confused about the meanings of "is" or commit category errors. And unlike eliminativism, it does not rule out scientific investigation into conscious properties on the grounds that their irreducibility mandates their quarantine to avoid contaminating science with reactionary tendencies.

Multiple realizability and realization

The argument from multiple realizability tries to block reduction in one fell swoop by establishing that for correlations discovered between some conscious property and some physical property, there is either some different physical property in the same *individual* that subvenes and realizes the same conscious property; or some different physical property in some other *species* that subvenes and realizes the same conscious property; or some different physical property in a *non-biological entity* that subvenes and realizes the same conscious property. Given that different physical properties subvene and realize the same conscious property, it is thought to follow that the conscious property will never reduce to any one of the properties the reductionist suggests. It is a further claim, but one often made by non-reductionists, that explanations of conscious phenomena need not expect anything of real interest to come from investigating the behaviour and structures of the neural assemblies that compose the brain. For, given multiple realizability, conscious properties are irreducible to the behaviour of those structures, so the nature and behaviour of the former will never imply, nor be implied by, anything of great specificity about the latter. In brief, given multiple realizability, conscious properties are irreducible and, given irreducibility, explanations of conscious properties need not dip into neural or any other more basic properties for their explanation. Unfortunately, the multiple realizability argument is not that potent. In this chapter, the general sweep of the argument is assessed. In Chapter 8, the results of this assessment are applied directly to the case of conscious properties.

Reducing any property is a two-step process: first, the property is functionalized, described as a node in a causal network; second, that functionalized property is causally realized by some microphysical properties. So, if $(SNP)_F$ is true and a property is not exhaustively described as a functional property, or if $(SNP)_I$ is true and a property does not inherit all of its causal powers from some set of microphysical properties, then reduction does not go through. Each of these counters is explored in the contemporary philosophical literature about reduction. Some non-reductionists argue that certain properties, even if functionally describable, have other non-functional properties and so are not merely functional properties (Block 2005, [1995] 2007). Others claim that functionalized properties do not inherit all their causal powers from microphysical properties (Burge [1989] 2007; Fodor 1987). Multiple realizability can be used to defend either or both of these non-reductionist alternatives.

We concur with identity theorists that plasma brains are conceivable and that viral brains violate no law of logic. We also agree with them that the existence of such logical possibilities and science-fiction fantasies does nothing to buttress the claim that human conscious properties are not reducible to microphysical properties of neural assemblies. For, like them, we are interested instead only in the more prosaic question, are conscious properties multiply realized in our actual world? We thus distinguish the possibility of multiple realization – multiple *realizability* – from actual multiple *realization*. Our interest herein is in multiple realization.

Although multiple realization, causal inheritance and functionalization are usually wrapped up with each other in arguments for and against neural reduction, they are in fact independent claims. First, even if causal inheritance entails functionalization, functionalization does not entail causal inheritance. Accepting functionalization of a property does not entail that it inherits all of its causal powers from a set of subvening microphysical properties. Non-reductionists adopting this position use multiple realization to block reduction by rejecting causal inheritance. Second, even if multiple realization entails functionalization, functionalization does not entail *multiple* realization. If a functionalized property is realized by different microphysical properties at a time or over time or is realized by different microphysical properties across species, then the functionalized property cannot be reduced to any one microphysical property and perhaps cannot be reduced to any combination of microphysical properties. This form of the argument tries to show that since there is a one–many relation between a functionalized property and microphysical properties and since identity requires a one-to-one relation, that functionalized property cannot be reduced to any set of microphysical properties. However, even if a functionalized property inherits all of its causal powers from a microphysical property, the functionalized property may have but one microphysical realizer. If so, then there is a one-to-one relation between functionalized property and microphysical properties and reduction goes through.

Teasing multiple realization, causal inheritance and functionalization apart helps explain why multiple realization has been at the centre of the reduction debates for the past twenty-five years. Type identity theorists and eliminativists reject non-reductive physicalism for not being hard-nosed enough and use functionalization and causal inheritance to argue against multiple realization, while non-reductive emergentists reject reductive physicalism for being too hard-nosed and use multiple realization to argue against causal inheritance or to argue against it and functionalization.

Tokening and realizing a property

It is undeniable that plenty of functional types *are* multiply realized. It does not matter much what a desk is made of (wood, steel, aluminum, stone or bone will do), or how many legs it has (one, two, three, four or more), or even whether it has legs at all (some desks protrude from walls). So long as what it is made of has a physical structure that is sufficiently rigid to form a platform at the right height and is of the right size or is in the right range of sizes, any material and any design will do. But some functional types are realizable by but a few physical types, and some by only one physical type. There are only a few realization types of electric toasters (pop-up toasters, toaster ovens, pincher toasters, swinger toasters, flopper toasters and conveyor belt toasters), two realizations of an internal combustion engine (the spark ignited gasoline engine and the compression ignited diesel engine), and only one realization of being a Phillips head screw.

"Wait a minute," you may be thinking, "surely there are thousands of different realizations of the property of being a Phillips head screw – big ones, little ones, brass ones, steel ones, blue ones, silver ones, ones for sheetrock, ones for wood, ones for metal, and so on." But these are different *tokens* of the type, not different *realizations* of the type. A token of a type is a spatiotemporally distinct individual instance of the type. A realization, on the other hand, is a subvening physical property, an instance of which has causal powers that exhaust the causal powers of the functional property supervening on it. The physical property that realizes a Phillips head screw, for example, is the pair of slots set at right angles to each other and intersecting at each other's midpoint. So long as that configuration of slots is tokened on a screw head, it is a Phillips head screw. The supervening functional property of being a Phillips head screw is causally realized by that subvening physical property because the causal powers of the latter are identical to and therefore sufficient for the causal powers of the former. In such cases, the functional property inherits its causal powers from its subvening physical property pair because the causal powers of the physical property determine those of the functional property.

Without noting the difference between tokens and realizations it is easy to take considerations that apply to the one as applying to the other. Take any two tokens of some type – these two desk chairs in my office. Here is one, and there is another. What makes them two tokens of the same type is that they are manufactured by the same company, have the same uncomfortable design, are made of wood, and have four legs and slatted backs. They are more or less duplicates of the type. Of course, they also differ in some ways – this one is here, and that one is there; this one has six slats in the back, while that one has lost a slat and has five; for some reason, this one has been painted fuchsia, but that one still has its original stain. But two tokens do not two realizations make. Multiple realizations are different *ways* of being a type, not different *examples* or *instances* of a type. Two tokens of a desk chair can, of course, also be different realizations of a desk chair, but if they are, the reasons they are different realizations are distinct from those in virtue of which they are different tokens of a desk chair. For example, the colour of a wooden desk chair, while pertinent for distinguishing two tokens of the type wooden desk chair, is not pertinent for distinguishing two realizations of the type, since the colour of the chair is not causally implied in fulfilling the function of being a desk chair. If there were two distinct physical properties, each of which determined that the chair's function is fulfilled, then the two chairs would be not just distinct tokens but also distinct realizations. Suppose, for example, that the stained chair has lost all of its legs and is stacked on cinder blocks. Then, arguably, the differences between the two would imply that they are multiple realizations of being a desk chair.

Given the difference between tokening and realizing a property, a supervening functional type is *multiply* realized when there are two or more distinct physical property types, instances of either or any one of which determines all the causal powers of the supervening functional type instance. Compare Phillips head screws with internal combustion engines, where there are two realizations – gasoline spark ignited and diesel combustion ignited. In a gasoline engine, a high-voltage spark ignites the air–fuel mixture in the cylinder, while in a diesel, compression and engine heat ignite the air–fuel mixture in the cylinder. Two distinct types of physical mechanism realize the same functional property in this case, so there are two realizations of the functional property. Again, compare internal combustion engines with corkscrews, of which there are quite a few realizations – waiter's, double-lever, screw-pull, double-prong and CO_2 injection, to name five. Each of the five extracts a cork from a bottle, but each does it using a mechanism distinct from the next. The first two use distinct kinds of lever action, a screw-pull corkscrew relies on brute opposing force, a double-prong corkscrew relies on torque and CO_2 injection corkscrew relies on an expansive gas propelling the cork out of the neck. So, there are five mechanisms and five distinct realizations of being a corkscrew (Shapiro 2004).

Requiring of tokens of functional types that they exhibit distinct physical properties that bestow the same causal powers makes a more precise understanding of multiple realization available:

(MR) A functional property F is multiply realized by physical properties $P_1, P_2, \ldots P_n$ if and only if (a) each of $P_1, P_2, \ldots P_n$ is a distinct physical property; and (b) each instantiation of $P_1, P_2, \ldots P_n$ is such that its casual powers are sufficient for the causal powers of an instance of F.

63

(For our purposes, one physical property is identical with another whenever they have the same causal profile and distinct when they do not. Hence, P_1 and P_2 are distinct if P_1 is caused by something that P_2 is not caused by or causes something that P_2 does not cause. It is consistent with P_1 being distinct from P_2 that each is individually causally sufficient for the causal powers of F.) Given (MR), the special case for the multiple realization of conscious properties by the neural properties they supervene on can be formulated:

> (MRC) A functionalized conscious property C is multiply realized by neural properties N_1, N_2, ... N_n if and only if (a) each of N_1, N_2, ... N_n is a distinct neural property; and (b) each instantiation of N_1, N_2, ... N_n is such that its casual powers are sufficient for the causal powers of an instance of C.

(MRC) blocks reduction of a functional property to any one of its physical realizers because although it is allowed that the causal powers of P_1, P_2, ... P_n are each sufficient for the causal powers of F, they are not also each necessary for the causal powers of F.

(MR) and (MRC) critics can reject either (a) or (b) or both (a) and (b). Type identity theorists and eliminativists reject (b): they argue that the causal powers of a realizer are not just sufficient for but identical with those of the realized property, so necessity is, contrary to what the multiple realization advocate claims, also implied. Emergentists also reject (b), but they go in the opposite direction: they argue that the causal powers of a subvening realizer, even if necessary, are not sufficient for those of the supervening functional property. Rather than rejecting (b), it is possible instead to reject (a). It may be that (a) is true less frequently than multiple realization advocates think. This is a debunking argument, and there are many instances of the type, some directed against the general case of (MR), some focused specifically on (MRC). In its latter form, the argument is that functionalized properties are realized by microphysical assemblies and that nothing other than microphysical assemblies have the physical properties that determine the causal powers of the functionalized property. Shapiro (2004) develops this kind of argument in an especially clear manner. Finally, it is also possible to reject (a) and (b). Shapiro and Andy Clark (1997, 2008) both develop such arguments. We investigate them later, in Chapter 10.

It is too early in the development of empirical research into the bases of conscious properties to assert that every candidate of multiple realized conscious properties will, upon further consideration of the evidence, turn out to be disconfirmed. But it is not too early to insist that the days of appealing to multiple realizability as an *a priori* proof against reduction are over. Plasma consciousness and hydraulic consciousness are both conceivable and neither violates any law of logic, but if that is all that multiple realizability comes to, philosophically minded neuroscientists and neuroscientifically minded philosophers interested in conscious properties will be forgiven for ignoring them. If multiple realizability's plausibility is a result of nothing more than a lack of detailed knowledge of neuroscientific evidence plus a dollop of philosophical imagination, then paying greater attention to the evidence is preferable. Of course, requesting that evidence be consulted before making philosophical pronouncements should not be taken to prove too much. Since we do not know whether every conscious property is or will be realized singly rather than multiply, thinking that multiple realization is never defensible except by scientifically ignorant philosophical speculation is also a mistake. Those impressed by multiple realizability typically use it as a pre-emptive strike against the possibility that empirical work can support reduction of conscious properties. *That* use of the argument is unsuccessful. Other uses of the argument are not thereby threatened. Hence, even if this section's arguments are sound and most of the wind in the sails of multiple realizability disappears, the reductionist's sails are not thereby puffed up to full.

THE ANOMALY ARGUMENT FOR NON-REDUCTION

Another reason for denying the reducibility of consciousness is to argue for (NRC)$_P$ and one way to do that is to argue that conscious properties are causally anomalous, that is, anomological (that is, not lawful). If so, then, since neural properties are causal properties and causal properties are lawful, conscious properties cannot be reduced to neural properties.

Causal laws are universally quantified conditionals. For instance, the sentence "For all humans x, whenever x swallows arsenic, death ensues for x" is arguably a causal law. Discovering causal laws is common in the physical sciences. It is well known that not all generalizations are causal laws. Suppose that every time a nominating speech is given for National TV Nation Day in the US Senate, a European head of state dies. Then:

> For all speeches on behalf of National TV Nation Day in the US
> Senate, if such a speech is given, then a European head of state dies

is also a true generalization. Of course, that generalization is true only because there has been just one nominating speech ever given on behalf of National TV Nation Day. It is a mere coincidence that the death of a European head of state occurred on the same day.

Some additional property is needed to distinguish accidentally true generalizations of this kind from causal laws. The standard candidate is that a causal law supports counterfactual conditionals while an accidental generalization does not. A counterfactual conditional is a proposition that states something contrary to fact. If the counterfactual derived from a generalization is true, then there is reason to suppose that the generalization is a causal law. So, from:

> For all humans, whenever someone swallows arsenic, death ensues

we can derive the counterfactual that were I to drink arsenic, death would ensue. But from:

> For all speeches on behalf of National TV Nation Day in the US Senate, if they are given, a European head of state dies

a corresponding counterfactual does not seem so obvious. It hardly seems likely that were the senator to have spoken on the following day, a European head of state would have died. Using this difference between generalizations that can and those that cannot support counterfactuals, Davidson argued that no generalizations about conscious events support counterfactuals (Davidson 1980a, 1980b, 1993). There can be all kinds of interesting psychological generalizations about conscious events, but none can be causal laws. If so, then conscious events are, unlike physical events, anomalous. Since physical events are governed by causal laws and conscious events are not, conscious event types cannot be reduced to physical event types.

The most widely discussed version of this line of thought is Davidson's *anomalous monism*, according to which conscious and physical token events are identical while conscious types are distinct from and supervenient upon physical types (see Davidson 1980a, 1980b). Most of the details of anomalous monism need not detain us, but one implication of the view is relevant. If anomalous monism is true, then conscious events do no causal work because of the conscious properties they have. Take two conscious events, the conscious thought that it is raining and the conscious thought that since I do not want to get wet, I will take my umbrella. According to anomalous monism, these two events are conscious events because they fall under a conscious type. If conscious types are anomalous, there can be no strict causal laws linking conscious types. Since conscious events cause other conscious events and since conscious types are anomalous, it follows that the first does not cause the second because it falls under a conscious type but only because it falls under a physical type. But if no conscious events ever cause other conscious events because they fall under a conscious type, then conscious events do not cause others in virtue of being conscious. That is one way of saying that anomalous monism entails epiphenomenalism of conscious types (McLaughlin 1989).

In the previous paragraph, *property* was replaced with *type*, and *having a property* was replaced with *falling under a type*. This is no accident: anomalous monism cannot be stated in any other way. Given various other commitments necessary for the view, the only way for anomalous monism to be consistent

with the token identity of conscious and physical events and the type distinctness of conscious and physical types is to think of token events as concrete particulars and to think of conscious types as descriptions true of those concrete
events or under which those concrete events fall. The view that conscious properties are epiphrastic is, recall, the claim that all conscious properties are nothing more than descriptions that contain conscious terms. (Obviously enough,
views of conscious properties according to which they are to be distinguished
from concepts or predicates are *non*-epiphrastic views of conscious properties.)
If conscious properties – that is, conscious types – are not distinguished from
predicates or concepts, then they are descriptions *true of* or *satisfied by* events
or concepts that events *fall under.*

This way of looking at properties has the benefit that an event's satisfying or
failing to satisfy a conscious predicate or falling under or failing to fall under
a conscious concept will not affect its identity as the event that it is. After all,
what things are and do is one thing; what things are called and how they are
conceptualized are two quite different things. So, the epiphrastic view of properties underwrites the difference between conscious and physical event types
and the identity of conscious and physical event tokens. This is why anomalous
monism is also known as the *token identity theory*: token conscious events are
identical to token physical events, but conscious types are different from and
irreducible to physical types. But anomalous monism pays a heavy price for
affirming token identity. Conscious types are descriptions, hence epiphrastic,
and, because they are epiphrastic, conscious types are also *pleonastic*, namely,
ersatz entities induced by but extending no further than a linguistic predicate.
As pleonastic, conscious types are *ipso facto* washed out of the causal network
of events, so any causal claim made on their behalf is false. Thus, no event has
any causal powers because of the conscious types under which it falls.

Defenders of anomalous monism have turned somersaults trying to convince
sceptics that anomalous monism is not guilty of epiphenomenalism. They argue
that supervenience of the conscious on the physical guarantees the relevance of
conscious types to the causal powers of an event and that relevance is sufficient to
avoid epiphenomenalism (Davidson 1993). But all that supervenience amounts to
in anomalous monism is a relation between predicates or concepts, and the considerations that warrant predicate and concept supervenience concern relations
such as definability, analysability and nomological irreducibility. Supervenience
of the conscious on the physical entails either that conscious predicates are not
definable in terms of physical predicates, even if the meaning of the former supervenes on the meaning of the latter, or that conscious concepts are not analysable
in terms of physical concepts, even if the former supervenes on the latter. What
supports these claims is the nomological irreducibility of mental predicates and
concepts to the predicates and concepts of physics. The problem is that unless
an event's causal powers are thereby affected, conscious supervenience does not
make a causal difference. And those causal powers cannot be so affected, since

conscious types are epiphrastic and pleonastic while causal powers are neither epiphrastic nor pleonastic. Hence, even if conscious types supervene on physical types, conscious types are epiphenomenal (Welshon 1999).

Another problem with anomalous conscious events is more serious. If there are neural substrates for conscious properties and conscious properties are distinct from neural properties, then there must also be causal relations between events instantiating properties of the two types, and these psycho-physical and physico-psychological causal relations must either be anomological or nomological. But there may be no way for them to be anything other than anomological, and if they are anomological, then there is an explanatory gap and, depending on how that explanatory gap is resolved, they may even be epiphenomenal. The argument for this conclusion is due to Jaegwon Kim (Kim 1985).

Suppose we have two propositions, p and q; p is the proposition "R.W. is less than seven feet tall" and q is the proposition "R.W. is less than eight feet tall" (for the record, I am 6'1" tall). If you believe that p, then on the assumption that you are rational, you also believe that q. So, in general for persons x reading this book:

(i) For all persons x reading this book, if x were to believe that p, then x would also believe that q

Now, if there are neural correlates for all beliefs, then p and q both have neural correlates, say neural properties N_1 and N_2, instantiated in activity of certain assemblies of your brain. If so, there is then a nomological causal relation between, respectively p and N_1 and q and N_2, as follows:

(ii) As a matter of scientific law, for all persons x reading this book, x believes that p if and only if N_1 is instantiated

(iii) As a matter of scientific law, for any person x reading this book, x believes that q if and only if N_2 is instantiated

If both of these are true, then the following seems also to be derivable:

(iv) If N_1 were to be instantiated, then N_2 would be instantiated

In short, the rationality requirement of belief attribution appears to be alone sufficient to infer a physical prediction about the neural properties of brain activity.

Surely this is a little too quick: what explains (iv)? There appear to be but three alternatives. Either (a) it is a fundamental physical law; or (b) it is a derived physical law; or (c) it has no physical explanation. But there just are not any *fundamental* physical laws connecting beliefs and neural activity, so (a) is a non-starter. Unfortunately, (b) is also implausible: if what explains the truth of (iv) is another more fundamental physical law, then that more fundamental physical law explains (iv) and the rationality requirements of belief attribution encoded in (i) are superfluous. And (c) is also implausible: if there is no physical explanation of (iv), then the only alternative is that it is explained by some logical principal on which (i) rests, which means that the truth of a counterfactual whose singular terms refer only to physical entities is dependent upon logic. That cannot be correct. Given that none of the alternatives work, then if these are the only alternatives, it follows that neither (ii) nor (iii) are causal laws. Generalizing to relevantly similar cases, not only are there no psychological laws, there are no psychophysical causal laws either. If so, then conscious types are, by the argument already provided, epiphenomenal.

This argument is a good deal more troubling than Davidson's anomalous monism, for it does not rely on anomalous monism's epiphrastic interpretation of conscious properties. The problem that it poses can be stated as the conclusion of a short argument. Conscious belief properties are irreducible and distinct from the neural properties with which they correlate and on which they supervene. Moreover, all causation is governed by causal law. However, there are no causal laws governing the relation between a conscious belief property and a neural property. And if there are no causal laws governing the relation between a conscious belief property and a neural property, then the relation between a conscious belief property and its subvening neural property is anomological. Unfortunately, since the relation is anomological, conscious belief properties are therefore epiphenomenal. For those interested in defending the irreducibility of conscious properties and the causal efficacy of conscious belief properties, this conclusion is unacceptable. So at least one of the premises leading to that conclusion must be rejected. But which premise is the best candidate for rejection? It turns out that every answer to this question is unattractive. Rejecting the nomologicality of causation has been the most popular, for the vagaries of the relation between conscious belief properties and neural events are generally acknowledged. But it is also possible to reject the claim that the absence of causal laws between conscious properties and neural events implies the epiphenomenality of conscious properties. This option is explored by emergentism. We return to these issues later.

THE SUPERVENIENCE ARGUMENT AGAINST EMERGENCE

In the last chapter, we introduced emergentism as an option for modelling the causal relations between some kinds of properties. Reductionists reject emergentism, focusing in particular on emergent and downwards causation. Their suspicion finds expression in an argument for the conclusion that any emergent that supervenes on some subvenient basal is epiphenomenal. This argument, known as the *supervenience argument*, is among the strongest arguments against the viability of any non-reductive physicalism, for, if sound, it undermines the causal independence of any and all emergents (Kim 1992b, 1998, 2000, 2005).

The supervenience argument has two steps: the first shows that causation between emergents must be replaced by downwards causation; the second shows that downwards causation must be replaced by causation between basals. It will be helpful to keep the following notions in mind (apologies for all the subscripts – they have to be included to keep the various times clear):

(OEE)   *Overestablishment* of emergents: Where there are events E_n, P_{n+1} and E_{n+1}, E_n and P_{n+1} overestablish E_{n+1} if and only if E_n claims to cause E_{n+1} and P_{n+1} subvenes E_{n+1}.

(ODB)   *Overdetermination* of basals: Where there are events P_n, E_n and P_{n+1}, P_n and E_n overdetermine P_{n+1} if and only if E_n and P_n both claim to cause P_{n+1} and only E_n or P_n (and not both E_n and P_n) cause P_{n+1}.

The supervenience argument relies on premises assessing the causal efficacy of overestablished emergents and overdetermined basals. These are:

(DE)   *Disqualification* of emergent causes: If E_n and P_{n+1} overestablish E_{n+1}, then E_n is *disqualified* as a cause of E_{n+1}.

(PE)   *Pre-emption* of emergent causes: If E_n and P_n overdetermine P_{n+1}, then E_n is *pre-empted* as a cause of P_{n+1}.[3]

And if an event is either disqualified or pre-empted, then it is *excluded* from being a cause.

Suppose an emergent event claims to cause another emergent event; that is, E_2 lays claim to cause E_3. Now, E_3 has a basal on which it supervenes, namely

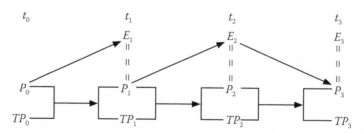

Figure 3.2 Disqualifying emergent causation.

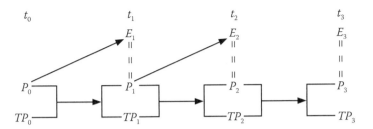

Figure 3.3 Pre-empting downwards causation.

P_3, and E_3's supervenience on P_3 also guarantees E_3's instantiation. So, E_2 and P_3 overestablish E_3. The way to solve this problem is to say that E_2 causes not E_3 but P_3, on which E_3 supervenes; hence, that E_2 is disqualified as a cause of E_3. Figure 3.2 represents the proposal. Since E_2 is *disqualified* as a cause of E_3, emergents are *excluded* from being causes of emergents.

Consider now downwards causation: E_2 supervenes on P_2 and P_2 claims to cause P_3. It appears that both P_2 and E_2 each cause P_3. So, P_2 and E_2 overdetermine P_3. The solution just proposed points the way to a solution of the problem: downwards causation from emergent to basal may be redescribed as causation between basals and supervenience of subsequent emergent on basal. In Figure 3.3, E_2 is *pre-empted* and thus excluded as cause of P_3. In short, emergents are disqualified as causes of other emergents, pre-empted as causes of basals, and therefore excluded from being either emergent or downwards causes. From exclusion, emergent epiphenomenality follows directly. Emergent causal powers are identical after all to those of the basals on which they supervene and so reduce to those of subvenient basals. That makes diachronic emergentism indistinguishable from reductive physicalism. Hence, strong diachronic emergentism is false.

Of course, reductionists can still throw disgruntled emergentists a bone. Emergents are causes after a fashion, since once supervenience is granted, their causal realization is warranted, reduction goes through, and the causal powers of emergents are redrawn as those of their causal realizers. In this way, the supervenience argument identifies the root problem with emergent conscious properties better than claiming that emergent conscious properties are anomalous. The problem with supervenient and emergent conscious properties is not that they are not governed by causal law whereas the physical properties on which they supervene and from which they emerge are governed by causal law. The problem with supervenient emergent properties is that they are either superfluous given the physical properties from which they emerge or are causally reducible to those physical properties. This is one of the reasons why arguments claiming that conscious properties are anomalous have disappeared – they pick out a non-essential feature of the relationship between conscious properties and physical properties.

71

Disqualification and overdetermination

The supervenience argument has stopped many emergentists in their tracks. But it does not work if either (DE) or (PE) are either irrelevant or false. And there is reason to think that (DE) and (PE) are both irrelevant *and* false.

One way to see the problems posed by the supervenience argument is to point out a frequently ignored consequence: the reasoning employed in it can be reapplied to the initial assumption that there is upwards causation from basals to supervenient emergent properties. Here too, if P_1 is alone sufficient for E_1, then P_0 is unnecessary as an upwards cause of E_1. Recall upwards causation (Fig. 3.4). Now, think about it: if basal causation plus supervenience replaces emergent and downwards causation, then basal causation plus supervenience can replace upwards causation (i.e. Fig. 3.5). P_0 is thus eliminated as an upwards cause of E_1. Hence, just as emergents are downwardly epiphenomenal, so basals are *upwardly* epiphenomenal.

Figure 3.5 illustrates a possibility. What is the argument that it represents something more than a possibility? Here are two things it cannot be. P_1's subvenience of E_1 cannot *disqualify* P_0 as an upwards cause of E_1, for were P_1's subvenience of E_1 to disqualify P_0 as cause of E_1, then P_1 would have to block P_0's causal work. But then P_1 would be a cause that works backwards in time, and if we are not prepared to defend backwards causation, this is a non-starter. For a

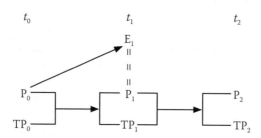

Figure 3.4 Upwards causation.

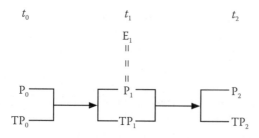

Figure 3.5 Eliminating upwards causation.

similar reason, P_1 cannot *pre-empt* P_0 as cause of E_1 either, for P_1 would then be a simultaneous cause, and that alternative is also a non-starter.[4] So, excluding upwards causation by disqualification or pre-emption is a non-starter. The only remaining reason is that upwards causation is *superfluous* given basal causation and supervenience: basal causation accomplishes all there is to accomplish, so upwards causation is superfluous and eliminable. Since basals do not upwardly cause emergents to begin with, there will never be any temptation to wonder whether emergents thus caused might after all do something.

Unless this is simply an assertion against emergents being causes, some reason for inoculating against supervenient causes (including supervenient emergent causes) must be found and that reason cannot appeal to either (DE) or (PE). The best and most frequently given answer is that supervenients are only misleadingly spoken of as properties – supervenient property talk is better replaced with talk of supervenient *designators* or *descriptions* (Kim 1998). If supervenient properties are descriptions, then there is no more to them than those descriptions and they are pleonastic. Then, just as in the case of anomalous monism, there is a direct argument to their epiphenomenality: since they are pleonastic, supervenients are *ipso facto* washed out of the causal network of events, so *any* causal claim made on their behalf is false. But note that, since the antecedent of (DE) will on this way of thinking about supervenients always be false, tolerating them long enough to disqualify them is a moot exercise.

That (DE) is moot for pleonastic supervenients does not show that causal inheritance is false for them, for although pleonastic properties neither inherit anything from their causal past nor bestow anything on their causal future, causal inheritance requires that emergent causal powers are identical with the causal powers of their subvenient basal present. Still, since the view is that what supervenes on basal events are *descriptions*, there is no causal power those supervenients *might* inherit from their cotemporaneous subvenient basal pair. Causal inheritance simply does not apply to pleonastic supervenients. Claiming otherwise is a category mistake. So, where supervenients are pleonastic, (DE) *and* causal inheritance are both moot.

Faced with the irrelevancy of causal inheritance for supervenient emergents, reductionists will be delighted, for the epiphenomenality not only of anything *other* than the physical but also from the physical *to* anything else vindicates their view that the physical is all there is. But not everyone is pleased with this result. Non-reductionists are typically willing to tolerate supervenient properties as something other than descriptions, and they typically want also to salvage upwards causation from basal events to non-pleonastic supervenient events. Doing so at least provides some set of entities from which supervenient properties might come. One consequence is that some basal events cause both basal and emergent events, so some causes have more than one effect. A corollary is that some basal causes have both supervenient and subvenient effects. These appear to be acceptable consequences (Lewis 1986b).

Suppose then that some group of basal events is an upwards cause and that what that group of events causes is the instantiation of a supervenient emergent property. If so, there is no good reason for claiming that an emergent event thus caused is subsequently disqualified as an emergent cause. Consider E_3's supervenience on P_3: supervenience establishes a nomological covariation between properties from different families at a time, not an instantaneous or backwards causal relation between them. If so, then that some properties supervene on others does not entail rejecting causal relations between supervenients or between basals and supervenients and does not entail disqualifying a supervenient property from having distinct causal powers from those of the basals on which it supervenes and does not disqualify the event of its instantiation from being a cause. In short, (DE) is false. So, to summarize the emergentist's counter to the supervenience argument to this point, either supervenient emergent events are pleonastic or they are not. If they are, then basals are eliminated as upwards causes and (DE) is irrelevant. If not, then emergents are not disqualified as causes and (DE) is false.

It is important to realize that from the falsity or irrelevance of (DE) it does not follow that strong diachronic emergentism is exonerated. All that has been accomplished is showing that emergents are, contrary to what is claimed, not disqualified as causes. The problem of overdetermination remains and may prove intractable, and the supervenience argument has real bite here. Even if emergent events *can* be causes of basal events, for any given emergent event laying claim to cause some subsequent basal event(s), there will always be some cotemporaneous basal event(s) that appear to compete with it. We can illustrate the problem by recurring to our little diagrams. E_2 emerges from P_1 and supervenes on P_2. So, where E_2 occurs, so too will P_2. Were E_2 and P_2 both to cause P_3, then there would be two causes of P_3 where there is arguably room only for one. That is overdetermination. Having P_2 pre-empt E_2 as cause of P_3 and affirming E_2's epiphenomenality looks like a good solution to the problem of overdetermination. So, even if the supervenience argument fails to show that emergents are excluded as causes, it does show, first, that where emergents are candidate causes, their candidacy will never go uncontested and, second, that they might lose every contest they enter. This dashes the strong emergentist's hopes for defending downwards causation.

The options open to the strong emergentist are limited. In fact, there are four. Either:

(a)　E_2 and P_2 conjointly cause P_3, and E_2 and P_2 overdetermine P_3, but overdetermination is not sufficient for pre-emption; or

(b)　E_2 and P_2 do not conjointly cause P_3, and E_2 and P_2 overdetermine P_3, but overdetermination is not sufficient for pre-emption; or

(c)　E_2 and P_2 conjointly cause P_3, and E_2 and P_2 do not overdetermine P_3, so P_2 does not pre-empt E_2; or

(d) E_2 and P_2 do not conjointly cause P_3, and E_2 and P_2 do not overdetermine P_3, so P_2 does not pre-empt E_2.

Recall that, in general, if E_n and P_n overdetermine P_{n+1}, then E_n is pre-empted as cause of P_{n+1} (that is (PE) from above). But if (a) or (b) is true, then the antecedent and the negation of the consequent are true. If so, (PE) is false. Likewise, if (c) or (d) is true, then the antecedent is false. If so, (PE) is moot. I think it is fair to say that showing that (PE) is false or moot is not going to be easy. Still, having cleared away the *a priori* claim that emergents *cannot* have distinct causal powers because they are supervenient and therefore disqualified from being causes, a landscape of emergent causation is revealed. It is pretty open country; explorations are less than ten years old and ongoing. This is where matters stand as this book goes to print – philosophers are currently debating these matters, and the dust has yet to clear. Here, we indicate some of the arguments offered for and against each alternative.

Consider the first three options. According to (a) and (b), overdetermination occurs but is not enough for pre-emption of overdetermining causes. The suggestion is provocative. Despite being a platitude that overdetermination is unacceptable, one might yet ask, is it really *that* bad? After all, given overdetermination, there is an embarrassment of causal riches: there will never be events popping into existence from nowhere or a slow ratcheting down to nothing due to a causal shortage. If one is prepared to live in this congested world, then (PE) is false, for overdetermination can be conceded without having to accept pre-emption. Moreover, the causal autonomy of conscious properties receives some support from such a view: species of causes other than the microphysical are useful given the preposterously complex collections of microphysical properties that would have to be invoked when explaining non-microphysical systems. Distilling emergent causal powers out of the gumbo of physics precludes having to identify such collections (Coady 2004; Sider 2003). On (c), while overdetermination is false, E_2 and P_2 are not competing causes of P_3 but conjoint causes of P_3. This option is true if E_2 and P_2 are cotemporaneous causes without each of which P_3 does not occur and with both of which P_3 does occur, a nice case of individually necessary and conjointly sufficient causes. But, if so, then the antecedent of (PE) is false and (PE) is moot: although pre-emption is prescribed for cases of overdetermination, E_2 and P_2 are not overdetermining causes. Hence, (PE) does not apply to supervenient emergent downwards causation and is irrelevant. However, even if there are individually necessary and conjointly sufficient causes, supervenient emergents and subvenient basals are not obviously members of the class (Kim 1998).

If none of (a)–(c) are promising, that leaves (d). On (d), E_2 and P_2 do not conjointly cause P_3, and E_2 and P_2 do not overdetermine P_3, so P_2 does not pre-empt E_2. This is true where E_2 and not P_2 causes P_3 or where P_2 and not E_2 causes P_3. Emergentists think the first disjunct is true; reductive physicalists think the second is true. The burden falls, then, on emergentists to identify how the first can be true. This issue is at the core of many current discussions of emergentism: it is one thing for emergent events not to be disqualified as causes in virtue of their supervenience and another thing to specify what, if anything, is that in virtue of which they *are* qualified as causes. Some emergentists simply announce that emergents are qualified as causes because they have causal powers distinct from those of their subvenient basals. Surely that just restates the problem. The best that can be said is that *if* emergents have causal powers distinct from those of their subvenient basals, then emergent events and their subvenient basal events do not always overdetermine subsequent events. If so, then the antecedent of (PE) is false, (PE) need not apply, and the supervenience argument's move against emergent downwards causation fails. But note the "if". It is a big "if", one to which we return in Chapter 11.

What has been accomplished to this point has been, for the most part, destructive: some of the most popular and influential arguments for certain positions in the consciousness debates are unsound. However, that certain arguments for or against a position are unsound does not imply that the position is itself mistaken or that there are no sound arguments for that position. We turn now to more constructive work that utilizes contemporary neuroscience to inform stronger arguments for certain positions. That work begins by introducing the representationalist theory of consciousness.

4. REPRESENTATIONALIST THEORIES OF CONSCIOUS PROPERTIES

A considerable amount of cross-disciplinary discussion between philosophers and scientists about conscious properties has occurred in the past twenty years. While all the cross-disciplinary discussion has yet to yield much consensus, it has yielded a set of working assumptions, shared by most neuroscientists and philosophers, about their kind (for want of a better word). One of these working assumptions is the representationalist understanding of conscious properties. Neuroscientists look for empirical support for conscious properties representationally understood; philosophers assess whether a representational understanding of conscious properties successfully captures all the features of conscious properties.

In contemporary philosophy, three versions of representationalism dominate discussion: computational representationalism, higher-order representationalism and self-representationalism. Philosophical critics of representationalism focus either on the alleged differences between the three versions of representationalism or on alleged problems that attach to every version of representationalism no matter how construed. A serious challenge comes from qualitative properties: if representationalism is correct, then qualitative properties must be representational. But they appear on all counts not to be representational properties. Similarly, subjective perspectivity appears not to be exhaustively analysed as the unity of represented content. These criticisms are discussed here in a philosophical context. Subsequent to introducing the neuroscientific evidence that has been discovered, we return to discuss them further in later chapters.

INTENTIONALISM, REPRESENTATIONALISM AND COMPUTATIONALISM

Representationalism is a species of intentionalism. According to *intentionalism*, conscious perceptual, affective, interoceptive, proprioceptive and cognitive processes are sequences of structured events composed of a subject, an object that is about something else, and a relation between the subject and the object.

Intentionalism holds that it is in virtue of having this structure that conscious perceptual, affective and cognitive processes enter into the causal roles that they do. Calling a theory intentionalist implies that every conscious event or entity is intentional, but it does not require holding that every intentional event or entity is conscious, for some intentional events and entities are not conscious. The typed word "cat" is about something and so intentional, yet "cat" is not conscious. To account for this wrinkle, Chisholm and Searle (Chisholm 1957b; Searle 1983, 1992) distinguish between *original* and *derived* intentionality. Original intentionality is conscious intentionality; derived intentionality need not be conscious. The typed word "cat" is a case of derived intentionality. Our interest is in original intentionality.

Representationalism is the specific intentionalist claim that perceptual, affective, interoceptive, proprioceptive and cognitive processes operate on events that refer to, map onto, or otherwise represent something else. A *representation* is something that is asymmetrically related to another entity such that (a) it is about the other entity but the other entity is not about it, and (b) it stands in for the other entity, and (c) it can guide behaviour in the other entity's stead (Haugeland [1991] 1998). Thus a limping gait represents injury, but injury does not represent a limping gait; a sculpture of a horse represents a horse, but a horse does not represent a sculpture of it; the word "wallet" represents wallets, but wallets do not represent the word "wallet". Representation's asymmetry distinguishes representation from resemblance, which is symmetrical. That a representation stands in for another entity implies that even in the absence of additional perceptual input or in the absence of the perceptual object altogether, the representation has sufficient saliency to guide – that is, cause – behaviour.

The category of representation is broad and includes images, symbols, maps, icons and models. Following Peirce (1976), a *sign* is the genus of which the others are species. A sign is some perceptual stimulus pattern that carries information or stands in for something else. Within the genus there are at three species: icons, indexes and symbols. An *icon* is a sensory representation of something, such as a painting or sculpture. An *index* is a stimulus-dependent sign that correlates particular perceptual information with or points to – indexes – something else. A limping gait indexes injury; a beeping car horn indexes danger; olfactory detection of pheromones indexes sexual availability; particular kinds of vocalization index danger or contentment; a wrinkled nose and scowl index disgust. A *symbol* is a stimulus-independent sign that has a conventional significance acquired through association with other symbols. Symbols, unlike indexes, bear no non-conventional relation to that which they signify. Thus the bald eagle (a bird) is a symbol that refers to the United States; "s" (an ink squiggle) refers to a particular phoneme; "grief" (a collection of ink squiggles) refers to a particular emotion.

The word "representation" can refer either to what represents something else or to the representing of something else or to the thing represented. That is a breeding ground for confusion, so we stipulate the following. There is, first, the *representation vehicle*, the entity or event that is a relatum of a representation relation. Second, there is the *representational feature*, the vehicle's property(ies) in virtue of which it is a relatum of a representation relation. Third, there is the other relatum, the *represented content*, which is the entity or event represented by a vehicle/feature pair. Fourth, there is the *representing relation* between the vehicle/feature pair and content such that the former is about the latter. Fifth and finally, there is the *representation mode*, the way or manner that the representational feature represents the content. In representationalist theories of consciousness, the set of representation vehicles and their representational features and modes are routinely assumed to be intracranial in some sense, and the represented content is assumed often to be extracranial. If so, then the representational relation is not entirely intracranial. Some think that a vehicle's representational feature(s) may not be intracranial either. These problems may be glossed over for the time being. We return to them later.

Computationalism is a species of representationalism. According to *computationalism*, perceptual, affective, interoceptive, proprioceptive and cognitive processes are computational processes, where a *computational process* is one for which there is an algorithm that describes it, where an algorithm is a procedure that produces a determinate answer in a finite amount of time. Computationalism holds that it is in virtue of having this structure that conscious psychological processes, states and events enter into the causal roles that they do. The most pervasive form of representationalism is computational representationalism (also known as the *representational theory of mind* and defended by Jerry Fodor [Fodor 1975, 1981, 2008; Fodor & Pylyshyn 1988]). Computational representationalism is the view that all conscious processes, states and events are structured in a particular way, with a subject, an object and various relations (cognitive, affective, interoceptive, proprioceptive or perceptual) between subject and object. That conscious processes, states and events are directed on an object that is about something else makes the view an instance of intentionalism. The object to which the subject is related represents something else, so the view is also an instance of representationalism. And computational representationalism is computational because the relations between subject and object – examples of which include belief, hope, fear, seeing, hearing, feeling – are identified with particular computational functions that take some input representation, manipulate it, and output either the same, or some distinct, representation.

Classicism

That at least a lot of our psychological life is representational should not lull us into thinking that representation is not remarkable, for consider that what in our heads are the representation vehicles are neurons or assemblies of them. This should be obvious – what else *could* it be? – and a little unbelievable – how *can* a neuron or an assembly of neurons, even a complex assembly organized into a neural pathway, be a representation vehicle at all, and what properties of a neuron or an assembly of them can be the representational feature(s) in virtue of which neurons represent? The parallel with the hard problem of consciousness is apparent. So too is the parallel with the explanatory gap problem: grant that a neuron or an assembly of neurons is a representation vehicle – still, how *does* that neuron or assembly of neurons do its representing such that the explanatory gap is closed? That is, what feature, if any, of a neuron or an assembly of them is the representational feature in virtue of which it or they represent something else?

Two solutions are offered by the representationalist theory of mind: classical and connectionist computationalism. *Classical computational representationalism – classicism* for short – claims that representation vehicles represent in virtue of their symbolic (usually linguistic) features and that the computations to which symbolic representational vehicles are subject are members of the same family of processes as those to which symbolic representations in a digital computer are subject. *Connectionist computationalism – connectionism* for short – claims that some representation vehicles represent in virtue of certain non-symbolic features and that some of the computations to which representation vehicles are subject are members of a family of processes that are distinct from those to which symbolic representations are subject in a digital computer.

Classicism depends upon certain assumptions underlying digital computation design. Chief among those assumptions is that cognitive processes (some extend this analysis to perceptual, interoceptive, proprioceptive and affective processes as well) are computational processes that operate over symbols. A *symbol* is a sign individuated by its form, where *form* is physical shape. Individual symbols group together into larger, molecular, sets of symbols by the rules laid down for their proper combination. Together, symbols plus combination and recombination rules compose an abstract computational system. A concrete computer is then:

> some chunk of the actual world [that] realize[s] the sequences of configurations of symbol types specified by the abstract system. This means that, at any given time, it must contain an appropriate configuration of *tokens* of the symbol types, and it must change sequentially from one such configuration to another in accordance with the rule of evolution. (Van Gelder 1995: 366)

This theoretical stance is transferred to the case of the human brain and its constituent neurons and neural assemblies, so that just as a concrete computer is a physical device that instantiates a symbolic computational system, so the brain is a physical device that instantiates a symbol computational system. So computers serve as exemplars of how a set of rules and symbols – two highly abstract categories – can find a home in the physical world: they do so by being instantiated or implemented or realized by an appropriate set of vehicles and transformations between them.

Commitment to symbolic computation finds expression in the claim, made famous by Fodor (1975), that there is a *language of thought*, a symbol system that is part of the brain's own basic functioning. When a person believes that, for example, the skiing last weekend was epic, what she believes is a sentence in her language of thought (or Mentalese) that is realized in some pattern of neural activity. The sentence of Mentalese in turn represents a proposition, an abstract object. The language of thought is at its most primitive level a system composed of syntactic squiggles rather than semantic symbols, since at the most primitive level these elements have not yet been interpreted as referring to or representing anything. And the relations between these elements are causal relations which, because between uninterpreted squiggles, also do not require interpretation of meaning. This claim is sometimes put into the slogan that a computer, and hence a brain as modelled on a computer, is a syntactic engine (Stich 1983).

Many neural models of consciousness assume some version of classical computational representationalism. And why not? Entire regions of conscious life are intentional, so if computational representation and intentionality are one and the same, then entire regions of conscious life are computationally representational. But note the "if" – subjective and qualitative features of consciousness have proven recalcitrant within a representational model, much less a classicist model, and even those regions of psychological life that are representational may not be conscious *because* they are representational. Representational models may pick out conscious events accidentally, the way that picking out a creature with a kidney picks out a creature with a heart without telling us much about having a heart.

Since most reductionists and non-reductionists accept neural assemblies as representational vehicles, whatever disagreements there may be between them must be about the feature(s) in virtue of which such assemblies represent. The current state of research in this area is diplomatically described as unsettled. One divisive issue is whether this feature is internal or external to a neural system, where an *internal* property is a property that does not entail the existence of another entity and an *external* or *relational* property is one that does entail the existence of at least one other entity. Connectionists, for example, claim that representational features are internal properties of neural systems, stable activation patterns in a neurally realized *parallel distributed processing* (PDP) network caused by or resembling things and events. For classicists, on the other hand, a neural system's representational features require fixing its place in a network of relations. Which relations are relevant is a matter of ongoing discussion. Covariance, causation and asymmetric determination have all been suggested.[1]

For classicists, conscious events are sentences of an internal language of thought to which individuals are related by various kinds of cognitive, affective, perceptual, interoceptive and proprioceptive relations. As an example, my belief that Utah's Biddlecome–Ekker Ranch is one of the most remote ranches in the lower forty-eight is analysed as a relation to the sentence "Utah's Biddlecome–Ekker Ranch is one of the most remote ranches in the lower forty-eight". Sentences are syntactically organized, semantically loaded and structurally complex entities, with molecular representations being syntactic concatenations of atomic representations and with the meanings of molecular representations being functions on the meanings of atomic representations. This way of thinking about the matter has numerous benefits, the most salient of which is that if thoughts are relations to internal sentences, then the things we *believe* are the things we *say*. Given that, all the considerable resources of contemporary logic and philosophy of language can be brought to bear on the fine-grained nuances of belief and other psychological kinds.

Connectionism

Connectionism starts its explanation of representation with the nature of an idealized neuron and its connective properties. Neurons are input–output devices that receive signals from the environment or other neurons, integrate and manipulate the signals they receive, and output a signal to another neuron (or other cells). Neurons are massively interconnected with one another. Millions of neurons at any one time may be variously connected to one another, forming a dense mat of interconnections. Such a system is a PDP system, one kind of a *neural network* (or neural net).

That a neural network processes signals in parallel pathways distributed across space explains neither how they compute nor how, if at all, they represent. To be computational, there must be some internal neural feature or external neural activity in virtue of which neurons or assemblies of them map signals of one type to signals of another type. And to be representational there must likewise be some internal neural feature or external neural activity in virtue of which neurons or assemblies of them, by mapping signals, convey information about something. Identifying that representational feature (or those features) or that activity is what distinguishes connectionists from classicists.

A representational vehicle/feature pair is, recall, asymmetrically related to another entity (the represented content) such that the vehicle/feature pair is about the content, stands in for it, and can guide behaviour in its stead. Connectionists reject the pervasiveness and necessity of symbolic representation. Relying on evidence from neuroscience that there simply is no symbolically structured encoding to be found in cortical neural activity, they chide classicists for being out of touch with reality. Classicists respond that their commitment to symbolic coding is instead helpful at an appropriate level of description and that the neural level is not that level. Of course, that does not really solve the problem – it *moves* it: after all, what level is the classical computational level and how, if at all, does it illuminate the neural level, and how, if at all, is it illuminated by the neural level? There are currently no answers to these questions – Searle calls it the dirty secret of computational models (Searle 2000).

However, a question, expressed by among others Haugeland (1978) (see also Eliasmith 2003; Van Gelder 1995), may be pressed against connectionists: if *not* in virtue of symbols, then how *do* connectionist neural systems represent, if at all? Connectionists respond that neural nets have three kinds of neurons – input, output and hidden neurons. *Input neurons* receive signals from something external to the net, which signals are then processed; *hidden neurons* do the processing; and *output neurons* take the processed signals and do something with them. So, just as a single neuron is a functional unit, so too a neural network is a functional unit. Consider a simple feedforward network. Input neurons have *activation values* or *activation levels*, where an activation level or value is the probability of generating an action potential spike down an axon. Each connection has a connection *weight* that measures the strength of the connection. Positive activation levels and connection weights are measures of neural excitation; negative activation levels and connection weights are measures of neural inhibition. Together, activation values and connection weights condition the flow of a signal through a network of neurons. Neural networks can add as much complexity as needed – layers of hidden neurons within any given network and feedback neural connections from higher to lower levels. Realistic networks of anything more involved than the simplest kinds of processing are monstrously complex, involving multiple feedforward/feedback loops, each composed of neurons and patterns over them, each with their own activation weights. Such complex feedforward/feedback networks are *recurrent networks* or *re-entrant networks.*

Re-entrant networks are PDP neural networks operating over neurons and assemblies of them. What then is it for a neural process to be *distributed*? One candidate is that a single message is stored across numerous neurons and neural ensembles rather than one (Kosslyn & Hatfield 1984). If so, then there can be no "grandmother neurons", that is, neurons that alone and singly represent only one entity, such as one's grandmother, or only one event, such as her riding a horse. But spatial distribution cannot be sufficient for representation, for if the message thus stored has no representational feature, then, regardless of the number of storage locations, it cannot be a representational vehicle. Hence, some other feature must supplement spatial distribution.

If PDP networks subserve conscious processes and conscious processes are representational, then PDPs are representational vehicles. If so, then those vehicles have some internal feature in virtue of which they represent content. What in the description just provided of a connectionist network is a likely candidate for that internal feature? The most popular candidate for the connection-ist representational feature is a pattern of neural activity – an *activation pattern* – over multiple neurons or neural ensembles (see, among others, Bechtel & Abrahamsen 1991; Eliasmith 2003; O'Brien & Opie 1999a, 1999b, 2001; Rosenfeld & Touretsky 1988). Activation patterns emerge from signal transmission through connections variously weighted. Distinct entities and events correlate with the occurrence of distinct activation patterns that emerge over the same set of neurons and neural assemblies. Thus, a single neuron can be a component of numerous emergent activation patterns and so can represent numerous entities and events at the same time. In this way, distinct activation patterns *superpose* on one another. The crucial feature of superposition is captured in a metaphor that Van Gelder develops:

> In the ideal filing cabinet every distinct item to be represented is encoded on a separate sheet of paper, and the sheets are then placed side by side in cabinet drawers. Because every item is stored separately, every item can be accessed independently of all the others, and the modification, removal or destruction of any one piece does not affect any others. If representation in the cabinet were fully superposed, by contrast, there would be no separate location for each discrete item; rather, the whole cabinet would be representing every item without any more fine-grained correspondence of sheets or locations to individual items. Accessing the representation of one item is, in an obvious sense, accessing the representation of all items; and modifying or destroying the representing of one cannot but affect the representing of all.   (Van Gelder 1991: 45)

For fully localized processing, there are no superposed activation patterns; for fully distributed processing, there is nothing but superposed activation patterns. Between the two poles, there is a continuum of processing types, some more, some less distributed. Somewhere on this continuum human processing appears as a partially distributed kind of processing.

All of this is interesting, but it is still not obvious that the feature in virtue of which a connectionist network is a *representational* vehicle, and hence, a vehicle of conscious intentionality, has been identified. If neural activation patterns are to be the representational feature, then there must be something about them in virtue of which they represent. There are thought to be two options: first, activation patterns represent some thing or event in virtue of their being *caused* by that thing or event; second, activation patterns represent some thing or event in virtue of their *resembling* that thing or event. Opie and O'Brien nominate resemblance. According to their view, a conscious event is identical to a stable pattern of activation in a neurally realized PDP network (or networks) that resembles something or some event (O'Brien & Opie 1999a,

1999b). Of course, this does not entail that neurons share first-order physical properties with that which they resemble; it requires instead that neural activation patterns preserve certain kinds of information provided by whatever that activation pattern putatively resembles. In particular, what is shared between an activation pattern defined over neurons and what it resembles is a specific structural pattern of relations defined over the elements of what is represented. So, for instance, a topographic map cartographically preserves certain physical relations between mountains and valleys, and the human face-recognition neural pathway neurally preserves certain physical difference relations between male and female faces.

Higher-order representationalism

Higher-order representationalist theories of consciousness claim that representationalism as so far understood misidentifies what makes psychological events conscious. For the higher-order theorist, nothing about a representation *per se* makes it conscious (Kriegel 2006). The existence of, for example, Freudian unconscious desires and beliefs confirms for the higher-order theorist that there are plenty of unconscious representational events. But Freudian cases are just the tip of the iceberg – postulating unconscious representations is ubiquitous in contemporary cognitive neuroscience, from the unconscious representations of the various stages of perceptual work-up to unconscious thought, as when we "sleep" on a problem. All such examples are fuel for the higher-order theorist's claim that there must be something distinct from a psychological event's representational properties that makes a psychological event conscious. So higher-order theorists partition representational events into *first-order* events with representational content and *higher-order* conscious events that target the first-order event (Rosenthal 2002). That targeting relation – whatever it is – then becomes the locus of consciousness. So, what makes a psychological event conscious detaches from the vehicle and migrates to the relation.

Higher-order theorists frequently nominate *awareness* as the relation that makes some representations conscious while others languish as unconscious or non-conscious. A more precise statement of the higher-order theory can then be stated: a person's first-order psychological event is conscious if and only if there is a higher-order psychological event such that the latter is being aware of the former (Carruthers 2005; similar views are expressed by Rosenthal (2002) and described but rejected by Kriegel (2006)). Take, for example, my hope that it will be sunny and not too windy tomorrow. That hope is the *conscious* hope that it will be sunny and not too windy tomorrow whenever the hope that it will be sunny and not too windy tomorrow is accompanied by the higher-order awareness of having the hope that it will be sunny and not too windy tomorrow. If that makes your head swim, you're not alone. But it is crucial to state the view with all that prolixity because otherwise it looks benign, and it is not benign. To repeat and putting the matter bluntly, without the higher-order awareness of the hope, my hope is unconscious.

Awareness is understood either as a kind of inner perception or as a kind of inner thought. Higher-order perception (HOP) models conceive of it as an internal monitoring or perception-like event, while higher-order thought (HOT) models conceive of it as an internal thought-like event. HOP theories take the awareness relation to be relevantly similar to sensory perception, interoception and proprioception. Like these processes, higher-order perceptual awareness also provides information relevant to our well-being. So HOP theories claim that in addition to events of sensory perception, interoception and proprioception, there is an internal, higher-order perception-like scanning of those events and the information they contain. On the occurrence of (or the disposition to have an occurrence of) such a higher-order inner scanning event, the representations provided by sensory perception, interoception and proprioception become conscious. HOT theories, on the other hand, take the awareness relation to be relevantly similar to thought. Just as first-order thoughts are complexes composed of a subject, a relation such as belief, desire or fear, and a representation (which, in turn, is related to that which it is about), so higher-order thoughts are complexes composed of a subject, a unique, non-inferential relation of awareness, and the representation believed, desired, or feared. On the occurrence of (or having a disposition for an occurrence of) such a higher-order thought, the representations provided by sensory perception, interoception and proprioception again become conscious.

Higher-order theories have frequently been accused of trying to impose upon *all* kinds of consciousness conditions that apply only to *some* kinds of consciousness. The requirement that there must be some distinct higher-order awareness for a psychological event to qualify as a conscious event at all seems to entail falsely that much more of our ordinary ongoing psychological life is unconscious than we would typically think. We are aware that we are in the psychological state we are in only intermittently (not every thought about my son Calvin is accompanied by awareness that I am having the thought), and yet many such thoughts seem conscious, even if not in the way higher-order theorists claim they must be. If so, higher-order views are too strong – that is, their necessary condition is false – because they prevent consciousness from being attributed to thoughts that are otherwise thought to be conscious. Surprisingly, higher-order views may also be too weak – that is, their sufficiency condition is false. Since nothing intrinsic to a psychological event is that in virtue of which it is conscious, and since awareness is sufficient for a psychological event being conscious, being aware of events other than psychological events seems to make *them* conscious (Byrne 1997; Dretske 1995, 1997). Being aware of the dust collecting on the leaves of the plastic plant in my office appears to make the dust collecting on the leaves conscious. No one but a panpsychist could tolerate this result.

These criticisms are far from final. Against the charge that higher-order theory is too strong, a reply is that if we reconsider thoughts unaccompanied by higher-order awareness, our temptation to attribute consciousness to them will waver and be seen as nothing more than a consequence of the loose way we use "conscious" and "consciousness" in natural language. And against the charge that higher-order theory permits plastic leaves to be conscious, a reply is that such a charge ignores the crucial fact that in order to be conscious, an event must first be a psychological event. But the first response smacks of semantic legislation, and the second requires more defence to be persuasive, for if there is nothing internal to psychological events that makes them candidates for higher-order consciousness, then there must be something external to them that makes them candidates. If so, the higher-order theorist is obliged to say what it is. It must also be allowed that even if higher-order theories of consciousness are too ambitious, not all their ambitions are bankrupt. Indeed, higher-order representationalism is an attractive model for (not surprisingly) monitoring consciousness and other kinds of reflexive consciousness. Both appear to be reiterative in just the way that the higher-order theory claims all of consciousness is.

Self-representationalism

Self-representational theories of consciousness try to take the best features of representationalism and higher-order theories and avoid their worst errors (Van Gulick 2006). Higher-order theories claim that a psychological event is conscious whenever there is a numerically distinct representation or awareness of that event. Self-representational theories suggest instead that a psychological event is conscious whenever there is a particular way it is represented (Kriegel 2006). Like all representationalist views, self-representationalist views affirm that a psychological event must be representational if it is to be conscious, and like higher-order versions, self-representationalist views affirm that awareness is necessary for a psychological event to be conscious. Unlike higher-order views, self-representationalist theories deny that awareness is a distinct psychological event, and unlike first-order representationalist views, self-representationalist theories deny that a psychological event's representational properties are sufficient for being conscious. Self-representationalist views and higher-order views are therefore united in opposing first-order representationalist views such as computationalism but disagree with each other on what must be added to capture consciousness.

Some of the arguments marshalled by self-representationalists against higher-order views of consciousness are based on logical features and some on what are claimed to be unfortunate implications of the higher-order view for the causal efficacy of conscious events. Take them in order. Higher-order theories affirm that a psychological event and the awareness of it are logically independent, while self-representationalism denies that logical independence (Kriegel 2006). Put otherwise, higher-order theories deny that the relation between the two is *constitutive*, while self-representationalist theories affirm that it is. This difference fuels the objection mentioned above that higher-order views render unconscious much of our ongoing conscious life because they set the bar for being conscious so high. It seems wrong that, for every psychological event, there must be a numerically distinct awareness of it in order for the event to be conscious. Self-representationalists urge instead that while the awareness is necessary for the event to be conscious, the two are internally related to one another. An obvious candidate for that internal relation is that the awareness is a constituent part the event such that the awareness always comes attached to the event (for details, see Kriegel 2006; Mulligan & Smith 1985; Van Gulick 2006). Since the awareness is a constituent part and parts are internally related to one another, the awareness and the event form a complex.

Numerous logical and ontological niceties attach to self-representational views, but they are of less importance to us than the claim, made by Kriegel (2006), that of all two-level views, self-representationalism is the only one that avoids epiphenomenalism. If true, this claim is sufficient reason for rejecting the higher-order view, since any view that entails epiphenomenalism is, other things being equal, less attractive than any view that does not entail epiphenomenalism. The argument is this. According to the higher-order view, the higher-order awareness is distinct from the psychological event. One consequence is that consciousness migrates from a representation to awareness of it. If so, consciousness is not an internal property of a psychological event but an external or relational property. But if consciousness is an external or relational property of an event, then, Kriegel argues, it cannot be one of that event's causal powers, since only internal properties are candidates for being causal powers. On the assumption that an entity without causal powers is causally inert, it follows that higher-order consciousness is causally inert, an epiphenomenon. That is unacceptable, so higher-order representationalism is unacceptable.

This argument introduces issues concerning the causal efficacy of consciousness that we return to later. It is sufficient to point out here that there is no firm consensus yet as to which of these three versions of representationalism is correct. Of the three, higher-order representationalism appears to be in the most trouble as a general view of what makes psychological events conscious, for the reasons suggested above. This state of affairs could change, of course. But we go forwards with the thought that while it is perhaps a reasonable theory of higher-order conscious events, higher-order representationalism is a less attractive alternative for run-of-the-mill kinds of conscious events than either first-order representationalism or self-representationalism. In Chapter 12, we argue that contemporary neuroscience gives some empirical support to self-representationalism.

REPRESENTATIONALISM AND INTENTIONALITY

Some versions of representationalism are too restrictive as accounts even of intentionality, much less of the other conscious properties. Thinking that there is a language of thought in terms of which all psychological life is couched is, for example, probably too narrow, for not only are some intentional events not syntactically organized and semantically loaded, even some representations are not syntactically organized or semantically loaded – iconic and indexical representations are examples. An evolutionary/ontogenetic argument strengthens the point (Garson 2002). Linguistic representation is both a late phylogenetic add-on and a late ontogenetic arrival. Our best evidence strongly suggests that members of the genus *Homo* were, and babies are, conscious before linguistic representation appears. Neuroanatomically, too, both phylogenetically and ontogenetically, the evidence suggests that language co-opted already existing neural pathways that subserved other forms of representation prior to language emergence. Hence, either language-based representationalist theories of consciousness are mistaken or this empirical evidence is mistaken. Some are prepared to exclude prelinguistic members of the *Homo* line and prelinguistic infants from the class of conscious organisms rather than relax the syntactical and semantic requirements of the language of thought hypothesis (Carruthers 2005). The version of representationalism that, we shall assume, is representative of the class includes linguistic representation but does not exclude other species of representation such as icons, indexes and other kinds of representations.

All versions of classicist computationalism are subject to a criticism that, if sound, demonstrates that syntactic processing is not sufficient for representation and, so, for conscious intentionality. This criticism – the *Chinese room argument*, a thought experiment cooked up by John Searle – revolves around the distinction made above between original and derived intentionality. As originally developed by Searle, the Chinese room argument was used against a number of proposals from artificial intelligence. However, the argument generalizes to show that any classicist computationalism that identifies the intentionality of consciousness with computational properties and does not distinguish between original and derived intentionality cannot distinguish between what we consciously do when we understand symbols and what a computer does unconsciously when it manipulates squiggles that are symbols (Searle 2000, 2004).

Language is composed of a syntax and a semantics. Syntax is the set of rules that determine whether certain strings of symbols form words and whether certain strings of words form a sentence. Semantics is the set of rules that tells us how symbols are to be interpreted, that is, what those symbols symbolize. Every word of a natural language has a semantic interpretation – for example, "cat" refers to furry creatures who live with us and meow. That string of letters – "c" "a" "t" – could have referred instead to buffalo. It is a matter of convention what words refer to. Of course, once established, convention must be followed if we are to understand each other.

Consider, then, the argument. (Our version uses Cyrillic letters, so we really should call it the *Cyrillic* room argument; happily they have the same acronym: CRA.) Suppose you are a monolingual English speaker sitting in a room. To your left is a window through which batches of papers will be passed to you by someone. They have squiggles written on them, none of which has a semantic interpretation known to you. To your right is another window, through which you pass one sheet of paper with squiggles on it to someone. You are given rules (a)–(h), in English:

(a) "Д", "Ж", "Ч" and "Я" are true sentences;

(b) "Њ", "Щ" and "Э" can be used but only between "Д", "Ж", "Я" or "Ч" or between groups of them marked by parentheses to form sentences;

(c) "(" and ")" can be used only around "Д", "Ж", "Я" or "Ч" when they are joined by "Њ", "Щ" or "Э", to form sentences;

(d) "Ю" can be used only before "Д", "Ж", "Ч" and "Я" or before groups of those symbols marked by parentheses to form sentences;

(e) (1) is true;

(f) whenever (1) is true, tear up the piece of paper it is written on and pick up the piece of paper on which (2) is written;

(g) whenever you have picked up the piece of paper on which (2) is written, put it down and pick up the piece of paper on which (3) is written;

(h) whenever you have picked up the piece of paper on which (3) is written, take that piece of paper to the window and hand it out.

You puzzle over the meaning of the rules. Then you get a sheet, the following written on it:

Д, Ж, Ч, Я

"Aha," you say to yourself, "now I get it." By Rule (a), "Д", "Ж", "Ч" and "Я" are true sentences. Next you get another sheet, this time with the following written on it:

(1) (Д Њ Ж) Щ Я

By Rule (b) and Rule (c), "(Д Њ Ж) Щ Я" is a sentence. Again, you wait around until another batch comes in through the window. This time, you get:

(2) Я
(3) ЮЧ

Since (d) is a rule, (3) is a sentence. Since (e) and (f) are rules, you dutifully tear up the piece of paper on which (1) is written and pick up the piece of paper on which (2) is written. Since (g) is a rule, you put down the piece of paper on which (2) is written and pick up the piece of paper on which (3) is written. Since (h) is a rule, you get up, go to the window and hand the sheet with (3) written on it out. The person on the other side of the window thanks you. A man enters the room and arrests you: "ЮЧ" means "I confess without coercion that I stole the crown jewels of Cyrillia." You are horrified: you had *no idea* that "ЮЧ" meant anything, much less that you confessed to stealing the jewels.

You fail to understand Cyrillic because you fail to understand the semantic interpretation of its symbols. Since you fail to understand what the squiggles are symbols for, you fail to understand that the squiggles are symbols. Understanding what syntactic elements and complex strings of such elements are symbols for, that is, understanding what they represent (their *meaning* on one understanding of this notorious word), is an original intentional activity. The CRA shows that original intentionality is necessary for understanding language but that the information provided to the man in the room does not supply it. Now, in general, if x is claimed to be sufficient for y and z is distinct from x yet necessary for y, then x is not sufficient for y after all. That is what the CRA shows: computationalism claims that reliable manipulation of representational elements is sufficient for understanding a language, but the original intentional activity of interpreting those syntactic elements as symbols is distinct from such manipulation and yet necessary for understanding a language. Hence, reliable manipulation of representational elements is not sufficient for understanding them as representational elements.

The CRA has prompted continuous criticism from artificial intelligence proponents (see Cole 2004 for review and references to this sizeable literature). We are interested in the relevance, if any, of the CRA for consciousness, and so are interested in those uses and criticisms of the CRA that suggest something about original and derived intentionality. If so, only a few counters to the CRA make relevant points. One of these few (a version of the so-called systems reply) argues that since the man in the room is equivalent only to a computer's central processor running a program, and since a central processor running a program does not understand anything, it is not surprising that the man in the room does not understand Chinese. Rather, it is the entire system – including those outside the room as well – that understands. By itself, this counter is not persuasive against the CRA. You can stuff as much information into the man in the room as you like – make him the entire system – he still does not understand Chinese.

However, that failed counter leads to a better one, explored in the computationalist setting by Margaret Boden (1988) and Georges Rey (2002), and by many others for whom consciousness is embodied and embedded in an environment. If you are the person in the room, you do not understand Chinese because you do not know what the squiggles on the pieces of the paper represent. So, if a reply to the CRA identifies what must be added for your use of the squiggles to represent something, that is, for your use of the squiggles to be intentional, then that reply is of interest. Boden and Rey (among others) suggest that placing you in the room in a larger environment and adding causal relations – perceptions, overt behaviour and others – to that larger environment have the desired result. They use these amendments to argue that a computer placed in a mobile, sensory transducing and pragmatically engaged robot could enjoy intentionality. However that suggestion plays out in the case of robots (Searle is dismissive), the suggestion is directly applicable to human and other organismic consciousness: perhaps intentionality is not a property of any event subserved exclusively by a neural system but is rather a property of the entire organism embedded in its environment (Clark 1997; Hanna & Maiese 2009; Van Gelder 1995). We return to the issues this suggestion raises in Chapters 11 and 12.

REPRESENTATIONALISM AND QUALIA

Representationalism is well suited for describing intentionality. Qualitative properties and subjective perspectivity, on the other hand, present hurdles for the view. When I hear a clap of thunder, my auditory experience has a certain character – being a booming sound of a particular timbre, tone and volume – and that auditory experience, together with the other elements of experience that result from the proper functioning of the other perceptual modalities, are bound together as a multimodal experience. Likewise, it seems equally unlikely that the qualitative feel of sexual orgasm is nothing more than a representation. Even more, these qualitative features seem not to be *representational* features at all. If so, then representationalism appears to excise what makes conscious events conscious – namely, their felt character from the inside. This dispute over the prospects of reducing qualitative properties to some kind of content is such a firmly entrenched division in contemporary philosophy of mind and consciousness that the term "representationalism" is sometimes interpreted as a thesis concerning two ways of understanding qualitative properties. Those who support reducing qualitative properties to some kind of content are, on this interpretation, *qualia representationalists*, while those who reject reducing qualitative properties to some kind of content are *qualia phenomenalists* (or, more colourfully, *qualia freaks*).

One of the best cases for qualia representationalism is made by Michael Tye (Tye 1995, 2000, 2002; see also Dretske 1995). Tye argues that qualitative character is identical to a particular kind of represented content. That particular kind of content is: (i) poised (i.e. it is immediately ready and available for subsequent belief and/or desire); (ii) abstract (i.e. it is repeatable); (iii) non-conceptual (i.e. it can be experienced without having the corresponding concept – one can experience red without having the concept of being red); and (iv) intentional (i.e. experience can be of things that do not exist – one can experience unicorns). Putting the first letters of these properties together yields the acronym *PANIC* as a name for qualitative content. That conscious experience has qualitative character is, if Tye is correct, exhausted by its having *PANIC* content, and that two such experiences have different qualitative character is exhausted by the one having particular *PANIC* 1 and the other having different *PANIC* 2. The details of the view need not detain us. Suffice it to say that the heavy work is done by the properties of being poised and being non-conceptual: it is because an experience has this particular kind of content with these two features that it is qualitatively loaded experience rather than qualitatively bereft experience (Kriegel 2007).

A less controversial position than Tye's has it that representational thought typically has qualitative character, and perceptual experience typically has representational content. When I think of some of the things that a so-called friend of mine did last week, I am plenty mad; just so, when I hear a particular song, I hear it *as* the B-52s' "Love Shack", and when I get a mosquito bite, the itch is information about a particular region of my arm. Still, since not all representational events must come loaded with qualitative character and not all qualitative events must come loaded with representational content, representation and qualitative character are not the same property (Block [1995] 2007, 2007a). For this kind of representationalist, all conscious properties are mental *paint*, that is, properties that provide experiential vibrancy and have some representational properties, but not mental *latex*, that is, properties that provide experiential vibrancy and have no representational properties of any kind (Block [2003] 2007). We assume this less controversial position.

Absent and inverted qualia

Computers are often taken to be paradigm cases of phenomenological zombies that might satisfy representationalist conditions for being conscious but not qualitative conditions – they compute but do not experience a thing. But computers are only tangentially relevant. Humans who have representational psychological events that are not also qualitatively endowed are clearly more to the point. We consider these matters later, after introducing relevant neuroscientific evidence. Here, we introduce two problems for any representationalist view of qualitative character, the problems of absent and inverted qualia.

It is consistent with conscious properties supervening on microphysical properties that there are organisms with exactly the same complement of microphysical properties as us and *no* qualitative properties. This is the problem of *absent* qualia. To illustrate the possibility, suppose a molecule-by-molecule duplicate of you is created. Done: say hello to You-2. By assumption, supervenience is not bidirectional, so while a one-to-one mapping from qualitative to microphysical properties is required, a one-to-one mapping from microphysical properties to qualitative properties is not – qualitative differences entail microphysical differences, but microphysical sameness does not entail qualitative sameness. So, for example, it is nomologically possible that all of You-2's neural whirrings occur without the slightest glimmer of phenomenological what-it-is-likeness. Compared to you, You-2 is a *zombie* (a *philosophical* zombie, but a zombie for all that). Some have used this consequence as evidence that the subjective qualitative character of conscious experience is somehow suspect. After all, You-2 is indistinguishable from you in *every* respect except one: you possess and You-2 lacks these qualitative properties. Of course, you will never know that it lacks these properties because you will never be able to tell that there is no way that things feel to You-2 – it will respond to every prompt to expound on how it feels *exactly* as you do. We investigate this argument later, in Chapter 11.

It is also argued that representationalist accounts of perceptual experience are consistent with individuals for whom systematic qualitative shifts in experience cannot be behaviourally identified. This is the problem of *inverted* qualia. Consider two people, Bert and Ernie. Ernie sees colours as the vast majority of people do – trees are green, stop signs are red – while Bert sees things in a different way. For him, what Ernie sees as green, he sees as red; what Ernie sees as brown, he sees as white; and so forth. But, were representationalism correct, so the argument goes, then Bert's spectrum is not inverted, for Bert would utter "red" in all the same circumstances that Ernie would utter "red", even though what he experiences when he utters "red" would be what Ernie experiences when he utters "green". And, in general, all the objects that would cause Ernie's experience to be of red objects would cause all of Bert's experience to be of green objects, and the transformation functions from Ernie to Bert would map one-to-one. So all of Bert and Ernie's behaviour and all the other psychological states they enter into would be identical. Were this account of experiencing red sufficient for experiencing red, then Bert and Ernie would both see red. But, by hypothesis, they do not. So this account of experiencing red is not sufficient.

While many researchers assume that qualia are properties of conscious perceptual experience, some claim instead that qualia are properties of the objects that cause conscious perceptual experience. To draw the contrast bluntly, the first view says that qualia are the way objects are presented *in* consciousness and the second says that qualia are the way objects are presented *to* consciousness. A vocal minority opt for this latter view, one benefit of which is that the ineliminable subjectivity that attaches to qualia if they are conscious properties is immediately replaced by a more scientifically tractable set of questions. We return to this issue again in Chapters 11 and 12.

REPRESENTATIONALISM AND SUBJECTIVE PERSPECTIVITY

When I take a break from writing, I sometimes go outside and lean against the wall. Just now, I experienced, more or less all at once and with no particular salience ranking, the following: the wall pressed against my back; the heat of the day warmed the top of my head; a breeze flowed across my arms; a bolt of lightning flashed about ten miles away; a meadowlark trilled thirty feet to my right; my stomach grumbled; the minty taste of chewing gum in my mouth mixed with the odour of sagebrush invading my nostrils; the back of my eyeballs throbbed a little; a big fat raindrop hit my shirt, filtered through the fabric, and started to trickle down my back; and all the while I continued to struggle with one of the weird philosophical puzzles consciousness poses.

This conscious experience was perceptual (hearing the meadowlark, seeing the lightning, tasting the gum, smelling the sagebrush); interoceptive (feeling my stomach grumbling and the back of my eyes throbbing); proprioceptive (feeling my position in space with the wall behind me); cognitive (reflecting on the philosophical problem); and affective (struggling with that problem). The complex experience as a whole had represented content and each of its components had represented content – it was the top of my head that warmed up, not the bottom of my feet; the breeze flowed across my arms, not my brain; the raindrop trickled down my back, not my chest; the meadowlark's song came from there to my right, not from over there to my left; it was one weird philosophical puzzle, not another weird philosophical puzzle with which I was struggling. Moreover, the world thus revealed in that experience and each of its elements had qualitative character – tone, volume and timbre of the song, brightness of the lightning flash, mintiness of the gum, pungency of the sagebrush fragrance, throbbing of the eyes, rumbling of the stomach, struggling with the problem, and so on. The content of this multimodal perceptual experience was, furthermore, experienced from a particular perspective, *my* perspective, neither someone else's nor no one's. If representationalism is correct, then each of these properties must also be understood exhaustively as a kind of representational property.

Presentness and transparency

Subjective perspectivity has two constituent features that have become the focus of recent philosophical interest: presentness and transparency. It also has one constituent feature that has been the subject of philosophical interest for hundreds of years: unity.

For each distinct modality in perceptual experience, and for unified multimodal perceptual experience, what it is like to perceive is for represented content to be present in perceptual experience rather than presented as a property of perceptual experience. The same may also be said, somewhat more controversially, of qualitative character: what it is like to perceive qualia is for qualia to be present in experience as properties of things and events in the external world, not as properties of our perceptual experience caused by things and events in the external world but distinct from them. Such *presentness* is true in general of non-dysfunctional perceptual experience; it is "immediately responsive" to content and qualitative character (Crane 2005). For example, the meadowlark's song is provided to my auditory apparatus by the meadowlark itself, there thirty feet to my right, not a hundred feet in front of me or seventy feet to my left. When I think about a meadowlark, on the other hand, I can as easily imagine it perched on my head and bellowing like a walrus as being thirty feet to my right and trilling.

Presentness is closely related to a second feature of perceptual experience, transparency. What it is like to perceive qualia-endowed content is that it is present without any apparent intervening medium, that is, it is *transparent* (see, among others, Leeds 2002; O'Dea 2008; Siewert 1998, 2004; Smith 2008; and Tye 2002). The meadowlark's song is transparently present as a component of the environment rather than as a feature of my perceptual experience of the environment. Likewise, the song's qualitative characteristics are transparently present as properties of the song, not as features of my perceptual experience of the song. Moreover, when I reflect upon my experience of the song, what I discover are not features of my experience of the song; rather, I return again to the song. Putting presentness and transparency together yields the following: (a) when we perceive things and their qualitative properties, they are present *right through* perceptual experience, not as properties of perceptual experience, and (b) when we monitor or reflect on perceptual experience, what we encounter in such reflective or monitoring conscious events are, again, properties of the perceived objects and events, not properties of perceptual experience.

Presentness is a benign and uncontroversial feature, transparency less so. The world may be transparently present in perceptual experience, but thinking that upon reflection or monitoring all that we ever encounter are represented objects and their properties is dubious. Upon reflection, we can quite easily be presented with properties of experience. Illusions and hallucinations are obvious candidates, but equally telling are utterly mundane cases. If you have corrected vision and remove your glasses, your visual perceptual experience of the external world, not the external world itself, becomes blurry. This is not to deny that some objects have fuzzy boundaries. But sharply perceiving fuzzy edges, blurrily perceiving sharp edges, and blurrily perceiving fuzzy edges are distinct (Smith 2008). Likewise, when you cross your eyes, you can instantly create offset images of what you're looking at. Again, if you suffer from tinnitus, it is not that there is an external source of persistent ringing; the ringing is instead a property of the activity of your auditory apparatus whose functioning yields auditory experience.

Even in mundane cases, some qualitative properties are revealed upon monitoring or reflection to be properties of perceptual experience rather than the things and events present in perceptual experience. Given the variety and number of neuropsychological perceptual disorders (discussed in Chapter 6), acknowledging that both what we experience and our experience of it can host qualitative properties can lead one to wonder whether *all* the things and *all* the qualitative properties that are transparently present in perceptual experience as external are, as reflection reveals *some* qualitative properties to be, internal properties of perceptual experience. The result of this suspicion is a view of perceptual experience that has been dubbed the "grand illusion hypothesis" (see Rowlands 2006 for a critical review). But the generalization necessary to yield the grand illusion hypothesis is too hasty. Distinguishing between qualitative properties of things consciously experienced and the qualitative properties of conscious experience blocks the generalization, but there is no reason to think that the distinction puts us on a slippery slope to indirect realism or idealism. If anything, the distinction between qualitative properties of things consciously experienced and qualitative properties of conscious experience leads away from indirect realism and idealism and towards a more substantial embodiment of conscious experience. We return to this matter in Chapter 12.

Transparency and presentness probably entail the falsity of higher-order representationalism as a general account of conscious properties. If perceptual content is transparent, then the presented objects and events and their presented qualitative features exhaust what that perceptual experience is about. If so, then no other feature of that experience is necessary for that experience to be conscious. Hence, the requirement that there be a distinct higher-order event in virtue of which a first-order event is conscious, a defining feature of higher-order representationalism, is incorrect (Kriegel 2006). Self-representationalism is a more complex matter. As a part of the first-order representation of qualitative features of objects and events, the higher-order awareness may also be transparently presented in conscious experience. But then it is not the case that the subject is separable from its representational perceptual experiences. Since it is not separable from those representational perceptual experiences, there is no temptation to reify the subject as some thing that experiences the passing show of experience. Nevertheless, that the self is implicated in all conscious experience introduces one aspect of the unity of consciousness not yet considered.

Content binding and unity

Represented content is transparently present in perceptual experience and unified. What it is like to perceive content is that its elements are bound, both within and across perceptual modalities, into a single and transparently present multicomponential field. The beak on the meadowlark thirty feet to my right is the source of the song I hear thirty feet to my right. The meadowlark whose song I hear is the meadowlark that I see thirty feet to my right. The singing meadowlark and the drop of water rolling down my back are components of a single multimodal, multicomponential, content whose auditory, visual, tactile, olfactory and gustatory qualitative features are likewise bound in a single multimodal qualia field. Of course, content unity, qualia unity and content-qualia unity can each and separately be compromised in idiosyncratic ways, either by environmental factors or by sensory or neural dysfunction. The meadowlark might be hidden by intervening scrub oak; I might be listening to music on my earphones and not hear its song; I may be blind or deaf; I may be an apperceptive agnosiac who can experience parts of an object but not as bound together into the object of which they are parts.

Not only is content bound in conscious experience, conscious experience is bound across content, and this on at least two dimensions: (a) there are not separate events for each distinct modality of perceptual input, one event for, say, hearing the meadowlark, another for seeing it; and (b) there are not separate subjects of experience, one for hearing, another for seeing. Putting (a) and (b) together, we can say that the presence of the always-intimated subject of conscious experience is also unified across experience modalities with the content of that experience. Perceptual experience, interoceptive and proprioceptive experience, emotional experience, cognitive experience and, for that matter, a complex multimodal perceptual-interoceptive-proprioceptive-affective-cognitive experience as well, is the experience of a subject to which it is bound.

The philosophical intuitions getting pulled on here are the Kantian ones that all conscious experience is the conscious experience of a subject. Such unity is a third feature of subjective perspectivity. Some contemporary discussions are neuroscientifically informed (Bayne 2008; Dainton 2000; the essays collected in Cleeremans 2003; O'Dea 2008; Shoemaker 1996a, 1996b; Tye 2003). One strand of these discussions flies under the banner of the *co-ownership theory of unity* (Bayne 2004; Brook & Raymont 2006; Strawson 2000; Zahavi 2000a), two versions of which are available. On the first, unity of conscious experience is accounted for as the result of all such experience being the experience of a single body or brain; on the second, unity of conscious experience is accounted for as the result of all such experience being the experience of a single psychological subject. Philosophical objections to both versions are numerous and ingenious (for a tour, see Bayne 2004). Most of them rely on thought experiments designed to show that even if either bodily or psychological unity are necessary for conscious unity, there must be something added to both to yield conscious unity. We need not disagree with this assessment, for we are interested here only in the view that some dimensions of conscious unity are not content based, not that all dimensions of conscious unity are not content based. Only the latter carries with it any obligation to provide a sufficiency condition.

Representationalist accounts of subjective perspectivity are typically provided in terms of content that is inherently self-implicating. But this is not the only way that subjective perspectivity can be a component of a representationalist theory of consciousness. Recall the distinction between representational content – that is, what is represented – and representational mode – that is, the way content is represented. What seems to be true is that experience's subjectivity is not exhausted by describing represented content (nor, for that matter, by describing the vehicles of representing or the relation of representing). But there may well be a self-implicating way of representing content that underwrites the perspectivity of subjectivity and the subjectivity of perspectivity. What makes some representations different from others is that those made in the subjective mode have different causal consequences than others: they are representations presented from the inside, so to speak, and being presented from the inside is causally distinct from not being presented from the inside (Levine 2001). Subjective perspectivity is thus at least consistent with representationalism. This alternative is currently under investigation by Van Gulick, Kriegel and other self-representationalists (see the essays collected in Kriegel & Williford 2006).

As can be gauged, representationalism is an account of conscious properties with considerable explanatory power. Even the most strident representationalists admit that qualitative character and subjective perspectivity present challenges to the view, and solving these challenges is among the most demanding tasks in contemporary philosophical thinking about consciousness. We return to it in Chapters 11 and 12, but only after surveying recent empirical neuroscientific work on the neural correlates of conscious properties. We are now in a position to keep some version of the following question in the back of our minds: does all the neuroscientific evidence support the conclusion that these conscious properties are reducible to or identical with any property of a neural assembly, regardless of its complexity? If all conscious properties are representational properties and if representationalism entails rejecting neural reduction, the answer may well be "no". In that case, philosophical considerations will show that the empirical evidence is consistent with some kind of non-reductive physicalism. If empirical evidence shows that conscious properties are reducible to neural properties and if that entails the falsity of representationalism, the answer may well be "yes". In that case, the scientific evidence will show that representationalism has to be jettisoned. Of course, these alternatives may not be exhaustive. But before a decision can be made about these matters, the empirical work has to be introduced. To that task we now turn.

5. CORTICAL EVOLUTION AND MODULARITY

Neuroscience is the scientific study of the brain and nervous system. It is a large field and immediately splits into four subfields. *Neuroanatomy* is the scientific study of the form and structure of the brain and nervous system. *Neurophysiology* is the scientific study of the physical and biochemical processes of the brain and nervous system. *Neuropsychology* is the scientific study of the relationships between, on the one hand, the brain and nervous system and, on the other, perceptual, interoceptive, proprioceptive, affective and cognitive processes and functions. *Neuropsychiatry* is the scientific study of neuropsychological dysfunctions. Given these distinctions, we can put the relations between the subfields like this: neurophysiology studies the physical and biochemical processes that neuroanatomically identified things enter into, neuropsychology studies the psychological functions of neurophysiologically identified processes, and neuropsychiatry studies dysfunctions of neuropsychologically identified processes.

Evidence from neuroanatomy, neurophysiology, neuropsychology and neuropsychiatry that there are neural correlates of conscious properties is rapidly accumulating. In this and the next three chapters, select evidence for these correlates is presented. Most of it comes from neuroanatomical and neurophysiological fMRI and PET imaging studies of neural function, from comparative neurophysiology and neuropsychology, and from neuropsychiatric studies of neuropsychological dysfunction in humans. An *entrée* into this empirical work can be made by reviewing the evolutionary history of human brains. This chapter focuses on cortical evolution, the structural modularity of the brain, and the controversial claim that consciousness is an evolutionary module. Note: since cognition is routinely contrasted with perception, interoception, proprioception and emotion, in this and the next chapters perceptual neuroscience, affective neuroscience and cognitive neuroscience are distinguished.

A POTTED HISTORY OF BRAINS

The general pattern of evolutionary brain growth is radial and from inside to outside, from ancient subcortical hind- and midbrain structures to newer surrounding allocortex and mesocortex to even newer surrounding neocortex (for those unfamiliar with these and other terms, please consult the Appendix). Cerebral structures found in brains of, say, reptiles and conserved thereafter are very old and primitive; structures that appear with mammalian species and conserved thereafter are less primitive but still old; and those found only in primates and humans are newer still. Reptiles have well-developed hind- and midbrain structures, incipient subcortical forebrain structures such as amygdala, thalamus and hippocampus, minimal allocortex and mesocortex, and no neocortex. Mammalian brains have not only allocortex and mesocortex but neocortex as well. In mammals other than primates, neocortical development occurs only in areas abutting subcortical forebrain, allocortex and mesocortex. In higher primates and humans, neocortex balloons to remarkable proportions.

Reptilian, mammalian and primate brains

Reptile and insect behaviour is automated, and their psychology, such as it is, is characterized by reflexive responses to visual, tactile, auditory and chemical features of the environment. Box turtles put in front of a mirror will, for example, continue to attack their reflection as long as there is enough light for there to be a reflection or until they are exhausted (luckily, their enemy always collapses at the same time). A frog detects a fly and – fthp! – flicks its tongue out to catch it. If it misses, it waits. Nothing else ever comes into its head: it just sits there until another fly passes within range and – fthp! – out goes the tongue again.[1] Turtle and frog behaviour is routinized, special-purpose, encapsulated, modular and algorithmic. The reptilian parts of the human brain – hindbrain (pons, cerebellum and medulla), midbrain (tectum and tegmental area) and hypothalamus – control many of the body's autonomic systems, such as breathing, heart rate, movement and the fight-or-flight mechanism. Herd behaviour, hoarding, nesting, preening, mating displays, fear, lust ("horniness" and "being turned on"), rage and contentment can be as reactive and impersonal in us as in a lizard. Of course, we are also conscious, rational, self-aware beings, with massively developed neocortex. We can, do, and often should resist reptilian responses.

Most hindbrain and midbrain regions are of little interest to neuroscientists studying consciousness. The hypothalamus is an exception. Appearing in many phyla predating mammals, the most important of its functions are regulating pulse, blood pressure, emotional arousal, and physiological conditions such as hunger, thirst, pain response, pleasure, sexual satisfaction, rage and dominance. In humans and other primates, the hypothalamus sends electrochemical messages to the rest of the body to control autonomic functions. Short-circuiting or stimulating hypothalamic pathways alters expression of hunger and satiety, rage, pleasure, sadness and lust, thus demonstrating that activity routing through the hypothalamus is causally necessary for instantiating some conscious properties.

It is not obvious that animals without neocortex – such as insects and reptiles – are conscious. Their neural architecture is certainly sophisticated enough for sensory information processing and for producing responses to that information, but sensory processing and responding to such processed information may not be all that is required for a brain to host conscious events. After all, thermostats process and respond to environmental information as well, and few would agree that a thermostat's processing is conscious. It lacks qualitative character and subjective perspectivity – there is no way the world is *for* the thermostat and nothing it is like to *be* a thermostat. It is also true that conscious animals cannot be conscious without the reptilian parts of their brains, but, again, these reptilian parts are not all that is required for conscious properties to be instantiated. After all, conscious animals cannot be conscious without hearts either. If the reptilian parts of the brain serve the same kind of supporting or facilitating role as a heart, reptilian cerebral structures are, at best, necessary preconditions for consciousness.

Certain brain structures and neural pathways are the heritage not of our shared reptilian ancestry but of our shared mammalian ancestry. These include subcortical regions such as the thalamus and basal ganglia, allocortical regions such as amygdala, hippocampus and pyriform cortex, mesocortical regions such as insular, cingulate, orbitofrontal and parahippocampal cortices, and neocortical regions such as primary sensory and associative cortex in occipital, parietal, temporal and frontal regions. This thicket of capsules, bulbs, nuclei, formations, bodies, bands, tracts and fissures, and even the mesocortical areas nearest them, are old, the compact and closely knit results of a protracted route through evolution. The subcortical and allocortical parts of primate cerebrum are like tangled neighbourhoods in an old city: lots of smallish structures, each with lots of smallish rooms, linked by numerous specialized paths to other similar structures. In comparison, mesocortex is like early-twentieth-century suburbs before cars became ubiquitous, and neocortex is like late-twentieth-century suburban sprawl. As should be expected, most of the differences between ours and other primate brains occur in these newer areas.

The allocortical and mesocortical neural assemblies and pathways subserving perception, memory, interoception, and more than a few kinds of emotion and motivation are likewise similar across primates. These pathways – in hippocampus, amygdala and parts of cingulate cortex – together form what is commonly called the *limbic system*. "Limbus" is Latin for ring, and the limbic system encircles the hindbrain and midbrain structures of the reptilian brain and is in turn encircled by neocortex. Limbic components are evolutionary add-ons to the reptilian brain shared across mammals and highly conserved across primates. Pathways circuiting through these assemblies underwrite more complex psychological and behavioural responses than those available to animals without them. Surrounding limbic components but interior still to neocortex is mesocortical *paralimbic cortex*: orbitofrontal cortex, insular cortex, temporal pole of temporal cortex, parahippocampal cortex (entorhinal and perirhinal cortex and subiculum) and parts of cingulate cortex. Between allocortical hippocampus and amygdala and neocortical frontal/prefrontal cortex, these mesocortical assemblies have more neural layers than allocortex and fewer than neocortex.

Although simply assuming that limbic, paralimbic and perceptual pathways have remained unchanged since the time of our primate ancestors masks evolutionary developments, significant stretches of neuroscientific research on limbic, paralimbic and perceptual pathways is done on rhesus and other varieties of macaque monkeys, and homologies between their and our versions of even these pathways are well established. Moreover, recent findings in comparative neuroanatomy have yielded further evidence that, in addition to massively preserved allocortex and mesocortex, many neocortical structures are homologous across a number of primate species (Matsuzawa *et al.* 2006). Since many of these more primitive structures are replicated in more advanced versions, then, so long as nothing is known to have changed in the interim, a rough-and-ready primate baseline can be established.

Human brains

Many of our psychological resources have been in place for a long time, some of them emerging deep in our mammalian past, others in our more recent primate past, others with the appearance of our *hominin* ancestors, and others only with *Homo sapiens*. If conscious properties are to be explained naturalistically, they too must fall into this pattern. Determining where intentionality, qualitative character, and subjective perspectivity and unity appear in the evolutionary story is a big challenge, for although contemporary human brains host these properties and are all over the place, none are more than a few decades old, and even the few preserved ones that loiter in ether do not inform us about our prehistoric past. Likewise, direct inferences from contemporary correlations between behaviour/ability and brain region to pre- and protohuman correlations between behaviour/ability and brain region are also blocked, for such inferences assume mistakenly that there have been no changes in brains between now and then. All that is left to study for the entire sweep of human development to the emergence of reflection on consciousness 3,000 years ago is our prehistoric ancestors' skulls. The period from four million years ago to 100,000 years ago is very sparsely represented. Of course, our nearest primate relatives, bonobos and chimpanzees, are still around as a reminder of how things may have been neurologically when humans first split off from the rest of the primate lineage, and their brains are intensively studied. Evidence from human neurophysiology, comparative neurophysiology, evolutionary psychology and cognitive archaeology concerning brain size, architecture and function across humans and primates is now extensive enough to circumscribe the functional and anatomical features of primate and human brain most likely associated with consciousness.

The great apes are *hominids*. Orangutans branched off the *hominid* lineage 12 to 15 million years ago, gorillas eight million years ago, and the common ancestor to chimpanzees and humans seven million years ago. Ancestors of and contemporary chimpanzees and ancestors of and contemporary humans constitute the *hominins*. About five million years ago our near ancestors, protohuman *Australopithicus afarensis* and *Australopithicus africanus*, first appeared. Their brain size was about 400 cubic centimetres (cm³). The early species in the *Homo* line, *Homo habilis* (human who is handy), *Homo erectus* (human who walks standing up), and *Homo ergaster* (human who works), are found about 2.5 million years ago. *H. habilis* is probably the oldest of the three and had a brain about 550 cm³ in size. *H. ergaster* emerged about two million years ago with a brain of about 850 cm³. *H. erectus* was the last to emerge, about 1.9 million years ago, and had the largest brain of the bunch at about 1000 cm³. *H. erectus* travelled out of Africa and survived for hundreds of thousands of years (the most recent fossils, from China, are less than 100,000 years old). It appears that only minimal brain size increase occurred within the line over its long run. *Homo heidelbergensis* (human from Heidelberg), probably a descendant of *H. habilis* or *ergaster*, emerged about 750,000 years ago and is the last common ancestor to Neanderthals and *Homo sapiens*. About six feet tall and muscular, *H. heidelbergensis* had a brain of about 1200 cm³. Subsequent to *H. heidelbergensis*, the line diverged to *Homo neanderthalensis* (human from Neander Valley) and *Homo sapiens* (human who knows). Archaic *Homo sapiens* is in turn the direct ancestor of us, we who are *Homo sapiens sapiens* (human who knows that it knows).

The oldest *H. neanderthalensis* fossil is about 350,000 years old; *H. sapiens* appeared in Africa some time more recently than 200,000 years ago. Both species probably migrated out of Africa no earlier than 100,000 years ago and perhaps no earlier than 60,000 years ago. They moved through the Levant into Asia and Europe and coexisted for many thousands of years. Neanderthals had large brains – they average about 1500 cm³, which is at least as large as, if not a little larger than, the average contemporary human brain. Despite their advances, it was all over for Neanderthals by 25,000 years ago. Whether through competitive attrition, loss of habitat, reproductive isolation, or a unique evolutionary advantage of *H. sapiens sapiens*, Neanderthals disappeared from the face of the earth and left us as the only remaining species of the genus. *H. sapiens sapiens* has a brain that averages 1400 cm³, about the same size or a little smaller than *H. neanderthalensis*. *H. sapiens sapiens* continued to roam and eventually colonized the world. We were in Australia by 40,000 years ago, the Arctic by 20,000 years ago, North America 10,000 years ago, and in the Pacific Islands 2,000 years ago. If ever there was a weed species, we are it.

EVOLUTIONARY DEVELOPMENTS IN HUMAN NEURAL STRUCTURES

Overall brain size tends to scale allometrically with body size. Relative to other primates, however, our brains have also increased in size *non*-allometrically. Non-allometric brain growth is a function of non-allometric growth in particular cortical regions, and here a similar rule applies: just as brain size scales predictably with body size, so too a cortical region's proportional size in comparison to other cortical regions scales predictably with brain size (Arbib 2001; Striedter 2005). Hence, individual cortical areas tend to enlarge together rather than separately, and it is rare and noteworthy when particular cortical regions enlarge disproportionately to others. As cortical regions increase in size, internal structural changes also occur. First, cortical regions tend to fractionate into smaller assemblies, and new cortical assemblies are added. The additional anatomical complexity thus introduced into gross cortical architecture engenders increased functional specialization, which for some psychological processes improves performance. A correlated change occurs within each assembly. Sheetlike fields of neuronal columns become structurally preferable to clumplike nuclei of neurons because the parallel and right angle connections found in the constituent columns tend to minimize dendrite and axon length, thus minimizing connection length and conserving space and energy. Such laminar structures have convergently evolved numerous times across vertebrate orders as brain size increases (Striedter 2005).

When the number of neurons in a brain increases, connection density – the proportion of neurons directly interconnected to other neurons – tends to decrease. One convincing argument for functional modularity follows from this phenomenon. As brains and cortical regions grow, the conductivity and computational power of their constituent neurons becomes increasingly less efficient as the length of the axons increases and neuronal connectivity decreases. Eventually, full connectivity across neurons is abandoned, and neural assemblies reorganize into smaller functionally specific assemblies, namely, modules (Shapiro 2004). As has been noted, increasing modularity is pervasive: if a brain is enlarging and increasing its computational power, it must go modular or it will go bust (Solé & Bascompte 2006; Solé & Valverde 2008). However, increased neuroanatomical fractionation and functional modularity are themselves good only up to a point, for decreasing neural connectivity threatens smooth operations, resulting in inefficient neural coordination across modules. As brains get bigger, they get more modular, and as they get more modular, the number of neural connections required for one module to interact with another increases, thus slowing down the overall processing times for all the processes that require activity in multiple neural assemblies. So too, as efficiency improves for each modularized function, coordination between and among modularized functions suffers. So, both neurally and functionally, as brain size increases and modularity proliferates, the degrees of separation between modules increases (Streidter 2005), eventuating in a brain that is good at a number of separate tasks but hopeless at accomplishing anything more sophisticated.

This problem has been solved in the mammalian brain in general, and in the human brain in particular, by adopting what is known as a *small world architecture* (Solé *et al.* 2003; Solé & Bascompte 2006; Streidter 2005). A small world neural architecture makes the best of the situation imposed by mutually opposed modularization and coordination tensions. Where elements are organized in a unidirectional chain, integration is low; where elements are organized so that each is connected to the other, integration is high; and where elements are organized so that some but not all are connected to others, integration is intermediate. Suppose we have a system of five elements, 1, 2, 3, 4 and 5. If 1 can cause 2, 2 can cause 3, 3 can cause 4, and 4 can cause 5, and no other causal relations between the five elements obtain, we would have the unidirectional causal system shown in Figure 5.1. Consider, now, another organization, in which 1 can cause 2 or 3, 2 and 3 can cause each other, 2 can cause 4 or 5, 4 can cause 5, and 5 can cause 3. We would have a partially integrated causal system such as that shown in Figure 5.2. Figure 5.2 represents a partially integrated system, with some forward, some lateral, some feedback and some reciprocal causal relations.

The system represented in Figure 5.2 is a simple example of small world architecture. As connection length shortens for most neurons as modularization increases, some neurons with long connections – notably the myelinated

Figure 5.1 A unidirectional causal system of five elements.

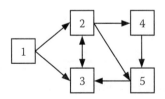

Figure 5.2 A partially integrated causal system of five elements.

neurons of the various fasciculi – are augmented and others newly added. These provide connection shortcuts between otherwise distant and disconnected neurons. Deacon (1990) and Striedter (2005) hypothesize that they connect with neighbouring regions that in ancestral cortical architectures were unconnected, invading them with information they previously lacked, thus making the enlarged assembly increasingly essential.

Brain size and new regions

It is tempting to think that at some point in the development of *Homo* a particular brain region first appeared, or a particular brain size was first achieved in virtue of which the lights of consciousness suddenly turned on. Unfortunately, this is false. Consciousness is not new with humans, and many of the offered candidates for thinking that it is new just do not work.

One explanation of the emergence of consciousness that does not work is that our brains are bigger than other species. Yet certain whales and elephants have larger brains and more convoluted cortex than humans do (Gibson 2002). Of course, they are also much bigger animals than humans, but even corrected for body volume and weight, human brains are smaller than the brains of some dolphin species. It is true that, in comparison to other primates, human brains are larger than expected. Were chimps our size and weight, their brains would be larger than they are but still smaller than ours (Bush & Allman 2004; Oxnard 2004). So there is some difference between us and them. In addition, it has been established that many particular structural components, including the medulla oblongata, hippocampus, amygdala, cerebellum, and some regions of neocortex are disproportionately larger in human brains than in other primates. But what has been thought to be our pride and joy – frontal/prefrontal cortex – is not, it appears, proportionately larger in us than in chimps. Both total volume of frontal/prefrontal cortex and relative volume to other regions of the brain are more or less the same in us as in chimps: about 38 per cent of all cortex in humans and orangutans is frontal/prefrontal; in chimpanzees and bonobos, it is about 35 per cent, and in gorillas, about 37 per cent (Semendeferi *et al.* 2002).

Even in the *Homo* lineage, Neanderthals had a brain larger than ours, and they had it 200,000 years ago; moreover, their frontal and prefrontal cortex was as big as ours. Although Neanderthals had a sloping forehead, it was not the result of poor frontal/prefrontal cortex development. Rather, their faces protruded whereas ours have dropped, retracted, and become more vertically oriented. Neanderthal craniums held a brain no smaller than and of roughly the same shape as ours, and, in all probability, with much the same neural architecture as well. So far as sheer size is concerned, then, modern brains and the brains of early humans and protohumans have not changed much over at least 200,000 years (Torey 2009).

Perhaps the addition of new brain structures is what matters. Unfortunately, all the human brain's major regions and structures were probably already in place in our shared primate ancestor when we separated off from them (Kirkcaldie & Kitchener 2007; Semendeferi *et al.* 2002). The most frequently mentioned candidate for a new brain region is the angular gyrus in the temporoparietal region, which helps compose Wernicke's area. In the vast majority of right-handed people and even in most left-handed people, these areas, lateralized to the left side of the brain, correlate with language comprehension. Since we are the only species that speaks and since Wernicke's area is required for speech comprehension, one might think that we alone have Wernicke's area or that we alone have lateralized Wernicke's area. However, chimps and bonobos, who do not speak at all, not only have brain regions holomorphic to those identified in us as Wernicke's area, but their versions of it are also lateralized. (Homologous areas in orangutans are not as well developed as in chimps and bonobos, so some changes appear to have occurred in more distant primate phylogenesis.) This is not to say that there are no differences between human temporoparietal region and the homologous area in bonobos and other primates. Ours have a more columnar organization than theirs, and new and different synaptic pathways to and from these regions have been added during our development (Torey 2009; Wilkins & Wakefield 1995). The only other candidate ever mentioned for a cortical region new with humans is the frontopolar region of prefrontal cortex, at the very front of the brain. But, again, it appears that even this region was already in place when we separated off from the chimps and bonobos, both of whom have them (Torey 2009). Ours are larger and better connected, not new.[2]

Neuron number, dendrite proliferation, extended ontogenesis, myelination

If neither larger brains nor brand new brain parts explain phylogenetic developments in human forms of consciousness, is there something else that does and, if so, what is it? One candidate is non-allometric growth in particular brain regions. For example, it appears that *H. sapiens* and *H. neanderthalensis* have larger and wider parietal cortex in the angular gyrus than their *H. erectus* ancestors (Bruner 2004; Lieberman *et al.* 2002; Torey 2009). In *H. neanderthalensis* and *H. sapiens*, this part of parietal cortex appears to have bulged, making the overall shape of the brain less egglike and more globular. This finding is a weaker version of the discredited claim that superior temporal cortex and angular gyrus in parietal cortex are new with humans. They are not new, but these findings do suggest that they are larger in Neanderthals and in us even than in earlier *Homo* members. Since posterior and inferior parietal and superior temporal cortex are loci of neural pathways implicated in visual and spatial integration, auditory integration, proprioceptive information integration, verbal communication, working memory and motor task planning, their non-allometric growth is likely to correlate with improvements in some subset of these abilities (Andersen & Buneo 2002; Colby & Goldberg 1999).

Archaeological evidence buttresses the claim. With *H. heidelbergensis*, tool-making improved significantly. Among other things, their tools were not only radially and rotationally symmetrical, but also congruently symmetrical across three dimensions – one side is a mirror image of the other. This advance was made possible by a change in construction method. *H. erectus* simply knocked flakes off a chunk, or core, of flint, but *H. heidelbergensis* used the core as a resource for numerous additional flakes, which were then worked further to their more refined shapes. This is a change from *"façonnage"* (French for "shaping") to *"debitage"* (French for "flaking") (Wynn 2002). The finer edges and improved functional plasticity afforded by *debitage*-produced tools in turn allowed increased sophistication and craft, one result of which is the carved wooden spears found in Germany, dating to 400,000 years ago and attributed to *H. heidelbergensis*. It is likely that *H. heidelbergensis* was able to visually represent multiple perspectives of the stone tools they created as they were creating them and were able to engage in hierarchical and sequential production procedures. The shift from *façonnage* to *debitage* also implies abilities to move attention from the knapping activity to one of its by-products, to apply procedures to that by-product, and to reconsider what they were doing. Just as importantly, they could probably instruct others how to do what they were doing, for *debitage* techniques are, it has been argued (Wynn 2002), too complicated to be acquired by observation alone. That has suggested to some a rudimentary protolanguage. Even if language was not required for instruction (one can imagine non-linguistic means of getting a pupil to pay attention, such as a grunt, a pat on the knee, or a slap on the head), shared attention to the procedure seems almost certain. Neanderthals advanced again, becoming expert enough to pass their skills on to apprentices. Hafting points to spears and Levallois technique imply sequential and hierarchical thinking and the ability to implement plans.

Wynn and Coolidge generalize from these archaeological findings to the claim that *H. heidelbergensis* and subsequent members of the *Homo* lineage had an enhanced form of working memory over their *H. erectus* progenitors (Welshon 2010; Wynn 2002; Wynn & Coolidge 2004; working memory is discussed in greater detail in Chapter 7). The additional complexity of *debitage* probably required enough capacity in the visuospatial sketchpad to hold in mind perspectival images of the core for some number of seconds. Likewise, if successful instruction of *debitage* required shared attention to the procedure, a lengthening of working memory capacity over *H. erectus* seems implied. These in turn imply not only lengthier and ramified working memory but also increasingly sophisticated long-term procedural memory governing skill, muscle memory and non-cognitive emotional memory. Although Neanderthals may have had some protolanguage – a few words for things and activities, perhaps, or food stuffs – even if they did not, their additional working and procedural muscle memory capacity suggests developments over *H. heidelbergensis* (Boë *et al.* 2002; Fitch & Reby 2001).

Suppose superior temporal and parietal cortices have grown non-allometrically in our phylogenetic career. In what does that growth – or growth of any cortical brain region, for that matter – consist? Does growth happen when there are more neurons, bigger neurons, reconfigured neurons, more connecting pathways, new connecting pathways, or reconfigured pathways? All are candidates. Human brains have more neurons than brains in other primate species; indeed, we have about twice the number of neurons that chimps have. Human neurons also have longer dendrites and axons and more synapses per axon than other primate neurons. Human brains also have more long myelinated neurons than other primate brains and more white matter tracts. Human brains also have more cortical regions with greater columnar organization than other primate brains. Finally, human brains take longer to mature than other primate brains. These differences entail that human brains have far greater connectivity capacity than do other primate brains. This additional connectivity is likely to be one of the bases of our additional flexibility, including our form of consciousness (Roth & Dicke 2005; Torey 2009).

The fact that our brains contain twice as many neurons as our nearest remaining primate relative is not predicted by our larger size. Something happened in protohuman and human development that resulted in this non-allometric increase. One suggestion, found in the work of Finlay *et al.* (2001), is that a small number of mutations, perhaps a single mutation, in regulatory genes accounts for the increases in neuron number. There are two stages of neuron growth. The first occurs when progenitor neurons are formed around the telencephalic ventricle. This stage is symmetric and exponential – every time cells divide, the number of progenitor cells doubles. The second stage of neuron growth occurs when each progenitor cell creates another progenitor and a neuron. All neurons that come from this stage of neuron growth stack on top of each other in columns. This stage of growth is neither symmetric nor exponential but asymmetric and linear. By the first process, cortex expands radially by exponentially increasing the number of neural columns; by the second, the thickness of neural columns grows. A mutation in regulatory genes that permits even a few additional rounds of symmetric cell division and delays the onset of neural column construction increases the number of progenitor neurons enormously.

In addition, all the extra neurons in human brains have longer dendrites and thicker axons and are arranged in more and longer neural columns than those found in other primate brains. We therefore have fewer neurons per square millimetre than other primates, so our brains have thicker and more convoluted cortex than other primate brains. Additional dendrite length makes hosting additional synapses possible, and in humans, synaptic proliferation has reached levels unmatched anywhere else in the animal kingdom. Adult mice, for example, have about 80 billion synapses; adult humans have anywhere from 100 to 500 trillion synapses, and more than double that number before synaptic pruning trims them in adolescence. More importantly, additional dendrite length makes hosting additional synapses necessary, for were the additional synapses not present, larger neurons would lose their antecedent level of connectivity to other neurons. Just so, additional dendrite thickness is likewise necessary to maintain conductivity cable properties (Kaas 2000).

Another difference between our brains and those in other primates and our common ancestor is that our versions of some neuroanatomical widgets have a different internal structure than their versions of the same widgets. First, primates have more feedback and top-down cortico-cortical pathways than other mammals, and humans have more than other primates (Neill 2007). Proliferating cortico-cortical feedback and top-down pathways correlate with input-independent direction of behaviour. Second, structural changes in neurons account for feedback and top-down pathway proliferation. Pyramidal neurons in layer III of neocortex become, as one climbs the phylogenetic ladder to *H. sapiens*, increasingly branched. Compared to other versions of pyramidal neurons, our heavily branched versions have increased neuroplastic potential (Elston 2003; Montagnini & Treves 2003; Stepanyants & Chklovskii 2005).

Such structural changes within neural regions and to neurons probably play some role in explaining interspecies differences across psychological abilities. Consider vocalization and speech. Vocalization is ubiquitous across primates. Even orangutans, who vocalize little, recognize conspecifics by sound. Bonobo chimps, perhaps our closest living *hominin* relative, also vocalize regularly, reliably and vociferously. They grunt, groan, peep, hoot, scream, whistle, bark, pout, pant and click in predictable ways in response to specific cues and in specific contexts. In addition, some bonobo vocalizations are tonally modulated, limited to short chunks, and organized as responses to communicative input from each other and from caretakers. However, bonobo vocalizations are not yet speech, for they are indexical rather than symbolic, stimulus-dependent rather than stimulus-independent, and emotionally bound to motivational state rather than cognitively liberated from motivational state.

Although a structural difference in Wernicke's and Broca's areas is not alone enough to explain speech, that human Wernicke's and Broca's areas are more columnar in structure does correlate with the appearance of speech. Changes in synaptic connectivity are thus probably a necessary condition for speech (Barbas 2005; Fitch 2000; Fitch *et al.* 2005; Hauser *et al.* 2002). But other neural changes are also required, for all the vocalizing among other primate species is emotional, associated with limbic structures such as the amygdala and hippocampus, and has but trivial cognitive content and trivial involvement of prefrontal cortex. Much of human vocalizing is, on the other hand, highly cognitive, associated with prefrontal pathways. So long as our precursors' vocalizing remained a limbic indexical accompaniment, as it still is in bonobos, it was not speech. At some point in our past, it appears that neural pathways in prefrontal cortex hijacked limbically based vocalizing for cognitively controlled rather than emotionally controlled vocalization, making vocal behaviour more than emotional outbursts.[3]

In addition, working memory and the neural pathways correlated with it also had to change to accommodate increased storage in working memory so as to comprehend and produce the syntactically complex and semantically meaningful sentences characteristic of speech. Vocalization dominated by limbic system pathways was not likely to have been symbolic. Indexing facial expression or vocal outburst to emotional state (itself a significant neuropsychological development that needs more comparative research) is not a *symbol* that refers to it. Symbolic reference requires a cognitive ability to use one kind of thing – an auditory squawk or a visual squiggle – as a representation of, or stand-in for, another kind of thing.

An interesting finding from comparative neuropsychology makes the point. Bonobos are not speakers but they are arguably language competent. Some bonobos have vocabularies approaching three hundred words (about what a two-year-old human child knows), and some teach conspecifics the elements of what they know by showing them lexigrams on the computers they use to communicate. Moreover, they can put symbols together to form more complex symbols. Savage-Rumbaugh even suggests that at least one bonobo – the famous Kanzi – can distinguish between sentences such as "put the tomato in the bowl" and "put the bowl on the tomato", which suggests that he at least may have some understanding of syntax and spatial and causal order (Savage-Rumbaugh *et al*. 2004).[4] That some bonobos engage in symbolically loaded and protogrammatical activities *sans* speech suggests that for them the ability to speak is not necessary for symbol use. Hence, at least in enculturated bonobos, the cognitive abilities required for engaging in symbolic activity do not appear to depend causally upon speaking ability.

Of course, symbolic competence is not yet *semantic* or *grammatical* competence. Language, unlike symbol use, is recursive – it loops back on itself and embeds clauses within clauses (as in this sentence) – and it is almost uncontrollably productive. While competence in assigning a referent object to a symbol is necessary for recursion and productivity, they require in addition the ability to compositionally embed and extend discrete linguistic units (Fitch 2000; Fitch *et al*. 2005; Torey 2009). Children over two years in age are already more advanced than the most advanced bonobo at comprehending and constructing grammatically complex and semantically rich utterances. Moreover, *understanding* a symbol and *using* that symbol to communicate with others are distinct. Given what is now known about working memory, auditory comprehension and vocal production neural pathways (discussed further in Chapter 7), care must be taken to avoid thinking that evidence for one is also evidence for the others. Recent bonobo studies try to account for the distinction and are the first to offer credible evidence that species other than *H. sapiens sapiens* comprehend and communicate with symbols.[5]

One reason for thinking that some of our kinds of highly nuanced emotion, cognition and perception are a consequence of synaptic proliferation is that as synapses multiply, each neural region becomes responsible for smaller scale, ever more local, comparisons and discriminations (Kaas 2000). Attractive as this argument is, it is inconclusive. If a mouse's 80 billion synapses are not enough to generate our kinds of emotion, cognition and perception, why should 100 trillion or 500 trillion (or a gazillion) synapses be enough? Without an explanation that appeals to the uniqueness of synapses and an argument for the conclusion that a critical number of them are sufficient for the appearance of new, more complex, psychological processes, it is just more of the same old, same old. Of course, there are such arguments, usually employing complexity, emergence and self-organization, and we investigate them later.

Two other related differences between humans and other primates are ontogenetic maturation rate and percentage of myelinated pathways. Human brains take longer to mature than any other primate (comparative neurophysiological studies of whale and elephant brain ontogenesis are almost unheard of, so it is hard to say much about them). Human brains develop rapidly and continuously from early in the embryonic state but, unlike all other primates, whose brains are set by six years of age, human brains continue to add neural resources throughout childhood into adulthood. Dendritic growth, more than anything else, is responsible for epigenetic brain enhancement. During this "exuberant period", lasting from the age of two to pre-adolescence, poorly connected neurons create synapses at a remarkable rate – sometimes as many as two million synapses per *second* are added. Starting first in motor and sensory cortex and spreading eventually to associative cortex, the processes of the exuberant period produce a quadrillion synapses by age five, laying down pathways that help the child become competent to survive and flourish. Concurrent with synaptic proliferation, synaptic pruning occurs. Environment plays a crucial role in pruning. If a baby's environment is severely degraded, permanent impairment will result from neural pathways pruned because they are underutilized in the degraded environment. Interestingly, impairments are not global. In vision, the ability to perceive fine detail – acuity – and the ability to uses both eyes together – binocularity – are affected by environmental degradation, but colour perception is not, and in the case of language, grammar and phonological abilities are affected by environmental degradation, but vocabulary size is not.

By age three, many cortical neurons are myelinated, which colours them white and creates the white matter of the brain. Myelination occurs first in primary motor and sensory cortex and spreads into neocortex only later. In certain temporal, parietal and prefrontal cortex regions (phylogenetically the youngest regions of neocortex), myelination is not complete until the mid-twenties.

Only mammals have myelinated neurons at all, primates have more of them than other mammals, and humans have more of them than other primates. Myelination is a response to expanding allocortex and, especially, neocortex. As axons lengthened and synapses proliferated, neocortex in primates and, especially, humans expanded dramatically. Had signal-transmission speed remained unchanged during axonal lengthening, perceptual, affective and cognitive processing times would have become increasingly sluggish, and brains without lots of myelinated neurons would then have had the natural selection chips stacked against them. Correlatively, primate, protohuman and human brains with lots of myelinated neurons had quicker signal-transmission speeds, which enhanced their survival.

CONSCIOUSNESS AS A MODULE

In the past thirty years, the belief that many abilities of the mind are modular has come roaring back into respectability. It is an odd development, on a par only with the re-emergence of interest in consciousness, for prior to the cognitive revolution of the 1960s psychology was thoroughly associationist, anti-innatist and antimodular. In those days, psychology affirmed the importance of learning over innate native endowments and actively sought general purpose mechanisms rather than specialized ones. But linguistic arguments from Chomsky in the 1970s and perceptual arguments from Fodor in the 1980s reintroduced modularity and innatism into linguistics and philosophy, and in the 1990s evolutionary psychologists reintroduced modularity and innatism into explanations of complex social-psychological abilities.

Both modularity and evolutionary psychology – a specifically named scientific movement with which modularity claims are frequently associated – are at this point highly charged research areas. The debates between evolutionary psychologists and their critics are among the most vituperative in contemporary science, and ideologically revved-up participants on both sides are drawing lines in the sand. Our interest in these squabbles is tangential, for even if evolutionary psychology can provide modular explanations for the occurrence of any number of perceptual, cognitive and affective abilities, it is a leap from success in those domains to success in the case of conscious properties. We could establish this conclusion by rejecting evolutionary psychology's explanations even in cases where evidence is strongest. We could, but we will not – attacking on these grounds is a big job (see Buller 2005a), and we do not need to do it, for even if modular evolutionary psychological explanations are appropriate for some domains, conscious properties are almost assuredly not in those domains. Whether conscious properties, even if not modules, are adaptations is a much more delicate question.

Phenotypes, genotypes and adaptations

In order to appreciate the implications of claiming that consciousness is an evolutionary module, some technical concepts from evolutionary science have to be introduced. Without these tools, the risk of running together different kinds of modules is simply too great. Running these different senses of the term "module" together makes it much too easy to conflate claims and conclusions about one kind of module with claims and conclusions about other kinds of module.

Phenotypic differences are observable physical differences across individuals in a species; *phenotypes* are observable physical properties of individuals. In order for phenotypic differences to be subject to evolutionary explanation, they must be subject to the evolutionary mechanisms of genetic drift, random mutation, or natural selection. Of these, the first two are the most widespread, but the latter is of greatest interest to those defending modularity claims. In order for phenotypic differences to be subject to natural selection, they must have a genetic basis, for what is inherited from parent to offspring is a particular genetic code and not the phenotype that results from the implementation of that code in an organism embedded in an environment. But it is the genotype as phenotypically implemented by an organism in an environment upon which natural selection acts. Phenotypes that enhance an organism's chances of surviving to mating age are *survival phenotypes,* and phenotypes that enhance an organism's chances of mating are *competitive phenotypes.* Survival and competitive phenotypes together compose the class of *adaptive phenotypes* and are selected for. Phenotypes that either inhibit an organism's chances of surviving to mating age or of mating itself are *maladaptive phenotypes* and selected against. Phenotypes that neither enhance nor inhibit survival and mating are *neutral phenotypes* and are neither selected for nor selected against.

Of all phenotypes, some are genetically coded for and inheritable, while some are not genetically coded for and are not inheritable. Inherited adaptive phenotypes are *adaptations.* Where A is an adaptation, then (a) at some point in the past, some individuals had a particular genotype G for A and some did not; (b) those with A and G for A were more likely to survive to reproductive age and to mate than those without; and (c) G codes for A's development. Inherited maladaptive phenotypes are *maladaptations*; inherited phenotypes that are neither adaptations nor maladaptations are *non-adaptations.* Adaptations include bipedalism, opposable thumbs, noses and skin pigmentation. Non-adaptations include wisdom teeth, male nipples, little toes, chins, navels and baldness. Maladaptations include sleep apnea, Huntington's chorea, haemophilia and, perhaps, colour blindness. Evolution has nothing to say about non-inheritable adaptive phenotypes. Since they are epigenetic, they are epiphenomenal from an evolutionary perspective. If one person gambles and loses money and another gambles and does not lose money, the first person has a maladaptive phenotype but not a maladaptation. Again, a consequence of better nutrition now than before is that average human height in the twentieth century has increased significantly. Suppose that greater height is adaptive; still, because it is not inherited, it is not an adaptation. In short, even if a phenotype *is* adaptive, directly inferring that it is an adaptation is fallacious.

Some inherited phenotypes are currently adaptive and have always served the *same* adaptive function. These are *fixed adaptations*. Some currently adaptive inherited phenotypes served no adaptive function at the time they emerged and were neutral by-products of another adaptation. Such phenotypes are *spandrels* or *co-opted by-products*. An example of a co-opted by-product is the ability to read. It is currently adaptive, but the brain's evolutionary changes were already set when reading was invented, so whatever they were adaptive for, they were not adaptive for reading. Again, some currently adaptive inherited phenotypes served a distinct adaptive function at the time they emerged and were a distinct adaptation. Such reapplied adaptations are *co-opted adaptations*. Feathers are a paradigmatic co-opted adaptation, originally an adaptation to aid thermal regulation and only later an adaptation for flying. Together, co-opted by-products and co-opted adaptations constitute the class of *exaptations*. (A third class may be mentioned. This class is inherited phenotypes that, while currently non-adaptative or maladaptative, were once adaptations. Our taste for fats and sweet things is an example. It was once adaptive – when fatty and sweet food was scarce – but is now maladaptive – when fatty and sweet food is plentiful.)

Consciousness as a module

The term "module" began its relevant life as a term of art in computer science and linguistics, where it refers to a system that is special-purpose, encapsulated and domain-specific. A system is *computational* if its processing of information is algorithmic and syntactic; a system is *special-purpose* if it performs one rather than a number of functions; a system is *encapsulated* if it is informationally isolated, having no additional input from other systems; and a system is *domain-specific* if it operates on information inputs of one (generally speaking, species-relevant) kind, rather than a number of distinct such kinds (Fodor 1983). Providing an agreed-upon definition of "domain" has proven to be difficult (the Introduction to Hirschfield and Gelman 1994 provides reasons for the difficulties). Nevertheless, it is generally agreed that a module's special-purpose dedication and domain-specificity allows it to be fast, that its computational operation allows it to be reliable, and its encapsulation allows it to chunk away in isolation from other modules. The concept of modularity eventually leaked out of computer science and linguistics and infiltrated biology and psychology. In its original use, the term *biological module* referred to a module implemented in a biological system in a living organism. Biological modules are, then, special-purpose, domain-specific and encapsulated mechanisms whose development and functioning is genetically coded for rather than being a causal consequence of interactions between the system and the environment.

Neural modules are a subset of biological modules, individual neural assemblies or pathways found in particular regions of the brain. However, neural modularity describes certain neural processes and neural functioning as well. Neural myelination is a modular process, for it is genetically coded, follows a schedule largely independent of environmental input, and does only one thing. On the other hand, epigenetic development of heteromodal associative cortex is not a modular process because it is not encapsulated – heteromodal associative cortex must be a part of a living being embedded in a rich perceptual, affective and cognitive environment in order to develop at all. (Humans are in no uncertain terms sensory junkies – we *need* stimuli for synaptic connectivity to develop – severely degraded sensory environments entail permanent neural deficiencies in sensory pathways.)

Many subcortical regions – not only in hind- and midbrain but also in certain forebrain regions – contain encapsulated neural pathways dedicated to particular physiological and psychological functions. Thalamic, amygdaloid, some other limbic pathways, and the various nuclei, clusters, bodies, formations and glands of subcortical forebrain are fairly specialized and isolated from others. Likewise, perceptual pathways have obligatory entrance points and are blind to the activity of other perceptual pathways. However, once feedforward neural processing reaches heteromodal, transmodal and supramodal associative cortex, its information becomes the shared property of an enormous network of synaptic connections, and heteromodal, transmodal and supramodal activity in turn re-enters the tops of affective and perceptual pathways. Most of the pathways in heteromodal, transmodal and supramodal associative cortices are neither encapsulated nor special-purpose, and associative cortex hosts at least 70 per cent of the neural pathways in a human brain. It does not follow that the remaining 30 per cent of neural pathways *are* modular, but it does narrow candidates for neural modularity down considerably. Still, there are *lots* of neural modules, and to the extent that any psychological event is correlated with *some* neural pathway, every psychological event follows some route through cortex and not another.[6]

A *psychological module* is a kind of module whose inputs, outputs and transformation functions are specified in terms of some psychological theory. If there are psychological modules, they can be further subdivided into cognitive, affective, interoceptive, proprioceptive and perceptual modules, depending upon the nature of their inputs, outputs and transformation functions. For example, given an appropriate description of a perceptual psychological module, some psychological activity is arguably modular. Since each primary sensory processing pathway is genetically encoded, has an obligatory entrance and a single function to perform, and since results from each are fed forwards to other psychological pathways without having received input from other such pathways, it is likely that primary perceptual pathway function is modular. Visual processing, for example, starts in V1 and progresses forwards, correlated with a particular group of neural assemblies. Primary visual processing does not on occasion migrate to another set of neural assemblies; nor do the assemblies constituting the primary visual pathway correlate every once in a while with auditory or gustatory processing. But secondary and other associative perceptual processing, not to mention the rest of associative processing, are not psychological modules, for even if special-purpose, they are neither encapsulated nor inherited.

Were it to follow the above characterizations, an *evolutionary module* would also be a kind of module – neural, psychological, or otherwise – that is either an adaptation or an exaptation, and an *evolutionary psychological module* would be an evolutionary module whose inputs, outputs and transformation functions are specified in terms of some psychological theory. Surprisingly, this is *not* what evolutionary psychological modules turn out to be. Part of the explanation for this difference is that an unfortunately multivocal, sometimes equivocal, use of "module" has seeped into discussions. What qualifies a neural pathway or psychological ability to be a "module" is not always clear within evolutionary psychology, and failure to acknowledge its equivocal reference has caused considerable and confusing disagreement within evolutionary psychology and between it and its critics.

Some evolutionary psychologists are trending towards a view on which precious few of the properties that characterize computational and biological modules will be salvaged. First, although widely assumed, it is an open question how well computational models fit psychological processing. It is not clear, for instance, that all psychological systems, processes and pathways are algorithmic, and it is clear that cognitive processes at least are not merely syntactic (more on these matters in later chapters). Second, domain-specificity has all but dropped out as a property of evolutionary psychological modules. Early discussions used the term "module" to describe certain complex psychological phenomena that have turned out not to be domain-specific even if they are problem-specific. The only domain-specific psychological mechanisms are likely to be subcortical and primary perceptual and affective pathways. While the processing in these pathways may be inherited and their functioning may even be an adaptation, evolutionary psychologists have typically been after much more complex targets, cognitive and affective abilities such as detecting cheaters, preference formation for particular hip/waist ratios in women, mating and kinship strategies, and social abilities. These are not domain-specific abilities. Finally, it is not clear that any psychological processing for which evolutionary explanations seem well suited can be encapsulated (for discussion, see Ermer *et al.* 2007).

What is left is bare-boned: an evolutionary psychological module is a special-purpose psychological mechanism that is either an adaptation or an exaptation, and, likewise, an evolutionary neural module is a special-purpose neural mechanism that is either an adaptation or an exaptation. Of course, since domain-specificity, computationality and encapsulation are, if this view is correct, no longer required for a process to qualify as a module, it is much easier to assess the modularity of conscious properties. So, if any of the properties of consciousness are evolutionary psychological modules, then they are either special-purpose fixed adaptations or special-purpose exaptations, either spandrels or co-opted adaptations. And if a given property of consciousness is not one of these, then it is not an evolutionary psychological module. The same applies to evolutionary neural modules: either a conscious property is realized by a special-purpose mechanism that is a fixed adaptation or an exaptation (spandrel or co-opted adaptation) or it is not an evolutionary neural module.

We could go through each of intentionality, qualitative character and subjective perspectivity to determine whether each is realized by a special-purpose neural mechanism and, on the condition that it is, determine whether that mechanism is a fixed adaptation or an exaptation, and if the latter, determine whether it is a co-opted adaptation or a spandrel. Since modules are special-purpose and a thing is special-purpose only if it performs one rather than a number of functions, the burden of proof is on the modularity advocate to prove the case. It may be difficult to shoulder the burden successfully, for except for perceptual qualitative properties, where at least early stages of perceptual processing are carried out in special-purpose neural assemblies, other conscious properties correlate with later, heteromodal, multimodal and supramodal neural assemblies that are not special-purpose. Even in the case of perceptual qualitative properties, the likelihood of there being special-purpose evolutionary modules is low, for while early perceptual processing may be special-purpose, later stages of perceptual processing are not. If qualitative character properties correlate with later rather than with early stages, then they would not be subserved by neural modules. And if they are not subserved by neural modules, then they are not subserved by evolutionary modules either. Similar reasoning applies to intentionality and subjective perspectivity: their instantiations are unlikely to correlate with special-purpose neural assemblies since they too correlate with heteromodal, multimodal and supramodal neural assemblies, none of which is special-purpose.

While all evolutionary modules are adaptations, not all adaptations are evolutionary modules, so even if conscious properties are not subserved by evolutionary modules, conscious properties may yet be adaptations, that is, adaptive phenotypes that are genetically coded for and inherited. The work discussing these issues is at this point speculative as there is little research on evolutionary explanations of intentionality, subjective perspectivity and qualitative character (but see the essays collected in Fetzer 2002). We can do no more here than identify options. The first step is to eliminate those that rest on mistakes. Among the mistakes is inferring from their pervasiveness that conscious properties are adaptations. Arithmetic, logic, dance, writing, torture and slavery are

or have been universally or nearly universally shared across human populations for some time, but since they are not inherited, they are not adaptations.
Second, just as not everything adaptive is inherited, not everything inherited is
an adaptation – schizophrenia is inherited and maladaptive and wisdom teeth
are inherited and non-adaptive. So even if consciousness is inherited, argument
must establish that it is an adaptation (Polger & Flanagan 2002). We conscious
ones might be successful not because we are conscious but because we have
some other adaptation on which consciousness happens to be a neutral free-
rider, a spandrel, or we might be successful because some or all the features of
consciousness are co-opted adaptations that originally served a function distinct from that which they now serve.

Third, current adaptiveness does not entail past adaptation. There is no
direct argument from a neural feature being correlated with some currently
shared conscious property to the conclusion that that neural feature is an adaptation for that conscious property. Broca's area is no more an adaptation for
speech production than the opposable thumb is an adaptation for tool grasping.
Bonobos have a Broca's area and produce no speech; gibbons have opposable
thumbs and use no tools. Rather, Broca's area and opposable thumbs are adaptations or by-products co-opted for a current function – speech production and
tool grasping, respectively – from a past function or gratuity. Since there is no
direct argument from current adaptivity to its past selection for that adaptive
function, we may set reverse engineering arguments about conscious properties
to the side until their need is demonstrated.

Fourth, the category of consciousness is too coarse-grained, even ambiguous, to provoke substantive answers about its evolutionary status. Trying to
determine whether consciousness is an adaptation is like trying to determine
whether buoyancy is an adaptation. Buoyancy is an adaptation in birds (inherited and selected for) and a non-adaptation in scorpions (inherited but neither
selected for nor against), so buoyancy *simpliciter* is neither an adaptation *nor* a
maladaptation. Moreover, what is inherited and selected for when buoyancy is
an adaptation in birds is a particular genetic code for the development of bones
with certain densities and wings of certain shapes composed of feathers with
certain mass. It is not buoyancy but bones and feathers and certain properties
of those bones and feathers that are inherited and selected for. At this point, a
parallel move from consciousness to its properties – intentionality, subjective
perspectivity, qualitative character – needs to be made.

Suppose these mistakes are avoided and we have identified the conscious
properties for which we hope to find an inherited genotype. The next step is
to determine whether a particular conscious property is an adaptation or an
exaptation, and if the latter, whether it is a spandrel or a co-opted adaptation.
Here a distinction must be drawn between conscious properties and the neural
properties, if any, with which they correlate. If there are no neural correlates
of *any* conscious property and neural properties are the *only* candidate for an

inheritable basis for conscious properties, then no conscious property is inherited. Second, even if neural properties are the only candidate correlates for an inheritable basis for conscious properties and there are neural correlates for every conscious property, conscious properties may yet be epigenetic developments on those neural correlates. Suppose, for example, that subjective perspectivity is an adaptive phenotype that always occurs whenever some neural adaptation, fixed or exapted, occurs. Subjective perspectivity may yet be a by-product that accompanies the neural property as an epigenetic development. If so, subjective perspectivity does not occur without the inherited adaptation, and, moreover, given that adaptation placed in an appropriate environment, subjective perspectivity can and will occur. Still, since the inherited adaptation is necessary for epigenetic subjective perspectivity and not sufficient for it, whatever the inherited adaptation may be, it is not subjective perspectivity. If so, then subjective perspectivity is not inherited. If so, then it is neither an adaptation nor an exaptation, although its neural correlates are.

Again, even if there are neural correlates for every conscious property, it may be that those neural correlates are themselves epigenetic developments and, again, neither adaptations nor exaptations. Such would be the case if all conscious properties correlate with neural properties that are not instantiated until some particular level of neural connectivity is achieved. Or perhaps the neural properties that correlate with conscious properties are themselves neither adaptations nor exaptations. The issues here are threefold. First, not knowing very much about any of the neural correlates of conscious properties, it is premature to offer much more than suggestions and promissory notes about properties, assemblies, pathways, systems and regions being adaptations or not. Second, it is not clear where we should expect to find evidence for neural adaptation or exaptation. Perhaps the neural correlates of conscious properties are entire neural networks whose activity produces them only given a particular epigenetic environment. Third, if the neural differences between our brains and the brains of our nearest primate ancestors were caused by a relatively small number of genetic mutations and there is a determination relation between neural changes and conscious properties, then no *specific* conscious property cascading from those few mutations will be separately selected for or against. Given those few genetically encoded changes and an appropriate environment, an entire suite of phenotypes may have arrived all at once, no one of which is *separately* selected for. What may have been selected for is the whole kit and caboodle.

Consider speech comprehension and production activity, which are positively correlated with activity in Wernicke's and Broca's areas. Such correlation does not establish that speech comprehension and production, much less the intentionality of language, are adaptations. Granted, there is suggestive evidence that speech comprehension and production may in part be inherited. Dysfunctional neural activity in Broca's area correlates with a specific genetic mutation in the Forkhead Box P2 (*FOXP2*) gene (Corballis 2004; Démonet *et al.*

2005; Marcus & Fisher 2003; Okanoya 2007). The mutation results in a nucleo-tide change, which in turn correlates with certain behavioural – phenotypic – symptoms. Affected individuals have difficulty articulating certain phonemes and are compromised in their ability to comprehend sentences with complex grammatical structure. In these individuals, there are observable differences in the activation of left (and right) Broca's area. (No results are yet available for activation patterns in Wernicke's area.) *FOXP2* is a member of an entire genus of *FOX* genes, all of whose members are transcription genes involved in cel-lular differentiation, proliferation and pattern formation. *FOX* genes are found in all mammals (and other animals and fungi), and the number of *FOX* spe-cies increases with increasing body complexity. As a transcription gene, *FOXP2* controls activation of genetic programs in other cells, telling them to start their programmes, thus resulting in a cascade of programme activation. Its work is not exhausted by its impact on areas now implicated in language comprehen-sion and production; *FOXP2* also controls heart and lung development and breath control.

All of this is interesting but of no obvious relevance for the evolution of speech or language or intentionality. Luckily, the story gets more interesting. It has been claimed that *FOXP2* became fixed in *hominins* less than 200,000 years ago, four million years after the human line split off from other primate lines, during the span of *H. neanderthalis* and roughly coincident with the emergence of *H. sapiens*. That is a curious coincidence, for if *FOXP2* controls genes that direct neural development and breathing control, whose proper functioning is, in turn, necessary for the fine motor control of vocalizing that is, in turn, neces-sary for forming the range of phonemes necessary for speech, then widespread speech among our archaic ancestors *prior* to 200,000 can be *ruled out*. If true, that is an interesting discovery, for it suggests one prerequisite for speech pro-duction and, perhaps, speech comprehension. But it is still leagues away from the conclusion that the intentionality of language is an adaptation. And since conscious intentionality is not reducible to the intentionality of language, this discovery is still leagues away from the conclusion that conscious intentionality is an adaptation.

This chapter has addressed certain broad issues in the evolution of human brains, their structure, and their constituent neural assemblies and pathways, and it has introduced certain other and even broader issues concerning the evolution of conscious properties. It should be clear that we still have a long way to go before it is possible to determine when and how conscious properties evolved into their current form, for even if they did so evolve, some of the argu-ments offered on behalf of that conclusion are not nearly as convincing as they could be and none of the arguments are nearly as convincing as they should be. Incomplete comparative knowledge about the neural basis of conscious prop-erty evolution is a particularly serious obstacle. Still, as serious as it is, it is only one part of the problem. Another part of the problem is presented by our still incomplete knowledge about the neural assemblies and brain structures in animals that are conscious now. Luckily, we know significantly more about the way current brains are composed, so we can be more confident about establishing the current neural correlates of conscious properties. We may not know enough yet about where we came from to know how we got from there to where we are now, and we may not know enough even about where we are now to know that the neural correlates of conscious properties currently being bandied about are the final word. But at least we have a set of proposed neural correlates. We turn now to introducing them.

6. AROUSAL, PERCEPTION AND AFFECT

The neurophysiology and neuropsychology of cortical assemblies and pathways is complex enough without having to overlay on to them the difficulties introduced by conscious properties – qualitative character, intentionality and subjective perspectivity. And yet this nest of issues is exactly what must be analysed if the properties of neural assemblies and pathways are to be taken seriously as contenders for the substrates for, or realizers of, conscious properties.

In this chapter, we focus on perceptual and affective conscious events. Both have been intensively studied by neurophysiologists, neuropsychologists and neuropsychiatrists. This work provides neural correlates for each of the perceptual modalities and for many interoceptive, proprioceptive and affective modalities. For the most part, neuroscientists have approached these conscious events and processes by focusing on the neural correlates for particular sensory modalities, such as vision or olfaction, or on affections, such as disgust or empathy. Little of this enormous body of research has tried to isolate the conscious qualitative features of perception and affection. But that is not to say that there is no work on these topics. So, in addition to outlining neural pathways for the sensory modalities and some affections, a smaller subset of these studies that purport to isolate neural correlates of the qualitative features of two sensory modalities, taste and smell, a pair of interoceptive phenomena, thirst and pain, and a pair of affective phenomena, fear and disgust, are also reviewed. We begin, however, with the physiological states of arousal and alertness, both of which are preconditions for conscious experience, and the default mode, a state superficially similar to alertness.

AROUSAL, TONIC ALERTNESS AND DEFAULT MODE

All of us arise every day as we awaken and go temporarily quiescent when we sleep. The *arousal* process is associated with activity in the ascending reticular activating system, most of whose constituent neural assemblies are phylogenetically ancient components of the reptilian brain. The ascending reticular activating system is a loosely individuated neural pathway ascending from the pons and medulla through the thalamus and hypothalamus into cortical regions. A crucial function in this system is served by the thalamus. In general, the thalamus is a relay station where myelinated neurons coming from various places are redirected to go to various other places, in particular to other regions of cortex. Hence, it plays a role in a variety of other cerebral activities. Particular subregions of the thalamus are, for example, the final location in the brain for most incoming sensory input before it is directed to cortex (an exception is olfactory sensory input, most of which bypasses the thalamus and goes directly to primary olfactory, or pyriform, cortex).

Thalamocortical neurons reach into many cortical regions. Neurotransmitter activity in these pathways excites a specific cortical region, which region returns the favour by sending excitatory messages back to specific locations in thalamus. As this activity rebounds and amplifies, synchronous and phasic oscillations in electrochemical neural behaviour emerge. The integrity of ongoing neural activity in this *ascending reticular activating system* and its synchronous behaviour are causally necessary for maintaining an awakened state. Haemorrhages, tumours, abscesses and lesions to thalamic regions and the ascending reticular system cause *stupor*, a deeply unresponsive state interrupted only by applying repeated and forceful stimuli, and, more seriously, *coma*, a similarly unresponsive state that continues uninterrupted despite repeated and forceful stimuli. Another superficially similar disorder, *vegetative state*, is caused by thalamic or bilateral cortical or white matter insult, such as occurs when the brain is starved for oxygen (anoxia) (Owen 2008). In vegetative state, wakefulness and the sleep–waking cycle are preserved, but there is no ongoing higher-order mental activity. An animal suffering from vegetative state is awake but featureless, like a television turned on to the blue screen.

The ascending reticular activating system is routinely implicated as the lowest neural system required for explaining conscious experience. However, while white matter assemblies projecting from thalamus to neocortex and projecting back from neocortex to thalamus are numerous and important in initiating and maintaining awakened and aroused states, neither any component of nor the entire ascending reticular activating system itself generates conscious experience. It is, rather, a necessary causal prerequisite of conscious experience – without its proper functioning, conscious experience cannot occur, but even if it is properly functioning, conscious experience need not occur. For, as vegetative state demonstrates, even if the reticular system is functioning, circadian rhythms are intact, and eyes are open, other malfunctioning prerequisites can undermine conscious experience. The reticular system thus provides the neural milieu from which conscious experience can, in concert with other causal prerequisites, emerge.

When the ascending reticular activating system and other neural regions are all functioning properly, a state characteristic of much of waking life obtains. This state is variously called *tonic alertness, tonic attentiveness, intrinsic alertness, vigilance, sustained attention, diffuse attentional system*, or *baseline awareness* (Fan *et al.* 2005; Filley 2002; Mesulam 2000; Raz & Buhle 2006). Shifting reference of, in particular, "arousal", "vigilance" and "sustained attention" across authors suggests that a distinct term is preferable (Oken *et al.* 2006). We use *tonic alertness*. Tonic alertness is that state of psychological activation that (a) obtains only if arousal has obtained, (b) contains no specific content, and (c) underwrites the processes of sustaining a coherent line of thought or action (Filley 2002). Tonic alertness is distinct from *phasic attention*, events of augmented alertness wherein affective and cognitive orientation to, selection of, and concentration upon, an area in the field of experience occurs. Tonic alertness is thus intermediate between being aroused and being phasically attentive.

The neuroimaging work being conducted on tonic alertness remains in a state of development. However, enough has been learned to suggest that, in addition to the pathways of the ascending reticular activating system, tonic alertness is correlated with widespread activity in pathways in ventral anterior and posterior cingulate cortex, dorsolateral prefrontal cortex (hereafter DLPFC), dorsomedial prefrontal cortex (DMPFC), middle and superior temporal cortex, white matter tracts, thalamus, tegmentum, locus coeruleus and amygdala (Filley 2002; Foucher *et al.* 2004; Mesulam 1981; Oken *et al.* 2006; Sturm & Willmes 2001). There is a clear need for more work here, for this default level of brain activation is necessary for other cognitive, affective and perceptual activity to occur. It is, therefore, an obvious candidate for the neural correlates of at least some properties of conscious experience.

Tonic alertness is also distinct from the state of conscious experience characteristic of daydreams, reveries, fantasies, wanderings and the other "desultory concoctions" of spontaneous inner experience (Klinger 1971: 347). This latter state is the *default mode* (Greicus *et al.* 2003; Raichle *et al.* 2001; Raichle & Snyder 2007; a helpful review is Buckner *et al.* 2008). When in default mode, the brain is not tasked with any particular perceptual, cognitive, affective or interoceptive task but is, rather, left to its own devices to keep itself busy. As with tonic alertness, the default mode's neural correlates are still in the process of being identified. But it increasingly appears that they make up a network that partially overlaps that of tonic alertness. This network includes ventromedial prefrontal cortex (VMPFC), DMPFC, posterior cingulate cortex, inferior parietal cortex, lateral temporal cortex and the hippocampus (Buckner *et al.* 2008). Functional extensions of the default mode have also been suggested. Comparing brain activation maps during the default mode with other brain activation maps while it is engaged in autobiographical memory, belief attribution to others, envisioning the future, and moral decision-making reveals strong overlap, leading to the claim that the default mode is a core correlate of the subjective perspectivity characteristic of conscious experience (Buckner *et al.* 2008).

THE PERCEPTUAL BRAIN

Perception is experience of the surrounding environment caused by the activity of the visual, auditory, olfactory, gustatory and tactile sensory neural assemblies. It is sufficient for our purposes to start with neural pathways as they emerge from the thalamus on their way to cortex, for it is only subsequent to that point that unconscious sensation becomes conscious perception. *Perceptual neuroscience* studies these processes.

Although our interest lies in the transition from preconscious and unconscious sensory processing to qualitatively endowed, perspectivally subjective, intentionally structured perception, some familiarity with the neural assemblies that correlate with sensory processing is required. Otherwise, honing in on the transition from preconscious and unconscious sensory processing to conscious perception and conscious perceptual experience, if there is one, will be impossible, leading to the confusions about perception that plagued Aristotle, Aquinas, Descartes, Locke and behaviourism. In what follows, primary and unimodal sensory pathways, heteromodal associative sensory pathways and integrative transmodal perceptual pathways are described for each sensory modality. In general, sensation is first processed by domain-specific neurons in dedicated pathways, the results of which processing projects to non-prefrontal regions for heteromodal integration with other sensory information, the results of which integration projects again to various regions of prefrontal cortex for transmodal integration with emotion and cognition and, if needed, from there to premotor and motor cortex for action. Somewhere in this tangle of pathways and assemblies conscious perception emerges.

Primary unimodal perceptual pathways

Primary sensory cortex is devoted to neural processing of environmental input functionally organized along the five sensory modalities. Each modality process is correlated with particular cortical regions and with cortex types. Primary olfactory cortex is allocortex, while primary visual, auditory, gustatory and touch cortices are mesocortex and idiotypic neocortex.

Vision
Most visual signals project from the retina through the optic nerve to the lateral geniculate nucleus of the thalamus, where they are directed to the occipital lobe's primary visual cortex for working up into visual perception. Their first destination is V1 (Visual Area 1, also known as primary visual or striate cortex), neurons in which respond to simple shapes. Primary visual cortex sends a large proportion of its connections to V2, secondary visual cortex (all cortex subsequent to V1 is extrastriate cortex). Neurons in V2 respond both to simple shapes, as do

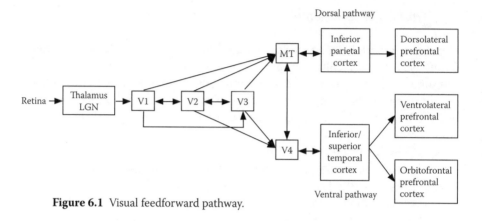

Figure 6.1 Visual feedforward pathway.

V1 neurons, and to more complex shapes. From V1 and V2, neural information projects to V3, where spatial location and sequential movement information begin their route through the dorsal "where" pathway, while colour, shape and texture information begin their route through the ventral "what" pathway (this characterization is contested; see Chapter 9). The dorsal pathway projects from V3 to V5/MT (Medial Temporal Area), in which movement is processed. V5/MT also receives input from V1 and V2. V2, V3 and V5/MT together compose the unimodal areas for vision. V5/MT in turn projects to heteromodal associative areas in temporoparietal regions and then to dorsolateral prefrontal cortex. The ventral pathway projects from V2 to unimodal V3 and V4, where colour and shape are further processed. From V4, projections head to inferior and superior temporal cortex and then to temporoparietal regions before projecting again to ventrolateral and orbitofrontal prefrontal cortex. The visual pathway is shown in Figure 6.1.

The bidirectionality of many of the visual processes, in particular, those from parietal and temporal cortex back to earlier stages in occipital cortex (V1–V4 and MT) indicates that, in addition to *feedforward* pathways that go from simple processing of object features to unified object perception, there are *feedback* pathways that constrain and modify those feedforward pathways. Although it is tempting to think of visual processing as strictly hierarchical and linear, going from V1 to V2, from V2 to V3, from V3 to V4 or MT, from them to parietal or temporal cortex and then forwards to prefrontal cortex, all visual areas are active within 40 milliseconds of initial V1 firing and all continually send information to the others in selectively parallel feedforward and feedback pathways.

Audition

Auditory neural pathways project from the inferior colliculus of the midbrain to the medial geniculate nucleus of the thalamus, and from there to primary auditory cortex in posterior temporal cortex. This area, A1, is active when presented with pure tones. In comparison, the areas surrounding A1 are less active when presented with pure tones and more active when presented with tones of increasing complexity along the dimensions of tone, volume, pitch and intensity. These areas, analogous to V2 and V3, surround A1 like a belt and further process sound. As with visual perception, there are dorsal and ventral auditory pathways in auditory processing. There is a dorsal pathway from A1 to a unimodal caudal-medial area (CM) and a unimodal caudal-lateral area (CL) immediately behind A1. Neurons in these areas project to posterior parietal cortex for subsequent heteromodal associative and integrative processing before projecting to dorsolateral prefrontal cortex. There is also a ventral auditory pathway, from A1 to unimodal rostral (R) and anterolateral (AL) areas immediately towards the front of the brain from A1. Neurons in these areas project towards superior temporal cortex and inferior parietal cortex for heteromodal associative processing, and then project to orbitofrontal and ventrolateral prefrontal cortex. The auditory pathway is shown in Figure 6.2.

As with visual perception, the dorsal auditory pathway is thought to be dedicated to sound location and the ventral auditory pathway to sound identification. Auditory information that locates objects and identifies movement and direction projects dorsally from inferior parietal and superior temporal cortex (Wernicke's area, roughly) to dorsolateral prefrontal cortex. Complex sound properties and vocalization patterns that help identify objects and what they are like – their qualitative features – project ventrally from inferior parietal and superior temporal cortex – again, Wernicke's area – to ventrolateral prefrontal cortex (Broca's area) and to orbitofrontal prefrontal cortex. In monkeys and other primates, the ventral auditory pathway presages speech abilities, for it is particularly sensitive to frequency modulation and conspecific calls. Monkeys

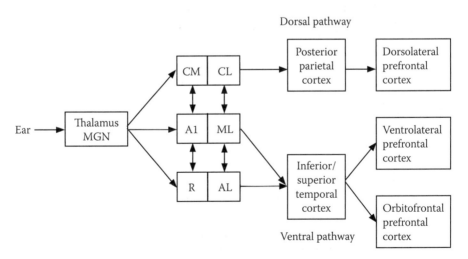

Figure 6.2 Auditory feedforward pathway.

and primates are adept on the basis of tone, volume, phonetic structure and frequency at recognizing conspecifics, at distinguishing between individual conspecifics, and at distinguishing between kinds of calls from individual conspecifics. For primates, area AL has been implicated in processing conspecific calls and in distinguishing between kinds of calls (Rauschecker & Tian 2000).

Gustation

Taste information travels from the tongue and pharynx along three different pathways to the parabrachial nucleus of the pons and from there to the ventral posterior nucleus of the thalamus. From there, taste information projects to primary gustatory cortex in the tongue area of somatosensory cortex and to insular cortex just beneath the tongue area (Rolls *et al.* 2003). From this primary gustatory cortex area, projections lead to secondary somatosensory cortex in parietal lobe, to the amygdala, to cingulate cortex and to orbitofrontal cortex, in which secondary taste association cortex is located (Saper 2002). The gustatory pathway is shown in Figure 6.3.

For primates, there are five primary taste sensations: sweet, sour, salty, bitter and savoury (umami). Many combinations and shades of tastes and flavours are of course possible; moreover, flavour perception commingles with and includes olfactory information.

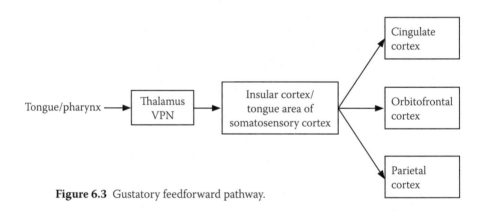

Figure 6.3 Gustatory feedforward pathway.

Olfaction

As one climbs up the phylogenetic ladder, olfaction's importance wanes and demands fewer cerebral resources. Smell is far less important in humans and other primates than it is for other mammalian species. Given all the psychological energy we expend on smelling food, each other and our surroundings, and given all the money we spend on perfume, soaps and air fresheners, this may be hard to believe. But were we to devote as much brain power to odours as dogs devote to odours, and were we to spend accordingly, we would spend next to nothing on clothes, some on food and things to chase, and the rest of it on smells and smell technologies.

In comparison to other sensory pathways, olfactory pathways are simple and direct. Most olfactory information projects from the olfactory bulb through the olfactory tract to primary olfactory cortex, with no thalamic interposition. Some olfactory information goes from olfactory bulb to amygdala. Primary olfactory cortex (also known as pyriform cortex) is located at the very rear and bottom of prefrontal cortex in the parahippocampal region of medial temporal cortex. Pathways from pyriform cortex project to entorhinal associative cortex in temporal lobe, which in turn projects to the hippocampus's dentate gyrus, a crucial area for memory implantation and consolidation. A phylogenetically young and distinct olfactory pathway, present in primates and humans, routes from pyriform cortex through the dorsomedial nucleus of the thalamus and thence to insular and orbitofrontal prefrontal cortex, where secondary and tertiary olfactory processing occurs. From orbitofrontal cortex, bidirectional pathways project to other heteromodal associative areas in prefrontal and parietal cortex, hippocampus, amygdala and other subcortical regions. Emotional responses to olfaction found in working memory are correlated with left hemispheric posterior orbitofrontal pathways, and qualitative features of olfactory perception and olfactory identification in working memory are correlated with right hemispheric ventral orbitofrontal pathways (Rolls 2000; Royet & Plailly 2004). The olfactory pathway is shown in Figure 6.4. There are hundreds of different olfactory sensations, all processed by dedicated pathways. The sensory discreteness of odour is one of the reasons why odours are so easily coded for in long-term memory and so often associated with specific declarative and episodic memories.

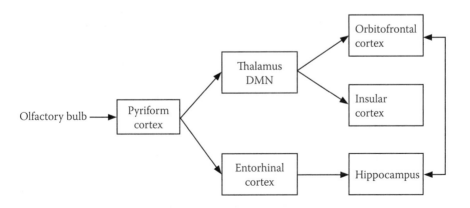

Figure 6.4 Olfactory feedforward pathway.

Moving between taste and smell is the primary means for primates to determine whether the substance in front of them is edible or inedible, nutritious or toxic. It is also the neural basis for flavour, for the area in which olfactory and gustatory information converge into flavour is located in orbitofrontal cortex. Another convergence area appears to be anterior insular cortex, located immediately adjacent to the convergence zone in orbitofrontal cortex. From these two areas, pathways project to other heteromodal and transmodal associative areas in prefrontal cortex.

Touch

Somatosensory information arrives at the thalamus from distal regions of the body via pathways in the spinothalamic tract. From the thalamus, two distinct touch pathways emerge. Pathways from the ventral posterior nucleus carry most somatosensory information to primary somatosensory cortex in the vertically aligned strips of superior parietal cortex immediately behind the central fissure, where there is a complex somatosensory map. Somatic information projects from primary somatosensory cortex to heteromodal associative cortex in insular cortex and orbitofrontal cortex. Of particular interest are the somatosensory features of texture and fatty substance, both of which activate specific orbitofrontal neurons, and the tactile somatosensory features of painful and pleasant touch. These correlations suggest that orbitofrontal cortex is directly involved in somatosensory working memory. Pathways from the thalamus's intralaminar nuclei also project to the basal ganglia and then to widely diverse cortical areas for heteromodal associative processing. The somatosensory pathway is shown in Figure 6.5.

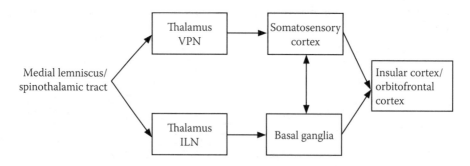

Figure 6.5 Somatosensory feedforward pathway.

Heteromodal processing, integration, binding

In addition to primary, secondary and tertiary unimodal sensory areas, some cortical areas are associated with sensory information processing but not dedicated to processing individual modalities. These are the *heteromodal* (*multi*modal or *poly*modal or *cross*modal) associative areas. Heteromodal associative regions are distal from primary, secondary and tertiary areas and connected to them by white matter tracts. The resultant loops of neural activity are huge in number, variously reinforcing and inhibiting within and across pathways, subject to perturbation from multiple intra- and interpathway sources, and high in complexity. In general, neural pathways in unimodal sensory cortex are similar across primates, but differences between humans and other primates emerge in heteromodal associative cortical pathways. Our knowledge of these differences is dramatically incomplete. This is an area of explosive research growth – some has been accomplished, a lot is being done right now, a lot remains to be started.

There are three heteromodal association areas (Mesulam 2000). The first is scattered across the intersection of parietal, temporal and occipital cortex (the temporoparietal junction area), the intraparietal sulcus and ventral premotor cortex. This heteromodal area is responsible for integrating sensory information into complex multimodal sensory perception. The second heteromodal association area is located in limbic cortex, clustered around hippocampus, orbitofrontal cortex, inferior parietal and temporal cortex and cingulate cortex. This heteromodal area is responsible for emotion, memory and motivation integration. The third heteromodal area is properly a *trans*modal (or *supra*modal) association area. Transmodal or supramodal processing differs from heteromodal processing. Heteromodal sensory processing integrates sensory information from the various sense modalities into a bound multimodal sensory bundle, and heteromodal affective processing likewise integrates emotional, memory and motivation information into a bound bundle. Transmodal processing, on the other hand, integrates such multimodal sensory and affective bundles with cognitive information for planning and voluntary behaviour. This transmodal processing area is located in dorsolateral and ventrolateral prefrontal cortex and the frontopolar region of prefrontal cortex. Together, these heteromodal and transmodal regions make up the largest part of the human brain.

What work there is on human heteromodal perceptual integration suggests a feedforward pathway from unimodal perceptual pathways to the heteromodal convergence zone in temporoparietal junction, intraparietal sulcus and ventral premotor cortex. However, imaging evidence shows only that these particular brain regions are active when heteromodal processing occurs; it does not show that heteromodal integration occurs *in* these regions (Macaluso & Driver 2004). It is consistent with existing imaging evidence that unimodal perceptual pathways from multiple perceptual modalities converge in a region and, once there, continue to run parallel to each other without interacting, like parallel highways that have no exit or entrance ramps. Yet our perceptual experience is of a unified, coherent scene, in which objects are integrated within a perceptual modality and integrated across perceptual modalities. In normal circumstances, we do not see a tree as a blob of green floating near a collection of leaf edges that are separate still from waxy surfaces; we do not hear a guitar solo as a discrete volume distinct from pitch, in turn distinct from tone. We listen to a guitar solo while we are looking at the tree, and it is all one, coherent, perceptual experience.

Somewhere in all the unimodal–heteromodal perceptual activity a little *magic* occurs, magic that turns discrete, dispersed, unconscious and preconscious, electrochemical sensory information into unified conscious perceptual experience. One part of this magic is perceptual binding, and the cluster of difficulties surrounding this part of the process has come to be known as the *perceptual binding problem*. The perceptual binding problem is providing an account that both specifies neural pathways correlated with psychological processes causally implicated in creating our unified, coherent perceptual experience of integrated objects located in space and time and explains how those neural pathways accomplish their task. The perceptual binding problem is only one of a number of binding problems.

The workup in visual and auditory pathways is piecemeal and accomplished via activity in parallel feedforward pathways that convert sensory input into experience of a featured object. A number of distinct perceptual binding problems in this process arise, some attaching to activity in unimodal pathways, some to activity in heteromodal pathways. Among the visual binding processes are: (i) *spatial binding*, by which sensory input from an external object is synthesized as being from one and the same object; (ii) *location binding*, by which the perceived object is located in egocentric space; (iii) *feature binding*, by which the qualitative characteristics of colour, texture, luminance and coherent motion get bound together; (iv) *part binding*, by which spatial parts of an object are synthesized into a whole; (v) *sequence binding*, by which objects are synthesized diachronically as the same object over time; (vi) *scalar binding*, by which dimensions on a scale are represented; (vii) *conditional binding*, by which conditional relations between events are represented; and (viii) *what/where binding*, by which the "what" and "where" information from the dorsal and ventral pathways is synthesized (Revonsuo 1999; Treisman 1998, 1999).

Binding processes occur both in unimodal sensory assemblies and in heteromodal and transmodal assemblies. Some binding processes involve attention. A standard binding process is that which integrates contours to shapes, such as lines and angles into a square. This is accomplished unconsciously in V1 and V2. Likewise, temporal integration of repeated visual input is accomplished unconsciously. Individuals who suffer from dysfunctional unimodal visual pathways, such as visual agnosiacs, are functionally blind despite the fact that their visual field is not empty. Similarly early unimodal auditory and gustatory dysfunction has also been investigated in some detail. Less is known about olfactory and somatosensory pathways (Robertson 2003; Treisman 1998, 1999).

More complex processing provides evidence for multimodal binding. Imaging experiments have compared brain activity while individuals either see lip movements for a story being read, listen to the story being read, or watch and listen to the story being read (Macaluso & Driver 2004). Various measurement techniques show different cortical areas identified as heteromodal processing areas. Given the linguistic nature of the task, the left temporoparietal junction – Wernicke's area – is the only area that satisfies the most stringent measurements. On less stringent standards, however, bilateral temporoparietal junction, lateral parietal, intraparietal sulcus and ventral motor areas are also implicated. These areas are the same as identified in other non-human primate studies. More importantly, since these areas are active in a bimodal perceptual task, support for integrative binding activity in these areas is strengthened. Other experiments yield similar results for complex visual-somatosensory perceptual tasks. These experiments also provide evidence that information resulting from heteromodal processing feeds back into unimodal pathways (see Raftopoulos 2005). For example, multimodal audiovisual information has been shown to backtrack and modulate unimodal auditory processing, and, similarly, multimodal somatosensory-visual information affects activity in unimodal extrastriate visual cortex.

Perceptual disorders: blindsight and agnosia

Our focus is on two post-thalamic disorders of vision – blindsight and agnosia. Discussion of three other post-thalamic disorders – aphasia, alexia and apraxia – is postponed to the next chapter because they involve more than perceptual pathways. We also postpone discussion of unilateral neglect until the next chapter because it is more properly an attentional disorder.

Blindsight

Blindsight is a disorder in which individuals have no qualitatively endowed visual perception but remain able to discriminate objects and events in the unseen field. Blindsight is most frequently associated with dysfunction in or destruction of the visual pathway's V1. Damage to V1 causes a black spot (scotoma) in the visual field. If all of, say, left V1 is damaged, the right visual field will be black. While individuals deny seeing anything in the visual field contralateral to damaged V1, they can if forced identify an object's location in that field with considerable, albeit still abnormally low reliability. Other features of blindsight are equally curious. Some blindsighted individuals, for example, report that they are aware of something they do not perceive and that they perceive visual after-images of items they do not see (Cowey 2004; Milner & Goodale 1995). These discrepancies between lack of qualitatively endowed visual perception and behavioural performance are interesting but, as we learn more about visual pathways, increasingly unsurprising. For, it turns out that V1 does not receive all the visual information from the thalamus's lateral geniculate nucleus. Although the bundle of fibres leading from the thalamus's LGN to V1 numbers in the millions, several distinct pathways bypass V1 altogether on their way to extrastriate visual regions V2–V4 and MT, and one pathway of about 10,000 fibres travels directly to the superior colliculus in the hindbrain. These pathways subserve some unconscious discriminatory performance (Cowey 2004).

Agnosia

Visual *agnosia* is a disorder in which an individual is incapable of recognizing or identifying visually sensed objects (Tonkonogy & Puente 2009). Auditory, gustatory and olfactory agnosias also occur, but we do not discuss them (for details, see Tonkonogy & Puente 2009). Visual agnosia is not caused by damage either to the eye, the optic tract, the thalamus, or primary visual cortex in V1. Agnosias are caused by damage to: (a) extrastriate unimodal cortex (V2–MT) in occipital or occipito-temporal cortex; (b) the white matter tracts connecting extrastriate unimodal cortex to heteromodal associative cortex; or (c) heteromodal associative cortex itself. Agnosias are reliably subdivided into apperceptive and associative agnosias. *Apperceptive agnosias* are those in which visual perception and recognition abilities are lost because there is dysfunction in unimodal visual cortex and between unimodal visual and heteromodal associative cortex ((a) and (b) above). Within apperceptive agnosias, three subspecies are often distinguished: visual form agnosia, ventral simultanagnosia and dorsal simultanagnosia, shown in Table 6.1.

Visual form agnosia is functionally characterized by poor recognition and discrimination of shapes and is correlated with damage to local occipital and temporal cortex white matter tracts. *Ventral simultanagnosia* is characterized by intact perception of objects but an inability to recognize more than one object at a time and is correlated with damage to posterior temporal cortex. *Dorsal simultanagnosia* is characterized by poor perception of more than one object at a time and an inability to locate perceived objects in the visual field. When a dorsal simultanagnosiac perceives an object, it floats in the visual field

Table 6.1 Apperceptive agnosias.

Type	Visual form	Ventral simultanagnosia	Dorsal simultanagnosia
Symptoms	Poor recognition and discrimination of shapes; unable to copy	Poor recognition of multiple objects at a time; unable to copy	Poor perception of multiple objects at a time; poor location of object in visual field; unable to copy
Affected brain regions	Occipito-temporal cortex; local white matter tracts	Posterior temporal cortex	Bilateral parietal & superior temporal cortex

without specific location, or the visual field contracts to the space occupied by the perceived object (Revonsuo 1999). One dorsal simultanagnosiac was subject to preserving movements in her visual field – actions were perceived as repeating until, over a span of minutes, they faded. It is correlated with bilateral damage to assemblies in parietal and superior temporal cortex.

Associative agnosias are those in which visually based recognition abilities are lost even though visual perception pathways are intact through unimodal visual cortex and even though recognition abilities based on other sensory modalities are intact. Associative agnosias result from compromised functioning in heteromodal associative cortex ((c) above). Within the class, three kinds are typically distinguished: colour agnosia, topographical agnosia and prosopagnosia (Tonkonogy & Puente 2009), shown in Table 6.2.

Unlike apperceptive agnosias, which are caused by dysfunction in unimodal cortex, associative agnosias are caused by dysfunction in heteromodal cortex and are functionally characterized by intact copying ability conjoined with an inability to recognize what has been copied. *Colour agnosia* is characterized by an inability to recognize a colour just copied or to pair object and colours. Colour agnosiacs may find black apples to be as normal as red apples; they may not be able to identify bread until they taste it; they may be unable to identify a watch as a watch even though they can use it to tell time. *Topographical agnosia* is characterized by an inability to move around a familiar room even though there are intact memories of the spatial relations between furniture items in the room. *Prosopagnosia* is characterized by an ability to recognize familiar others by voice or smell and an inability to recognize them by looking at their faces. Individual parts – a nose, a mouth – can be perceived and identified, but they do not add up to a face. Although prosopagnosiacs cannot recognize familiar others visually by their faces, they do exhibit emotional responses to those familiar others whom they do not visually recognize, thus revealing that the visual and limbic pathways responsible for emotional response are intact despite disavowal of familiarity. This suggests that there is a level of unimodal and heteromodal visual processing sufficient for engaging some preconscious affective pathways but insufficient for engaging some conscious cognitive pathways (Bauer 1984).

Table 6.2 Associative agnosias.

Type	Colour	Topographical	Prosopagnosia
Symptoms	Various; poor naming and discrimination of colours; able to copy	Poor use of visual cues for movement; able to copy	Poor recognition of familiar human faces, familiar cars, animals, etc.; able to copy
Affected brain regions	Heteromodal visual cortex; occipito-temporal cortex	Right posterior cingulate cortex	Right and bilateral occipito-temporal cortex (fusiform cortex)

A unique set of perceptual disorders targets our sense of self. *Asomatognosia* is the loss of awareness and denial of ownership of a body part, usually an arm; it frequently accompanies hemispheric neglect (Feinberg *et al.* 2009). Asomatognosia correlates with dysfunction in parietal cortex, in particular the right supramarginal gyrus, occipital lobe, thalamoparietal white matter tracts and posterior insula damage. *Somatoparaphrenia*, defined as asomatognosia plus confabulations about ownership of body part, is additionally correlated with temporal lobe and orbitofrontal damage (Feinberg *et al.* 2009). Related disorders are autoscopic hallucination, heautoscopy and out-of-body experience, disorders in which there are illusions of duplication of one's body in extrapersonal space. Blanke and Metzinger (2009) characterize the three species as follows. In *autoscopic hallucination*, one is subject to an illusory visual duplication of one's body in extrapersonal space from one's own embodied perspective. In *heautoscopy*, one is subject to an illusory visual duplication of one's body in extrapersonal space from an indeterminate perspective intermediate between one's own embodied perspective and the autoscopic body. In *out-of-body experience*, one is subject to an illusory visual duplication of one's body in extrapersonal space from the perspective of the autoscopic body. In autoscopic hallucinations, there is no sense of disembodiment, the hallucinations are from a body-centred perspective, and the subject acknowledges the hallucinatory content. In heautoscopy, on the other hand, there is no acknowledgment of the hallucinatory content, the sense of disembodiment is ambiguous, but the sense of body-centredness is maintained. And in out-of-body experience, there is, like heautoscopy, no acknowledgment of hallucinatory content, but unlike heautoscopy and autoscopic hallucination, there is clear disembodiment and the subjective perspective changes from one's corporeal body to the autoscopic body.

THE QUALITATIVE/AFFECTIVE BRAIN

Some philosophers have restricted the class of qualitative properties to those presented in perception and perhaps, at least in the case of pain, to interoception. This restriction is a mistake (Damasio 2000; Graham & Horgan 2002; Hanna & Maiese 2009; Panksepp 2003, 2005; Thompson 2007). There are qualitative properties of visual, auditory, gustatory, olfactory and somatosensory perceptual events, of interoceptive events such as thirst, food and air hunger, and sleepiness, proprioceptive events such as balance and kinesthesia, and emotional events such as grief and elation. We therefore stipulate the following. *Perceptual qualitative properties* are those that perceptual events have and that are correlated with the activity of the five sensory modality mechanisms (vision, audition, olfaction, gustation and touch) and caused by stimuli from outside the body. *Interoceptive qualitative properties* are those that interoceptive events have and that are correlated with the activity of interoceptive mechanisms (thirst, food hunger, air hunger, sleepiness, temperature control, micturition (the urge to uri-nate), sexual orgasm and pain) and caused by vegetative stimuli from within the body. (For reasons of space, we do not discuss *proprioceptive qualitative properties* further – narrowly defined, proprioceptive events are related to the sense of bodily position in space; broadly defined, proprioceptive events are included in the class of interoceptive events.) *Emotional qualitative properties* are those that emotional events have and that are correlated with the activity of limbic mechanisms and caused by salient internal and external events. Emotional experiences make up an enormous set, but on any list the basic emotions of fear, disgust, rage, pleasure/playfulness/happiness, care, lust and surprise/panic would certainly be included.

The neuroscientific discipline that comes closest to studying qualitative properties as understood by philosophers is *affective neuroscience*. Affective neuroscience purports to discover the neural underpinnings of more kinds of qualitative properties than are typically of interest to many philosophers, but, as just noted, on this score at least the philosophers are probably wrong. Affective neuroscience broke off from cognitive neuroscience about fifteen years ago as an attempt to compensate for the lack of neuroscientific work on what are known as affective processes (Panksepp 2003, 2005). As the discipline has devel-oped, distinctions between it and perceptual and cognitive neuroscience have become increasingly complex, sometimes muddy. In this section, some findings forthcoming from affective neuroscience concerning qualitative properties are presented. We restrict attention to what affective neuroscience has to say about taste, smell and flavour, types of perceptual qualitative properties, thirst and pain, types of interoceptive qualitative properties, and fear and disgust, types of emotional qualitative properties.

Perceptual qualitative properties

Perceptual qualitative properties have driven neural-minded philosophers and neuroscientists to distraction. Both wonder where, if anywhere, in the neural pathways of perception qualitative character makes its appearance. Our target perceptual qualia are taste and smell, and flavour, the commingling of taste and smell. Similar accounts could be given for vision, audition and touch.

Taste
Having established the unimodal and heteromodal pathways activated during taste events, we focus now on those assemblies and pathways that appear to be uniquely correlated with the qualitative properties of taste. As noted, from primary taste processing in insular cortex and the tongue area of somatosen-sory cortex, there are projections to secondary somatosensory cortex, amygdala, cingulate cortex and orbitofrontal prefrontal cortex. This insular-orbitofrontal

cortical pathway is thought to be crucial for the emergence of conscious perception of taste and for food cravings. Evidence for the role of orbitofrontal cortex in taste qualitative properties comes from a variety of studies that show that two separate areas in orbitofrontal cortex respond differentially to fat, the first to its neurochemical properties, the other to its textural properties such as creaminess, juiciness and smoothness (see, among others, Kringelbach 2004; Kringelbach *et al.* 2003; Rolls 2004, 2005; Verhagen *et al.* 2003). Similar evidence suggests that orbitofrontal pathways are correlated with sweet, salt, bitter, sour and umami tastes and also with astringent and acidic tastes.

Smell
Primary olfactory cortex is located at the bottom of prefrontal cortex and in the parahippocampal region of medial temporal cortex. Pathways from there project to entorhinal associative cortex in temporal lobe, which in turn projects to the hippocampus's dentate gyrus, a crucial area for memory implantation and consolidation. A distinct primate olfactory pathway projects from primary olfactory cortex through the thalamus to insular and orbitofrontal cortex. As with taste, evidence suggests that activity in the orbitofrontal pathway is correlated with the qualitative features of smell. For example, lesions to, and dysfunction in, orbitofrontal cortex routinely results in compromised odour detection and identification abilities, and imaging studies of sensitivity to peppermint and banana aromas show significant activity in both orbitofrontal and temporal cortices (Levy *et al.* 1999). Different cortical regions respond to unpleasant odours. Cingulate cortical pathways are routinely more active during unpleasant odour experience than during pleasant odour experience, and truly offensive odours activate not only cingulate cortex and orbitofrontal cortex, but amygdala as well (Rolls *et al.* 2003).

Flavour
Flavour is the combination of taste, smell and, to a lesser extent, somatosensory feel, texture and temperature. Studies show correlations between both unimodal taste and smell modalities and activity in orbitofrontal cortex and between heteromodal association across taste, smell and mouth feel modalities and activity in orbitofrontal cortex. Qualitative features of flavour are correlated to activity in these pathways. It is significant, then, that orbitofrontal cortex contains neural pathways some of which are unimodal and others of which are heteromodal. It has been estimated that 34 per cent of orbitofrontal neurons respond only to taste, 14 per cent respond only to smell, 21 per cent only to appearance, 13 per cent to smell and appearance, 13 per cent to taste and smell, and 5 per cent to smell and appearance (Rolls & Baylis 1994).

Interoceptive qualitative properties

Neurophysiology of interoception is now sufficiently well developed to map out some of the neural activity thought to correlate with interoceptive qualitative properties. Our target interoceptive qualia are thirst and pain. Similar accounts are available for food hunger, air hunger, sleepiness, temperature control, micturition and sexual orgasm.

Thirst

Even if not as ancient as to be part of the reptilian brain, being thirsty is still a phylogenetically old phenomenon. We all know what it is like to be thirsty: a dry mouth, dull headache, muscle tightness in the face, swollen tongue and a craving for water. We quench thirst typically within three to five minutes of starting to drink, long before the water cycles through our system sufficiently to lower sodium levels, a process that takes anywhere from fifteen minutes to two hours.

Thirst is activated by an intracellular loss of water and the resultant increase in sodium levels in extracellular blood plasma and brain fluid when water re-enters the cells to correct the intracellular imbalance. When extracellular sodium levels increase sufficiently, receptor cells in the lamina terminalis on the surface of the third ventricle detect the change and precipitate a cascade of neural activity. Lesions to this region cause *adipsia*, the loss of thirst. The receptor cells of the lamina terminalis activate pathways in subcortical hypothalamus, thalamus, parahippocampus, amygdala, mesocortical insular cortex, anterior and posterior cingulate cortex, and orbitofrontal cortex. If the need for water is not satisfied, thirst intensifies and additional activity in neocortical intraparietal associative regions occurs. Upon wetting the mouth, activation begins in prefrontal cortex and deactivation begins in parahippocampus and posterior cingulate cortex. When water is drunk to satiety and the experience of thirst wanes, deactivation of corpus callosum, posterior cingulate cortex, insular cortex, orbitofrontal cortex and thalamus occurs (Denton 2005; Denton *et al.* 1999; Egan *et al.* 2003). Figure 6.6 shows the thirst pathway.

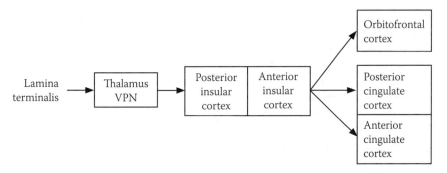

Figure 6.6 Thirst feedforward pathway (adapted from Damasio 2003).

With the exception of the prefrontal areas (activated only as a consequence of wetting the mouth), the areas correlated with the qualitative properties of thirst are subcortical, allocortical and mesocortical rather than neocortical. True enough, when the need for water becomes dire and thirst dominates our conscious thoughts, neocortical intraparietal regions correlated with attention and other cognitive resources are enlisted to resolve the threat. But the antiquity of the neural pathways that correlate with the experience of paradigmatic qualitative thirst properties suggests that any mammal with similar activation/deactivation patterns has qualitative thirst properties.

Pain

The identification and description of pain has been controversial for as long as people have been talking about it. Nowhere is the controversial nature of pain more readily seen than in the long-standing debates about the relation between pain experience and correlated neural systems that carry the somatic information without which pain experience does not occur. Recent research identifies and describes the neural pathways of pain in detail. These accomplishments help sharpen investigations into possible cortical correlates of pain qualia.

The route of pain information begins with the activation of Aδ-fibres and C-fibres, found in all bodily tissues. These fibres convey information about the physiological status of tissues to lamina-1 of the spinal cord, a bundle of long fibres that help compose the spinothalamic tract. Some lamina-1 fibres, the nociceptive specific (NS) fibres, respond to sharp pain, others, the polymodal nociceptive (HPC – heat, pinch, cold) fibres, respond to burning pain. Lamina-1 fibres stream upwards to the ventral posterior nucleus (VPN) of the thalamus. VPN is small in monkeys and becomes increasingly large as one moves from monkeys to primates; in humans, VPN is very large. VPN stimulation in humans provokes pain, cooling and visceral sensations. In addition to transmission to VPN, gustatory, chemical and other visceral information is transmitted from the nucleus of the solitary tract and from the parabrachial nucleus to the basal part of VPN (VPNb). Together, information from VPN and VPNb represents all interoceptive information, which then projects to mesocortical posterior insular cortex, where, on the dorsal margin, cortical representations of sharp and burning pain, muscular and visceral sensations, touch, hunger, thirst, itch and air hunger are produced. From this area, projections lead to mesocortical orbitofrontal cortex, somatosensory cortex and anterior cingulate cortex, the latter of which is correlated with motivation and initiation of behavioural responses. In addition, re-representation of interoceptions in anterior insular cortex also occur (Craig 2002, 2003, 2004). Figure 6.7 shows the pain pathway. As with thirst, the neural pathways correlated with pain are phylogenetically old. So, again, if these pathways are necessary and sufficient for the qualitative property of pain, then the qualitative experience of pain goes back a long way. That is hardly surprising.

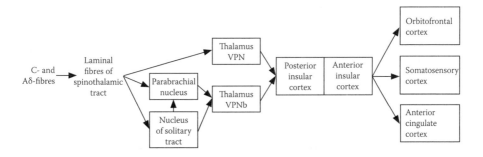

Figure 6.7 Pain feedforward pathway (adapted from Damasio 2003).

Before leaving the topic, mention of *phantom pain*, a bizarre clinical syndrome, needs to be made. At least half of all amputees experience phantom pain. From immediately to within a few weeks after amputation and lasting from a few weeks to decades, most phantoms occur with arm and leg amputations, but there are reports of phantom ulcers, breasts, face parts, erections and menstrual cramps (Lotze *et al.* 2001). While most phantoms are experienced as fixed in position, some move as a result of stimulating different parts of the remaining limb. Fine-grained experiences of moving, grasping, reaching and squeezing frequently accompany phantom hands and are likely to persist even when the rest of the phantom arm attenuates. Such individuals report that although their experience is as-of an arm that over time becomes shorter, their experience over the same stretch of time continues to be as-of a hand involved in activities. Many individuals with recently amputated arms experience as-of hand pain of a remarkably specific kind, needles or nails being stabbed into the palm of the hand (burning, cramping and crushing are also described). The amount of pain experienced in the limb or body part prior to its amputation correlates with the phenomenological intensity of phantom experience after amputation (Ramachandran & Hirstein 1998).

Ramachandran has hypothesized that since the input that would have gone to hand areas of somatosensory cortex no longer does so once a hand or arm is amputated, areas in somatosensory cortex nearest hand areas remap the cortical areas that no longer receive input. Imaging studies now provide evidence for the truth of this hypothesis. A strong correlation exists between phantom pain as-of a hand and activity in the facial area of primary somatosensory cortex, which lies immediately next to hand areas in individuals who still have their hands (Flor *et al.* 1995; Karl *et al.* 2001; Lotze *et al.* 2001). Other studies by Ramachandran and colleagues have provided additional evidence of cortical remapping by demonstrating that individuals with recently amputated arms and hands report phantom sensory experience in specific fingers when specific regions of their cheeks are touched.

Emotional qualitative properties

Emotion is the centrepiece of contemporary affective neuroscience. It is a huge field and one in which a lot of work needs still to be done before many general implications can be derived. To get a quick idea of how enormous the field will have to be to be comprehensive, consider a partial list of human emotions and moods: accomplishment; affection; agitation; aggression, alarm; altruism; ambivalence; amusement; anger; angst; annoyance; anticipation; anxiety; apathy; apprehension; arrogance; awe; bashfulness; benevolence; bitterness; boldness; boredom; caution; chagrin; comfort; compassion; compulsion; confidence; contempt; contentment; courage; coyness; coziness; craving; curiosity; cynicism; delight; delirium; depression; derision; desire; despair; diffidence; disappointment; disdain; disgust; dismay; distrust; dizziness; dread; ecstasy; elation; embarrassment; empathy; emptiness; ennui; enthusiasm; envy; euphoria; exaltation; excitement; fatigue; fear; flirtation; forgiveness; friendship; fright; frustration; fury; generosity; giddiness; gladness; glee; glory; gratitude; grief; grumpiness; guilt; happiness; hate; hilarity; homesickness; honour; hope; horror; hostility; humiliation; humility; hysteria; impatience; indignation; infatuation; irritability; joy; jealousy; kindness; loathing; loneliness; longing; love; lust; magnanimity; mastery; melancholia; mercy; modesty; nausea; nervousness; nostalgia; obsession; panic; paranoia; patience; perturbation; pity; pleasure; pride; queasiness; rage; regret; relaxation; relief; remorse; repentance; repugnance; repulsion; resentment; sadness; sarcasm; satiety; satisfaction; scepticism; self-pity; serenity; shame; shock; shyness; sorrow; shock; stress; sublimity; subservience; suffering; sullenness; surprise; suspense; suspicion; sympathy; terror; unhappiness; vulnerability; well-being; worry.

No doubt every reader can add others to the list, and no doubt some will think that some of those on the list are not really emotions or moods. No matter: what is immediately apparent is the impressive heterogeneity of intensity, phenomenology, valence and degree of cognitive involvement across the affective kinds.

Neuroscience of emotion is an active research area, and long-standing psychological categories, such as those listed above, are colliding head-on with neuroscientific categories. In such an environment sparks are bound to fly. For example, it is virtually axiomatic that emotions are conscious phenomena. Neuroscientific researchers frequently insist that conscious experience of emotion must be distinguished from its neurophysiology, that emotion must be operationalized, or that the subjectivity of emotional experience must be quarantined and left out of scientific discussion. But these methodological demands easily culminate in equivocation, as terms familiar from everyday life are imported into scientific discussions without their familiar referents. The term "emotion" can be found even in the most behaviouristically rigorous programmes, but in such work it refers not to an event loaded with qualitative character at all but to a kind of observable behaviour, such as facial expression. "Affect" and "feeling" are likewise subject to shifting definitions across researchers and methodological scruples. These methodological concerns put everyone in a bind, since the phenomena of interest are emotion's consciously experienced qualitative properties, its feeling. It is quite true that the qualitative character of emotional experience *might* be exhaustively explained by, equivalent to, caused by, or identical with, electrochemical activity of neural assemblies reliably correlated with that character, but such a claim requires defence. After all, when Anna, say, feels happy, it is not at all obvious that her qualitative feeling is nothing but electrochemical activity in a limbic system pathway. The qualitative character of an emotion is one thing; the content of an emotion is another thing, and what subserves qualitative character and content is still another thing, or perhaps another two things. We cannot simply assume that evidence for any one of these phenomena is evidence for all of them.

We focus as much as possible on the qualitative character of emotion and the neural events with which that qualitative character correlates. We are not directly interested here in the causal prompts of emotion. To avoid misunderstanding, we stipulate that "affect" refers to temporally short neural events that have valence and intensity; "valence" is either positive or negative, as an emotion is either attractive or aversive; "intensity" refers to the degree of attractiveness or aversiveness; "feeling" refers to conscious experiences associated with such brief affect episodes; and "emotion" refers to affect–feeling pairs. The term "mood" refers to temporally longer affect–feeling dyads. Emotions are frequently intense and short in duration; moods are typically less intense but long-lasting. We discuss two emotions, fear and disgust.[1]

Fear

No credible evidence entails that the amygdala is solely responsible for even basic emotions, much less for all emotions. Still, fear at least involves activity in the amygdala. As has been noted, the amygdala, hippocampus and anterior cingulate cortex form the central neural pathways of the limbic system. The amygdala receives input from the hindbrain, olfactory bulb, thalamus, hypothalamus, hippocampus, perirhinal cortex, insular cortex, primary and secondary sensory cortex, and orbitofrontal cortex. In turn, amygdala sends projections to all but one of the above areas (the exception being sensory cortex) plus the basal ganglia structures of caudate nucleus and putamen (the striatum), nucleus accumbens, ventral tegmental area (in midbrain), locus coeruleus (in hindbrain) and septum. This impressive connectivity and wide-ranging reciprocity hints at the phylogenetic significance of affects circuiting through it.

The amygdala plays a role in fear production and recognition. Consider a sensory stimulus, say of an approaching unknown member of one's own species (a conspecific). That complex visual and auditory stimulus is taken up from the sensory cortex by the thalamus. In response, the thalamus projects messages both to the amygdala directly and also to orbitofrontal prefrontal cortex, which in turn projects to the amygdala. The first, short, route of fear permits a rough estimation of danger and the opportunity for immediate and precognitive response. The second, long route of fear permits a more nuanced, cognitively refined, executive back-up and check on the short route. In the long route, the perceived object's sensory modalities route first through primary sensory cortex and orbitofrontal prefrontal cortex, the latter of which projects a worked-up representation of the object back to the amygdala. Pathways from orbitofrontal cortex also direct messages to the hippocampus, where comparisons are made and contexts established. That enriched representation is communicated back to the amygdala for modulated response.

Figure 6.8 shows the fear pathways. Thick arrows represent the short pathway from sensory input to amygdala and hypothalamus, and thin arrows represent the long pathway. Upon detecting danger (through either route), the amygdala projects to the striatum, hypothalamus and pituitary, which alter adrenaline levels, initiating the cascade of autonomic changes characteristic of fear – increased heart rate and blood pressure, sweaty hands, dry mouth, tense muscles and being frozen in place. All of us respond to perceived danger rapidly, often before we are aware of or think about it. That is an example of the short route. Usually, after initially responding with a start, we modify our response. That is an example of the long route. The long route is an advance over more primitive fear responses, and it reveals that the amygdala is part of a phylogenetically advanced association circuit with the hippocampus, wherein current dangerous input is compared to and put into context with past input.

Substantive differences are found between human amygdala function and monkey and other primate amygdala function. Humans with lesioned amygdala are particularly bad at recognizing facial expression of emotion. The impacts of lesioned amygdalae on monkey and non-human primates are much more severe. Without an amygdala, monkeys are utterly tame, have no discernible fear, eat almost anything, visually react to almost everything, put anything they can lift into their mouths, and try to have sex with almost everything (monkey

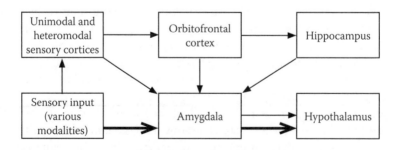

Figure 6.8 Short and long fear feedforward pathways.

and otherwise) most of the time. Non-human primates without amygdalae are also rendered socially incompetent. Since vocalization routes directly through the amygdala, removing it from a chimp results in inappropriate or absent vocalization. Moreover, since non-human primate vocalization is not routed through prefrontal cortex at all, insult to the area of their brain homologous to our Wernicke's area has little or no impact on their vocalization. In humans, the reverse is true: loss of amygdala causes no discernible disruption of vocalization and insult to Wernicke's area results in incoherence. These neurofunctional differences reveal an interesting difference between us and other primates, noted in the last chapter: for all other primates, vocalization is almost entirely a limbic system affair, while in humans alone, most vocalization, and especially speech, is routed directly and massively through prefrontal neocortex.

Disgust

The cross-cultural universality of some of the cues for disgust has recently been confirmed (Curtis *et al.* 2004): visual, tactile, olfactory, or gustatory detection of insect activity, decomposing flesh, faeces, urine, putrid odours, bodily secretions, and viscous, oozing, festering, sticky and slimy substances. Responses vary, but all mammals have both autonomic responses and behavioural responses. In humans and other primates, autonomic responses include decreasing blood pressure and decelerating heart rate, and behavioural responses include a universally shared and instantly recognized facial expression – contorted nose and mouth – sniffing, snorting, vocalizing ("eeew!" "gross!"), withdrawal and sometimes vomiting.

Disgust is correlated with activity in insular cortex and the basal ganglia. Recall that insular cortex is reciprocally connected to the thalamus, amygdala, orbitofrontal cortex and primary sensory cortices and that the basal ganglia (striatum, globus pallidus and substantia nigra) receive inputs from cortex, thalamus, amygdala and hippocampus and send outputs to brainstem and thalamus and thence back to cortical areas. Phylogenetic antiquity for both insular cortex and basal ganglia is suggested by input, internal and output pathways, which are shared across a wide range of mammalian species, and by their allocortical and mesocortical cytoarchitecture.

The neural pathways associated with disgust response vary somewhat across mammals, but in humans incoming perceptual information and interoceptive information routes from sensory cortices through thalamus to anterior and posterior insular cortex. Individuals with lesioned anterior insular cortex have impaired disgust experience; stimulating anterior insular cortex produces disagreeable taste and nausea; and neuroimaging methods show that anterior insular cortex is active when disgust is produced by odours and slimy objects. The presence of external cues is not necessary for disgust, and even self-induced disgust correlates with activity in insular cortex (Torunchuk & Ellis 2007). The basal ganglia are active during behavioural responses and expressions of disgust.

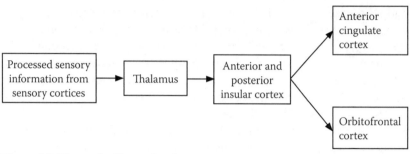

Figure 6.9 Disgust feedforward pathway.

Evidence comes both from neuroimaging measurements and from individuals with Huntington's disease, a genetically based degenerative disease that causes cell death in the caudate nucleus of the striatum. Such individuals show a marked inability to recognize facial expressions of disgust in others and demonstrable deficits in responding to disgusting tastes and smells. Figure 6.9 shows the disgust pathway. One striking similarity across the perceptual modalities, interoception, and the emotions that we have reviewed is the presence of correlations between qualitative properties and neural activity in insular cortex and orbitofrontal cortex.

The neural correlates for qualitative properties discussed above represent a tiny fraction of the evidence currently available that supports the claim that qualitatively rich experience has neural correlates. We did not even mention most of the emotions and we mentioned none of the *social* emotions, such as love, solidarity, pride and compassion, which many consider to be important for distinguishing us from other mammals. Moreover, the neural correlates proposed for the perceptual, interoceptive and affective states we did investigate are far from complete. Significantly more is known now about the neural correlates for taste, smell, thirst, pain, fear and disgust than five years ago, and compared to twenty years ago the comparison is even starker. Having said that, more work needs to be done, for it is increasingly clear that many past studies failed to distinguish qualitative character from other properties of perception, interoception and affect or reduced the former to the latter without so much as a by-your-leave. As will be seen in later chapters, this temptation weakens claims sometimes made on behalf of neural reduction of qualitative character.

7. ATTENTION, WORKING MEMORY, LANGUAGE AND EXECUTIVE FUNCTION

Cognition presents topics of long-standing interest to psychologists and neuro-psychologists. Cognition encompasses a huge array of processes, including attention, working memory, and language understanding and production. Some cognitive processes are executive functions. Accounts of executive function vary enormously (Jurado & Rosselli 2007), but its component processes typically include inhibiting behaviour; learning; formulating goals; sequencing actions; integrating information; remembering; generalizing and abstracting; understanding; knowing; analysing; monitoring; introspecting; discriminating; evaluating; creating; deliberating; planning; decision-making; judging; choosing; and directing – in short, much of our daily conscious lives.

Evidence increases monthly that there are neural correlates for attention, working memory, language understanding, and for each and every one of the constitutive processes of executive function. Cataloging all the evidence is too big a job for this book. Instead, we first discuss attention, focusing on top-down forms of attention, and we introduce the paradigmatic neurological attentional disorders of acute confusional state and unilateral neglect. Second, we introduce working memory. Third, we discuss language understanding, focusing in particular on semantic understanding, and on the neurological language disorders of aphasia and alexia. Finally, we address some of the executive functions and introduce frontal lobe syndrome. Many other cognitive processes are important for determining whether conscious properties have neural substrates, but there is an enormous amount of work on memory, attention, language processes and executive function, and the points we want to make are best made by discussing them.

ATTENTION

More than a thousand articles a year with "attention" in the title are published (Raz & Buhle 2006). All of this work has resulted in increasingly fine-grained descriptions of attention and a proliferation of distinctions between attention and related phenomena. All these species of attention and their neural correlates are directly relevant for understanding conscious properties, for both overlap significantly with ordinary conceptions of consciousness and its properties (Cavanna & Nani 2008; Posner 1994).

Kinds and components of attention

Phasic attention is distinct from arousal, for while a deficit in arousal entails a deficit in attention, a deficit in attention does not entail a deficit in arousal. Comatose individuals cannot attend to anything because they are not aroused, but individuals suffering from persistent vegetative state (PVS) can exhibit normal circadian rhythms and other measures of arousal despite engaging in no phasic attentional processes. Phasic attention is also distinct from tonic alertness. While distinct from tonic alertness, phasic attention (hereafter "attention") presupposes tonic alertness. Individuals suffering from acute confusional syndrome are tonically alert but unable to engage in any attentional processes. (As noted in Chapter 6, the relations between the neural correlates of tonic alertness and those of attention are not yet well understood.)

Attention can be characterized across a number of dimensions. There is to begin with the voluntary/involuntary dimension. *Voluntary* or *endogenous* or *goal-driven* or *top-down attention* is prompted by internally initiated voluntary cognitive activity. *Involuntary* or *exogenous* or *stimulus-driven* or *bottom-up attention* is prompted by features of perceptual, interoceptive and proprioceptive experience intruding upon ongoing cognitive activity.[1] Second, attention can be overt or covert. *Overt attention* directs a sense organ or sense organs to that which is attended; *covert attention* does not. We can attend to a feature in our visual field, for example, without turning our eyes ("foveating") to the feature. Similarly, we can attend to a particular sound or smell without turning our heads to its source. Third, attention can be internally or externally directed. *Internally directed* attention is attention turned on some cognitive, affective, perceptual, interoceptive, or proprioceptive event; *externally directed* attention is attention on some feature of the perceptually given environment. Fourth, attention can be either *short-term* or *sustained*.

There are then four general kinds of attention, each with subvarieties: voluntary overt; voluntary covert; involuntary overt; and involuntary covert. *Voluntary overt* attention is attention caused by some intention and is demonstrably turned on some object, either endogenous or exogenous (as when I decide to turn my head to better hear the yipping of a coyote). *Voluntary covert* attention is caused by some intention and not demonstrably turned on some endogenous or exogenous object (as when I decide to listen to the coyote's yipping while typing). *Involuntary overt* attention is caused by some feature in the field of experience, endogenous or exogenous, and is demonstrably turned on some object (as when I visually discern the coyote moving in the scrub oak twenty yards from the window and turn my eyes away from the computer towards it). *Involuntary covert* attention is caused by some feature in the field of experience, endogenous or exogenous, and is not demonstrably turned on some object (as when I catch the coyote out of the corner of my eye) (Knudsen 2007; Peelen *et al.* 2004; Posner 1994).

Attention is a temporally extended process with phases, each comprised of component cognitive processes. An influential model, proposed by Posner, claims that attention is a tripartite process of alerting, orienting and execution (Posner 2004). The *alerting* or *vigilance* phase of attention is the process of transiently increasing response readiness to a stimulus and of maintaining that state of readiness for a short time. Such *phasic* alertness is distinct from *tonic* alertness, discussed in the previous chapter. Second, there is the *orienting* or *scanning* phase, the processes of selecting and concentrating upon some feature of the field of internal or external experience. Third, the *executive* phase is the process of monitoring and resolving conflicts between the outputs of other perceptual, affective and cognitive processes and activities. Its constituent processes include standard executive functions – planning, decision-making, risk calculation, integration, reflection and error detection. The executive phase of attention looks a whole lot like the central executive of working memory. Indeed, they are the same, as argued below.

Neural correlates of attention

Imaging and neuropsychological studies suggest that voluntary attention and involuntary attention are both correlated with neural activity in a network involving multiple brain regions. Formation of spatial representations correlates with activity in bilateral superior parietal cortex near the intraparietal sulcus and right (and, to a lesser extent, left) inferior parietal cortex in the temporoparietal junction area; coordination of motor exploration correlates with activity in left (and, to a lesser extent, right) premotor and supplementary motor cortex, including insular cortex, and left ventrolateral prefrontal cortex (VLPFC); and motivational valence correlates with activity in bilateral anterior cingulate cortex and some cerebellar regions and other subcortical regions, such as the reticular formation, colliculus, globus pallidus, thalamus and locus coeruleus (Awh & Jonides 2000; Desimone & Duncan 1995; Peelen *et al.* 2004; Sturm & Willmes 2001).

Phasic alerting typically correlates with activity in right, and to a lesser degree left, inferior parietal cortex in the temporoparietal junction area, colliculus, locus coeruleus and thalamus (Fan *et al.* 2005). Overt and covert orienting, regardless of sensory modality, correlates with activity in parietal areas surrounding intraparietal sulcus, anterior cingulate cortex, right DLPFC, supplemental motor area, cerebellum, locus coeruleus and globus pallidus (Fan *et al.* 2005; Hopfinger *et al.* 2000; Mesulam *et al.* 2001; Raz 2004; Raz & Buhle 2006). Orienting associated with particular sensory modalities also correlates with modality-specific cortical regions. The frontal eye fields and the thalamus's pulvinar are, for instance, activated primarily when voluntary or involuntary overt attention precipitates a shift in eye movement to a particular area of the visual field.

If both voluntary and involuntary attention are composed of the same component alerting and orienting processes, each of which is in turn correlated with the same neural pathways, how then are they distinct? There must be *some* distinction between the two. Most agree that activity in the subcortical globus pallidus is correlated only with voluntary attention. Beyond that, there is considerable disagreement. Some claim that in voluntary attention alone there is activity in superior and dorsal parietal cortex surrounding the intraparietal sulcus and in DLPFC (Corbetta *et al.* 2002; Sturm & Willmes 2001). Others claim that in voluntary and involuntary attention alike there is widespread shared neural activity even in these areas (Peelen *et al.* 2004). On this alternative, there are different *levels* of activity in DLPFC and superior parietal cortex in voluntary and in involuntary attention and different *patterns* of activity in those regions, but not *in-kind* differences. This debate is not resolved, although the additional fine-grain in task selection and resolution in more recent studies suggests that, while neural differences exist between voluntary and involuntary attention, they may not be the differences that have hitherto been described.

Even greater disagreement surrounds neural correlates of executive attention. What is common ground across a number of investigations is that, when taken collectively, *all* the processes constitutive of executive attention are correlated with neural activity clustered in right DLPFC and VLPFC, anterior cingulate cortex and regions of parietal cortex. Beyond that, conflicting evidence, incomplete evidence and disagreement are common. Some claim that error detection is correlated with activity in the front of (or rostral) anterior cingulate and that conflict resolution correlates with activity in dorsal anterior cingulate cortex. But it has also been claimed that many cognitively based executive attention processes, not just conflict resolution, correlate with dorsal anterior cingulate cortex, and that what is correlated with rostral anterior cingulate cortex is not just error detection but a whole range of affectively based executive processes. Again, others (Miller & Cohen 2001) suggest that monitoring conflict but not resolving conflict is correlated with a complex pathway involving anterior cingulate cortex but also DLPFC, locus coeruleus and ventral tegementum. Still others suggest that the kind of conflict resolution correlated with anterior cingulate cortex is restricted to response conflicts and that another neural pathway in DLPFC is associated with heteromodal conflict resolution (Raz & Buhle 2006).

Neurological attention disorders: acute confusional state and unilateral neglect

Cognitive activities constitutive of attention cause quicker and more accurate cognitive processing than when that activity is absent. For example, when individuals are asked to attend to motion changes rather than colour changes in an experiment, activity in V5 is greater than when they are not asked to so attend. Interestingly, this neural activity is higher *before* the stimulus is even presented. Parallel results for the case of attending to colour and activity in V4, another unimodal pathway, have also been reported. Both results suggest that attending to an upcoming stimulus initiates downwards feedback into unimodal sensory pathways, a noteworthy counter to views in which early unimodal pathways are held immune from such infiltration (Gazzaniga *et al.* 2002; Kastner *et al.* 1999; Knudsen 2007; Pessoa *et al.* 2003).

The causal efficacy of attention can also be established by noting the consequences of cortical dysfunctions that correlate with acute confusional state and unilateral neglect (also known as visual hemi-neglect, hemispatial neglect or spatial neglect). In *acute confusional state*, an individual's ability to focus, maintain, or shift attention is compromised. It is correlated with lesions to and other dysfunctions of the thalamus, caudate, temporal cortex and internal capsule. *Unilateral neglect* (also called *hemispheric neglect*) is a disorder in which an individual is incapable of paying attention to one half of the egocentrically oriented perceptual field. Individuals with left neglect may shave or apply makeup only to the right side of their faces, may eat only from the right side of the plate, may reach for the phone only if its ring is strongly in the right auditory field, may read only the right page of a book, the right side of a page of a book, or even the right side of a word. There can be compromised manual exploration and unwillingness to intentionally direct movement to the neglected half of egocentrically oriented space. The neglected side can even come to lose emotional and motivational saliency such that individuals are surprised when anything of importance emerges from the field they ignore.

Like blindsighters, numb touchers, deaf hearers and achromatopsiacs (colourless vision), neglecters can, upon instruction, identify what they claim does not exist in the neglected field. But whereas blindsighters, numb touchers, deaf hearers and achromatopsiacs acknowledge the deficits to their qualitative experience, neglect individuals do not. Their deficit is caused by dysfunction in attentional rather than perceptual pathways. Neglect patients qualitatively perceive and are experientially sensitive to objects and events in their neglected field, but they cannot attend to them, and since they cannot attend to them, they do not notice that their conscious experience has a deficit. In short, neglect patients are both experientially and informationally sensitive but attentively insensitive, which shows that endogenous attention, while a characteristic accompaniment of many conscious events, is distinct from and can dissociate from what makes those events conscious (Flanagan 1992, 1998; Lamme 2003, 2004; see also below, Chapter 9).

Unilateral neglect is most frequently reported as lateralized to the left half of the visual field because most reported instances result from dysfunction in heteromodal associative areas in right posterior parietal cortex. But the phenomenon is restricted neither to the left side of the visual field nor to damage to right posterior parietal cortex. All modalities of attention and all components of the neural network subserving attention are implicated in unilateral neglect, so, just as the phenomenological symptoms of unilateral neglect are diverse, so too can its neurological causes be diverse. Neglect individuals have intact perceptual pathways up to heteromodal perceptual association areas in right posterior parietal cortex, damage to which is routinely correlated with the deficit. But damage to dorsomedial prefrontal cortex (the frontal eye fields and supplementary frontal eye fields), cingulate cortex, striatum and even the thalamus can also result in unilateral neglect. Unilateral neglect usually affects the left egocentrically oriented perceptual field because it correlates with right parietal damage. When right parietal pathways are compromised or destroyed, the heteromodal representations of external space mediated by those pathways are undermined. However, neglect caused by right dorsomedial prefrontal damage is just as debilitating as parietal damage, often more so, to the point that it is indistinguishable from blindness. And damage to right cingulate cortex can result in a diminished sense of the contralateral field's motivational saliency (Mesulam 1999).

Some disorders related to unilateral neglect affect our sense of agency and body-ownership. *Anarchic hand syndrome*, a disorder characterized by spontaneous non-intentional limb movements, results in conscious experience of one's limbs being alien from oneself. An amusing fictional example is Doctor Strangelove from the Kubrick film of the same name, whose right hand routinely shoots into a Nazi salute at the most inopportune moments. Whenever this occurs, Strangelove has to knock the saluting arm down with his other hand. Similarly, an individual reported in Schwabe and Blanke (2007) picks up a pencil and starts scribbling on the wall with it. When she attends to what her hand is up to, she pulls it down to stop it with her other hand, declaring that the offending hand just refuses to do what she wants it to do and instead does what it wants to. A related disorder is *diagonistic apraxia*, in which abnormal movements of one hand accompany intentional actions of the other hand. Again, Schwabe and Blanke (2007) report a case in which a patient, asked to remove his underpants, reaches down with his right hand and starts to pull them down while his left hand pulls them back up. The same patient, when asked to pick his pants up off the floor, reaches down with his right hand to lift them while his left hand starts to unbutton his shirt. Both disorders are thought to be due to frontal cortex damage and damage to the corpus callosum.

WORKING MEMORY

Memory is composed of two systems, *short-term memory* and *long-term memory*. Since it comes closest to describing certain features of ongoing conscious events, our interest lies primarily in short-term memory. The term "short-term memory" has been superseded in the past twenty years by "working memory". While "short-term memory" marks a direct contrast with long-term memory, it suggests misleadingly that the ongoing bubble of awareness within which our lives proceed is not much more than a relay station for information on its way to long-term memory. *Working memory* avoids this implication and suggests instead our ability to integrate, coordinate, maintain and manipulate complex information in real time. But even "working memory" is in some ways misleading, for it suggests that the ongoing bubble of awareness within which our lives proceed is primarily a storehouse of memories that only last a few seconds. "Working consciousness" might be more accurate for the set of processes that standard models of working memory actually describe. Fear of "consciousness" probably prevents its acceptance.

Baddeley–Hitch working memory

Working memory includes the processes in virtue of which, among many other things, you understand that the sentence you are currently reading is a single unit (the other processes go to understanding the sequence of words *as* a sentence; see below). Of course, being able to understand a sentence as a single unit is just symptomatic of working memory's activities. Generalizing, *working memory* is the set of processes that temporarily represent and retain very recently experienced or retrieved information in consciousness when this information is no longer present in the environment. Working memory establishes spatial and temporal continuity from the very recent past to the present and maintains and integrates the complex of occurrent incoming information into a unified experiential field. Without it, we would be trapped in an evanescent and fractionated present; with it, our experience has an ever-overlapping past that folds seamlessly into the present and allows us to anticipate the future.

The most influential views on working memory are those developed by Baddeley and Hitch. (Of the 16,000 articles on short-term memory published in the past twenty-five years, more than 7,000 of them refer to Baddeley and Hitch (Jonides *et al.* 2007).) Baddeley originally conceived of working memory as composed of three systems: the multimodal central executive, the phonological loop and the visuospatial sketchpad (Baddeley 1986). The *phonological loop* is composed of two subsystems, the *phonological store* and the *articulatory loop*, the first of which is a temporary storehouse of sounds and the second of which is responsible for sound production. The *visuospatial sketchpad* (or scratchpad) is likewise composed of two systems, the first devoted to processing qualitative pattern information such as colour, texture and shape, the second devoted to processing spatial location and sequential movement information. The *multimodal central executive* is responsible for attention, behaviour inhibition, decision-making, sequencing and integrating the information from the phonological loop and the visuospatial sketchpad.

The phonological loop's two subsystems – the phonological store and the articulatory loop – are taken to explain how we think subvocally. Read the words "I'm dreaming of a white Christmas, just like the ones I used to know" – you probably hear them in your head, perhaps attached to a melody. Now, with your eyes closed, repeat the sentence silently to yourself. Again, you probably hear the words (and melody) in your head. The *phonological store* is the set of processes that store information by sound properties; the *articulatory loop* is the set of processes that rehearse such stored information to keep it freshly in mind. As we repeat the sentence to ourselves, the stored information is rehearsed and refreshed. Although interacting, the phonological store and articulatory loop are distinct systems that work independently.

The visuospatial sketchpad is also composed of two subsystems, a qualitative or non-spatial component and a spatial component. The qualitative component keeps pattern, colour, shape and texture information in mind, and the spatial component keeps location, movement and distance information in mind. Think of someone – say your favourite elementary school teacher. You can form an image of this person and the way she/he looks and her/his location in the classroom. If you close your eyes and focus on the image, you can keep the image alive. That is the visuospatial sketchpad at work. While the existence of a visuospatial sketchpad is confidently asserted by cognitive scientists and neuroscientists, there is disagreement about what spatial and qualitative features are captured by its component subsystems. Baddeley's original model was based on a pattern/location distinction, but others prefer a static/dynamic distinction, and still others an object/spatial distinction. No distinction has proven demonstrably better than the others.

An odd feature of the standard model of working memory is that it limits working memory to what is seen and heard. What about the other senses – smell, touch and taste? Is there a tactile-textural touchpad, an olfactory palette, a gustatory store? Ongoing experience is rich with tactile, olfactory and gustatory perceptual information held online. We poke and squeeze fruit and vegetables; we smell babies' heads, flowers and rain; we educate our palate until we can distinguish hints of strawberry from hints of raspberry in wine. It would be bizarre were these components not part of working memory. Luckily, there is no inconsistency in extending working memory to these other sensory modalities. Most such attempts are in the developmental stages.

The central executive is a bit of a problem. While the most important of working memory's three systems, it is the least understood. In part, this is a result of so much being attributed to it. The standard constitutive cognitive processes of the central executive include selecting, maintaining, updating, switching (or rerouting), planning, sequencing and decision-making. But, in so far as it includes selection, central executive function bleeds into attention; in so far as it includes updating, it bleeds into cognitive control; in so far as it includes switching, the central executive starts to look like a system of cognitive monitoring; and in so far as it includes planning, sequencing and decision-making, the central executive looks like a metacognitive process. Depending on the author, this multitasking is taken to be either a reflection of the central executive's ineliminably complex role or an artifact of a misguided analogy with a computer's central executive.

One particularly forceful way of putting these problems is to note that the central executive's various functions threaten to compose a *homunculus*, a little person inside the brain that replicates the activity of the big person with that brain. A homunculus merely shifts the locus of explanation from something big to something small. We do not, for example, explain our ability to scramble eggs by identifying a little egg scrambler in our brain. For, what then about the little egg scrambler – does *it* have an even smaller egg scrambler in *its* brain? The reiteration of ever-smaller egg-scrambling homunculi never stops: where there is one homunculus, there is a bunch of them. To the extent that the central executive is a homunculus, to that extent does it merely shift the locus of explanation from something big to something small, a shift that explains nothing. For consider: what then about the central executive's homunculus – does *it* have a central executive? And, if it does, does it have a homunculus too? And, if it does, does it have a central executive? The reiteration of ever-smaller homunculi never stops.[2] If, then, regress of homunculi is to be avoided, it must be dissolved at the first step, and for that, neural mechanisms are required.

As originally conceived, the central executive is responsible for integrating information from the phonological loop and the visuospatial sketchpad. Our conscious experience is routinely and normally *unified* – what we consciously perceive, think and feel is experienced as a bound, integrated whole and not as a series of discrete elements. Since the phonological loop and visuospatial sketchpad provide the only – and separate – storage locales over the temporal period governed by working memory, it is not clear how the central executive accomplishes its integrating function, for, without storage capacity, the central executive cannot hold the elements of experience in place to integrate them. Recently, Baddeley has allowed that an additional component is required – the *episodic buffer* – which integrates and temporarily stores information from different sources, including long-term memory, as a bound episode. The episodic buffer is still under central executive control, which can retrieve the stored information in conscious awareness, reflect on it, and modify it if needed (Baddeley 2000, 2002, 2003). Further discussion of executive function is provided later in this chapter.

Neural correlates of working memory

As described thus far, working memory is a cognitive system that specifies a set of cognitive processes by identifying their informational inputs, manipulations on those inputs, and informational and behavioural outputs. Armed with these functional specifications, neuroscientists have for the past twenty years been busy trying to confirm the neural basis of its various components.

One of the key features of working memory for which neural correlates must be found is its capacity to hold things "in mind". Were working memory no more than another node in perceptual feedforward pathways, we would be unable to do this, and our cognitive and affective experience would be a sequence of evanescent episodes. But things do *not* disappear or cease to exist in consciousness when they cannot be seen, smelled, heard, tasted or touched. We can attend to the image of a remembered friend for many minutes, savour the smell of fresh snow when skiing, mull a problem in logic over and over in our minds, brood about an insult for hours, and, in general, manipulate the contents of our mind almost endlessly. These processes must, if we are physically minded about consciousness, be subserved by some neural mechanism. The best candidate

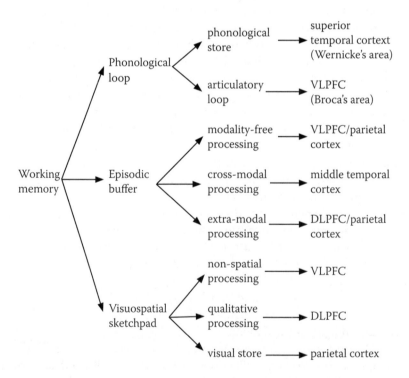

Figure 7.1 Neural correlates of a standard working memory model (excluding central executive).

for that mechanism is now acknowledged to be sustained activity in prefrontal cortex. Fuster and others demonstrated that neurons in monkey and human DLPFC and VLPFC sustain their activity for up to 20 seconds after the environmental input that initially caused that activity has been removed (Fuster 1973, 2000, 2001). Goldman-Rakic, among others, integrated this neuroscientific and behavioural evidence with the cognitive psychological work on working memory (Goldman-Rakic 1987, 1990, 1996), setting the stage for the past fifteen years' explosion of cognitive neuroscientific work on working memory.

Perceptual and affective information feeds forwards from unimodal associative sensory and limbic cortical areas to heteromodal associative regions in parietal and temporal cortex. Goldman-Rakic's seminal papers on working memory replicate the dorsal/ventral distinction found in the model of visual and auditory perception pathways that she was instrumental in developing. According to her, posterior DLPFC processes locational information arriving from dorsal visual and auditory pathways originating in parietal cortex, transforming perceptual information into egocentric representations. Posterior VLPFC and orbitofrontal cortex, on the other hand, process qualitative information arriving from ventral visual and auditory pathways originating in temporal cortex, transforming retinotopic neural information into semantic and qualitative representations of objects (Baddeley 2000; Courtney 2004). Goldman-Rakic's model is shown in Figure 7.1.

LANGUAGE UNDERSTANDING

The complexity of language perception and production follows from its multimodal perception and production. But there is a good deal more to language than its perception and production, for as complex as these may be, they are nothing as compared to the complexity of language comprehension. Language is a phonological, syntactic and semantic medium of communication composed of spoken symbols that have meaning, which meanings must be learned, remembered and understood, and which often come loaded with and cause responses that in turn have affective content. Given this complexity, it should come as no surprise that the field of cognitive neuroscience of language is in an almost continuous uproar.

Understanding symbols and meaning

Written language comprehension – we shall use *understanding* – follows visual perceptual pathways, and spoken language understanding follows auditory perceptual pathways into heteromodal associative areas. But perceptual pathways do not exhaust language comprehension. Language understanding is more demanding than perception, for it also contains phonological, syntactic and semantic elements.

Phonology studies a language's sound system and classifies its sound components. The processes constitutive of phonological perception parse incoming acoustic signals for their phonemic components and represent the first extension beyond basic auditory pathways. Written language perception is a ready point of comparison. Written language is easy to perceive in part because words are separated from each other by blanks. Consider for example the following sentence: "Four score and seven years ago, our fathers brought forth on this continent a new nation, conceived in Liberty, and dedicated to the proposition that all men are created equal." Were that sentence to be represented without spaces between words it becomes the more demanding: "Fourscoreandsevenyearsagoourfathers broughtforthonthisContinentanewnationconceivedinLibertyanddedicatedto thepropositionthatallmenarecreatedequal." Compare also the ease of listening to people who speak clearly to the difficulty of listening to those who slur their words, a difficulty that results from not producing identifiable phonemes.

Syntax is the set of rules that govern the proper combination of linguistic elements to form larger elements: letters combine to form words according to certain syntactical rules, words and punctuation combine to sentences according to certain other syntactical rules. In English, for example, there must be a proper combination of verb phrases and noun phrases in a string of words – "the dog chased the cat" is a sentence of English; "the dog the cat" is not. Again, there must be a proper placement of articles, prepositions and other linking devices in a sentence – "the dog chased the cat" is a sentence of English; "dog the the chased cat" is not. And there must be a proper placement of noun phrases – "John massaged Jane's shoulders" is distinct from "Jane massaged John's shoulders". There must also be agreement between verb and subject – "the children of the woman who was dehydrated yelled" is distinct from "the children of the woman, who were dehydrated, yelled". All languages have syntactical features, and every language has unique syntactical features. To be a competent user, every last one of them must be understood.

Semantics is the set of features of a language in virtue of which its functional units – words and sentences – have meaning. We shall, for the time being, leave "meaning" undefined. That we do so should cause alarm bells to go off – something dangerous is nearby. "Meaning" is a notorious word, a word whose meaning we presuppose every time we listen to another talk, speak ourselves, read or write, but which defies any straightforward analysis.

Neural correlates of language understanding

Thousands of neuroimaging and lesion studies have tried to identify the neural correlates of language understanding. The orthodox view is that spoken and written language understanding is dominated by left hemispheric pathways that feed forwards from and back to Wernicke's area in left temporoparietal cortex (hereafter lTP) and Broca's area in left VLPFC (for review, see Poeppel & Hickok 2004 and Démonet *et al.* 2005). This orthodox view is undergoing revision, prompted by recent studies that pry phonology, syntax and semantics apart. These studies suggest, first, that deficits in speech sound perception contribute minimally to the speech production deficits characteristic of damage to lTP and, second, that dysfunction in lTP does not result in speech perception or understanding deficits. As a result of this work, there is at present no universally accepted account of either syntactic or semantic neural pathways, although there is emerging consensus on some crucial matters. One thing *is* clear: the "virulent left-hemisphere imperialism" (Poeppel & Hickok 2004: 10) that has been widely assumed for years is in trouble, for the more complex language tasks of understanding metaphors, drawing inferences, generating sentence endings, repairing syntactical mistakes, detecting inconsistencies and discerning narrative sequencing enlist right as well as left hemispheric pathways (Jung-Beeman 2005).

Phonological understanding is measured in studies that dissociate phonological elements from other elements of language. This dissociation has established that acoustic analysis and phoneme identification and representation are associated with a heteromodal network of activity that includes bilateral posterior and middle superior temporal cortex, left supramarginal gyrus of parietal cortex, posterior superior regions of left VLPFC, and left supplementary motor area cortex (Friederici & Kotz 2003; Gold & Buckner 2002; Hickok & Poeppel 2007). A similar heteromodal pathway is discernible for visually experienced language, starting with input to left occipito-temporal cortex and feeding forwards to left superior temporal cortex and left supramarginal gyrus and terminating in left VLPFC (for review, see Démonet *et al.* 2005). We do not discuss these processes further.

Neuroimaging studies that measure syntactic comprehension use a variety of techniques that dissociate syntactical understanding from semantic understanding. Among these techniques are inflectional studies (Sahin *et al.* 2006) and studies employing "jabberwocky" sentences, sentences that are grammatically correct but composed of pseudowords – "the delarish geratur snoffened cistardly" – or that instantiate category mistakes – "Taffer's ventral speech flies a snide anchovy to the four" (Friederici & Kotz 2003). Using these techniques, it has been found that syntactic word form identification is associated with heteromodal activity in bilateral posterior superior temporal cortex and inferior parietal cortex, while word category identification is correlated with activity in anterior superior temporal cortex and inferior portions of left VLPFC (Dapretto & Bookheimer 1999; Grodzinsky & Friederici 2006; Sahin *et al.* 2006; for doubts, see Kaan & Swaab 2002 and Spitsyna *et al.* 2006).

Lesion and other neuropsychological studies of syntactic understanding show that none of the regions that correlate with syntactic processes are syntax-specific. Lesions in Broca's area have been shown to be neither necessary nor sufficient for syntactic deficits: those who score low on syntactic tests do not have a common lesion in Broca's area, thus showing that damage to Broca's area is not necessary for the deficit, and some individuals who have damage to Broca's area do not show syntactic deficits, thus showing that damage to Broca's area is not sufficient for the deficit (Kaan & Swaab 2002). Moreover, syntactic deficits correlated with dysfunction in Broca's area attach not to simple syntactic competence determinable by word order, but only to competence at complex syntax. Broca patients typically do not struggle with sentences that have simple subject–predicate structure; rather they find it difficult to parse sentences such as, "Which rioter did the police officer, who was directed to keep order by the parade director, handcuff, and which did she drag across the street?" This has led to the worry that what is being measured in syntax comprehension studies is working memory demand and nothing specific to syntax. If so, Broca's area is not the only syntax-understanding region of the brain, is not solely devoted to syntax understanding, and may not even *be* a syntax understanding region.

Understanding meaning activates an entire suite of cognitive and affective processes that distil semantic information from phonologically structured acoustic signals into forms that permit access to items stored in the meaning lexicon (Poeppel & Hackl 2008). The cognitive processes constitutive of semantic understanding are generally thought to correlate with heteromodal activity in posterior aspects of middle and superior temporal cortex, aspects of the left temperoparietal region, and left VLPFC (Bookheimer 2002; Démonet *et al.* 2005; Hickok & Poeppel 2007; Jung-Beeman 2005; Rodd *et al.* 2005; Spitsyna *et al.* 2006). Beyond these general agreements, opposing perspectives on the role of other cortical regions in semantic understanding have recently emerged. Some argue that semantic understanding is correlated with activity restricted to the areas just listed (Hickok & Poeppel 2007; Rodd *et al.* 2005), others that semantic understanding is additionally correlated with activity in anterior aspects of superior and inferior temporal cortex (Spitsyna *et al.* 2006), others still that not only activity in left superior and middle temporal cortex but activity also in right superior and temporal cortex is associated with semantic understanding (Federmeier & Kutas 1999).

In part, these disagreements are a result of studies measuring different tasks – word ambiguity, full sentence comprehension, divided attention to speech integration – and there may be neural differences across tasks. In part, disagreement flows from different measurement techniques and experiment design. In part, disagreement stems from the ambiguity of "meaning" itself. Poeppel identifies three distinct meanings of "meaning" – *conceptual meaning* (knowledge of the attributes of entities falling under a concept), *lexical meaning* (knowledge of the formal properties of single words), and *compositional meaning* (knowledge of the way that words combine to form sentence meaning) (Poeppel 2006). Philosophers and linguists can easily identify any number of additional meanings that "meaning" has: conceptual role meaning, referential meaning, use meaning, truth-conditional meaning, situational meaning, externalist meaning, pragmatic meaning, intentional meaning. Without agreement on which meaning of "meaning" is in focus, there can be little hope for agreement on neural correlates of understanding meaning.

Hickok and Poeppel (2004, 2007) argue that language understanding is decomposable into a ventral and a dorsal pathway. At the earliest stages of language understanding, primary auditory processing in bilateral middle to posterior superior temporal cortex parses incoming auditory input for phonemic structure. Output then splits into a ventral stream and a dorsal stream. The strongly left-hemisphere dominant dorsal pathway starts when phonological input from bilateral superior temporal cortex projects to ITP, a heteromodal association area, and then feeds it forwards to left VLPFC, supplementary and premotor areas, and insular cortex (other heteromodal and supramodal areas). The dorsal pathway is responsible for mapping understood phonological elements to articulate motor representations in speech production. The weakly left-hemisphere dominant ventral pathway takes phonological input from bilateral superior temporal cortex at a point in posterior middle and inferior temporal cortex, a heteromodal area hypothesized to be the lexical interface area for mapping phonological elements to semantic meanings, the latter of which are stored in diverse cortical regions. This semantic information is bidirectionally connected to anterior middle and inferior temporal cortex, a supramodal

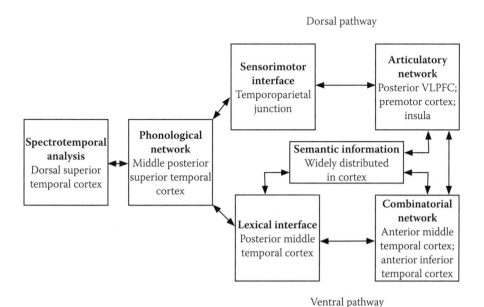

Figure 7.2 Language pathway (adapted from Hickok & Poeppel 2007).

area hypothesized to be a "combinatorial network" for understanding structured semantic units, such as sentences. The language pathway is shown in Figure 7.2.

A model suggested by Obleser, Wise, Scott and Spitsyna is similar, with the exception that the ventral pathway includes anterior middle and inferior temporal cortex not just for accessing complex sentence meaning and binding sentence constituents together but for all semantic understanding as well. On this model, phonologically processed acoustic signals feed forwards to posterior middle temporal cortex and then also to anterior middle temporal cortex (so-called temporal pole) and anterior inferior temporal cortex ("fusiform gyrus") (Obleser *et al.* 2007; Spitsyna *et al.* 2006). It is not obvious that these models are incompatible with one another, for there may instead be a range of temporal cortex enlistment, varying as a function of input complexity. Jung-Beeman (2005), for example, suggests that semantic understanding has three levels of resource demand: activation, integration or binding, and selection. *Semantic activation* permits initial access to distributed semantic representations and occurs bilaterally in temporoparietal and posterior superior and middle temporal cortex. *Semantic integration* determines the amount of semantic overlap across multiple semantic domains and detects and refines higher-order semantic relations. Semantic integration correlates with activity in bilateral anterior superior temporal cortex, extending to anterior middle temporal cortex. *Semantic selection* is the cluster of executive processes of retrieving and sorting competing semantic meanings and concepts and selecting one from them and correlates with activity in left VLPFC. This model can be used as an overarching framework that eases the apparent contrasts between the other two models.

Neurological language disorders: aphasia and alexia

While agnosia is a perceptual disorder, aphasia and alexia are disorders of language processes and reading processes. Some of the affected processes in language competence are perceptual, but others are perceptual *and* cognitive, either deficits in attention, working memory, understanding, or production. For ease of exposition, we keep the aphasias and alexias together rather than segregate those that are purely perceptual from those that are both perceptual and cognitive. *Aphasia* is a loss of language abilities, *alexia* a loss of reading abilities. Aphasias are typically subdivided into perisylvian aphasias and transcortical aphasias. *Perisylvian aphasias* result from damage to cortical regions immediately adjacent to the sylvian fissure separating temporal cortex from prefrontal and parietal cortex. The prototypical perisylvian aphasias are Broca's, Wernicke's, conductive and global aphasias. *Transcortical aphasias* result from damage to cortical regions surrounding Broca's and Wernicke's areas rather than direct damage to them.

Table 7.1 Perisylvian aphasias (adapted from Nolte 2002).

	Broca's	Wernicke's	Conduction	Global
Spoken language symptoms				
Comprehension	Good	Poor	Good	Good
Fluent production	Poor	Good	Paraphasic	Poor
Naming	Poor	Poor	Poor	Poor
Repetition	Poor	Poor	Poor	Poor
Other associated symptoms				
Right-side hemiplegia	Yes	Yes	No	Yes
Sensory deficits	Rare	Common	Common	Common
Writing production	Poor	Good	Usually good	Poor
Reading comprehension	Good	Poor	Good	Poor
Affected brain region(s)	Broca's (left ventrolateral pfc); insular cortex	Wernicke's (left superior temporal/inferior parietal cortex)	Superior longitudinal fasciculus; external capsule	Left ventrolateral pfc; left temporal cortex

Table 7.2 Transcortical aphasias (adapted from Nolte 2002).

	Transcortical motor	Transcortical sensory	Transcortical mixed	Anomic
Spoken language symptoms				
Comprehension	Good	Poor	Poor	Good
Fluent production	Poor	Good	Poor	Good
Naming	Poor	Poor	Poor	Poor
Repetition	Good	Compulsive	Compulsive	Good
Other associated symptoms				
Right-side hemiplegia	Yes	Yes	Yes	No
Sensory deficits	Rare	Common	Common	Rare
Writing production	Poor	Good	Poor	Good
Reading comprehension	Good	Poor	Poor	Good
Affected brain region(s)	Pfc around Broca's	Parietal cortex around Wernicke's	Pfc around Broca's and parietal cortex around Wernicke's	Left pfc; mid-temporal cortex, angular gyrus

Wernicke's aphasia is also known as *receptive aphasia* because it compromises the ability to comprehend speech. Individuals with Wernicke's aphasia often produce grammatically correct, properly intonated word salad, utterly meaningless in context with the other words being produced. This deficit is a direct result of being unable to distinguish between distinct phonetic units and the consequent inability to embed those units in auditorily received words.

Wernicke's aphasia can be divided into subspecies. First, there are those receptive aphasias characterized by reasonably good visual comprehension of language and severely compromised auditory comprehension of language. This is *pure word deafness* and is caused by dysfunction in auditory cortex adjacent to Wernicke's area in left superior temporal cortex. Another receptive aphasia is characterized by the converse phenomenon, reasonably good auditory comprehension of language and severely compromised visual comprehension of language. This kind of aphasia is *alexia* or *pure word blindness without agraphia* and is typically caused by dysfunction in visual cortex or in white matter pathways feeding forwards from visual cortex. One curiosity of alexia without agraphia is that individuals can write but cannot understand what they have written. Since alexia without agraphia is not caused by damage to Wernicke's area, it is also frequently categorized as an agnosia rather than as an aphasia. While some alexias are not accompanied by agraphia, others are. *Alexia with agraphia* is the inability to produce written language. Such alexias are associated with damage to left VLPFC (Broca's area). Alexia without agraphia is a deficit entirely within visual pathways and may have nothing uniquely to do with linguistic deficits, so it may be better categorized as an agnosia. However, alexia with agraphia is triggered by the inability to produce written language and so is properly categorized as an aphasia.

Broca's aphasia is also known as *expressive aphasia* because it compromises the cognitive processes that produce fluent speech. Broca aphasiacs speak haltingly and incompletely, for they are unable to include all the components necessary for a complete sentence. Broca aphasiacs frequently report that they know what they want to say and cannot figure out how to say it. One associated kind of aphasia is *aphemia* or *pure word dumbness*, in which comprehension, reading and writing are intact but muteness prevents verbal repetition and naming. Pure word dumbness is caused by dysfunction in the supplementary motor area or, occasionally, in Broca's area itself.

Transcortical sensory aphasiacs comprehend auditory speech poorly but produce verbal speech fluently. The single most salient symptom is paraphasia, the substitution of one word for another not on phonetic lines but on meaning lines. Transcortical sensory aphasiacs will frequently substitute words from the same category, for example, "Ford" for "Chevrolet" and "pen" for "stapler". Transcortical motor aphasiacs have all but one of the symptoms of Broca aphasiacs: the former have good repetition abilities, since their superior longitudinal fasciculus is intact. Conduction aphasiacs comprehend auditory speech and speak fluently, albeit with paraphasia, but they cannot repeat what they hear if asked to do so. Since they comprehend what they hear, they typically recognize their mistake and try to rectify it, but, since the white matter connections between Wernicke's and Broca's areas are compromised, they do not succeed. Global aphasiacs sometimes are mute and sometimes cannot write. They sometimes retain simple speech, frequently limited to highly emotive words, such as profane words. The neuroscientist has a ready explanation for this quirk as well: as it turns out, one of the neural pathways preserved in global aphasiacs is an assembly external to Broca's area that is part of the limbically based vocalization route found in non-speaking but emotionally vocal species, such as chimpanzees and bonobos, and preserved in us.

EXECUTIVE FUNCTION

The qualifier "executive" in *executive function* is ambiguous, calling to mind on the one hand the kind of ongoing oversight, review, analysis, assessment, goal setting and planning that corporate executives do, and on the other hand initiating and implementing – that is, executing – activity. The impact of this ambiguity on the development of the neuroscientific understanding of working memory, attention and semantic understanding, each of which deploys particular subsets of these processes, cannot be overestimated. Characterizations of executive functions vary widely as the focus falls on one rather than another meaning of "executive".

In the most general terms, executive functions are all the cognitive processes that together constitute the evaluation and control of cognitive, interoceptive and affective processes (adapted from Shimamura 2000). Most executive functions are *metacognitive*. As metalevel phenomena, metacognitions are distinct from object-level cognitions. Object-level cognitions include basic information processing operations, such as encoding, rehearsing, maintaining, retrieving and understanding. A metacognition is a cognitive process that is about another, object-level, cognitive process – that is what makes it *meta*cognitive. What we monitor when we monitor is other thoughts, beliefs, fears and hopes, and what we do when we monitor them is adopt a distinct cognitive attitude towards them, analysing their causes and consequences, for example, and assessing their fit within our overall psychological economy. To take an example, when we resolve to correct a cognitive error, we first identify a particular object-level belief before we analyse it for its truth or falsity; then, having determined that the belief is false or unjustified, we conjoin the knowledge of its falsity or lack of warrant with a desire to eliminate error if possible, which desire, if not corrupted by a weakness of will, results in a decision to jettison the offending belief. In all of this activity, metacognition is for the most part access asymmetric: metacognitive events have access to object-level cognitive events, but object-level cognitive events lack access to metacognitive events.[3]

We take a wide view of executive functions, including within the category both cognitive and metacognitive processes. First, there are cognitive processes involved in *voluntary attentional control*, such as orienting and shifting. Second, there are cognitive and metacognitive processes that can be grouped together as *monitoring* processes, including information updating, organization and integration, memory retrieval, switching and inhibition. Third, metacognitive processes constitutive of *rational thought* must be included, processes such as logical thought, generalization and abstraction, propositional knowledge, analysis, introspection and reflection. Fourth, executive functions also include metacognitive *planning* processes such as goal setting, action sequencing and strategy formation. Fifth, the metacognitive *evaluative* processes of conflict and error detection and resolution, deliberation, discrimination and assessment must be included. Sixth and finally, there are the cognitive and metacognitive *executing* processes such as decision-making, judging, choosing and directing (see Jurado & Rosselli 2007). This order is premised on the following idealized sequence. We are first conscious of some input, whether perceptual, interoceptive, proprioceptive, affective or cognitive. Having become conscious of that input, we organize and integrate it into the ongoing flow of psychological activity. We then think about it (if necessary), make a plan (if necessary) and deliberate about options (if necessary). Finally, we decide on an action and execute that action.

Neural correlates of executive functions

An accurate characterization of the current state of affairs in attempts to locate neural correlates of executive functions is that, beyond a few narrowly circumscribed areas, the field is a tangled mess of contradictory, inconsistent and confusing experimental results, falsified generalizations and overly ambitious theoretical model building. This state of affairs, while unsatisfying, is significantly better than it was thirty years ago, when there were almost no results to report. As with affective neuroscience, neuroscience of the executive functions is currently exploding, with significant advances made monthly.

The monitoring processes of updating, shifting and inhibition are found in most accounts of executive functions. There appears to be a growing consensus on the neural correlates of at least these processes. It appears, for example, that activity in some cortical regions correlates with all three processes and that activity in other cortical regions correlates with one or another of the three. The common areas for updating, switching and inhibition have been tentatively identified as left superior parietal cortex and parietal cortex in the right intraparietal sulcus area, left DLPFC and left VLPFC (Collette *et al.* 2005; Jurado & Rosselli

2007; Ridderinkhof *et al.* 2004). In addition to these shared regions, updating also correlates with activity in frontopolar cortex, superior frontal cortex, orbitofrontal cortex and anterior cingulate cortex (Collette *et al.* 2005; Jurado & Rosselli 2007). Shifting additionally correlates with activity in right DLPFC, right supramarginal parietal cortex and left precuneus (Badre & Wagner 2007; Jurado & Rosselli 2007; Ridderinkhof *et al.* 2004). And inhibition additionally correlates with activity in dorsomedial prefrontal cortex, right orbitofrontal cortex, left posterior parietal cortex and frontopolar cortex (Collette *et al.* 2005; Jurado and Rosselli 2007; Ridderinkhof *et al.* 2004).

Rational thought includes inductive and deductive reasoning, and proposed neural correlates of inductive and deductive reasoning are representative of rational thought's neural correlates. Designing experiments that test specifically for inductive and deductive reasoning as distinct from language understanding has not been easy. But the attempt has been made, and for good reason: language understanding, while a prerequisite for logical reasoning, does not exhaust logical reasoning. Put otherwise, logical reasoning does not reduce to language understanding. Recent experimental designs are making headway in making the necessary distinctions (for discussion, see Goel 2007 and Monti *et al.* 2007). Goel and Dolan note the confusion that has resulted from failing to distinguish inductive from deductive reasoning (Goel & Dolan 2004) and from using different kinds of deductive arguments of varying degrees of complexity. For example, different regions activate when the measured task is a categorical syllogism task rather than a conditional syllogism (Goel 2007). Having noted the disagreements, there is widespread agreement across imaging studies that bilateral occipital cortex, bilateral posterior, inferior and superior parietal cortex, bilateral posterior superior and inferior temporal cortex, left VLPFC and DLPFC, frontopolar and superior prefrontal cortex are all involved in logical reasoning.

That a cortical region is involved in logical reasoning does not imply it is that in which logical reasoning consists. Parsons and colleagues (Monti *et al.* 2007) recently reported on a set of experiments that try to isolate deductive reasoning skills. Using tests formulated in jabberwocky, they have designed experiments and deployed various statistical methods for identifying neural regions that correlate specifically with such skills. Regions correlating to language understanding – left superior temporal cortex, occipital cortex, left VLPFC – and regions correlating with attention – such as right posterior parietal cortex – are then factored out. This still leaves a significant number of regions that correlate with deductive reasoning. Arguing that support regions that distil and maintain logical form in working memory are distinct from core regions involved in deduction, they partition the two kinds. Support regions, such as posterior left DLPFC, bilateral intraparietal sulcus and inferior parietal regions, and left VLPFC, correlate with processes necessary for deductive reasoning, such as representation and maintenance functions (left VLPFC) and information updating,

comparison, judgement and spatial attention (left DLPFC and the bilateral parietal regions). Factoring the support regions out presumably leaves regions that
correlate with processes that are that in which deductive reasoning consists.
The candidates they identify as core deductive regions are left frontopolar cortex and superior medial frontal cortex. Frontopolar cortex is the most anterior
region of cortex in the brain, has neurons with high dendritic branching, is
reciprocally connected to other supramodal regions, is among the latest regions
to mature, and has expanded disproportionately in recent evolution. Superior
medial frontal cortex is routinely correlated with top-down control cognitive
mechanisms and monitoring processes (Monti *et al.* 2007).

Similar findings have been reported for planning, evaluation and executing
components of executive functions. Planning and goal setting routinely implicate bilateral DLPFC and medial superior frontal cortex as neural correlates
(Bunge *et al.* 2001; Jurado & Rosselli 2007). The various component evaluation
processes have proposed neural correlates as well: risk assessment correlates
with orbitofrontal cortex; error and conflict resolution correlate with anterior
cingulate cortex, posterior medial frontal cortex and DLPFC; and rewards and
punishment judgements correlate with insular cortex and the caudate nucleus
of basal ganglia (Jurado & Rosselli 2007; Ridderinkhof *et al.* 2004). Finally, execution processes as a whole correlate with activity in frontopolar cortex, orbitofrontal cortex, insular cortex, and dorsal and rostral anterior cingulate cortex
(Duncan & Owen 2000; Ridderinkhof *et al.* 2004).

Neurological disorders of executive functions

Frontal lobe syndrome is a family of disorders, some affective, some cognitive,
all of them correlated with frontal and prefrontal cortex dysfunction. As more
is learned about correlations between particular cognitive and affective deficits and particular affected regions, new terms have been introduced, and the
umbrella term "frontal lobe syndrome" has become less useful. Still, so long as
knowledge remains unsettled, it is probably easiest to describe what has been
ascertained using this term. Paradigmatic frontal lobe syndromes are those in
which either behaviour inhibition or initiation is compromised. In the former,
individuals lose nothing in performance on typical cognitive function tests but
start to behave in unusually provocative ways – they swear, exhibit impulsive
sexuality, impulsive eating and impulsive drinking, plan poorly, and are prone
to aggressive displays, giggling fits, emotional lability and disorganization. This
cluster of symptoms is variously called *frontal disinhibition syndrome, orbitofrontal syndrome, dysexecutive syndrome* or *executive dysfunction syndrome*.
In the latter, individuals again lose nothing in performance on cognitive function tests but behave in featureless and apathetic ways – they have impaired
concentration or concern for details, they exhibit apathy, engage in repetitious

behaviour and display attenuated emotional affect. This is variously called *frontal abulic syndrome, frontal disinitiation syndrome, frontal convexity syndrome,* or *dorsolateral syndrome* (Lyketos *et al.* 2004).

Although frontal disinhibition syndrome is frequently correlated with damage to left orbitofrontal cortex and frontal disinitiation syndrome with damage to left DLPFC, individuals with at least some symptoms of one type typically also have at least some symptoms of the other type. Furthermore, the symptoms themselves can be correlated with more than one cortical region. For example, even in the absence of frontal lobe damage, lack of verbal control can occur after caudate nucleus damage, disinhibition after thalamic damage, apathy after globus pallidus damage, and all three symptoms after stroke damage in subcortical white matter tracts (Lyketos *et al.* 2004). Moreover, frontal lobe symptoms have been described in people with a wide variety of diseases, such as Huntington's chorea, closed head injury, stroke, Parkinson's disease, AIDS, Alzheimer's, and frontotemporal degeneration and dementia, each of which damage neurons in different ways. In addition, *frontotemporal dementia*, a condition caused by the deterioration of myelinated pathways in frontal and temporal cortex, often has many of the same behavioural and psychological symptoms.

This concludes our review of current neuroscientific work on neural correlates for select perceptual, interoceptive, affective and cognitive processes. Together, the findings from neuroscience provide strong inductive support for the conclusion that there are reliable correlations across individuals between the instantiation of intentionally structured, qualitatively endowed and perspectively subjective conscious properties and neural activity located in assemblies and pathways at fairly fine-grained cortical locations. We turn in the next chapter to discuss a more global neuroscientific approach to these conscious properties.

8. NEURAL MODELS OF CONSCIOUS PROPERTIES

The research reviewed in previous chapters establishes neuroanatomical correlates for particular perceptual, affective and cognitive processes that happen also to be conscious. This approach, by far the most prevalent in neuroscience, identifies neuroanatomical correlates for specific processes, hoping thereby to capture consciousness in the process by capturing it in the processes. Another approach that works from general properties of consciousness to neural correlates for those properties has also gained considerable traction in the neuroscience community. This approach, which provides neural models of consciousness and conscious properties, is this chapter's topic.

A noticeably high incidence of disagreement permeates this research. Granted, many of the views share certain commitments. Chief among them are the following: (i) neuroanatomical correlates of conscious properties provide evidence that particular kinds of neural activity are the substrates of conscious properties; (ii) at least some conscious properties are necessary for some kinds of information processing; (iii) intentionality is representational and computational; and (iv) qualitative properties are distinct from content properties. But there is dissent, especially from (iii) and (iv). Those who claim that intentionality is computational often look askance at qualitative properties and argue that they must be computational or at least representational, while those who claim that conscious properties are biological sometimes argue that qualitative properties cannot be computational or representational. Others also split content and qualitative properties off from higher-order, monitoring, self- and reflective-conscious properties, arguing that none is reducible to the others and that one or another or all are or are not scientifically tractable.

VEHICULAR MODELS

Neuroanatomical and neurophysiological correlates of conscious properties establish that neural activity of some kind at some place systematically covaries with conscious property instantiation. However, neural correlates do not explain neural subservience of conscious properties. Most neuroscientific research programmes about conscious properties routinely grant that something more than neuroanatomical and neurophysiological correlates are required to understand why they are also plausible neural substrates and realizers of conscious properties. To identify what that something is, each of the proposals canvassed here offers a model of anatomically specified neural assembly activities and physiologically specified processes that are thought to be relevant for understanding the neural substrates and realizers of conscious properties. In general, a *model* of *x* is an entity distinct from *x* that is: (a) better understood than *x*; (b) relevantly similar to *x*; and (c) because of (a) and (b), used to understand *x*. Models can be concrete, like a model airplane, or abstract, like a mathematical formula or a conceptual framework. Models of the neural substrates of conscious properties are mathematical formulae or conceptual models of neural assembly activity better understood than that activity, relevantly similar to it, and used to understand it. Neural models of consciousness embed neural activity in a conceptual framework that helps us understand how that activity subserves a conscious property. They thus play a role in filtering the welter of empirical data concerning neural correlates, putting those correlates into a format that can find a home in a full-fledged theory (Chemero 2009).

We adopt a categorization scheme that distinguishes models across two dimensions: the vehicle/process axis and the specialized/non-specialized axis (Cleeremans 2005; O'Brien & Opie 1999a, 1999b; the former distinction is from Dretske 1988). According to *vehicle models*, conscious properties are reducible to, or identical with, internal properties of active individual neurons or assemblies of them. *Process models* claim instead that conscious properties are reducible to, or identical with, causal or computational properties that active neurons or assemblies of them instantiate. Alternatively put, for a vehicle theory of conscious properties, what makes a psychological event conscious are internal properties of neural events, whereas for a process theory, what makes psychological events conscious are extrinsic causal or computational relations that neural events enter into with other such events. According to *specialized models*, conscious properties are reducible to, or identical with, activity of neural vehicles or processes dedicated to the purpose, whereas *non-specialized models* claim that conscious properties are reducible to, or identical with, activity of non-dedicated neural vehicles or processes. A *dedicated* vehicle or process has one functional role to fulfil; a *non-dedicated* vehicle or process has more than one functional role to fulfil. Hence, there are four different kinds of neural models of consciousness: (i) specialized vehicle models; (ii) non-specialized vehicle models; (iii) specialized process models; and (iv) non-specialized process models.

Each has advocates, although the specialized vehicle model is now marginalized. Most models are process models rather than vehicle models. One reason is that process models align more closely with computationalism and representationalism than do vehicle views. A second connected reason is that vehicle models are more abruptly reductionist than process models and thus easier to falsify. Vehicle models identify conscious properties with internal properties of neurons or neural assemblies. That is more ambitious than identifying conscious properties with something that happens to or in neurons or neural assemblies, as proposed by process models. Likewise, specialized vehicle models are more ambitious than non-specialized vehicle models, since for them the only relevant neural properties are those from a specific region of the brain or those with a particular profile. As a result of the demands that such a model must meet, there are few specialized vehicle models of consciousness.

One specialized vehicle model

The best-known specialized vehicle model is Atkinson and Shiffrin's proposal that conscious properties are identical with neural activity responsible for short-term memory (Atkinson & Shiffrin 1971). This proposal is a vehicle model because it identifies conscious properties with neural processing that has the internal property of being sufficiently strong, and it is a specialized model because it restricts conscious properties to the processing that is part of short-term and working memory stores. Yet, even if some conscious properties are straightforwardly identical with the neural pathways of short-term and working memory, it has become clear in the past twenty years that not all conscious properties are, so we do not discuss this view further.

Non-specialized vehicle models

Two non-specialized vehicle models have gained wider currency. First, there is a connectionist model, developed variously by O'Brien and Opie, Cleeremans and Jiménez, Lloyd, and Mangana. Second, there is a quantum mechanical model, championed by Hameroff and Penrose.

Connectionism

As noted in Chapter 4, connectionist neural models identify conscious processes with internal emergent patterns of interconnected activity across neurons or neural assemblies. Although some connectionist neural models are intentionalist without being representationalist, most are not only intentionalist but representationalist and computationalist. Clearly, identifying the internal properties of neural assemblies are crucial steps in understanding what connectionism entails. Most connectionists nominate stable activation patterns of neural network activity as representational vehicles (Maia & Cleeremans 2005; McClelland

& Cleeremans 2009), and at least Opie and O'Brien argue that these stable activation patterns are identical to the qualitative character of experience (O'Brien & Opie 1999a). If true, it appears that both represented content and qualitative character are exclusively features of our internal virtual reality and not properties of external reality at all (Metzinger 2009a). As will be argued in Chapter 11, this consequence is unattractive.

Connectionists have struggled to apply their analysis of neural processing to conscious properties. It is generally acknowledged that connectionism is equipped to account for the inaccessibility of much of neural processing: unconscious processing is inaccessible because its activation patterns are not sufficiently stable over time ever to become consciously experienced. Just as importantly, connectionists appear to have neuroanatomy and neurophysiology on their side: as they note, both neuroanatomy and neurophysiology are demonstrably connectionist in their architectural properties. Moreover, the connectionist analysis of representations as stable activation patterns over networks is respectfully neural sounding to be persuasive when compared to some of what the classicists suggest. Still, the gap between what connectionism can actually model and what it would need to model were it to be a competent model of conscious properties is pretty wide (Fodor 2008). It remains an open question, for example, whether, and if so to what degree, developed connectionist networks accurately model neural networks of the human brain (Bechtel & Abrahamsen 1991; Eliasmith 2003). Connectionism also has real trouble making sense of certain aspects of cognition. Fodor and Pylyshyn (1988) argue that connectionism cannot account for cognition's productivity (the ability to represent a huge number of propositions), its semantic systematicity (the ability to understand some sentences as intrinsically related to one another), its semantic compositionality (complex propositional meaning being a function of the meaning of simpler components), and its inferential systematicity (the ability to recognize any inference of similar logical type). Whether these alleged shortcomings are real or, if they are, whether they are fatal to connectionist models of cognition, is a matter of ongoing debate (see, among others, Chemero 2009; Garson 1994; Skokowski 2009).

Most of these debates are not directly relevant. However, it is to be noted that anyone concerned with identifying the neural correlates of conscious properties has to acknowledge that those neural correlates cannot just be convenient caricatures that fit handily into a pre-existing conceptual framework. If those correlates are to be that which conscious properties reduce to, they must be the real working things with their real working properties, not a model of neural assemblies and their properties pieced together according to a theoretical blueprint that has no counterpart in the brain's structural elements. So, since the brain is a network of neurons whose architecture is demonstrably connectionist, the neural correlate programme must accommodate those features. Accommodating the connectionist architecture of the brain has been thought to have three consequences. First, it has been argued that the category of representation at use in classical computationalism is a mismatch with whatever kind of representation feature a neural assembly might have. In particular, connectionists argue that the classicist's assumption that representations are symbolically structured entities, transformations between which are best modelled by logic and mathematics, has to be replaced with something that is not symbolically structured. Second, connectionists sometimes argue that conscious properties cannot be properties of representations because the brain is not in the business of producing representations in the first place. If so, then either conscious properties are representational properties and attach to something not found anywhere in the brain and so are not neurally realized or, contrary to classical computationalism, conscious properties are not properties that only representations can have. Third, connectionists sometimes argue that the brain's architecture is consistent with, perhaps an implication of, the dynamic coupling of the brain with its body and the environment in which it is embedded. Thus, the debate between connectionism and classicism is an opening skirmish in a much broader attempt to rethink the relationship between the conscious mind and the rest of the world. Dynamicism is introduced later in this chapter, but most of these matters are discussed in Chapters 11 and 12.

Quantum mechanics

Perhaps the most astonishing vehicle models of conscious properties are those that invoke quantum mechanics. *Prima facie* the claim is incredible: conscious properties seem about as far removed from quantum mechanics as anything natural can get. But three lines of argument implicate quantum mechanics, and two of the three are interesting. The first line of argument can be summarized as follows: quantum mechanics is peculiar; conscious properties are peculiar; therefore conscious properties must be quantum mechanical. The argument is fallacious: just because two things are peculiar does not imply that they are the same thing. Variants of the argument type are plentiful, focusing here on quantum indeterminacy and the indeterminacy of free will, there on quantum non-objectivity and the subjectivity of conscious properties, and elsewhere on quantum coherence and subjective unity. We decline engagement with all of them.

The other two proposals are not obviously non-starters. One of them suggests that conscious properties are subserved by subneuronal quantum mechanical behaviour in an axon's microtubules, the other that conscious properties must be invoked in explanations of quantum behaviour. These are complementary strategies. The one is a *quantum model of conscious properties* that builds quantum phenomena into a model of conscious properties. Hameroff and Penrose adopt this approach (see, among others, Hameroff & Penrose 1995; Penrose 1990, 1994). The other is a *conscious model of quantum behaviour* that builds conscious properties into a model of quantum phenomena. Stapp is the best-known advocate of this approach (Stapp 2004). As interesting as conscious models of quantum behaviour may be, they are not relevant here. Our interest is in models that take conscious properties to be the *explanandum* (what is explained) and quantum behaviour to be part of the *explanans* (what does the explaining). Building conscious properties into a model of quantum phenomena flips the direction of explanation, making quantum phenomena the *explanandum* and conscious properties part of the *explanans*. So, we do not investigate these arguments either.

Hameroff and Penrose's proposal is that conscious properties correlate with subneuronal subatomic quantum behaviour in the microtubules that compose a neuron's cytoskeleton. Microtubules are components of the protein networks of the cytoskeleton, which in turn determines the physical form of the neuron and regulates synaptic connections. Microtubules are hollow, their walls composed of protofilaments, each one of which is composed of a series of subunits called tubulins. Tubulins are building blocks 8 nanometres (nm) long, composed of two 4 nm monomers, each of which has an electrical charge determined by the behaviour of the billions of electrons of the billions of atoms composing them. There are about 10^{18} – a quintillion – microtubules.

Of particular interest to quantum mechanics are the properties of position, momentum and velocity. Position is location in space; momentum is the product of a body's mass and its velocity; velocity is a vector property whose magnitude is speed and whose direction is the body's motional direction. Quantum mechanics is interested in a particle's position and velocity in a three- (or four-) dimensional space of atomic and subatomic particles. The familiar picture of an electron's behaviour as it orbits the nucleus is of a planet orbiting the sun. However, an electron is just as much like a continuous vibrating guitar string suspended around the nucleus of the atom. This equivalence is known as *wave-particle duality*. Now, it turns out that electron orbits are determinate in a peculiar way: an electron can be in one orbit A or another orbit B somewhat larger or smaller, but in no orbit intermediate between A and B. This suggests that the energy behaviour of electrons is quantized, that is, it comes in discrete packets between which there is no intermediary state. Thus the quantum of energy in an electron predicts that there is no continuous travel between possible orbits. On a macro scale, this would be like stepping out of your door at home on to the moon.

As interesting as wave-particle duality is, another discovery about quantum behaviour, made by Heisenberg, is more celebrated. There is an ineliminable indeterminacy in the measurement of quantum behaviour – the more precise the measurement of an electron's position is, the less precise must be the measurement of the electron's momentum be, and when one fixes the position of an electron in its orbit, one loses the ability to measure its momentum altogether. Since momentum and position are both necessary to measure velocity, it follows that an electron's velocity cannot be fixed. Moreover, the actual position of an electron in its orbit is, prior to measurement, only some*where* in that orbit rather than at a particular some*place*. Only upon measurement is the electron's position fixed. Correlative findings occur if the wave-model is used: when electronic position measurements are made, wave behaviour ceases. Position measurement nullifies an electron's wave behaviour, thus nullifying the unique wave function that describes the electron's behaviour. This is *wave function collapse*.

Since quantum indeterminacy persists until measurement, prior to measurement there is no particular way quantum phenomena are. This consequence is dramatically illustrated by two thought experiments, Schrödinger's cat and Wigner's friend. Suppose there is a cat – Schrödinger's cat – locked in a box in a superposition of life and death. Quantum indeterminacy implies that only upon unlocking the box and investigating is the cat alive or dead. Wigner's friend iterates the problem. Suppose Wigner's friend measures Schrödinger's cat while Wigner is out of the room. Wigner then determines the state of Schrödinger's cat only upon re-entering the room and quizzing his friend. If, now, a mechanical device is substituted for Wigner's friend, then, since it is physical, it is in a superposition of states. Only when a conscious observer, such as Wigner, measures the measuring device does the superposition resolve into a single state. Of course, this is generalizable: everything is in a superposition of quantum states until some conscious measuring event compels wave function collapse.

The consequence that superposed quantum states last indefinitely is most unusual, and it is a matter of ongoing debate. For our purposes, it is sufficient to note that if the Hameroff-Penrose proposal were committed to this consequence, it would be circular, for, as noted above, the offered quantum model would entail that conscious properties must be invoked to model the quantum behaviour found in the entities postulated as their substrate. Hameroff and Penrose reject the indefinite length of superposed quantum states, suggesting instead that state reduction (wave function collapse) is induced by gravity itself, which, by hypothesis, is not a conscious phenomenon; so, circularity is avoided. However, the price thus paid for avoiding circularity is extraordinarily high, for the claim that state reduction is objectively induced by gravity requires, as some have noted, nothing less than a new theory of nature (Wiseman & Esiert 2007), a theory for which there is no evidence and even no agreed-upon interpretation. There are other problems with quantum models of consciousness, but we pass over them (see Koch & Hepp 2006). The model's current status is so uncertain that it may be set aside until such time as persuasive argument suggests bringing it back to the table.

PROCESS MODELS

Process models claim that conscious properties are reducible to or identical with certain processes that neurons or assemblies of them engage in. Since most neural activity is electrochemical message transmission, and since such transmission is dynamic, the attraction of process models for conscious properties is readily apparent. After all, the interconnections of conscious psychological events and the dynamic nature of cognition, affection, perception and interoception map quite happily to such a view. For that reason alone, it can just *seem* right to think of conscious properties realized by dynamic neural activity.

Specialized process models

Specialized process models affirm that processes become conscious when they are the causal consequences of particular dedicated neural mechanisms realized in the brain. We investigate three candidates: the global workspace model, the field model and the corollary discharge model.

The global workspace

The core idea of the *global workspace* model is that a psychological event is conscious if it is widely accessible to other cognitive processes, such as long-term memory, attention, cognitive control, metacognition, deliberation, decision-making and action selection. As Bernard Baars puts it, the global workspace theory claims that consciousness is "a fleeting memory capacity that enables access between brain functions that are otherwise separate" (Baars 2005b: 46). Baars's own development of the global workspace model is often informal and analogical, suggesting that we think of the mind as a working theatre in which intentionality is a spotlight of perspectival attention directed on certain lead actors in information processing. Those in the attentive spotlight are surrounded by a penumbra of supporting actors and chorus members held on the stage of working memory. The spotlighted actors broadcast to the other actors and chorus members in working memory; to the audience members (long-term memories, procedural memories, motor behaviour, other subconscious and unconscious processes) who do with the information what they will; and to the stagehands, those unconscious information processing systems without whose context-setting activity nothing comes forwards to the stage and whose activity is sometimes dictated by the goings-on in the spotlight. The primary function of conscious properties is thus "to allow a theater architecture to operate in the brain, in order to integrate, provide access, and coordinate the functioning of very large numbers of specialized networks that otherwise operate autonomously" (*ibid.*: 47).

So long as the theory remains a cognitive-functional theory, there is no pressing need to articulate it to specify the neural correlates of the processes it implicates. The processes thus integrated and coordinated – the unconscious work of the stagehands that sets the context for consciousness – can be identified as those perceptual, affective, interoceptive, proprioceptive, cognitive and long-term memory processes that provide the contents of conscious events.

The processes to which conscious contents are sent – the unconscious work of the audience members – can be identified as the motor and speech processes *via* which intentions are implemented and all the other learning, visual imagery, episodic memory, attentive and executive function processes whose behaviour can be affected by consciousness.

The global workspace model's attractiveness has provoked both computationally minded and neurally minded researchers to propose implementing neural models of the theatre of consciousness. Dehaene and Changeux offer perhaps the most articulated neural models. They begin by distinguishing between the *state* of consciousness – the intransitive use of "consciousness" that identifies whether an organism is alert or awake – and the *content* of consciousness – the transitive use of "consciousness" that identifies what an organism is conscious of – and thereafter limit their neural model of the global workspace to the contents of consciousness (Dehaene & Changeux 2004; Dehaene *et al.* 2006). The distinction between state and content is unfortunate in this context, for it conflates a species of consciousness – state versus creature consciousness (recall Chapter 1) – and a constituent component of consciousness – what a conscious event is about. The trouble is that whenever one is conscious, one is conscious of something, even if it is no particular something. A better distinction is between tonic alertness (Dehaene and Changeux's *state* of consciousness) and phasic attention (their *content* of consciousness). Tonic alertness is that state of psychological activation that (a) obtains only if arousal has obtained, (b) contains no specific content, and (c) underwrites the ability to sustain a coherent line of thought or action. Tonic alertness is distinct from phasic attention, events of augmented alertness during which affective and cognitive orientation to, selection of, and concentration upon, an area in the field of experience occurs.

Dehaene and Changeux propose that spontaneous gamma frequency (20–80 Hz) oscillatory electrical activity occurring in a dynamic array of thalamocortical networks is the neural substrate of tonic alertness (Dehaene & Changeux 2005; Dehaene *et al.* 2006). Tonic alertness is a bottom-up neuromodulatory process that starts in the tegmentum, feeds forwards to the thalamus, and expands to cortical areas, including dorsomedial and ventromedial prefrontal cortex, anterior and posterior cingulate cortex, and lateral parietal and superior temporal cortex. Having achieved minimal tonic alertness, the thalamocortical system can continuously increase in alertness up to a threshold, beyond which there is a discontinuous and non-linear transition or jump that ignites widespread, long-lasting, self-amplifying and phase synchronous gamma band activity in prefrontal areas, cingulate cortex, parietal cortex and temporal cortex, with particular areas even more active than others depending upon the nature of the input – sensory, interoceptive, affective or cognitive. The ignition to and sustaining of global neural activity is the neural substrate of conscious properties.

What makes the Dehaene–Changeux neural model a specialized process model is their hypothesis that there is a class of neurons, widely dispersed across cortical and certain subcortical regions, that constitute the dynamic neural network and which ignite when tonic alertness makes its non-linear jump to phasic attention. These *workspace neurons* have a large number of synaptic connections in prefrontal, parietal and cingulate cortices. Among others, pyramidal spindle cells in anterior cingulate cortex, long axon white matter cells connecting distal cortical areas, and long axon white matter cells connecting cortical and thalamic areas all appear to be candidate components of the workspace neural network (Dehaene & Changeux 2004).

When acting together to subserve consciousness, workspace neurons sustain only a single neuronal representation at a time, which implies that we are conscious of only one thing at a time. Binocular rivalry and certain visual illusion experiments provide evidence that this is the case. In binocular rivalry, distinct images are presented to each eye simultaneously. Rather than consciously perceiving one image superimposed upon the other, we consciously perceive one image followed closely by the other image. This will continue for as long as one continues to be presented with the images – they never stabilize as one image. Another familiar example is the Necker cube illusion (Figs 8.1 and 8.2). Consider Figure 8.1. We see it in one of the two ways seen in Figure 8.2. But we do not see it as *both* of the possibilities at the *same* time.

On this model, phasic attention is in a strict sense necessary for consciousness (Dehaene & Changeux 2004; Dehaene *et al.* 2006). That is, without phasic attention, consciousness does not occur. Here is the reason. Recall that there are both top-down endogenous conscious events and bottom-up exogenous conscious events. On the model, workspace neural networks are endogenously or exogenously activated to amplify and maintain a particular neural representation. In either case, conscious events are those for which a particularly salient neural representation has sufficient strength to reorient ongoing endogenous processes. Endogenously activated conscious events engage workspace neural assemblies in prefrontal areas, parietal areas and temporal areas, and exogenously activated conscious events additionally engage workspace neural assemblies in brainstem, insular cortex and affective regions such as amygdala and periaqueductal grey (Baars 2005a).[1]

The Baars–Dehaene–Changeux model of conscious events has appeal because it effectively models some of the most obvious facets of accessibility

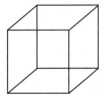

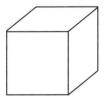 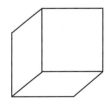

Figure 8.1 Necker cube.   **Figure 8.2** Two ways of seeing the Necker cube.

in a way that connects consciousness with a developed research programme on attention. Criticism has come from those, including Block (2005, 2007a), who argue that in addition to access properties, conscious events also have distinct and dissociable qualitative properties, and from those, including Koch and Tsuchiya (2007) and Lamme (2005, 2006), who reject the necessity of attention for consciousness. Both criticisms have far-reaching implications about the nature of conscious properties. Discussion is deferred until Chapter 9.

CODAM

The corollary discharge of attention movement (CODAM) model, developed by John G. Taylor, provides a neural model for the properties of subjective ownership, global accessibility and infallibility. On the model, subjective perspectivity is caused by neural processes as a kind of by-product of attentional control. Subjectivity and attention are thus so closely related that a better understanding of the former is possible only given a firm understanding of the latter.

On the model, attention brings subconscious neural processing to consciousness. Endogenous attention focuses on subconscious processing and thereby amplifies that activity to the point that it enters consciousness. If, on the other hand, attention is exogenous, salient subconscious processing breaks through to awareness and intrudes into consciousness. Either way, attention is the neuro-cognitive process by which the content of subconscious processing becomes conscious. Attention is thus a controller that sends amplification/inhibition signals to other processing pathways, stimulating attended inputs and inhibiting non-attended inputs, filtering salient from other information and holding it in working memory buffers for further and more complex processing (Taylor 2003, 2005, 2006, 2007).

Little distinguishes the CODAM model from standard models of attention, at least to this point. Indeed, the description of attention offered by Taylor is functionally equivalent to descriptions found in Desimone, Duncan and Postle, discussed earlier. It is what Taylor adds to attention that makes CODAM a candidate model of subjectivity and consciousness. Taylor hypothesizes that in the brain there is a copy of the control signal generated by attentional pathways. This copy – the *corollary discharge* signal – feeds forwards both to a monitoring module for error detection and correction and to a corollary discharge buffer that holds the signal for predicting and anticipating subsequent input. This signal works in tandem with whatever attended information is currently being held in working memory to establish a sense of ownership that attaches to predicted and anticipated input information and as a guarantee that the attended information input is what is being attended. The sense of ownership is constitutive of subjectivity (Taylor 2005, 2006, 2007). Hence, just as activity in working memory's episodic buffer binds information into unified multimodal experience, the corollary discharge buffer binds multimodal information to a subject, thus creating unified, subjectively perspectival, experience.

Taylor offers both evolutionary and neuroanatomical arguments for the CODAM model. Consider the neuroanatomical evidence. The various neural correlates of the processes that provide input to attention and conscious content pathways are those identified by other neuroscientists who work on endogenous and exogenous attention, the various components of working memory and monitoring. They need not be reviewed here. However, it is pertinent to note that identifying the relations between the neural correlates of attention, working memory and monitoring is far from settled, so CODAM's assumption that the neural correlates of these cognitive processes are also neural correlates for the corollary discharge is unconfirmed. This is not the only speculative aspect of Taylor's arguments. CODAM's hypothesis that there is a corollary discharge buffer that works alongside other working memory buffers located in parietal cortex has also yet to be confirmed. In addition, the evolutionary evidence for CODAM is also speculative. On the model, the corollary discharge buffer amplifies working memory content, accelerates access to it, and provides a sense of ownership of that content, thus providing faster response times to informational input that has greater saliency than it would otherwise (Taylor 2007). This capacity is hypothesized to have provided some survival benefit over those organisms that lack it. If so, it would be helpful were the existence of the corollary discharge signal confirmed. In addition, the conscious properties the corollary discharge signal is assumed to be targeting – the sense of ownership and subjective perspectivity – sometimes dissociate, as depersonalization syndrome and autoscopic phenomena such as out-of-body experiences show (Blanke & Metzinger 2009). If so, it is not obviously the case, as Taylor appears to assume, that neural evidence of correlates for one is also evidence of neural correlates of the other. Likewise, it is not at all clear how a corollary discharge signal, even if it were to be discovered, would realize ownership or subjective perspectivity. Finally, given Taylor's assumption that phasic attention is necessary for conscious events to occur, a criticism can be levied against the view if that claimed necessity is false. In Chapter 9, we argue that the claimed necessity is in fact false.

Non-specialized process models

The greatest diversity in neural models of conscious properties is represented by the class of non-specialized process models, each of which claims that conscious properties correlate with certain kinds of non-dedicated neural assembly activities. We introduce four models: gamma oscillation, electromagnetic field theory, the dynamic core and vehicle externalism.

Gamma oscillations and synchronized neural activity

Francis Crick and Christof Koch more or less single-handedly got the whole neural correlate of consciousness enterprise off the ground in the early 1990s by hypothesizing that 20–80 Hz gamma oscillations in neocortical neural activity are necessary but insufficient for consciousness (Crick & Koch 1990). Subsequent research by Singer (1999, 2004) and Treisman (1996) on stimulus-dependent synchronized neural firing and binding seemed to offer additional empirical support for the proposal. However, further investigation has considerably damp-ened enthusiasm. To begin with, the evidence that synchronized oscillations are correlated with conscious activity is taken from anesthetized cats, and it is hard to see how unconscious cats might provide any evidence of a necessary or sufficient condition for consciousness. More seriously, synchronous oscillation precludes some of the rapid neural processing that occurs in the ventral stream of sensory processing (Rolls 2007). Such synchronous oscillation is doubly dis-sociable from the processing that yields conscious perception, so even if it were not to occur, conscious perception still can occur. Thus, synchronous oscillation is no more than a concomitant accompaniment to consciousness. As a result of this and related arguments, Crick and Koch have abandoned the hypothesis and replaced it with a more complex theory, similar to Tononi and Edelman's dynamic core model, discussed shortly.

Electromagnetic fields

A more recent model that focuses on the global nature of consciousness is the neural *field model*. The work of E. R. John (2001, 2005) may be taken as repre-sentative (for distinct developments, see McFadden 2002; Pockett 2002). As with most process models, the field model takes conscious properties to be fairly late and complex phenomena that presuppose a significant amount of antecedent neural processing. For example, multimodal and transmodal neural mechanisms subserving sensation are assumed already to have combined with those subserv-ing interoception and affection to form an exogenous/endogenous information system that feeds information forwards to the mechanisms subserving conscious property instantiation and which constitute content. The model likewise assumes that the information fed forwards to the conscious mechanisms is already bound along a number of dimensions into representations. Bringing things to conscious-ness is then the process of transforming such bound representations into per-spectivally subjective experience (John 2005). John calls this species of conscious experience *apperception*, a nod to Leibniz and, especially, Kant. Like Kant, he means by "apperception" the kind of unified or bound perceptual, interoceptive, cognitive and affective experience that we all enjoy, experience that integrates or synthesizes momentary and occurrent perception with the information available from working and episodic memory and which is perspectivally subjective.

The field model focuses on electromagnetic properties generated by wide-spread and distributed neural activity rather than on chemical signals relayed at individual synapses. Multimodal and transmodal exogenous and endogenous input produces non-random synchronous gamma activation patterns in localized and distributed neural regions. Such non-random synchronous activation patterns establish states of negative entropy spread across brain regions, where *negative entropy* refers to an organization of electrical activity far from default or ground energy settings. When these "islands" of local negative entropy themselves bind together, they form a system of dispersed neural assemblies whose electrical activity is coherent despite spatial separation. Thus, conscious experience emerges as an electromagnetic field property generated by neurally encoded information synchronously resonating in a sufficiently large number of neural pathways (John 2005).

Some of the implicated pathways have been tentatively identified by testing brain regions affected by anesthetic depression (Hameroff 2006; John & Prichep 2005). Both sets of authors note that it is not reduction of neural activity in any particular neural pathway but overall reduction of neural activity across a distributed neural network that results in episodic memory loss, depression and loss of consciousness levels, and, finally, in complete immobilization. Regions in this distributed neural network include multiple prefrontal regions (DLPFC in particular), anterior cingulate cortex, superior frontal cortex, superior parietal cortex, insular cortex, amygdala, basal ganglia and thalamus (John 2005). In addition, there is a pattern of neural decoherence at loss of consciousness. John and Prichep (2005) identify an abrupt change – in the range of 10–20 milliseconds – in gamma synchrony between frontal/prefrontal and parietal regions and a functional decoupling of left and right hemispheres when loss of consciousness occurs; a similarly abrupt re-establishment of synchrony between anterior and posterior regions and functional recoupling of the hemispheres occurs when consciousness returns. Mashour (2004, 2006) calls this phenomenon *cognitive unbinding* and has proposed that the general function of anesthetics is to degrade and disrupt cognitive binding processes, from the cellular to the global.

The field model has been developed in an experimental environment that quantifies levels of consciousness and maps them to levels of anesthesia. This work relies on neurotransmitter electrochemical properties and the effects of anesthetic chemicals upon those properties. John substantiates this physiological evidence with evidence from neuropsychological disorders, such as attention deficit disorder, dementia, mood disorders, obsessive-compulsive disorder and schizophrenia, each of which also correlates with deficiencies and excesses of neurotransmitter levels. These studies help circumscribe baseline modes of synchronous electrical organization in the brain from which deviations can be identified. Some deviations, such as those found in anesthesia and psychiatric disorders, are pathological when sustained over time. However, when modulated in a phasic or momentary manner across brain regions, such synchronous deviations from baseline activity constitute the manner in which information is represented and hence constitutes conscious content (John 2005). This is a little mysterious: how do synchronous deviations from baseline neural activity constitute representation and, thus, content?

Two other concerns reinforce the one raised in the previous paragraph. First, John works from an understanding of consciousness as "subjective awareness of momentary experience interpreted in the context of personal memory and present state" (John 2003: 244). Although there is nothing inherently wrong in focusing on subjective awareness of momentary experience, even if – contrary to what appears to be the case – the electromagnetic field theory were to provide definitive neural correlates of representational content and subjective perspectivity, the neural correlates of qualitative character remain completely unspecified. So, at best, the theory is incomplete. Moreover, it is not clear that the electromagnetic field's focus on electromagnetic properties of neural assembly activity theory adds anything to other non-specialized process hypotheses (Pockett 2002). Since the only way to differentiate the electrochemical model from other process models is to generate a hardware version of the field and insert a wetware head into it to determine whether it experiences the content putatively encoded by the hardware field, and since that is currently impossible, the unique benefits of the model cannot currently be assessed.

Neural Darwinism, the re-entrant dynamic core and Φ

On Edelman and Tononi's *dynamic core* proposal, re-entrant neural paths in the thalamocortical system subserve conscious property instantiation. The dynamic core model takes the integrative access properties of consciousness as central to its biological function, so the model is of conscious experience as characterized by multimodal sensory binding, stability over time, subjectivity, reportability, allocentricity and adaptability. Edelman (2003) hypothesizes that conscious organisms have an advantage over unconscious organisms since they integrate massive amounts of complex sensory input with memory, affective valence and planning to produce highly adaptive motor responses. But such integration was not directly selected for; rather, natural selection has acted on the neural assemblies from which it emerges. Consequently, Edelman provides a neural model of those neural assemblies. The *theory of neural group selection* (TGNS), also known as *neural Darwinism*, is a model of evolutionary neural selection according to which ontogenetic brain development is characterized by the proliferation and subsequent pruning of neural pathways according to their experiential benefits (Edelman 1987). As we have seen in Chapter 5, this process of proliferation and pruning allows the brain to strengthen certain synapses and weaken others without changing underlying neuroanatomy. The process is constrained by, and in turn constrains, ongoing input from the limbic system, thus providing evaluative salience. These two processes – developmental and experiential neural selection – help shape conscious properties phylogenetically and ontogenetically.

Neural Darwinism is an account of the phylogenetic development of neural structure. The structure or architecture thus developed also requires a more synchronic description. A current trend suggests that neural architecture is essentially dynamic, non-linear and self-organized (Strevens 2005a, 2005b; Van Gelder 1998; Von der Malsburg 2002, 2004). An *organized system* is a set of entities structured to realize a function or maintain a particular configuration. A *self-organized system* is a set of entities structured to realize a function or maintain a particular configuration and whose structure is not imposed by an external cause. Organization in general and self-organization in particular are *global* properties of groups of entities rather than *local* properties of each of those entities. In one sense of the term, they are emergent higher-order properties of a system rather than properties of any of the components of a system. (We investigate emergence further in Chapter 10.)

Some self-organized systems are static, others dynamic. An example of a *static* self-organized system is a magnetized hunk of iron (Heylighen 2003). Molecules composing the hunk are all little magnets – so-called spins – each with a north and a south pole. At high temperatures, spins move randomly, anarchically repelling and attracting each other. However, as the hunk's temperature lowers, a spontaneous alignment appears such that the spins all line up in a single orientation, south-north-south-north and so on, creating a strong magnetic field across the hunk. This self-organization is an emergent global organization of the system of iron molecules that compose the piece of iron: it is the hunk of iron as a whole that is magnetized with a north and a south pole. It is true that the north and south poles of the individual molecules do not disappear when the hunk magnetizes, and it is also true that the hunk's poles would not be as they are were the molecules' poles not as they are, but the *hunk's* poles are not the aggregate of the *molecules'* poles. A *dynamic* self-organized system is a self-organized system whose configuration or function is in constant motion. The Bénard phenomenon provides a useful contrast to magnetism (Heylighen 2003). In the Bénard phenomenon, a liquid evenly heated from below will, after an initial state of disorganization, self-organize into a series of columnar rolls, with ascending hot water on one side of a roll and descending cold water on the other side of a roll. The liquid's molecules are in constant motion, competing and cooperating with one another, leading to self-amplifying constellations of motion that subserve the emergent roll pattern.

Just as some self-organized systems are static while some are dynamic, some self-organized systems are linear and some are non-linear. A *linear* system is one whose causal outcomes are roughly proportional to causal inputs, whereas a *non-linear* system is one whose causal outcomes are disproportional to causal inputs. Throwing a javelin is a linear process: if you throw the javelin with a given level of force, it will go, say, thirty feet; if you double the force, it will go about twice as far. Were throwing a javelin non-linear, on the other hand, there would be a point where an incremental increase in the force with which the javelin is thrown would result in it going, say, 5,000 feet. Non-linear processes are the result of positive and/or negative feedback loops. A *feedback loop* occurs when the results of some node in a causal process feed back to an earlier node of that very causal process. A feedback loop is *positive* when what feeds back augments or amplifies the causal process; a feedback loop is *negative* when what feeds back limits or cancels the causal process. Positive feedback engenders instability; negative feedback engenders stability.

The centrepiece of Tononi and Edelman's model of conscious properties is the postulation of a set of dynamic, non-linear and self-organized processes that they call the *dynamic core* of re-entrant neural processing. *Re-entrant processing* is a non-linear cycle of reciprocal feedforward and feedback signalling between cortical regions, especially the massive bidirectional pathways between thalamus and prefrontal cortical areas. The synchronized activity of distributed neural groups across functionally specialized cortical areas is a direct result of re-entrant signalling, and this synchronization subserves binding and integration of perceptual and motor pathways into subjectively unified and allocentrically organized experience (Edelman & Tononi 2000). A metaphor may help to clarify the view. Imagine:

> a peculiar ... string quartet, in which each player responds by improvisation to ideas and cues of his or her own, as well as to all kinds of sensory cues in the environment. Since there is no score, each player would provide his or her own characteristic tune, but initially these various tunes would not be coordinated with those of the other players. Now imagine that the bodies of the players are connected to each other by myriad fine threads so that their actions and movements are rapidly conveyed back and forth through signals of changing thread tensions that act simultaneously to time each player's actions. Signals that instantaneously connect the four players would lead to a correlation of their sounds; thus, new, more cohesive, and more integrated sounds would emerge out of the otherwise independent efforts of each player. This correlative process would also alter the next action of each player, and by these means the process would be repeated but with new emergent tunes that were even more correlated. Although no conductor would instruct or coordinate the group and each player would still maintain his or her style and role, the players' overall productions would tend to be more integrated and more coordinated, and such integration would lead to a kind of mutually coherent music that each one acting alone could not produce.
>
> (Edelman & Tononi 2000: 49)

So, just as the musicians' playing will eventuate in a coherent and integrated production, so too neural firing in a re-entrant network will eventuate in coherent and bound, integrated experience.

The coherent and bound experience described above and made possible by re-entrant processing in the thalamocortical system is *primary* consciousness. Edelman and Tononi attribute primary consciousness to mammalian species other than humans and perhaps in attenuated form also to birds. One noteworthy feature of primary consciousness is that it is qualitatively loaded (Edelman 2003), so any mammal capable of primary consciousness also has qualitative conscious experience. Rare among neuroscientists, they hypothesize that sets of neurons in inferior temporal cortex are selectively activated when an organism senses particular colours. So, for example, one set of neurons is activated when an organism senses red and inhibited when it senses green; likewise for blue and yellow and for light and darkness. Their neural firing rates define a three-dimensional space wherein each colour corresponds to a distinct point in that space (Edelman & Tononi 2000). Generalization to other sensory modalities is possible but, to date, neither Edelman nor Tononi have offered details.

As so far portrayed, the dynamic core model of qualia is a bit underdescribed, and it hardly provides either an account of qualia or a neural foundation of their reduction. How does the location of a colour in a three-dimensional space realize the quale of that colour? Edelman and Tononi recognize the problem and suggest that if the three-dimensional space is enlarged to an N-dimensional space, where N is the number of neuronal groups that constitute the dynamic core at a time, then we will have a candidate neural realizer of colour. N is a large number, between a thousand and a hundred million. The components of N form a functional cluster of highly integrated neural pathways that cannot be decomposed without loss of information (Edelman & Tononi 2000). So, for instance, in addition to neuron sets that fire selectively for particular colours, other neuron sets fire selectively for, say, motion, shape, texture, edges, and so forth. Colour qualia are then particular points in this N-dimensional space defined by the integrated activity of all the neuron sets that constitute the dynamic core at the time the quale is experienced.

Edelman and Tononi claim that what distinguishes humans from other mammals is not that we alone have qualitatively rich experience. As already noted, many mammals have qualitatively rich experience. If not that, then what does distinguish us? Edelman (2003) suggests that we also enjoy *higher-order* consciousness and a self that is self-conscious. Higher-order consciousness is characterized by additionally complex and recursive cognitive and affective processes such as self-consciousness, monitoring, reflexive consciousness, symbolically encoded thought and affective regulation.[2] Consistent with the re-entrant processing hypothesis, these additionally complex forms of consciousness are neurally realized in the brain by nothing more magical than additional re-entrant loops. Likewise, our kind of subjective perspectivity is initially a result of re-entrant processing carrying interoceptive and proprioceptive information about the body and its motor systems that distinguishes between action initiated from within (such as when I push a button to turn on the radio) from motion induced by something external (such as when my finger ends up push-ing the button because someone bumps into me). But subjective perspectivity is not exhausted by such phenomena, for we are, in addition, self-conscious. Self-consciousness arises only with the emergence of recursively structured lan-guage and higher-order forms of consciousness that take other psychological events as their content and do something further with them. We return to these issues in Chapter 12.

The dynamic core hypothesis is further augmented with a *measure*. The measure, called "Φ" (the Greek symbol "phi"), is equal to "the amount of caus-ally effective information that can be integrated across the informational weak-est link of a subset of elements" (Tononi 2004: 1). While the mathematical details of Φ need not concern us, the logic of the need for and some of the features of the measure bear comment. The measure applies to a system (where a system is, recall, a structure of a large number of elements that enter into dynamic events or states that are forwards, backwards and laterally depend-ent upon the events or states of the other elements of the system). Φ is, then, a measure of the interdependence and integrative binding of the system's ele-ments and the information carried thereby. Consider a system of photodiodes, simple, two-state devices that measure the presence or absence of light. We can compose a sensor chip of, say, a million such diodes, each tuned differently to distinct luminosity. The chip would then have a million diodes, each one of which has a repertoire of two states, and the chip would be remarkably sensi-tive to small changes in luminosity. Still, there is no causal interaction between the photodiodes composing the chip: each photodiode is an independently act-ing sensor. So, the chip has no causally interdependent elements. Since it has no causally interdependent elements, the chip is not capable of integration, and its Φ measure is zero.

Compare the chip made up of a million photodiodes with the dynamic core in the thalamocortical system, and, more specifically, some subsystem therein composed of, say, a million neurons. Suppose that these million neurons have initial causal input from afferent sensory, interoceptive, proprioceptive and lim-bic pathways. The subsystem's neurons then enter into forwards, backwards and lateral interactions with each other, many of them reciprocal, and re-entrant interactions with the thalamus, forming an ever-changing network of causal interdependencies. Since each of these causal pathways is at the same time an information pathway, this subsystem can also be thought of as a network of informational interdependencies whose initial inputs are from sensory, intero-ceptive, proprioceptive and limbic cortical systems feeding forwards to it. Of course, each of the sensory, interoceptive, proprioceptive and limbic pathways feeding into the thalamocortical system is in turn decomposable into its own subsystems. The auditory system, for instance, is decomposable into the ventral and dorsal informational pathways, each of which is in turn decomposable into more specialized pathways, one for pitch, one for volume, one for location, and so forth, each of which carries information that is subsequently integrated – bound – with information from the other dedicated auditory pathways to create an integrated sensation of sound. That bound auditory sensation is in turn bound with the other sensory modalities and with interoceptive, proprioceptive and limbic information to compose an integrated multimodal conscious perceptual experience of the surrounding environment (Tononi & Sporns 2003).

Systems with high Φ scores have high informational integration; those with low Φ scores have little informational integration. On the basis of these differences, the dynamic thalamocortical core that subserves the emergence of conscious events can be distinguished from the activity of other cortical and subcortical regions of the brain that play a non-constitutive role in the emergence of conscious events. The ascending reticular activating system, for example, is necessary since if it is lesioned conscious events collapse, but the proper functioning of the ascending reticular activating system is necessary only because it is necessary for the proper functioning of the thalamacortical system, not because it supplies any of the contents or establishes any of the qualitative or perspectivally subjective dimensions of conscious events. Its work is, rather, that of an external on-off switch or a transient booster of thalamacortical firing (Tononi 2005). Likewise, cortical input and output systems, such as retinal visual input neural systems and motor pathway output neural systems, while connected to highly integrated thalamocortical systems, are, even if necessary for there to be particular conscious contents (as in the case of the retinal visual input system), not for that reason themselves conscious systems. For, the composition of the integrated system into which the input is sent and from which the output is forthcoming does not change; it is, rather, the composition of the system composed of the integrated system plus the input system or the output system that changes.

The activities of the basal ganglia and various cortico-subcortical loops can also be shown not to be substrates of consciousness. The basal ganglia, for example, contain many complex pathways cycling through dorsolateral and orbitofrontal prefrontal cortex, anterior cingulate cortex, and motor and frontal eye field cortical regions. But these basal ganglia pathways are structured in parallel rather than as integrated, and they cycle into and out of the integrated thalamocortical systems without changing the composition of the integrated system. As in the case of input and output systems, what is changed is instead the composition of the system composed of the integrated thalamocortical system plus the basal ganglia. Likewise, the various cortico-subcortical loops that implement dedicated subroutines for unconscious processes that can be influenced by and can influence conscious experience are also distinct from the integrated thalamocortical system. These cortico-subcortical loops include those devoted to all the myriad actions – riding a bike, typing, shooting a basketball – that we first learn consciously, slowly and by making mistakes, but then with practice perform without much conscious awareness (Tononi 2005).

The thalamocortical system itself has many circuits that are not part of the highly integrated dynamic core, so many circuits that are not part of consciousness. Activity in unimodal sensory pathways, while necessary for supplying the multimodal regions of associative cortex with its contents, is not therefore conscious. What we are conscious of, as described above, is a multimodally integrated perception that is bound with interoceptive, proprioceptive and affective information. Unless we suffer from dorsal simultagnosia, we do not visually experience objects floating in space disconnected from their background; unless we suffer from Wernicke's aphasia, we do not hear gobbledygook when someone talks to us; unless we suffer from Broca's aphasia, we do not produce gobbledygook when we talk to someone. Rather, we see objects against a background; we hear words in well-individuated chunks with their meanings attached; we produce words in well-individuated chunks with their meanings attached. All the processing that feeds forwards to the regions of the thalamocortical dynamic core occurs in more or less dedicated circuits that are, since they are not sufficiently integrated with other circuits, unconscious rather than conscious, and it is only with their dysfunction that their necessity for what we take for granted in conscious experience becomes apparent.

External consciousness

Tononi and Edelman's dynamic core hypothesis is a neural model of conscious properties that identifies dynamic intracortical neural assembly activity as the system that correlates with conscious property instantiation. But the dynamic core model is only a relatively modest way of incorporating dynamicism into a model of conscious properties. Other, more far-reaching proposals similarly committed to modelling conscious properties as dynamic systems properties are also out there. On one of the most widely discussed of these more far-reaching proposals, the relevant system that correlates with conscious property instantiation is neither neural activity of a complex cortical assembly nor the neural activity of the central nervous system taken as a whole, nor the activity of the central nervous system taken as a whole in conjunction with other systems of the body. Rather, the relevant dynamic system that correlates with conscious property instantiation is the embodied central nervous system embedded in an environment.

The family of views coalesces around the idea that conscious psychological activity is embodied and embedded in an environment. Call the family *externalism* (the family name is also called *situated cognition* (Robbins & Aydede 2009)). Some members of the externalist family are more radical than others. All of them affirm both that the brain's work is much less frequently devoted to symbol manipulation than computationalism assumes and that representational states are far less ubiquitous in the brain than representationalism assumes. The more conservative members are *semantic externalism* (Burge 2007) and *wide computationalism* (Wilson 2004; Wilson & Clark 2009) or, as it is also known, the *extended mind hypothesis* (Clark 2008; Clark & Chalmers 1998). These views are semantic claims about how to distinguish contents from one another. On all three, contents of representational states, events and processes are sometimes individuated by extracranial and extrasomatic events and objects. (Differences between Burgean externalism and wide computationalism need not delay us.) The radical member of the family is *radical embodied cognitive science* (Chemero 2009). For reasons that will become clear, we refer to the radical of the family as *vehicle externalism*. In this section, we introduce a model that vehicle externalists propose for conscious property instantiation. In Chapters 11 and 12, we discuss the various views that claim membership in the externalist family and scrutinize the challenges that vehicle externalism in particular poses to computational representationalism and other neural reduction programmes.

Vehicle externalism's starting point is that conscious psychological events are constitutively dependent upon being embodied and embedded in an environment. This constitutive claim is distinct from the weaker claim that conscious psychological events are causally dependent upon being embodied and embedded in an environment. Conscious psychological events are *causally dependent* upon being embodied and embedded in an environment whenever they are causally coupled with the body and the environment (Prinz 2009). Two systems are *causally coupled* whenever causal relations between them are non-linear, and causal relations between two systems are non-linear when they have various positive and negative feedforward and feedback loops. So the claim is that conscious events are constituents of a larger dynamic causal system and that conscious events are best described as causally coupled with that larger dynamic causal system. On this alternative, conscious events are, for all their causal coupling with the extracranial body and environment, nevertheless intracranial and can even occur without causal input from the extracranial world; think of dreams, abstract thoughts, hearing a tune in your head, hallucinations, and so forth. (Of course, those conscious events that have no extracranial causes usually have a different phenomenological feel than those that have extracranial causes. We return to these matters in Chapter 12.)

Since causal coupling is consistent with conscious events occurring intracranially, it poses no new threat to the neural reduction programmes and is, therefore, not what is revolutionary about vehicle externalism. The uproar is caused rather by the claim that conscious events are constitutively dependent upon being embodied and embedded in an environment. One system is *constitutively dependent* on another when the one is constitutively coupled with the other, and systems are *constitutively coupled* whenever the resulting conjoint system is non-decomposable (see Bechtel 1998, 2009; Bechtel & Richardson 1993; Strevens 2005b). A system is *constitutively decomposable* when it is composed of constituents whose causal powers are *not* a one-to-one function of the causal powers of the other constituents, where a one-to-one function from one system to another is a mapping from the one to the other such that no element of the one maps to more than one element of the other. For example, a physical system is constitutively decomposable as to its spatial extension, since the spatial extension of any constituent spatial part of the system can be fixed independently of fixing the spatial extension of any distinct constituent spatial part of the system. So, the causal powers of the spatial extension of a physical system are a simple aggregation of the causal powers of the spatial parts composing the physical system.

The situation is otherwise with a constitutively non-decomposable system. A system is constitutively *non-decomposable* whenever it is composed of constituents whose causal powers *are* a one-to-one function on the causal powers of the other constituents. Examples of constitutively non-decomposable systems are a single day in your life, the flow of a river, photosynthesis and explosions. Each of these systems is composed of constituent elements whose causal powers vary as a one-to-one function of the other constituents. Pretty clearly, claiming that psychological events are conscious only if they are constituents of a larger constitutively non-decomposable dynamic system is controversial, for if true, conscious events are in a quite literal sense spread out beyond the brain (for variations on this proposal, see Chemero 2009; Noë 2004; Noë & Thompson 2004a; Thompson 2007).

It is generally agreed that two degrees of spread are possible. On the first, conscious properties are embodied without being embedded, and on the second, conscious properties are both embodied and embedded. According to the more moderate alternative, conscious properties are higher-order properties that are constituents of a constitutively non-decomposable dynamic system whose realizers include extracranial but otherwise intra-organismic elements (other systems of the body). Conscious properties are instantiated only by this body-wide system. Still, conscious events are body-wide events rather than events of the brain or even the central nervous system. On the second view, conscious properties are emergent higher-order properties of and realized by a non-decomposable system made up of lower-order properties instantiated intracranially by neural assemblies, extracranially but intra-organismically by other bodily systems, and extra-organismically by events and objects in the environment.

Suppose I see a book on the desk in front of me. On computational representationalist accounts of conscious visual experience, the extracranial and extra-organismic book, my extracranial but intra-organismic sensory organs and my intracranial neural apparatus are causally related, perhaps even causally coupled. The vehicle externalist means to say something different and, initially at least, a little counterintuitive. He means to say that the extracranial book is literally a constituent element of the conscious visual experience of it. He readily grants that the book is causally coupled with my sensory organs and my neural apparatus such that were the book not there I would not visually experience it. But he is also saying that book, sensory organs and neural apparatus are causally coupled *because* all three are constitutive elements of a dynamic and non-decomposable system of conscious visual experience spread across and emergent from those constitutive elements. So, the activated neural assemblies and processes, the electrochemical states of my eyes, other intra-organismic systems and the book's various properties (such as spatial position, reflectance properties plus whatever else must be thrown into the pot) are each such that their causal powers are one-to-one functions of the causal powers of the other component elements.[3] This is quite an extraordinary claim, which we investigate in greater detail in Chapter 12, after unpacking what causal powers are in Chapter 10 and discussing causal coupling again in Chapter 11.

This completes our summary of contemporary neural models of conscious properties. Some models are admittedly more plausible than others. The least plausible – the attention model, the quantum mechanical model, CODAM – have been assessed in this chapter. We will not return to them. Those that remain – some of the process models – form the focus of subsequent analysis. What is impressive about most of these models is their serious engagement with the long-standing philosophical issues that consciousness poses to the naturalist. Even if a particular proposal only waves its hand at one of these entrenched difficulties, that it even acknowledges the issue is a significant change from the state of cognitive neuroscience twenty years ago, when these issues were routinely dismissed as irrelevant or misguided philosophical grousing. Whether any of these neural models provide sufficient warrant for reducing any conscious property to neural assembly activity remains to be seen. We turn now to the philosophical arguments concerning these issues.

9. MEASUREMENT, LOCALIZATION, MODELS AND DISSOCIATION

The previous chapters show that there are systematic correlations between conscious processes, events, states and properties and neural events, states, processes and properties and that these correlations are to varying degrees localized to particular cortical regions. The ever-growing mountains of evidence for such localized systematic covariations are grist for the reductionist's mill, suggesting that conscious properties do not just covary with activity in localized neural assemblies but that the latter are neural substrates of the former. It is a relatively quick, albeit contentious, argument from the claim that neural properties and events are substrates of conscious properties and events to the claim that the latter are realized by, and hence reduce to, the former. Consciousness neuroscience thus fulfils its role as the harbinger of reductive physicalism.

Admittedly, the neuroscientific study of conscious properties is not much more than twenty years old, and plenty of gaps remain. Disagreements about evidence strength, data interpretation, experiment replicability and preferability of competing neural models and theoretical frameworks are plentiful. However pointed these shortcomings and disagreements may be, they occur against the background assumption that scientific investigation into consciousness will ultimately be successful in reducing conscious properties to something neural. To think these efforts are missing something essential may seem pig-headed. This view is mistaken, and many of the best reasons for thinking so come from philosophically minded scientists and scientifically minded philosophers. In this and the next three chapters these reasons are investigated. In this chapter, certain epistemological and conceptual issues are hashed out.

MEASUREMENT AND LOCALIZATION

Presenting a welter of neuroimaging and neuropsychological evidence about the anatomical location and physiology of neural assemblies and processes that correlate with psychological events which instantiate conscious properties is admittedly a little stupefying. It was necessary to dispel any lingering doubts that evidence in this arena is piecemeal or *ad hoc*. It is neither – it is rapidly accumulating, broad, deep and interconnected. Since knowing where something occurs is often necessary for knowing how it works, all the neuroanatomical evidence is and will continue to be important for discoveries yet to be made. However, since knowing where something occurs is rarely sufficient for knowing how it works, the neurophysiological evidence and the various neuroscientific models of consciousness are also important.

Many people who read neuroimaging and neuropsychological studies about some perceptual modality or some cognitive process (or a dysfunction in some such process) come away persuaded that the evidence provided by the identified neural correlates of that particular conscious process provide everything needed for identifying the instantiation of a conscious property with some set of correlates. But it is best to view this inference with caution. A truckload of neuroanatomical and neurophysiological correlates is admittedly pretty impressive as evidence that something is going on just here in the brain and that that something is directly relevant for the instantiation of a conscious property. Nevertheless, that welter of correlational evidence is just that: a truckload of correlates. It is one thing to specify neuroanatomical and neurophysiological correlates of conscious properties; it is another thing to identify the instantiation of a conscious property with those correlates or to claim that the correlates are substrates or realizers of the conscious property.

Two considerations initially prompt the recommendation to be cautious. First, since neuroimaging studies measure only certain kinds of neural activity properties, argument is required to connect the measured properties with conscious properties. This is an instance of what we will call the *measurement* problem: correlation between a conscious perceptual, affective, or cognitive property, on the one hand, and measured neural assembly activity on the other does not prove that the measured quantity is the substrate for, or realizer of, a conscious property (Malach 2007). Additional premises must be added to close this inferential gap.

Second, while neuroimaging studies establish that conscious properties and processes correlate with certain kinds of activity in particular neural assemblies, they do not prove that conscious properties and processes correlate only with *that* activity in *those* neural assemblies. This is what we will call the *localization* problem: correlation between a conscious perceptual, interoceptive, affective, or cognitive property or process, on the one hand, and, on the other hand, activity of a particular kind in a particular neural assembly does not thereby prove that the property or process is localized to that neural assembly activity or that the neural assembly activity is dedicated to that property or process.

In addition, correlational studies do not distinguish kinds of conditions for the instantiation of conscious properties or processes. This is the *correlation* problem: correlation between an instantiated conscious perceptual, interoceptive, affective, or cognitive property or process and a particular kind of activity in a neural assembly at a particular location does not thereby distinguish between that neural activity being a necessary condition, a sufficient condition, or a necessary and sufficient condition for the instantiation of that conscious property or process.

In this chapter, we discuss the first two problems; in the next chapter, we discuss the third, much more complexly faceted problem.

Measurement problems

The measurement problem is actually a small family of problems, some of which arise from *what* gets measured, some of which arise from the *techniques* used to measure what gets measured, and some of which arise from the *inferences* derived from the measurements provided by the use of those techniques. Experiments that do not separate aspects of perceptual, interoceptive, affective and cognitive processes underscore the importance of acknowledging the first aspect. Correcting for these shortcomings requires teasing constituents of processes apart using increasingly fine-grained dissociation studies. Dissociation studies of language comprehension provide a ready example. Earlier studies that ran together auditory, phonological, morphological, lexical, syntactical and semantic properties are being replaced with studies that try to dissociate one property from the next, thus making earlier confounds apparent and providing more precise results. Still, despite the advances made on this front, few neuroscientific studies have tried to separate off the peculiarly conscious aspects of perceptual, affective, interoceptive and cognitive processes. Improvements on this score are urgently needed. The second aspect of the measurement problem – how what is measured gets measured – is perhaps of greater interest. It is, to begin with, readily acknowledged that none of the imaging techniques combine sufficient spatial and temporal fine-grain to precisely map neural activity in particular assemblies: EEG is temporally fine-grained but superficial and spatially coarse-grained; PET and fMRI are spatially fine-grained and temporally coarse-grained.

Evidentiary problems with imaging studies also attach to the logic of imaging studies, which can be described roughly as follows. The root assumption of such studies is that a difference across brain region activity when performing different tasks is evidence for the functional role of a brain region's activity in performing a task. So, finding a method for measuring that differential activity helps to identify the region's cognitive, affective, perceptual, interoceptive and proprioceptive functional roles. PET and fMRI imaging are just such methods. With PET and fMRI, patterns of blood flow in capillaries that surround neural assemblies in particular brain regions are measured. Those patterns correlate with increased electrochemical activity in those assemblies, which electrochemical activity in turn correlates with occurrence of particular kinds of perceptual, affective and cognitive processes that characteristically come loaded with conscious properties. Since blood flow patterns are not the neural properties in virtue of which neural assembly activity correlates with conscious property instantiation, some argument that links what is measured to whatever is that in virtue of which they correlate needs to be produced. This is a general problem: there is an inferential gap between measuring neural activity of some kind and claiming that what is measured is therefore the neural property in virtue of which events are conscious.

To clarify the point, consider a macro example. For the first twelve years following the Second World War, an increasing number of storks in the city of Copenhagen correlated with an increasing number of human babies born. But inferring that the increased number of storks in Copenhagen is therefore the causal property in virtue of which the number of human babies increased is pretty obviously mistaken. For, both the increased number of storks and the increased number of human babies are causal results of a common third cause – the increased population of Copenhagen following the end of the Second World War. That increased population caused an increase in the number of human baby makers and an increase in the number of buildings with the chimneys on which the storks nested. Similarly, properties of neural activity measured in PET and fMRI studies may correlate with instantiation of some conscious property, but their correlation does not entail that they are the neural properties causally or constitutively responsible for the conscious property.

One may think that the inferential gap induced by measurement results from PET and fMRI being indirect measures of neural activity. Although it is certainly true that they are indirect, this is not the source of the inferential gap. The indirectness of PET and fMRI measurements would be a problem if they were not to covary reliably with more direct measures. However, PET and fMRI measurements covary reliably, indeed linearly, with direct measures of individual and multi-unit neural electrical activity taken by inserting electrodes through the skull and into individual neural neurons and neural assemblies (Rees *et al.* 2002). Of course, this kind of single-cell research is highly invasive and raises a number of thorny ethical issues, so the development of indirect measures such as PET and fMRI that covary linearly with them has been an extraordinary boon. The indirectness problem actually runs a lot deeper. Even if PET and fMRI measurements covary linearly with single-cell measurements of electrochemical activity, those localized electrochemical activity properties may not be the neural properties in virtue of which neural events instantiate conscious properties. If so, even the measured electrochemical activities, much less the indirect PET and fMRI measures that covary with them, are neither substrates for, nor realizers of, conscious properties. Although the inferential gap is narrower, it is still open.

Another aspect of the measurement problem is particularly acute with fMRI images. Such images are produced when a magnetic resonance scanner tracks statistically significant differences in blood oxygen level dependent (BOLD) activity and maps such BOLD activity differences using statistical parametric maps. A statistical parametric map is a graphical representation of different levels of BOLD activity using distinct colours for distinct levels of BOLD activity. When such a statistical parametric map is overlain on to a brain model, the result is an fMRI image of statistically significant differential BOLD activity across regions of the brain. The method used in fMRI imaging to determine statistical significance is null hypothesis significance testing (NHST). If BOLD activity passes a NHST, it is statistically significant; if it does not pass a NHST, it is not statistically significant. BOLD activity that passes a NHST does so because it is activity that would be unlikely to occur were the null hypothesis true. The null hypothesis for BOLD activity in a particular brain region is the proposition that an experimental condition – say, a task assigned by the experimenter – has no effect on measured BOLD activity. The negation of the null hypothesis is the research hypothesis, that is, the proposition that an experimental condition – again, in the current case, the task assigned by the experimenter – has some effect on observed BOLD activity as measured by a magnetic resonance scanning device. The goal of the experiment is thus to falsify the null hypothesis and thereby to give the alternative research hypothesis inductive support. Neuroimages are produced by performing NISTs in each 3-D region (voxel) of BOLD data, the results plotted as statistical parametric maps. Statistical parametric maps thus show where rejecting the null hypothesis is warranted (Klein 2009).

Previous chapters have reviewed research that shows that the brain is a dense mat of interconnected neurons, feeding forward, feeding backward and feeding across widely distal brain regions. It can be difficult to accurately represent how pervasive the interconnectivity of neurons is: in general, there are no more than five synapses between any two neurons. That the brain is structured in this way in turn entails that it is *causally dense*, that is, it is a system in which there are causal paths between most neurons, regardless of the changes in explanatory variables (Klein 2009). Given causal density, we can find differential BOLD activity across many more brain regions for a given task set by the experimenter than are typically identified in an fMRI study. Granted, some of that activity is minimal and some of it adventitious. However, since the probability of getting differential BOLD activity data in many brain regions given even the null hypothesis is quite high, the measured differential BOLD activity data in particular brain regions of interest, while real, is and will always be complemented by differential BOLD activity in these other areas. Measured BOLD activity in the brain region of interest is thus less informative about that region's functional role than it is typically assumed to be.

The same point may be made even more directly (Klein 2009). Given the casual density of neural interconnectivity, the probability of getting differential BOLD activity data in many brain regions even on the null hypothesis is quite high, which is just to say that the null hypothesis is almost always false: it will almost never be the case that some assigned task has no measurable effect on BOLD activity. Since the null hypothesis is almost always false, rejecting it usually does not support the research hypothesis that differential neural activity is the result of different assigned tasks. But then the choice of one threshold of statistical significance is arbitrary, for one threshold is as good as the next. Unfortunately, using one threshold rather than another yields statistical parametric maps that vary dramatically in their depiction of neural activity. If so, then statistical parametric mapping will rarely resolve disagreements about the BOLD data that confirm some particular research hypothesis about differential brain activity.

In both cases, interpreting fMRI images as evidence of differential neural activity is compromised because such an interpretation ignores neural causal density. Since neural interconnections are causally dense, an image of a particular brain region being differentially active on a given task does not establish that neural activity in that brain region is the substrate or realizer of that task. All the measured BOLD activity may be something that points instead to neural activity that plays a necessary but non-constitutive role in the neural implementation of the task rather than a sufficient or constitutive role in the neural implementation of that task. Indeed, the measured BOLD activity may point to neural activity that is nothing more than an adventitious by-product of the neural activity that is core to the neural implementation of the conscious task, real but functionally irrelevant for implementation.

Localization problems

It is an unavoidable implication of neuroimaging and neuropsychological studies that some neural localization of psychological processes is significant, for otherwise we would find, contrary to what is the case, no difference between a scan of an individual counting sheets of paper and a scan of someone eagerly anticipating a raft trip down the Yukon. However, the reliability and pervasiveness of localization are up in the air. One reason is that despite all the neuroimaging studies from the past twenty years, too few metalevel integrative studies interpreting their results have been undertaken. Two recent meta-analyses highlight the issues.

First, two teams have independently called into question the reliability of correlations between complex psychological processes and activity in particular neural assemblies and pathways (Kriegeskorte *et al.* 2009; Vul *et al.* 2009; Vul & Kanwisher in press). Kriegeskorte and colleagues' version of the argument is particularly clear. They argue that the widespread practice of using data both for selecting regions of interest in the brain to study and for analysing the activity in the regions of interest thus identified runs the risk of yielding at least partially circular results. The problem is especially prevalent in neu-roimaging studies, where researchers responsible for 42 per cent of 134 fMRI papers published in *Nature, Science, Nature Neuroscience, Neuron* and *Journal of Neuroscience* in 2008 engaged in some form of non-independent analysis. In designing these studies, researchers hypothesized that a particular cortical region would respond more strongly to one condition rather than to another condition. Using the resulting image of differential activity rates to define the region of interest, researchers then used the same image to analyse and test the hypothesis (Kriegeskorte *et al.* 2009). The threat of circularity is apparent: in using the same images both for identifying a region of interest and analysing the activity in that region, such studies run the risk of overemphasizing the activity in that region and neglecting activity in other regions. Vul and colleagues use a similar argument to infer that the reported correlations are much higher than should be expected (Vul *et al.* 2009). Debate is ongoing (for a critical response to Vul and colleagues' article, see Lieberman *et al.* 2009).

Second, meta-analyses of neuroimaging and neuropsychological studies that review multiple studies with an eye to generalizing results have shown that localizing neural pathways that correlate with complex psychological processes has limits. Lloyd (2007) may be taken as representative (see also Hardcastle & Stewart 2002 for a similar analysis). Lloyd performed a meta-analysis of 959 papers that report on 4,221 neuroimaging and neuropsychological experiments. This meta-analysis reveals that for thirty-seven cognitive, perceptual and affec-tive processes (such as action inhibition, syntactical processing and comprehen-sion, reasoning, working memory, olfaction and emotion) and the forty-seven numbered Brodmann areas[1] of the human brain (ninety-four if lateralization is factored in), every process is subserved by more than one Brodmann area and every Brodmann area subserves more than one process (Lloyd 2007). As an example, consider the correlation of left DLPFC (Brodmann area 44) with audi-tion. Grant that neuroimaging evidence shows that whenever there is audition there is activity in left DLPFC. That correlation entails neither that left DLPFC is the only neural area correlated with audition nor that audition is the only psychological process correlated with left DLPFC. In fact, in addition to left DLPFC, audition correlates with activity in right and left superior, middle and inferior temporal cortex, ventromedial prefrontal cortex, dorsomedial prefron-tal cortex, superior parietal cortex, premotor and motor cortices, left angular gyrus and left anterior cingulate cortex. And, in addition to correlating with audition, left DLPFC also correlates with (among many others) imagination, inhibition, observation, musical comprehension and colour vision (Lloyd 2007).

This kind of result is replicable for *every* process/cortical region pair investi-gated: no region of cortex correlates with only one psychological process, and no psychological process correlates with only one cortical region. Indeed, psycho-logical processes in the investigated domains correlate with an average of twenty-two Brodmann areas, and each Brodmann area in turn correlates with an average of ten psychological processes (Lloyd 2007); similar results have been reported for some emotions (Wager *et al.* 2008) and working memory (Wager & Smith 2003). There do appear to be upper and lower bounds: every process appears to correlate with no fewer than three Brodmann areas and no process appears to correlate with more than twenty-eight Brodmann areas.

That thirty-seven perceptual, affective and cognitive processes correlate with activity in interconnected networks of neurons across a number of cortical regions supports the claim that localization of many psychological processes to single cortical regions is false. While some degree of localization is the norm – auditory processing does not routinely start in primary auditory cortex only to migrate on occasion to primary olfactory cortex – its limits may be no more fine-grained than entire pathways through a number of cortical regions, each of which carries information of various kinds. The problem with PET and fMRI is, as we have seen above, that neither provide the evidence to determine how much localization actually obtains. Hardcastle and Stewart (2002) use an analogy to highlight the evidentiary problem with localization efforts based on these technologies:

> We liken voxel and pixel analysis to having 1000 people in a large room. If you measure the oxygen consumed in this room you will not differentiate the following states, no matter how accurately you can measure the oxygen consumed: 500 people with red hats sleeping while 500 people with blue hats walk on a treadmill, 500 red hats on the treadmill while 500 blue hats sleep, or 250 red hats and 250 blue hats on the treadmill while 250 red hats and 250 blue hats sleep, and so on. In order to understand what is actually going on in the room, we need to know which people are sleeping or exercising, and why. Measuring gross oxygen consumption won't tell us that.
>
> (Hardcastle & Stewart 2002: S80)

Now, since psychological processes and functions are also often conscious, so long as there is nothing unique about the conscious properties such processes instantiate, using PET and fMRI to identify the neural correlates of those conscious properties at any level more fine-grained than entire pathways through brain regions may also be compromised.

Thinking that the neural correlates of conscious properties are to be found in some kind of activity in single neurons or highly specific and small neural populations is particularly unlikely. Again, Hardcastle and Stewart (2002) make the case for such scepticism. Single-cell measurements *must* ignore the complex feedforward and feedback processing rampant in the causally dense brain, for otherwise localization hypotheses cannot even get off the ground. Much less could these hypotheses be tested without bracketing that causal density. On the assumption that psychological processes are implemented in highly localized cell populations, measurements can be generated for activity in a single cell or a small population of cells. But the activities of cells surrounding that of the small populations measured in such studies are never measured, so it is not possible to determine from the measurement in that cell or those small populations exactly what facets of the psychological task being measured are actually being measured, or indeed if any facets of the psychological task are being measured. For, it is not possible to determine what role, if any, the connectivity of the single cell or small population of cells to other cells or larger populations is playing in the measurement being taken during the task. Thus, single-cell/small-population measurements systematically underestimate and misrepresent the responsive dynamics of even small neural assemblies, much less larger assemblies and pathways that are composed of millions and tens of millions of neurons. So the appropriate response to conclusions about complex psychological function being implemented in single cells or small populations of them is a sceptical one. As Hardcastle and Stewart wryly note, "brain imaging seems to support localist assumptions because we aren't very good at it yet" (Hardcastle & Stewart 2002: S78).

MODELLING PROBLEMS

While there are now reasonably well-established neuroanatomical and neurophysiological correlates of any number of conscious processes and even plausible candidate correlates for some of the conscious properties, there is not yet a comprehensive model of the neural substrates of conscious processes and properties. Given the complexity of both conscious processes and properties and cortical neuroanatomy and neurophysiology, this state of affairs should be neither surprising nor disappointing. After all, the enormity of the task at hand is only now becoming clear. Having a model of the neural substrates of conscious properties requires a reasonably clear understanding of the nature of conscious properties, reliable and replicable studies establishing neuroanatomical and neurophysiological correlates for the properties thus understood, and a plausible conceptual model into which all of that correlational work can be fed. The model must apply not only to neuroscientific studies that try directly to identify neural correlates of conscious properties but also to all the other parallel neuroscience studies of all the other relevant perceptual, interoceptive, affective and cognitive processes that are conscious.

The neural models of conscious properties discussed in Chapter 8 fall into four baskets: specialized and non-specialized vehicle models, and specialized and non-specialized process models. These neural models do not map directly to the philosophical views about conscious properties discussed earlier. The question thus arises: how are the neural models related to these philosophical ways of thinking about conscious properties? All neural models are, in a general sense of the term, functionalist models (as we will see in Chapter 11, some functionalist models are non-neural models), which is just to say that neural models all start from the assumption that conscious properties are functional properties, that is, higher-order causal properties. But the models disagree on what realizes those causally efficacious conscious properties. Vehicle models propose that conscious properties are realized by neural vehicles, either individual neurons or assemblies of them, and their properties. On this first way of thinking of things, the function of a particular neural assembly is, for example, to fire at a particular spiking rate, and that spiking rate contributes to the implementation or realization of some conscious property. On the second way of thinking of things, conscious properties are realized by processes of which those neural vehicles and assemblies and their properties are components. For process models, the function of a particular neural process is, for example, to fire in a particular range of synchrony, and that synchronous firing contributes to the implementation or realization of some conscious property.

Although vehicle and process neural models are often representationalist and classically computationalist, neither need be either. Granted, the specialized process global workspace model offered by Baars and John's electromagnetic field approach are both recognizably computationalist and representationalist. However, Edelman and Tononi's dynamic non-specialized process model is, at a minimum, neither classically computationalist nor representationalist, for its account of primary consciousness as an embodied dynamic system coupled with the external environment precludes the occurrence of isolable representational events. Likewise, Opie and O'Brien's connectionist specialized vehicle model is not classicist, even if it is a kind of representationalism. Penrose and Hamerhoff's quantum mechanical proposal is neither classicist nor connectionist; indeed, it is not even recognizably representationalist.

In some ways, then, the vehicle/process distinction is orthogonal to the other distinctions we have drawn. One way to understand the difference is this. The functionalist/non-functionalist distinction is the most general distinction: if conscious properties are not functionalist properties, then science is not the appropriate discipline to study them. Assuming that conscious properties are functionalist, the next set of distinctions – representationalism/non-representationalism, computationalism/non-computationalism and classicism/non-classicism – help identify which branches of science are the most appropriate branches for laying out the theoretical framework within which understanding conscious properties can make progress. And, finally, having settled those sets of questions, the vehicle/process distinction specifies the families of entities that are the best candidate for being the realizing family of entities.

Attention models

Attention and consciousness are closely related, and in ordinary language the two terms are sometimes used interchangeably. If we hear something but do not attend to it, we often say that although we are aware of the sound, we are not conscious of it. But ordinary language is not reliable, for it also rejects the coextension of conscious and attentive experience. Athletes who attend to their goal usually do not attend to the constituent bodily movements required to achieve that goal; they are, as we say, "in the zone", so tightly focused on making the basket or reaching the next handhold that the rest of their ongoing experience retreats in salience. They are for all that conscious, even if they attend to one thing and do not attend to others. As ordinary language commitments vary across researchers, various features of attention receive more focused coverage, the result being a *lot* of neural models of attention in cognitive, affective and perceptual neuroscience that utilize an impressive array of mathematical and conceptual resources, that are offered at many different levels of explanation, and that cover a number of distinct processes.

The neural correlates of attentional processes also overlap to a considerable degree with processes constitutive of and neural pathways correlated with working memory. It appears that the two are distinct for at least some species of phasic attention, for all species of phasic attention occur within the bubble of working memory but the processes of working memory can be triggered without engaging endogenous attention. However, the ways in which working memory and endogenous attention differ are far from being sorted out. In part, this is a consequence of a problem that attaches both to attention and working memory. Localization findings stemming from the alerting, orienting and executive model are influenced by ordinary language commitments that make attention a kind of spotlight directed upon a field of experience (Posner 1994; Posner & Petersen 1993). These assumptions encourage the view that, just as a spotlight has an on-off switch and a motion control, so too attention's alerting and orienting features are special-purpose, discrete neural pathways that look more like neural modules than distributed neural networks. But the spotlight metaphor and the view that attention switches on and off both may be misleading; if so, inconclusive and conflicting experimental findings about the modularity of attentive neural processes are an obvious consequence.

A distinct model of attention suggests that attention is an emergent property of ongoing dynamic biased competition across neural pathways and that it works in tandem with working memory. On this model, first proposed by Desimone and Duncan (1995), attention is not a special-purpose process that turns on and shines a cognitive beam on the field of experience; rather, it is an ongoing process that selects from the welter of information available at any moment a portion of it to merge with ongoing activity in working memory. Information that has relatively high signal strength rises to working memory; that which does not, does not. Signal strength, in turn, is determined by a combination of factors, including top-down biasing signals prompted by voluntary attention that enhance neural responses to attended stimuli and improve information quality from most regions of the brain and bottom-up saliency filters that likewise enhance neural responses to attended stimuli and degrade neural responses to unwanted information (Kastner & Ungerleider 2000; Knudsen 2007; Shipp 2004). Attention is thus more a matter of "tuning in" to an object's location or focusing on some feature of an object than of "turning on" a spotlight and directing it to a location or feature.

Working memory models

Parallel debates about the Baddeley–Hitch model of working memory have recently erupted. First, the organization of dorsal and ventral working memory pathways and even whether there are dorsal and ventral working memory pathways at all are both disputed. These disagreements can be traced to disagreements about the existence of dorsal and ventral perceptual pathways. Even if unimodal visual and auditory pathways divide labour into a dorsal "where" pathway and a ventral "what" pathway and even if heteromodal visual and auditory pathways likewise have dorsal and ventral components, there are not dorsal and ventral neural pathways for all perceptual information. Olfactory working memory, for example, is not structured along a ventral/dorsal distinction at all. As noted, primary olfactory processing in pyriform cortex projects directly to orbitofrontal cortex and insular cortex, on the one hand, and, on the other, to amygdala and hippocampus (there is a small relay to the thalamus's mediodorsal nucleus, but it does not divide into dorsal and ventral pathways either). The same is true of gustation: while taste information routes through the ventral posterior nucleus of the thalamus, it projects to insular cortex and to the tongue area of somatosensory cortex without dividing into separate streams. As a direct consequence, flavour – the combination of taste and odour – is likewise not divided into ventral and dorsal pathways. So, since not all perceptual modalities are organized into ventral and dorsal pathways, the generalization of that organizational principle to working memory assemblies and pathways is likewise jeopardized.

For those who think that the ventral/dorsal distinction makes sense for at least some perceptual pathways, other uses of the distinction remain disputed. The standard model claims that the ventral pathway leading to VLPFC is dedicated to holding qualitative properties of objects in working memory and that the dorsal pathway leading to DLPFC is dedicated to holding spatial properties of objects in working memory. VLPFC activity is then held to be responsible for temporarily maintaining qualitative representations, while DLPFC activity temporarily maintains spatial representations of objects. This "domain-specific what/where" hypothesis is replicated in a large number of studies. However, it is no longer clear that *any* perceptual pathway carries *only* spatial information or *only* qualitative information forwards to prefrontal cortex. Instead, it may be that all perceptual pathways carry multimodal perceptual spatial and qualitative information forwards (Dade *et al.* 2001; White & Wise 1999). Alternatively, while perceptual information feeds forwards to prefrontal cortex on dorsal and ventral pathways, the distinction between VLPFC and DLPFC may be that VLPFC encodes and retrieves information held in other, posterior, locations, while DLPFC monitors and manipulates the same information (D'Eposito 2008; Petrides 2000; Petrides *et al.* 2002). On this hypothesis, there is still a VLPFC/DLPFC distinction, but it is drawn not on a difference between domain-specific kinds of information, but on a difference between kinds of processing. Others still argue that what comes forwards to VLPFC and DLPFC is multimodal perceptual information that has been processed in posterior locations according to certain rules and that prefrontal areas process that information according to distinct rules (Miller & Cohen 2001; Romanski 2004).

Two of the most persuasive cases for moving beyond the standard model of working memory have been made by Jonides and colleagues (Jonides *et al.* 2007) and by Postle (Postle 2006). For Jonides, the standard model is mistaken on two broad fronts. First, storage and processing mechanisms for working and long-term memory are not, they claim, distinct. Instead, the cortical regions that store representations, both short-term *and* long-term, are the same cortical regions as those that process it. Second, overlap between attention and working memory neural assemblies is, they argue, so pervasive that a reassessment of the cortical regions subserving each set of cognitive processes is required. They argue that working memory is not decomposable into a number of modular storage buffers and a central executive; rather, bound chunks of perceptual, affective and cognitive information are held by attention and made immediately available for subsequent cognition. One consequence is that the standard model's reliance on short-term modular buffers, each with large storage processes, is no longer needed. Instead, the resources of long-term memory storage are hypothesized to serve the bulk of storage functions.

Postle's concerns are more far-reaching, raising both logical and empirical problems for the standard model. The standard model dissociates location and qualitative working memory processes from pathways for storage and processing. Postle reviews a considerable amount of neuropsychological and imaging evidence that suggests to the contrary that there is no domain-specificity to the prefrontal cortex's working memory storage mechanisms (Postle 2006). He also challenges the standard model's commitment to location and qualitative working memory storage and processing, noting that these are not the only dissociable processes or pathways. Similar dissociations can be made for working memory for manipulable and non-manipulable objects, for phonological, semantic and syntactic working memory, for auditory pitch, loudness and location, and for touch, olfaction and gustation. All of this cognitive fractionating requires increasingly specialized neural pathways for increasingly specialized cognitive processes. But the resolution of current imaging and lesion techniques is not sufficiently fine-grained to confirm that distinctness between psychological processes is mirrored by neural pathway distinctness.

Indeed, localization evidence is consistent with either of two alternatives: first, there is a direct mapping from particular processes to particular neural pathways that we will eventually discover with more fine-grained techniques, *or*, second, there is no mapping from process to pathway that will ever be discovered, regardless of measurement accuracy. Rather, consistent with Lloyd's findings, multiple processes are subserved by a single pathway and multiple regional pathways subserve a single process. Although current imaging technologies will no doubt be replaced by more precise technologies, what are now identified as evidential limitations may thus be symptomatic of a more fundamental and ineliminable complexity in the alignment of cognitive processes with neural pathways.

The standard model's domain-specificity claims threaten to fractionate cognitive processes wantonly, with an equally profligate fractionation of correlated subserving neural pathways. The result would be a cognitive architecture composed of thousands of "domain-specific buffers", each of which would encode a distinct kind of information in working memory (Postle 2006: 25). And this cognitive architecture would be replicated by neural architecture: prefrontal (and other) regions would be organized into a complex lattice of dedicated neural modules, each of which implements the processing of a distinct kind of information in working memory. In short, the commitment to domain-specific processing and implementing neural pathways threatens to splinter working memory into as many distinct neural pathways as there are conceptually separable kinds of information.

These theoretical objections are serious, serious enough to consider putting the standard working memory model up on blocks and go shopping for a new model. The model Postle proposes is one on which working memory is not a separate and dedicated system of prefrontal-temporoparietal pathways organized along domain-specific information kinds at all, but is, rather, "a property that emerges from a nervous system that is capable of representing many different kinds of information, and that is endowed with flexibly deployable attention" (Postle 2006: 29). On this alternative, attention and working memory are two aspects of one and the same process, a process subserved by a widely distributed and interconnected neural system that takes as input information from multimodal perceptual, affective, proprioceptive and interoceptive feedforward pathways, holds it "in mind", and manipulates it for some purpose. Since whatever neural assemblies are already implicated in attention are sufficient for working memory, there is no need for special-purpose memory storage modules or for isolable working memory neural pathways that implement storage of or processing on domain-specific kinds of information.

The disagreements about models of attention and working memory just canvassed reflect deep disagreements about whether attention and working memory – and, by extension, many other cognitive and non-cognitive neural processes – are classical computational systems or dynamic connectionist systems. On standard models, neural processes are described using architectural principles that devolve from classical computationalism. When modelled thus, attention and working memory are conceived as modular processes occurring in discrete cortical regions that play a specific role in a larger system of cognition. The alternative models conceptualize the constituent processes of attention and working memory as dynamic emergent processes that occur in cortical areas whose architecture is connectionist. When modelled thus, attention and working memory turn out to be emergent phenomena over large-scale interconnected neural activity that is embodied intra-organismically and embedded extra-organismically in an environment. Both are structured as non-modular, non-sequential, embedded systems that are coupled, through continuous and mutually determining interaction, with the intra- and extra-organismic environment. We discuss this alternative in greater detail in Chapter 11.

DISSOCIATION OF INTENTIONAL CONTENT, QUALIA AND SUBJECTIVE PERSPECTIVITY

We have assumed that qualitative character, subjective perspectivity, and intentionality are conceptually distinct properties. If so, then psychological events can have any of $2^3 = 8$ combinations of the properties. Where "Q" represents qualitative character, "C" represents accessible content, and "S" represents subjective perspectivity, we have:

(1) $Q + C + S$ (2) $Q + \neg C + S$ (3) $\neg Q + C + S$ (4) $\neg Q + \neg C + S$

(5) $Q + C + \neg S$ (6) $Q + \neg C + \neg S$ (7) $\neg Q + C + \neg S$ (8) $\neg Q + \neg C + \neg S$

Let us agree that psychological events that satisfy (1) are conscious and that those that satisfy (8) are unconscious. In the past ten years, neuroscientific evidence has emerged that suggests that at least some of (2) through (7) are actual, that is, that conscious properties actually dissociate from one another on occasion. If this evidence is reliable, then the search for the neural correlates and substrates of the conscious properties and events becomes additionally complex, for any research programme that assumes a monolithic concept of consciousness glosses over the possibility that intentional content, qualitative character and subjective perspectivity correlate with partially overlapping, partially distinct neural assemblies. One such debate concerns the dissociation of conscious and attentional events.

Dissociation of attentional and conscious events

Even if attentive events and conscious events overlap, it appears unlikely, as global workspace theory and CODAM have it, that conscious events are the same class of events as attentional events (Prinz (2000) claims that attention is necessary for consciousness, but on rather different grounds). Of course, many psychological events are both attentive and conscious. Obvious candidates are events that occur within the timeframe of working memory, such as attending to the nearby report of a gun or episodes of endogenous attention. Likewise, many psychological events are neither attentive nor conscious. Candidates include the formation of negative after-images, so-called zombie behaviours (Beilock *et al.* 2002; Koch & Tsuchiya 2007), rapid vision, and all kinds of proprioceptive and interoceptive information, such as peristaltic contraction in the digestive tract, each of which is relentlessly fed forwards to the brain yet remains beyond the reach of both attention and consciousness.

Cases in which we are conscious of something despite not attending to that something and cases in which we attend to something despite not being conscious of it are more interesting. If such dissociations occur, then attention is neither necessary nor sufficient for consciousness (Block 2007a; Burge [2006] 2007). Consider the claimed necessity of attention for conscious perception. If something is not attended to, does it follow that we are not conscious of it? Well, on one sense "attend" and one sense of "conscious", the answer is clearly *yes*. If the only kind of attention is voluntary attention, and higher-order consciousness the only kind of consciousness, then where there is no attention there is no consciousness either. But voluntary attention is not the only kind of attention, and the higher-order theory of consciousness is too strong for all kinds of consciousness.

Since attention is, on the one hand, both voluntary and endogenous, and, on the other, involuntary and exogenous, there are actually four cases to consider before establishing the dissociation of attention and consciousness issue. These are: (i) the necessity of involuntary and exogenous attention for conscious perception; (ii) the necessity of voluntary and endogenous attention for conscious perception; (iii) the sufficiency of involuntary and exogenous attention for conscious perception; and (iv) the sufficiency of voluntary and endogenous attention for conscious perception.

On (i): involuntary and exogenous attention is *not* causally necessary for conscious perception. In cases of change blindness, individuals do not attend to a change that has occurred in a scene despite being conscious of the change. A typical example is the following: two scenes, A and B, where B differs from A across some dimension(s), are visually presented to test individuals and they are asked to identify the changes. Many cannot do so, and their inability to attend to the change has been taken as evidence that they are unconscious of the change (Block 2007a). However, these individuals may be *qualitatively* conscious of the change even though they do not *attend* to it. If so, then there can be a kind of consciousness without attention. This phenomenon is so ubiquitous in ordinary life that it is sometimes shocking to have it revealed. But thinking that we have to be attentive to be conscious entails a mistake, for, as Lamme puts it, "arguing that change blindness is evidence for a limited sensory experience is ... the same as arguing that when someone has forgotten what he saw yesterday he was blind that day" (Lamme 2004: 864; the confound of reportability is discussed later in this chapter). In all such cases, exogenous attention does not occur, and conscious perception does occur. Hence, as claimed, exogenous attention is not causally necessary for conscious perception.

On (ii): voluntary and endogenous attention is *not* causally necessary for conscious perception. Koch and Tsuchiya (2007) support the non-necessity of voluntary attention for conscious perception with dual task research in which individuals are instructed to attend to some particular feature or region of a screen. While attending to their task, images of male and female faces or famous faces are projected onto a peripheral region of the screen. Despite these peripheral images not being attended to while the central task is attended to, subjects identify the faces as one gender or another and as famous or not. In these and similar cases, subjects have qualitative access to some features of the peripheral images despite not attending to them. Hence, as claimed, endogenous attention is not causally necessary for conscious perception.

On (iii): involuntary and exogenous attention is *not* causally sufficient for conscious perception. The causal effectiveness of subliminally flashing pictures in a timeframe shorter than can be consciously processed and registered – the so-called attentional blink (typically less than 50 milliseconds) – shows that stimuli exogenously attended to need not be consciously perceived (for reviews of attentional blink experiments, see, among many others, Dehaene & Changeux 2004 and Sergent *et al.* 2005; see also Block 2007a). Hence, we can exogenously attend to something and yet not consciously perceive it. Hence, as claimed, exogenous attention is not causally sufficient for conscious perception.

On (iv): voluntary and endogenous attention is *not* causally sufficient for conscious perception. Koch and Tsuchiya (2007) support the insufficiency of voluntary attention for conscious perception by appealing to masking research in which individuals are asked to focus on a screen, and male and female nudes are projected onto the screen with continuous flash suppression that makes them invisible. Heterosexual subjects attend to images of the other gender despite attention to the screen and despite the invisibility of the images. In such cases, subjects attend to something that is not consciously perceived. Hence, as claimed, endogenous attention is not causally sufficient for conscious perception.[2]

Dissociation of endogenous and exogenous attention from conscious perception has been described so far from a cognitive perspective. Only a few neural models of conscious perception and attention can accommodate the dissociation. These are models, such as Tononi's, that insist that conscious events require activity in re-entrant pathways, for it is only upon the occurrence of such re-entrant activity that short-term memories are formed, and the formation of short-term memories is essential for conscious events to occur (Lamme 2005 describes such a model). Since conscious events are subserved by activity in re-entrant pathways rather than feedforward pathways and exogenous attention is subserved by feedforward pathways rather than re-entrant pathways, the pathways subserving exogenous attention and consciousness are distinct. And since on the model some events are unreportable, there can be qualitatively endowed events that are not accessible. Conscious events are, thus, distinct from activity in unidirectional feedforward exogenous attention pathways that may produce automatic, intelligent and even complex behaviour, but behaviour that is for all that unconscious.

If attention and consciousness are distinct, a fourfold categorization of psychological process types is available (Koch & Tsuchiya 2007; Lamme 2005, 2006):

(i)   *unattended* and *unconscious* processes that activate at best a small number of feedforward associative pathways and do not activate any re-entrant pathways;

(ii) *attended* and *unconscious* processes that activate multiple feedforward associative pathways and do not activate any re-entrant pathways;

(iii) *unattended* and *conscious* processes that activate a few feedforward associative pathways and multiple re-entrant pathways;

(iv) *attended* and *conscious* processes that activate both multiple feedforward associative pathways and multiple re-entrant pathways.

Cases (i) and (iv) are common ground between those who think that attention is necessary and sufficient for consciousness and those who think it is not. But whereas the global workspace model marks a three-way dissociation between subliminal processing, preconscious processing and conscious processing, Koch and Tsuchiya, Tononi, and Lamme argue that this way of cutting the pie camouflages an important distinction. While they concur with the global workspace model that attentive and conscious processing deserves the name "conscious processing", they note that unattended but conscious processing is mislabelled on the global workspace model as "preconscious processing". For them, such processing is not preconscious but qualitatively conscious and unattended. Moreover, the global workspace model runs together two kinds of processing that should be distinguished. Unattended and unconscious processing and attended and unconscious processing are in global workspace models both subsumed under the category of subliminal processing, which fails to account for attended but unconscious processing altogether.

Unattended but conscious processes and attended but unconscious processes are not just laboratory curiosities but can make up significant parts of daily life. Conscious processes that lack endogenous attentional processing are characteristic of all those stretches of a day during which we engage in zombie behaviours such as typing at a keyboard. Endogenously attending to such habituated behaviours actually impedes and hampers performance of the behaviour. This point is further supported by noting that experts at some particular kind of trained behaviour – shooting a basketball, climbing a rock wall, skiing, swinging a golf club or tennis racket – who have their attention diverted from the trained behaviour outperform those who attend to that trained behaviour. Not surprisingly, the converse is true of novices, who perform better when attending to the behaviour than when not attending to the behaviour (Beilock *et al.* 2002, 2004). Likewise, attentional processes that lack conscious processing also help explain other curiosities, such as driving a car on "autopilot" and sleepwalking, during which we can move through a room and around furniture but about which we can recall nothing (Koch & Crick 2001).

Dissociation of qualitative character and accessible content

A qualitative property is the what-it-is-likeness of conscious experience. Although most of the philosophical debates have focused on perceptual qualia, emotional experience and interoceptive and proprioceptive experience are also qualitatively endowed. But even more is true, for *no* conscious experience is, at least in typical cases, entirely devoid of qualitative properties. Granted, the pleasure of finding an answer to a complex mathematical or engineering problem is muted in comparison to sexual orgasm, but it is a pleasure nonetheless. Likewise, although there is a difference between the cognitively based suspicion one feels when presented with certain arguments and the perceptually based suspicion one feels about the man who follows us down a dark street, both are species of the same genus. So, in general and typically, qualitative character is a feature of all conscious experience (Block 2007a; Zahavi 2008).

This general claim about typical circumstances does not imply that qualitative properties do not on occasion dissociate from other conscious properties. Indeed, neuroscientific accounts of perceptual processing provide evidence that perceptual qualitative properties actually dissociate from intentionality and subjective perspectivity. Blindsight provides an example. Where left V1 is damaged, individuals deny seeing anything in the contralateral visual field. While blindsighters deny seeing anything in the contralateral field, they can if asked identify an object's location with considerable reliability and, if instructed to do so, they can pick up and catch objects thrown through the blindfield (Holt 2003). Moreover, some blindsighted individuals report that they are aware of something they do not perceive and that they perceive visual after-images of items they do not see (Cowey 2004). Being aware of trucks not visually perceived, perceiving after-images of unseen coffee cups, catching balls thrown through the blindfield, and determining the colour of unseen flowers are, it has to be admitted, peculiar. It is this almost paradoxical quality that has most intrigued philosophers, for it implies that qualitatively endowed conscious experience is not necessary for some visual functioning. That implication runs counter to philosophical commitments and common sense, which suggest to the contrary that no part of visual function is possible without qualitatively endowed conscious experience. But philosophical commitments and common sense must yield to scientific discovery: blindsight is well established and reliably corroborated, and rejecting scientific discoveries to hold on to a set of philosophical commitments is like sticking one's head in the sand and denying that it is sunny.

One way to help common sense tolerate blindsight is to align the elements of visual functioning preserved in blindsight with intentional content to which there is access and align the elements of visual functioning not preserved in blindsight with qualitative features of that content. Distinguishing qualitative features from representational content is parallel to a distinction between *informational* and *experiential* sensitivity, the former a non-qualitatively based repertoire of information discrimination processes, the latter a qualitatively based repertoire of experiential discriminatory processes (Flanagan 1992). The neural elements of visual function preserved in blindsight preserve access to content (informational sensitivity), whereas qualitative features of vision are compromised because the neural elements that underwrite them are dysfunctional. Blindsighters are thus informationally sensitive and experientially insensitive. Block's distinction between accessibility and phenomenology and their neural correlates marks a relevantly similar, although somewhat narrower, distinction (Block [1995] 2007, 2007a). For Block, the blindsighter's perceptual experience has no visual qualitative character even though some kind of visual access is retained, even if it is not the kind of access sufficient to be used for subsequent psychological or behavioural activity.

A neuroscientific explanation of blindsight actually predicts the difference between informational and experiential sensitivity, access and phenomenology. After all, V1 does not receive all the visual information from the thalamus's lateral geniculate nucleus. Another bundle of neurons – the tectopulvanar pathway – bypasses V1 altogether, projecting directly from thalamus to extrastriate visual cortex in inferior parietal cortical regions. In addition, the neural pathway that routes from thalamus through V1 itself splits in V1 into the familiar dorsal and ventral pathways, the former assembly projecting to posterior parietal cortex and thence forwards to dorsolateral prefrontal cortex and the latter projecting to inferior temporal cortex and ventrolateral and orbitofrontal prefrontal cortex. If the dorsal stream is the "where" pathway and the ventral stream is the "what" pathway, an explanation of how people can pick up a pencil or catch a ball despite qualitatively bereft experience immediately falls out: such blindsighters have functional dorsal streams and dysfunctional ventral streams, so they can locate the ball in space even while being insensitive to its colour or even to the fact that it is a ball. Similar neural explanations of numb touch, deaf hearing, motion and change blindness, and achromatopsia (black, white and grey visual experience) are also available (Holt 2003). Each such explanation provides a causal account of highly specific deficits to qualitative perceptual experience by identifying neural pathways whose compromised activity results in the relevant qualitative dysfunction. Hence, neuroscientific evidence about blindsight supports accessible experience that has no qualitative character.[3]

Experience that is qualitatively loaded but inaccessible is supported by other kinds of evidence. Everyone is familiar with spacing out, daydreaming and highly focused attention. When otherwise not engaged, our mind sometimes "wanders", and during such default mode episodes qualitative features of perceptual experience can escape access. When, for example, we daydream, we may suddenly realize that the fax machine's out-of-paper beep has been firing every minute for some time. Again, when fully engaged in a hard mental problem, we may suddenly realize that someone has been standing in our visual field at our office door. Again, when we are directed to focus on a particular feature of our perceptual field, we may completely miss the man in the gorilla suit walking across our perceptual field. Again, athletes are often coached to do something distracting when training so that they do *not* attend to their muscle movements (Beilock *et al.* 2002, 2004). In each of these cases, features of perceptual experience register without thereby being made available for subsequent reasoning and emotional response.

If this evidence is reliable, there are both qualitatively endowed but inaccessible conscious events and accessible and non-qualitatively endowed conscious events. Thus, both (2) and (3) (on p. 210) are supported. Generalizing from such evidence, Block has argued that there are not one but two neural correlates of consciousness, one correlate for qualitative properties and one for content properties (Block 2005, 2007a). In the most general terms, qualitative features correlate with neural assembly activity in superior temporal and posterior cortical regions that subserve unimodal and early multimodal perceptual processing, whereas access features correlate with neural activity in more anterior prefrontal cortical regions that subserve later multimodal and transmodal perceptual processing and supramodal cognitive processing.

Block's contention has not gone unchallenged. Baars has argued that there is only one kind of consciousness – some events of which have, and some of which lack, qualitative character (Baars 2005a). On this account, access is essential to every kind of consciousness: if a psychological event is not accessible, then it is not conscious. Hence, contrary to Block, there are no qualitatively endowed conscious events that are not accessible. This view is buttressed by an argument for the conclusion that if there were qualitatively endowed conscious events that were not accessible, we could never know that there were. For, the only way to confirm such an event's existence would be to enquire of the subject what she was qualitatively conscious of, and the response thus received would confirm contrary to the hypothesis that whatever it was, it is accessible after all. In brief: if there are qualitatively endowed events that are not accessible, then we can never know that there are, and if there are not qualitatively endowed events that are not accessible, then the dissociability of qualitatively endowed events from accessible events collapses. Block calls this argument the *methodological puzzle of phenomenological consciousness* (Block 2007a). This is a puzzle all right, but it can be dissolved by noting that, first, reporting presupposes accessibility and so can be successfully used against qualitatively endowed but inaccessible conscious events only if there is no other corroborating evidence for qualitatively endowed and inaccessible conscious events, and by arguing that, second, the necessary condition is false: empirical evidence suggests to the contrary that there are at least two kinds of conscious properties, each with separate neural correlates (Block 2007a).

Dissociation of qualitative character and subjective perspectivity and of content accessibility and subjective perspectivity

Suppose that qualitative character and content accessibility dissociate. Do qualitative character and subjective perspectivity, and content accessibility and subjective perspectivity also dissociate? That is, are (4) and (5) (on p. 210) also true? Here, the evidence is much less clear, even equivocal.

Phenomena such as out-of-body experience, heautoscopy and autoscopic hallucination are, perhaps surprisingly, not directly relevant for showing that subjective perspectivity can dissociate from qualitative character and content access. In *autoscopic hallucination*, a person experiences a spectral reduplication at some distance from his body; in *out-of-body experience*, a person experiences his corporeal body from a perspective some distance from it; and in *heautoscopy*, a person experiences his corporeal body and a spectral reduplication from a perspective intermediate between them. Neural correlates for each of the phenomena have been proposed. Autoscopic hallucinations correlate with dysfunction in right parieto-occipital or right occipito-temporal regions, while heautoscopy and out-of-body experience correlate with dysfunction in, respectively, left and right temporoparietal junction regions (Blanke & Metzinger 2009; Blanke & Mohr 2005; Vogeley & Fink 2003). Note that the neural assemblies that correlate with autoscopic hallucination are upstream from those that correlate with heautoscopy and out-of-body experience. This neuroanatomical difference maps to qualitative differences across the phenomena: in autoscopic hallucination, one hallucinates a spectral body from the subjective perspective of the corporeal body; in heautoscopy, the subjective perspective is from either the spectral body or the corporeal body, or in some cases, rapidly alternates from one to the other; and in out-of-body experience, one experiences the corporeal body from a spectral subjective perspective.

These deformations to subjective perspectivity, while peculiar, are not, however, sufficient to show that subjective perspectivity dissociates from either content accessibility or qualitative character. For, in each of the phenomena, one's body – either the corporeal or spectral body – is experienced from a subjective perspective. In autoscopic hallucination, the experience is not of a spectral body from a subjectless perspective but rather is of a spectral body from an embodied subjective perspective. In heautoscopy, the experience is of a corporeal body and spectral body from a subjective perspective that alternates between the two. Even in out-of-body experience, the corporeal body is experienced from a disembodied subjective perspective. In each case, the subjective perspective remains even if its embodiment lapses. Moreover, in none of these phenomena do content accessibility or qualitative character dissociate from subjective perspectivity, even if the latter is disembodied.

Other neuropsychological disorders show more directly that subjective perspectivity can dissociate from content accessibility and qualitative character. Depersonalization syndrome and fugue states are obvious candidates. In *depersonalization*, individuals experience detachment from themselves, feeling that they are observers of themselves. Depersonalization patients describe themselves as being "detached" from their own body, "observing" their bodily behaviour from "outside", feeling "like a robot" and feeling like the world is "unreal". Similarly, electrical current administered to an epileptic patient resulted in the patient reporting a peculiar sensation of "not being present and floating away" (quoted in Tonkonogy & Puente 2009: 262–3). Depersonalization is tentatively thought to correlate with dysfunction in left temporal lobe and higher-than-normal activity in inferior parietal cortex and occipital cortex. *Fugue* is characterized by episodes of alert absent-mindedness of which there is little or no subsequent memory. During fugues, individuals may be coherent and competent, albeit vague about their identity and perplexed if asked more than simple questions (Tonkonogy & Puente 2009). Cortical localization studies have to date proved inconclusive.

Depersonalization and fugue states provide some evidence that states in which compromises to aspects of subjective perspectivity do occur. If so, then since qualitatively endowed experience can be ongoing during such episodes, some aspects of subjective perspectivity can dissociate from qualitative character. Likewise, since content accessibility need not be compromised during depersonalization episodes, as evidenced by the individual's ability to describe the episode, some aspects of subjective perspectivity can dissociate from content accessibility. Fugue states are equivocal: someone in a fugue can answer questions, thus supporting occurrent content accessibility, but subsequent to emerging from the fugue, there is rarely any memory of anything that occurred during it, thus supporting retroactive content inaccessibility.

In this chapter, some of the methodological and epistemological issues that the neuroscience of consciousness presents have been laid out. The localization problem is for the most part internal to neuroscience, which is to say that its resolution primarily requires more care by neuroscientists when they announce their results and derive inferences from those results. The modelling disputes are also largely internal to neuroscience, although given the nature of the disagreements between localization advocates, on the one hand, and emergence advocates, on the other, more global disagreements about the nature of conscious cognitive processes may be lurking. The measurement problem appears less serious than it actually is. While certain aspects of the measurement problem can be resolved by tethering imaging results to other kinds of neuroscientific evidence, the inferential gap exposed between any such measured neural property and the neural property or properties causally or constitutively implicated in the instantiation of conscious properties is stubborn. In the next chapter, this issue is discussed in greater detail.

10. CORRELATES, REALIZERS AND MULTIPLE REALIZATION

If microphysical neural reductionism gets things right, conscious properties inherit all their causal powers from the microphysical properties of certain neural assemblies and so are totally realized by those microphysical neural properties. A strategy for showing that conscious properties inherit all their causal powers from microphysical neural properties is the following. First, include subjective perspectivity, qualitative character and intentionality in the set of representational properties. Second, include representational properties in the set of functional properties. Third, survey enough of the neuropsychological, neuroimaging and evolutionary evidence to convince doubters that the neural correlates of such functionalized conscious properties are also neural substrates for them. Fourth, invoke a thesis such as (NR)[1] to warrant reducing those functionalized properties to certain microphysical properties of neural substrates. Successfully completing these steps provides a blueprint for the kind of arguments for any candidate conscious property to reduce to the microphysical properties of neural assemblies.

The central role of claims such as (NR) in this project is apparent. If (NR) is false, neural reduction collapses. There are three ways to argue that (NR) is false: first, use multiple realization of conscious properties against it; second, deny that conscious properties are totally realized by microphysical properties; third, deny that conscious properties are totally realized by neural properties, microphysical or not. In this chapter, multiple realization is rejected. In the final two chapters, we consider the second and third, considerably more challenging, objections.

CORRELATES AND SUBSTRATES

In addition to the measurement problem and the localization problem discussed in Chapter 9, deeper epistemological problems with the neural correlates of conscious properties programme remain. These concerns condense into a straightforward question: just what does the existence of all these neuroanatomical and neurophysiological correlates amount to? Answering this question leads to thorny discussions concerning correlates, causes, substrates and realizers.

Correlates and causes

A *neural correlate of consciousness* is a minimal neural event type, N, such that for some conscious event type, C, there is a correlation between C and N. A *correlation* is a measurement of association between two things, where "thing" is understood widely to include objects, events, states, processes, phenomena and measurements, gathered under a single term, *variable* (our preferred ontological categories are events and properties, but we will use processes and states as well). Calculating that measurement uses specific mathematical formulae, the details of which need not delay us. Correlation is frequently called *covariation* because wherever two variables correlate, there they covary. Developing myopia as an adult and going to sleep with the light on as a child correlate to a particular degree of probability: those who sleep with the light on as a child are more likely to develop myopia as an adult than those who do not sleep with the light on as a child, and those who develop myopia as an adult are more likely to have gone to sleep with the light on as a child than those who do not develop myopia. Correlations thus understood are a dime a dozen. The length of a desk correlates with its width; the shrinking thickness of the world's longest non-polar glacier, the Fedchenko, over the past five years correlates with the rising cost of gasoline in the United States over the past five years; the decrease in the number of pirates correlates with global warming (as followers of the Flying Spaghetti Monster have pointed out).

Correlations are easy to come by because correlation is such an inclusive relation: it is reflexive (everything correlates with itself), symmetric (if A correlates/covaries with B, then B correlates/covaries with A) and, in general, not transitive (it is not the case that if A correlates with B and B with C, then A correlates with C). Correlation's symmetry in particular is telling, since causation, emergence and reduction are asymmetrical. Despite its blandness, correlation is suggestive of something else in virtue of which that covariance occurs, for one answer to the question, "Why do two things, x and y, covary?" is, "They covary because one of them *causes* the other".

It is familiar that covariation does not imply causation. To begin with, covariance may be mere coincidence. Drinking orange juice as a child correlates with heroin use as an adult, but there is no causal connection between the two, and to think otherwise is an instance of the *cum hoc ergo propter hoc* ("with this, therefore because of this") fallacy. Again, some scientific studies do not distinguish between covariance and causation. Recall the recently mentioned study that established a correlation between myopia and sleeping with the lights on. Children who go to sleep with the lights on do so primarily because their *parents* leave the lights on because *they* are more likely to be myopic than parents who do not leave the lights on. Again, even if a study does distinguish between covariance and causation, it may not be able to distinguish between one thing causing another and the other causing the one. For example, periodontal disease correlates with heart artery plaque, but it is not clear which comes first in the causal order. Finally, even if a study does distinguish between covariance and causation and even if it establishes a causal order, there may be a *third variable* that causes both of the correlated variables. A frequently cited example is the correlation noted in Chapter 9 between increased human births and stork nestings in Copenhagen after the conclusion of the Second World War. Neither caused the other – a population influx to Copenhagen after the Second World War caused both additional human births and construction of additional buildings on which storks nested.

Were there no neural correlates of consciousness, neuroimaging and neuropsychological studies would just be wrong-headed. And were correlations between conscious events and activity in neural assemblies all that could ever be taken from neuroimaging studies and neuropsychology, both would be huge disappointments, for neural correlates of a conscious property are used to warrant the stronger claims that they are substrates or realizers of the property. What we are typically looking for are multiple neural conditions, each individually necessary and together conjointly sufficient for a conscious property's instantiation. Adopting this approach makes the neuroimaging and neuropsychological literature tractable. Neuropsychological studies provide a way to identify individually necessary correlates of conscious properties. Neuroimaging studies provide almost real-time indirect measurements of widespread ongoing neural activity that more or less correlates with, and so provides evidence that there are neural substrates of, ongoing conscious perceptual, interoceptive, affective and cognitive processes. These findings help identify the correlates that, when put together, are sufficient for conscious property instantiation.

It is tempting to infer from the correlation between some compromised conscious property and some localized neural assembly damage that activity in the *un*damaged neural assembly is alone responsible for the conscious property's uncompromised instantiation. However, although the conscious property may be compromised when a particular neural assembly is insulted or lesioned, it is more likely that the properly functioning neural assembly is not itself enough for the conscious property's instantiation. An analogy may help. Suppose there are three balls *a*, *b* and *c*, one in each of three rooms, *A*, *B* and *C*. The balls are supported two feet above floor by a latticework of a thousand ropes, all knotted together in relatively disordered ways, some of which extend through all the rooms, some of which occur only in one and some only in two rooms. Suppose I cut rope 134 in room *A* and that cut results in rope 785 in Room *C* losing so much tension that *c* falls off the rope lattice under it. Ropes 134 and 785 are then necessary for *c* to remain suspended, but, since *c* relies not only on them but also on other ropes in Room *C* to remain suspended (*c* is not held in place only by them), neither rope 134 nor rope 785 are sufficient for *c*'s being and remaining suspended.

Compare visual experience. It is well established that visual experience lapses when the thalamus or V1 are lesioned or otherwise compromised. That shows that without something that happens in the thalamus and V1, visual experience does not occur. Yet even if a lesioned thalamus or V1 is sufficient for the cessation of visual experience, by itself that does not show that what happens in the thalamus or V1 is sufficient for the activation or maintenance of visual experience. Much less does it make the thalamus or V1 the brain's vision centre. After all, there are assemblies and pathways later in the causal chain – unimodal regions in occipital cortex, heteromodal visual associative regions in occipito-temporal cortex, supramodal associative regions in prefrontal cortex, and certain of the white matter tracts connecting them – without which visual experience also does not occur. So thalamus, V1 and those other assemblies are each causally necessary but individually insufficient for visual experience (Rees *et al.* 2002 make this point as well).

As with perception, so too with interoception, proprioception, affection and cognition. Neuropsychological studies establish that acute confusion results from lesions of the thalamus, caudate, temporal cortex and internal capsule. AD/HD results from dysfunction in the smaller splenium of the corpus callosum, the caudate nucleus and globus padillus, VLPFC, and low synaptic levels of dopamine and norepinephrine. Anterograde and retrograde amnesias result from damage to the hippocampus, immediately adjacent temporal cortex, the medial thalamus and bilateral DLPFC. Frontal disinhibition syndrome results from damaged left orbitofrontal cortex, and frontal abulic syndrome from left DLPFC damage. Each of these neuropsychological explanations explains deficits to conscious experience by identifying neural assemblies whose dysfunction results in certain conscious properties being either compromised, subject to flickering, or altogether non-existent. But for all these processes, establishing that activity in a particular neural assembly is necessary for some conscious process to occur or for some conscious property to be instantiated does not imply that that activity is *all* that is necessary for that conscious process to occur or conscious property to be instantiated. There are probably dozens of similar causally necessary conditions. Hence, only a complete set of them qualifies as a sufficient condition for the conscious property to be instantiated.

In short, neuropsychological disorders identify a suite of necessary conditions for a conscious property's instantiation, but they are not alone enough to identify the assembly or pathway with which some conscious property correlates and so are not alone enough for identifying the minimal sufficient condition for that property's instantiation. What would establish a minimal sufficient condition is an exhaustive set of intrusive procedures designed to determine the interplay between each of the necessary conditions. It would be a huge, grotesquely invasive undertaking that will probably never be started.

Of course, it is important not to underemphasize the role that neuropsychological research plays either. The necessary causal conditions that neuropsychological studies discover are essential for moving beyond neural correlates to neural substrates and realizers of conscious properties. First, establishing necessary causal conditions for conscious property instantiation is important because a substrate covaries with a conscious property instantiation as a matter of scientific law, which immediately narrows research into the minimal sufficient causal condition of conscious property instantiation to already established neural substrates. Since a conscious property is not instantiated without a correlating neural assembly property that is also a substrate, the search for the neural assembly properties whose instantiation is sufficient for conscious property instantiation need extend no further than the neural assemblies identified by neuropsychological research (Rees *et al.* 2002). There may not be a neural realizer, of course, but neural substrates are the only candidates for one if there is.

Correlates and substrates

Not all correlates of conscious properties are substrates of those conscious properties. Yet conscious properties, events, states and processes reduce to their neural correlates only if correlates are neural substrates. What then is required for a correlate to qualify as a substrate? Informally, a neural substrate of some conscious property, state, process or event is a neural property, state, process or event *in virtue of which* a conscious property is instantiated, or *in virtue of which* a conscious event, state or process occurs.

One interpretation of the slippery phrase "in virtue of" is that such talk makes a causal claim. For example, one token event e occurs in virtue of another token event c occurring whenever c causes e, and a property G is instantiated in virtue of property F being instantiated whenever F's instantiation causes G's instantiation. Finding the neural substrates of conscious properties would then amount to discovering the neural causes of their instantiation. But this is not what most have in mind when they claim that neural events, states and processes are substrates of conscious events, states and processes. After all, this way of interpreting "in virtue of" is consistent with substance dualism – conscious events could occur in virtue of neural events and neural events could occur in virtue of conscious events even if conscious events were events of a soul and neural events were events of a particular neural assembly. This way of interpreting "in virtue of" is also consistent with the most robust forms of property dualism – conscious events could occur in virtue of neural events and neural events in virtue of conscious events even if all the properties that make conscious events conscious are of a distinct ontological category from any of the physical properties that make their neural causes physical events.

The phrase "in virtue of" is typically understood as making a different claim, one inconsistent with dualism. On this way of looking at the matter, neural correlates are important because they provide empirical evidence that conscious properties are implemented or constituted by properties of neural processes, events and states. If a neural correlate of a conscious property is also a neural substrate of that conscious property being instantiated, then the following is true:

(NSC)   A neural correlate N of a conscious event type C is a neural substrate of C if and only if there is a minimal neural event type, N, correlated with C, such that it is a scientific law that a being is in C if and only if it is in N.

The properties instantiated by C are conscious properties; those instantiated by N are neural properties. Conscious events of which (NSC) are true then have neural substrates. This is a near-standard way to understand what a neural substrate of a conscious property is (cf. Chalmers 2000; Block 2007a). (NSC) is broad enough to leave it open whether the neural event type involves a single neuron, a small family of neurons, a layer of neurons, a neural assembly larger than a layer, a pathway larger than an assembly, a structure of numerous neural assemblies or pathways, a region of the brain, the entire brain, or the entire central nervous system. It is also broad enough to leave it open whether the neural property is a quantum property, an electrochemical one such as spiking rate, a neurochemical one such as signalling, a computational one such as connection weight, activation level, or activation pattern, or indeed something else altogether.

As a biconditional, (NSC) is composed of a necessary condition:

(NSC)$_N$ For every conscious event type, C, there is a minimal neural event type, N, correlated with C, such that it is a scientific law that if a being is in C, then it is in N.

and a sufficiency condition:

(NSC)$_S$ For every conscious event type, C, there is a minimal neural event type, N, correlated with C such that it is a scientific law that if a being is in N, then it is in C.

Just as the indiscernibility of identicals establishes what is necessary for identity and what is sufficient for establishing when two things are distinct, (NSC)$_N$ establishes what is necessary for a neural correlate to be a substrate and what is sufficient for denying that a correlate is a substrate. If more than one type of neural event covaries with a given type of conscious event, that is, if conscious event types are multiply realized, then (NSC)$_N$ is not satisfied. Indeed, if multiple realization is true across individuals of a species and across times in an individual, the scope of the scientific laws mentioned in (NSC)$_N$ sharpens to a point: a token neural substrate n for a token conscious event c in a particular individual x's brain at a particular time t (Bickle 1998). But then all the neuroimaging work hardly seems worth the effort or the millions of dollars spent on an MRI machine. Such arguments, if sound, show that there is no scientific law that binds together the heterogeneous neural correlates across persons, across times, or across species and, hence, that conscious properties are anomalous. We consider such arguments shortly.

Another argument against neural substrates is that, in order for a correlation between some neural event type N and a conscious event type C to be backed by scientific law, there must be some shared property between N and C. But, it is claimed, there is no such shared property. So even if N correlates with C, that is all it will ever do. Here is a version of the argument. Consider a perceptual experience, the multimodal perceptual experience of watching, smelling and listening to a malodorous black bear stripping a blueberry bush of its fruit twenty feet away. If the properties of the neural assemblies that correlate with such an experience are also neural substrates of the content of that perceptual experience, that perceptual experience with that content must as a matter of scientific law correlate with some neural assembly activity that has such and such properties. But that implies that the content of the former must match the content of the latter. That is, a conscious experience has a neural substrate only if there is by scientific law some neural assembly whose activity has as its content the same content as that of the conscious experience. Suppose so. Still, if there are properties of the conscious content that the neural content lacks or properties of the neural content that the conscious content lacks, then the contents do not match. And surely there are properties of the conscious content of experiencing the bear that the neural content lacks. Naming such a property seems to be easy: subjective perspectivity is a property that the conscious content of my experiencing the bear has but which does not appear to characterize the activity of any neural assembly, regardless of complexity, that co-occurs with that conscious experience (Noë and Thompson [2004a] state the argument and provide references to neuroscientific studies that appear to assume it).

A well-known candidate for visual neural content, receptive field content (RF content), shows that neural assembly properties lack subjective perspectivity. The RF content of a neural assembly is the preferential spiking or firing rate of an assembly when presented with certain kinds of visual input rather than with certain other kinds of visual input. But RF content is not subjectively perspectival. Noë and Thompson put the matter succinctly:

> RF-content lacks the sort of perspectival self-consciousness that is
> the hallmark of perceptual experience .... [W]e do not understand
> how a neural representational system could have this sort of content.
> Indeed, it is difficult to see how anything other than a whole perceiver
> as an intentional agent could be the bearer of this sort of content.
>
> (Noë & Thompson 2004b: 90–91)

The point is generalizable: since the content of *all* conscious experience is subjectively perspectival and the content of *no* neural event is subjectively per-spectival – no matter how far along on the chain of processing it appears – the activity in neural assemblies that co-occurs with and correlates with a conscious event does not have the same content as the conscious event's content. Hence, given the matching content requirement, the neural activity that correlates with and narrowly subserves conscious experience is not its neural substrate. Since having a neural realizer is necessary for reduction, the neural reduction of sub-jective perspectivity fails.

Parallel arguments establish a similar conclusion for the cases of intentional-ity and qualitative character. Hence, in general, since having neural substrates is necessary for reduction and neural correlates of conscious properties are not their neural substrates, the neural reduction of consciousness fails. Of course, if either it is *not* a requirement that the neural event and the conscious event share a property or if there is some property that *is* shared, then this kind of argument collapses and correlation research is safeguarded against the threat. We consider such arguments in Chapter 11.

SUBSTRATES AND REALIZERS

Even if a neural event is a substrate of a conscious event, (NSC) does not estab-lish everything required for a conscious event to reduce to its neural substrate, which is just to say that being a (NSC) neural substrate is not sufficient for being a neural realizer. For, the covariation between conscious and neural events, states, and processes backed by scientific laws and described by (NSC) does not estab-lish that the causal powers of the latter are sufficient for those of the former. After all, not all scientific laws are laws about causal powers. Hence, there is a gap between being a neural substrate and a neural realizer. Note the echoes from supervenience. Just as supervenience ties supervenient conscious events down to their subvening basal events *via* a particular kind of covariance relation, so (NSC) ties conscious events down to their neural substrate events *via* scientific law, but just as supervenience is not sufficient for reduction, so (NSC) is not sufficient for reduction.

Realization, implementation and constitutive sufficiency

Realization is a central concept in contemporary philosophical arguments about reduction in general and hence about the reduction of conscious properties in particular. So long as it is accepted that if X is realized by Y, then X reduces to Y, the balance falls out neatly: first, show that a higher-order something correlates with some lower-order something and that correlation is evidence that the lower-order something is a substrate of the higher-order something; second, argue that being a substrate is, in conjunction with other requirements, sufficient for being a realizer; third, having gained realization, point out that the higher-order something inherits all of its causal powers from its realizer substrate. Since by hypothesis causal inheritance is sufficient for reduction, the higher-order something reduces to the realizing substrate, and there is nothing more to the former than the latter.

Recall from Chapter 2 that realization is the conjunction of two claims. According to the *functionalization thesis*, an instantiation of a functionalized supervening property is instantiation of a subvening property that satisfies a certain causal profile. According to the *causal inheritance thesis*, if a functionalized supervening property is instantiated in virtue of one of its subvening properties being instantiated at that time, the causal powers of the former are identical to the causal powers of the latter. The subvening property with that causal profile is that supervenient's *realizer*, and where a supervenient property has a realizer, the former's causal powers are identical to, and thus sufficient for, the latter's causal powers. The causal powers of a functionalized supervenient property thus reduce to those of its realizer(s).

Neuroscientific models of consciousness propose that the neural correlates of conscious properties are either *vehicles*, such as neurons and neural assemblies, or *processes*, such as particular kinds of electrochemical activity in and across neurons and neural assemblies. If a vehicle or a process is to qualify as a candidate realizer of a conscious property, two conditions must then be satisfied. First, the vehicle or process must be a substrate, which is to say that the instantiation of a conscious property covaries either with that vehicle or that process as a matter of scientific law. Second, the causal powers of either the vehicle or the process must be identical to the causal powers of that conscious property. Where both conditions obtain, the neural vehicle or neural process *implements* the conscious property. In general, X is implemented by Y – Y implements X – whenever the existence of Y is constitutively sufficient for the existence of X (Shoemaker 2007). So, for example, where being an artificial light source is a higher-order property and the flow of certain kinds of electrons across an enclosed vacuum implements that property, that flow of electrons across an enclosed vacuum is constitutively sufficient for the instantiation of being an artificial light source. What, then, is *constitutive sufficiency*? Sufficiency at least is clear enough: in general, if one thing is sufficient for another, then if you have got the first, then you are going to have the second. Constitution is another matter. For our purposes, it is enough to say that X is constituted by Y – Y constitutes X – whenever X is exhaustively composed of Y or whenever X consists in nothing but Y. So, where one property Y of a thing is constitutionally sufficient for another property X of that thing, that thing's instantiation of X is exhaustively composed of that thing's instantiation of Y.

Examples of implementation are easy to find. A diesel engine mechanically implements, and so realizes, being an internal combustion engine. A flow of a set of charged electrons of a certain kind across an enclosed vacuum electrically implements, and so realizes, being a fluorescent light source. Transmission of light rays through an eye to the brain optically implements, and so realizes, being a sensory transduction device for wavelengths of light. Synaptic neurotransmitter activity is an electrochemical implementation of, and so realizes, being an information transmission device. All these realizing implementations are not just tokens of a functional type; their existence is constitutionally sufficient for the existence or instantiation of the type. Of course, some types are multiply implemented, and some are singly implemented. For multiply implemented functional types, such as being an internal combustion engine, there are distinct physical properties whose instantiations are individually constitutionally sufficient for the functional type. And each of the distinct physical property's causal powers are alone sufficient for the causal powers of an instance of the functional type. On the other hand, for singly implemented functional types, such as being a fluorescent light source, there is only one physical property whose instantiation is constitutionally sufficient for the functional type. Fluorescent lights may have different chemical elements – argon, xenon, neon or krypton – in the tube, but the property of each that realizes being a fluorescent light source is the same across the elements.

Recall again the theses of reduction and neuroreduction of consciousness from Chapter 2. The first, (RPC), claims that:

> Physical events or parts thereof exhaust everything that is concrete, and there is a supervenience relation between all conscious properties and microphysical properties such that subvening microphysical properties are always the only realizers of supervening conscious properties.

The special case of neural reduction, as expressed by (NR), claims that:

> Physical events or parts thereof exhaust everything that is concrete, and there is a supervenience relation between all families of conscious properties and microphysical properties of neural assembly activity such that subvening microphysical properties of neural assembly activity are always the only realizers of supervening conscious properties.

Both (RPC) and (NR) are typical examples of what is known as *microphysical reduction*. On microphysical reductionist accounts, properties from a supervening family are *higher-order* functionalized systemic properties of complex wholes, while properties from the subvening family are *lower-order* realizing properties of that whole's simpler microphysical parts (where we have scientific theories about the two orders of property families and the two orders of entities, the higher-order theory reduces to the lower-order theory because the latter theory replaces the former theory). Microphysical reductionism about conscious properties insists that for every supervening conscious property, there is a set of microphysical properties of neural assemblies that are their only realizers. Any property other than a microphysical property of some neural assembly that claims to be the realizer of a conscious property instead earns its causal keep only through the good graces of that neural microphysical property.

With implementation added to the toolbox, something that is only implicit in (RPC) and (NR) can be made explicit. When a mechanism or process implements a higher-order property, what instantiates the realized property is not always what instantiates the realizing property. In some kinds of property realization, what instantiates both the realized higher-order property and the realizing lower-order property is the same thing, but in microphysical reduction, what instantiates the realized higher-order property is not what instantiates the realizing lower-order property or properties. Instantiation of a higher-order property by a big thing – a macroentity – may be realized by instantiation of a lower-order property by a smaller thing or group of smaller things. The lower-order property of that smaller thing or group of smaller things may in turn be realized by instantiation of another even lower-order property by still smaller things or groups of smaller things, and so on until we reach the smallest things – microentities – and groups of them. So, for example, a bird's being able to fly is realized by its wings having a certain lift-to-drag (L/D) ratio. Being a wing with a certain L/D ratio is in turn realized by groups of feathers being structured in a particular shape, a muscular structure that facilitates their synchronized movement, hollow bones, and so on. Being a bone is in turn realized by a complex structure of bone tissue, marrow, blood vessels, epithelium and nerves. Being bone tissue is realized by osseous tissue. Being osseous tissue is realized by collagen and calcium phosphate cells in a particular lattice structure. This process iterates until basic microphysical particles and their properties are reached. (NR) proposes that this general view is applicable to conscious properties; (NR) opponents reject this general view about conscious properties. We return to this issue shortly.

Core, total and differential realizers

Even the most ardent neural reductionists and type identity theorists will agree that neuroimaging and neuropsychological studies need to distinguish between coincidentally active neural assemblies and reliably and predictably active neural assemblies. (That is part of the worry behind the concerns of Kriegeskorte and Vul, discussed in Chapter 9). Only those neural assemblies that are reliably and predictably active are plausible candidate correlates of particular conscious cognitive, perceptual, affective, proprioceptive and interoceptive processes. But partitioning the coincidental from the reliable and predictable is not enough for differential between correlates that are necessary for those conscious processes and those that are sufficient for those processes. Nor is it enough to distinguish those correlates that are enabling conditions of conscious processes from those correlates that are their substrates.

Philosophers have been particularly alert to these gaps and have suggested that a distinction between core and total neural realizers be introduced. The root distinction is between core and total realizers. A *core realizer* of some property *P* is a property whose instantiation is a salient component of a total realizer, and a *total realizer* of a property *P* is a property whose instantiation is the minimal realizer sufficient for the instantiation of *P*. With that distinction in mind, core and total realizers of conscious properties can be provided. A *core neural realizer* of a conscious property *C* is a neural property *N* whose instantiation is a salient component of a total neural realizer, and a *total neural realizer* of a conscious property *C* is that *N* whose instantiation is the minimal neural realizer sufficient for the instantiation of *C* (Shoemaker 1996a, 1996b, 2007). Block (2007a) requires that a core neural realizer be that part of a total neural realizer that distinguishes events with one content or character from another event with distinct content or character. We shall instead refer to such a realizer as a *differential neural realizer*.

Parallel distinctions can be drawn between differential, core and total substrates and between differential, core and total correlates. Thus, a *core neural substrate* of a conscious property *C* is a neural property *N* whose instantiation is a salient component of a total neural substrate; a *total neural substrate* of a conscious property is that *N* whose instantiation is such that *N* and *C* covary as a matter of scientific law; and a *differential neural substrate* of a conscious property *C* is a neural property *N* whose instantiation is that part of a total neural substrate that distinguishes events with one content or character from another event with distinct content or character. Likewise, a *core neural correlate* of a conscious property *C* is a neural property *N* whose instantiation is a salient component of a total neural correlate; *a total neural correlate* of a conscious property *C* is that *N* whose instantiation is the minimal neural condition such that *N* reliably correlates with *C*; and a *differential neural correlate* of a conscious property *C* is a neural property *N* whose instantiation is that part of a total neural correlate that distinguishes events with one content or character from another event with distinct content or character.

Core, total and differential neural correlates of conscious processes and properties can be used to determine core, total and differential neural substrates and realizers of particular conscious processes and properties. There may be, for example, numerous core neural correlates for a conscious process or property, the set of which constitutes the total neural correlate of that process or property. Likewise, differential neural correlates provide the evidentiary backing to determine which, if any, of them are also differential neural substrates and differential neural realizers, and which are instead core but not differential substrates and realizers. Using the core/total distinction to organize meta-analyses of neuroimaging studies thus assists researchers to zoom in on what is crucial for instantiating conscious properties and to distinguish what is crucial for instantiating those properties from what is adventitious background noise or necessary enabling conditions.

Deploying these distinctions has barely begun in neuroscience. Despite having a long way to go, we can predict how the project will be carried out: the necessary meta-analytic work will be done, requisite follow-up studies undertaken, experiments performed and replicated, and some years down the road it will turn out that there is a huge number of confirmed distinct core, differential and total neural correlates of distinct conscious processes and properties. All those core neural correlates would be good evidence for establishing beyond a reasonable doubt that the activities of certain neural assemblies are core neural substrates of certain conscious processes and properties. It would be an extraordinary accomplishment for neuroscience. But it would still not be enough for reducing conscious properties to their neural substrates because there are arguments that allow that there are core neural substrates, and even that there are core and differential realizers of conscious properties, but deny that any neural substrate is ever a total substrate of conscious properties and hence deny that any neural substrate is ever a total realizer of conscious properties. We investigate these arguments in Chapters 11 and 12.

MULTIPLE REALIZATION OF CONSCIOUS PROPERTIES

In an earlier chapter, the multiple *realizability* argument against reductive physicalism was rejected. But the multiple *realization* argument – the argument that purports to show that conscious properties are in fact multiply realized across species, individuals or times – was left unanalysed there. Multiple realization purports to establish that there is an actual difference in the physical properties that realize a given conscious property across species, across individuals of a species, or across times in an individual. The multiple realization advocate must demonstrate that the physical property realizing a conscious property in one case is distinct from the physical property that realizes the same conscious property in another case. That can be accomplished only by appealing to empirical evidence. Having surveyed some of that evidence, it may appear that the prospects here look bright, for evolution and interindividual variability appear to guarantee that many higher-order psychological properties are and will continue to be multiply realized across species and across individuals of a species. The challenge appears to be not which candidate might satisfy the requirements of multiple realization, but which of the many obvious candidates to choose. However, even if inter-species and interindividual multiple realization is true for some psychological properties, the properties that subserve conscious properties are not obviously multiply realized, either across species, across individuals, or across times.

Interspecies multiple realization of conscious properties

The appearance and sustenance of brains capable of producing experience with conscious properties and their peculiarities must be consistent with natural selection, and explanations of conscious properties must likewise comply with the constraints imposed by natural selection on the kind of psychologies and the kind of brains that can evolve (Shapiro 2004). An obvious constraint is that the brain is an organ in a living being, an organ that works certain input up into per-ception, proprioception and interoception, and makes that available to affection and cognition. Another constraint is that even if the human brain and human psychology are, as it appears, unique in nature, we can and should expect a range of similar neural and psychological properties across related species. That there are such similarities across species provides inductive support for thinking that neurons, neural assemblies and their activity provide the most likely crucible for the emergence of conscious events and properties. That in turn supports reject-ing proposals that try to reduce conscious events and properties to anything more fundamental than neurons, neural assemblies and their activity.

Evolution stamps itself on organisms by natural selection, which starts work-ing as soon as there are organisms – that is, reproducing entities – to act on. Generally speaking, natural selection does not give a jot about the molecular or cellular structures that subvene phenotypes unless those structures are them-selves phenotypes on which natural selection acts or they are required for the phenotypes on which natural selection acts. So long as a phenotype has benefi-cial consequences for an organism's survival to reproduction age, then the genes that code for the phenotype will be selected for without attention to implemen-tation. So, for many kinds of phenotypes the complex cellular and molecular structures that subvene the phenotype are evolutionarily irrelevant. Natural selection's routine indifference towards cellular and molecular structure does not mean that multiple realization is guaranteed, but once that indifference is coupled with mutation and genetic drift, multiple realization is highly probable. Since many of the cellular and molecular structures that result from mutation and genetic drift make absolutely no difference to the organism's survivability to reproduction age even if they subvene functional phenotypic properties that do make such a difference, such cellular and molecular structures are opaque to evolutionary forces and diversify readily. Sufficient mutations and enough genetic drift are likely to produce different cellular and molecular structures subvening the same functional phenotypic property. In this way, mutation and genetic drift are mechanisms of multiple realization.

Given natural selection, independent evolution of similar phenotypes and the genotypes coding for them should be expected, and, indeed, the phenomenon is sufficiently widespread that there is a name for it: *convergent evolution*. Convergent evolution occurs when the same evolutionarily functional phenotype develops across separate genotypes. Such phenotypes are *analogous* phenotypes in distinct lineages. There is a parallel phenomenon within lineages. *Non-convergent evolution* occurs when the same evolutionarily functional phenotype develops across species in a single lineage. Such phenotypes are *homologous* phenotypes (Shapiro 2004). An obvious example of convergent evolution, and so an obvious candidate for interspecies multiple realization, is self-propelled flight. Self-propelled flight is tokened in a huge variety of ways in at least two separate *phyla* (insects and vertebrates), numerous *classes* of insects, three *classes* of vertebrates (birds, bats and fish) and thousands of *species* (most of them flying beetles). Moreover, airplanes, helicopters and zeppelins provide handy non-organic tokens of self-propelled flying machines as well.

Even if most of the organic instances are of homologous evolution from a common ancestor, neither insects and vertebrates, nor birds, bats and fish evolved from a common flying ancestor. Surely here, if anywhere, there is multiple realization. Yet, self-propelled flight is not multiply realized simply because bats, beetles, band-wing flying fish, blackbirds and B1 bombers all fly. Recall, multiple realization of a functional property occurs only when there is more than one physical property realizing it. A key question is, then, what physical property realizes self-propelled flight? If the domain is both natural and artificial flyers, it includes planes, helicopters and zeppelins, the first of which use wings to achieve lift, but the latter two of which use, respectively, high-speed rotors and lighter-than-air gases to achieve lift. Hence, if our domain is animals and these artificial self-propelled flyers, self-propelled flight is multiply realized. But at least to my knowledge, no flying animal uses high-speed rotors or lighter-than-air gases to achieve lift. They all use wings. If so, then self-propelled flight is not multiply realized in animals. (While it is true that flying squirrels do not have wings, they do not fly either – they glide.)

Having a wing is one candidate for the physical property that realizes self-propelled flight. But it is not the only candidate. Another candidate is that it is a wing's property of L/D ratio, a measurement of the amount of lift generated by a wing divided by the drag the wing creates by moving through the air. If so, then an L/D ratio in a particular range is an aerodynamic realizer of being a wing. So long as bats, beetles, band-wing fish and blackbirds all realize flying by having wings with an L/D ratio in that range, each realizes flight in the same way. Hence, again, animal flight is not multiply realized (Shapiro 2004).

Another candidate is that the properties that bestow their causal powers are instead the structural properties of the wing. So, L/D ratio, while the physical property that realizes the functional property of flying from the perspective of aerodynamics, is in turn a functional property from the perspective of another science, and, as such, is itself realized because there is at least one, perhaps more than one, property that realizes that ratio. In birds, L/D ratio is realized in a lattice of feathers, in bats it is realized in a sheet of skin, in a beetle it is realized in extensions of exoskeleton. So from the perspective of physiology, the property of L/D ratio is a functional property that is multiply realized in distinct physiological structures.

Compare flying properties with conscious properties. The occurrence of conscious events and conscious properties is overwhelmingly likely in multiple mammalian species (Seth *et al.* 2005). If so, what must be established to show that conscious properties and events are multiply realized across these species is that the physical properties from which those conscious properties inherit their causal powers differ across the species in which they occur. And to confirm that this is so, there is no substitute for comparative neuroanatomy, comparative neurophysiology, comparative cognitive science and comparative affective neuroscience. It might turn out that birds, for example, are qualitatively conscious and that the qualitative character of their visual experience is realized in a physiological structure distinct from that in us that realizes qualitative character. We do not have sufficient comparative evidence to know whether this hypothesis is true. However, given our homologous evolution from other primates, it is unlikely that these qualitative properties are differently subserved in any of the species in the phylogenetic line leading directly to us. "It is unlikely" – here again such claims can be confirmed only with relevant comparative evidence (Allman *et al.* 2002; Arbib 2001; Matsuzawa *et al.* 2006; Mithen 2007; Oxnard 2004).

Of course, our kind of conscious experience may have qualitative properties that differ from the qualitative features found in the experience of every other primate species; likewise, their conscious experience may have qualitative properties that our experience lacks. In such cases, interspecies multiple realization is moot. Since, in the first case, we are the only species whose experience has the property, there is no obligation to determine whether it is realized by different physical properties in another species. The relevant issue is, rather, whether homologous precursors to the conscious properties unique to us, if any, are found in those other species. Similar points apply to the other case: if bonobos are the only kind of primate to have experience with a particular qualitative property, there is no obligation to determine whether that property is realized by different physical properties in us.

Inter- and intra-individual multiple realization of conscious properties

Even if interspecies multiple realization of conscious properties is not well supported, non-reductive views of conscious properties might still claim support from the multiple realization of conscious properties in persons across times and across persons at a time. But empirical evidence suggests that conscious properties are not multiply realized across individuals at a time or across time in the same individual, as claimed.

Neuroimaging and neuropsychological evidence strongly suggests that *interindividual* multiple realization is false. As a general rule, it simply is not true that conscious processes are subserved by some particular neural assembly activity in one person and different neural assembly activity in another person. There is confirmed commonality on a significant scale across individuals and across a huge assortment of perceptual, interoceptive, affective and cognitive processes, including the neural correlates of qualitative character, subjective perspectivity and intentionality. The same kind of consideration applies to *intraindividual* multiple realization across time. One might think that a conscious property being subserved by activity in one neural assembly, N_1, at one time while being subserved by activity in a distinct neural assembly, N_2, at a different time is evidence of multiple realization. However, it is multiple realization only if the property instantiated by neural activity in N_1 is different from the property instantiated by neural activity in N_2, and, again, that is not something that can be known *a priori* from the philosopher's armchair. Empirical evidence has to confirm or disconfirm the claim. And, again, the neuropsychological and neuroimaging evidence augurs against the claim.

Admittedly, there are relevant differences depending upon whether the neural assembly is modular or non-modular. As noted in Chapter 5, early damage to modular neural assemblies and pathways, such as unimodal perceptual, affective, interoceptive and proprioceptive assemblies and pathways, is usually devastating and long-lasting, whereas comparable damage to the same neural ssemblies later in life need not be devastating or long-lasting. Non-modular assemblies and pathways, such as those in heteromodal and supramodal prefrontal cortical regions, present a different picture. For them, early damage is usually not devastating, whereas late damage often leads to unrecoverable deficits. These differences are directly relevant for interpreting some of the claims made on behalf of neural plasticity and its support for multiple realization.

When neural trauma occurs, some conscious processes migrate from one neural assembly to another such that the same conscious process is subvened by activity in one neural assembly prior to brain trauma and by activity in another neural assembly subsequent to that trauma. Even if true, such plasticity is evidence only that distinct neural assemblies instantiate the same properties that subvene the conscious process; it is not evidence that the same conscious process is realized by different physical properties being instantiated by distinct neural assemblies. Likewise, a single neural assembly can, again as a result of trauma, subvene one conscious process before and another conscious process after trauma (Shapiro 2004, reporting on work by Kaas 2000). Cutting the median nerve in the thumb half of the front portion of a hand causes reorganization of representation of the hand in primary somatosensory cortex. The somatosensory pathways that represented input from the outer and upper surfaces of the thumb and first two fingers before the cut reorganize after the cut to represent input from the inside and lower surfaces of the same thumb and fingers. So, what in those pathways used to represent one thing represents something else subsequent to cutting the median nerve. This is a case of distinct conscious processes being subvened by activity in a single neural assembly, not of a single conscious process being subvened by distinct properties of neural activity. Hence, it is not evidence of multiple realization of a conscious property.

Another kind of support might be thought to come from neural changes that result from becoming an expert. Professional musicians, for example, have more developed neural assemblies in motor pathways controlling executive finger movement than non-professional musicians have, and long-time taxi drivers have enhanced hippocampi in comparison to the rest of the population. While this is evidence for pretty remarkable changes in neural assemblies, it is not evidence for multiple realization. After all, there is a change not just in neural assemblies, but also in the conscious processes themselves: expert taxi drivers know more than the normal person about the streets of their city, and expert musicians have greater and more control of their finger movements than do non-musicians. Since intrapersonal multiple realization requires that a different physical property subserve a single psychological process across times, and since experts differ in both, changes in expert neural assemblies are not evidence for multiple realization. If anything, the neural changes characteristic of these kinds of expertise look like evidence *against* multiple realization of the conscious processes constitutive of expertise by the properties of the neural assemblies subvening the expert capacities.

The case of phantom pains is similar. Most phantoms are experienced as fixed in position (although some move as a result of stimulating different parts of the remaining limb). Qualitatively loaded experiences of moving, grasping, reaching and squeezing accompany phantom hands, and many individuals with recently amputated arms experience as-of hand pain of needles or nails stabbing into the palm of the hand, or the hand being burned or crushed. Phantom limbs and pain might be thought to provide evidence for multiple realization because the neural properties whose instantiation correlates with the instantiation of qualitative pain are gone altogether. But this is mistaken. While the input neural correlates are gone, neural correlates of the qualitative properties of pain and the qualitative properties themselves remain. Since, for example, the input that would have gone to hand areas of somatosensory cortex no longer does so once the hand is amputated, areas in somatosensory cortex nearest the hand areas remap the cortical areas that no longer receive input. A strong correlation exists between phantom pain as-of a hand and activity in the facial area of primary somatosensory cortex, which lies immediately next to hand areas in individuals who still have their hands. Individuals with recently amputated arms and hands report phantom sensory experience in specific fingers when specific regions of their cheeks are touched (Flor *et al.* 1995; Karl *et al.* 2001; Lotze *et al.* 2001). This kind of evidence suggests again that neural assemblies retrofit themselves to subserve conscious qualitative properties of pain experience. Again, this is evidence of multiple realization only if the neural properties whose instantiation migrates are different neural properties than those that originally instantiate pain. And, again, determining whether that is true requires empirical work.

Some of the strongest neuroscientific evidence for intra-individual multiple realization comes from neuropsychological experiments in which, due to severing connections in the pathways of one sensory modality, processing in that modality migrates away from its normal pathway to another pathway normally dedicated to processing input in a different sensory modality. The experiments cited by Shapiro (2004) are done on ferrets. Visual pathways are severed, resulting in rewiring that avoids the damage not by detouring around the damage and reconnecting back to visual pathways further down the line, but by rerouting visual input information entirely away from the inaccessible remainder of visual cortex. The new route goes through auditory cortex. Tests conducted when the ferrets become adults show that some visual discernment abilities, similar to those a blindsight individual might have, are preserved as a result of such rewiring. Here there appears to be multiple realization of visual processes, for the same psychological process is at least partially realized by distinct neural properties, the first visual neural types, the second retrofitted auditory neural types.

Yet scepticism may be appropriate even here. First, the visual function subvened by retrofitted auditory cortex is seriously impoverished when compared to that subvened by dedicated visual cortex. Second, the structural organization of auditory cortex that subvenes these impoverished visual processes changes from that found in dedicated auditory cortex to become more like that found in dedicated visual cortex (Shapiro 2004). If so, the same process is *not* subvened by distinct neural properties, and to the extent that the *same* visual process *is* subvened by auditory cortex after visual cortex is rendered useless, it is only because auditory cortex structure reorganizes to replicate visual cortex structure. If so, then if it is that structure rather than cortical location that is the property subvening the psychological process, the same process is not subvened by different properties.

Showing that half a dozen attempts to support multiple realization of processes that also happen to be conscious are unsuccessful does not constitute a knock-down argument against inter- or intra-individual multiple realization of conscious properties. No doubt other studies exist, and future studies may yet confirm inter- or intraspecies multiple realization of some processes or some of their conscious properties. So more scientific work specifically focused on qualia, intentionality and subjective perspectivity is required to determine whether their neural correlates can be teased apart from the neural correlates of the processes whose properties they are (see the interview with Vittorio Gallese in Metzinger 2009a, who makes a similar point). This much at least is true: getting the multiple realization argument to stick anywhere requires looking at the empirical evidence and having one's philosophical conclusions directed by that evidence. Philosophical reflection alone cannot show that multiple realization is true and so cannot show that conscious properties are not realized by physical properties.

Multiple realization and higher/lower order and macro/micro level cross-classification

For years multiple realization arguments have stood as bulwarks against the tides of reduction. One of the reasons these arguments have been so attractive is that scepticism about attributing higher-order conscious properties to the little things or groups of little things that instantiate a realizing lower-order property is relatively easy to generate. After all, some of the features of higher-order properties appear not to be features that the realizing lower-order property(ies) can have. For example, it can seem bizarre to attribute the reflexive loops of subjective self-reflection, or the nuances of enjoying the sound of Sonny Rollin's saxophone tone to electrochemical or microphysical properties of neurons and assemblies of them.

Multiple realization arguments are not as persuasive as they appear. Reductionist advocates need not attribute a higher-order property that a big thing instantiates to a little thing or groups of little things that instantiate the realizing lower-order property or properties in order for the former to reduce to the latter. Reductionists claim instead that the lower-order properties that the little things or groups of little things instantiate is all there is to the higher-order property that the big thing instantiates. Whatever residue of the higher-order property is left over can be eliminated as epiphenomenal. Consider a higher-order property of olfactory qualitative character instantiated by an experience that a conscious subject has and the property proposed as its total realizer. The total realizer is some microphysical property of biochemical activity, or some activation level, or some spiking rate of some complex neural assembly in orbitofrontal cortex. Reductionists need not claim that instantiation of the qualitative property by the subject is identical to the instantiation of some microphysical property instantiated by neural assembly activity in orbitofrontal cortex. Rather, they hold that there is nothing more to the former than the latter, that instantiation of the olfactory qualitative property by the subject is exhaustively constituted by instantiation of the microphysical property of the orbitofrontal neural assembly activity.

Whatever residue to the macroproperty there might be that is not captured by the microproperties of orbitofrontal neural assembly activity is eliminable because it is epiphenomenal.

Of course, the burden falls on the reductionist to demonstrate that the residue not captured by the lower-order properties *is* epiphenomenal. But since it is not just conscious properties that are subject to reduction – since, that is, *all* higher-order properties are realized by and so are reducible to microphysical properties – the properties studied by every science other than microphysics inherit their causal powers from those of the microphysical properties on which they supervene. This is as true for chemical properties as it is for conscious properties. Although every science quantifies over entities and describes properties in its own unique vocabulary and designs experiments using its own unique methods, the causal powers of any properties other than microphysical properties are inherited entirely from the causal powers of microphysical properties.

Microphysical reductionists and antimicrophysical non-reductionists and emergentists regularly share the assumption that there are discrete *levels* of property and entity families and that each level occupies a niche in a hierarchy of sciences, each science devoted to studying a property family and entity family at a given level (Oppenheim & Putnam 1958). Although there is nothing necessary about putting matters this way, it is undeniable that one image that immediately comes to mind when supervenience, multiple realization, reduction and emergence are discussed is going up and down a scale of levels. This image is as applicable across a wide array of otherwise distinct views.

Unfortunately, the concept of level is vexed (Hardcastle 1992; Kim 2003, 2005). Microphysical reductionism actually works along two dimensions, the higher-order/lower-order functional–realizer dimension and the higher-level/lower-level macro–micro dimension. Both dimensions help underwrite reduction. When the functional property–realizer property relation takes the lead, we get a distinction between higher-order properties and lower-order properties, that is, a distinction between a property of a property and a property. For example, the property of being a wing is a property that some structures with a particular L/D ratio have and some structures do not. When, on the other hand, the macro–micro dimension takes the lead, the distinction will be between higher-level properties that are properties of big things composed of parts, such as an internal combustion engine, and lower-level properties that are properties of one or more of the smaller things, such as camshafts or valve lifters, that are the big thing's constituents.

On the first way of looking at things, a hierarchy of conscious properties looks like this: my conscious hunger, for example, supervenes on certain properties of my neural assembly activity; those neural properties supervene on certain biochemical properties; those biochemical properties supervene on certain chemical and electrical properties; those chemical and electrical properties supervene on certain atomic-physical properties; and those atomic properties supervene on certain subatomic microphysical properties. On the other way of looking at the matter, my conscious hunger supervenes on certain properties of neural assemblies in particular regions of my brain; those neural pathway properties supervene on certain properties of the neural assemblies that compose the neural pathways; those assembly properties supervene on properties of the cells that compose the neural assemblies; those cellular properties supervene on certain properties of the molecules that compose the cells; those molecular properties supervene on certain properties of the atoms that compose the molecules; and those atomic properties supervene on the microphysical properties of the subatomic particles that compose the atoms.

Were the two hierarchies to mesh seamlessly, the result might look like this:

FUNCTIONALIZED MACRO-LEVEL F:
    My conscious hunger H

F_{-1} LEVEL: My conscious hunger H supervenes on neurological properties N_1 ... N_n of neural pathways p_1 ... p_n localized in brain region R.

F_{-2} LEVEL: Neurological properties N_1 ... N_n of p_1 ... p_n supervene on biochemical properties B_1 ... B_n of the neural assemblies a_1 ... a_n that compose p_1 ... p_n.

F_{-3} LEVEL: Biochemical properties B_1 ... B_n of neural assemblies a_1 ... a_n supervene on chemical properties C_1 ... C_n, and electrical properties E_1 ... E_n of cells c_1 ... c_n that compose a_1 ... a_n.

F_{-4} LEVEL: Chemical properties C_1 ... C_n, and electrical properties E_1 ... E_n of cells c_1 ... c_n supervene on chemical properties C_1 ... C_n, and electrical properties E_1 ... E_n of molecules m_1 ... m_n that compose c_1 ... c_n.

F_{-5} LEVEL: Chemical properties C_1 ... C_n, and electrical properties E_1 ... E_n of molecules m_1 ... m_n supervene on atomic-physical properties P_1 ... P_n of atoms t_1 ... t_n that compose m_1 ... m_n.

REALIZER MICROLEVEL R:
    Atomic-physical properties P_1 ... P_n of atoms t_1 ... t_n supervene on microphysical properties M_1 ... M_n of subatomic particles x_1 ... x_n that compose t_1 ... t_n.

It is a tidy picture. But it is a little too tidy.

The root problem is that the higher-order/lower-order function–realizer hierarchy and the higher-level/lower-level macro–micro hierarchy cross-classify properties (Kim 2003). Some properties are true of entities from more than one level, and some entities have properties from more than one level. Even the stitched-together hierarchy just presented exhibits this. Look at the F_{-4} level – even though it moves from a cell to a cell's constituent molecules, both cells and molecules exhibit electrical and chemical properties. This problem is a general shortcoming facing any hierarchy that tries to tie both property orders and levels to the size of a thing instantiating a property. Big and little things interact literally all the time. If you swallow LSD, your conscious experience will include hallucinations; if you are bitten by an infected mosquito, you will get Dengue fever and feel dazed and confused; if you step on a lizard, you will squash its internal organs and destroy its neural network (such as it is). Big and little things have lots of the same properties, and thing size has little if anything to do with property level or order.

It is, I think, time to consider jettisoning the micro–macro dimension of property level and make do with the higher-order/lower-order dimension alone. There are higher-order properties instantiated by big things and higher-order properties instantiated by little things; likewise, there are lower-order properties by big things and lower-order properties instantiated by little things. The relevant questions for the neuroscience of conscious property instantiation are then clustered around the issue of which lower-order properties of which neural mechanisms, if any, implement or realize higher-order conscious properties.

We started in this chapter with the epistemological issue posed by the inferential gap between, on the one hand, correlation between measured neural and conscious properties and, on the other, the neural property or properties in virtue of which conscious properties are instantiated. The stubbornness of that inferential gap in turn supported the worry that some neuroscientists and philosophers persistently overstate the ontological significance of neural correlates. To understand what that overstatement consists in, we dug deeper into the differences between correlates, substrates and realizers. In Chapter 11, these results are used to reject the claim that microphysical properties implement or realize conscious properties. In Chapter 12, these same results are used to assess the allegation that even non-microphysical neural properties implement or realize conscious properties.

11. MICROPHYSICAL REDUCTION, OVERDETERMINATION AND COUPLING

The rush to image the neural correlates of conscious events can look more than a little like high-tech phrenology (Uttal 2001). Although feeling bumps on the skull and producing cranial maps has been replaced by a lot of coloured pictures and intracranial neural maps, the drive to reduce consciousness to something small remains the same. Still, it would be surprising were there nothing at all to the correlational evidence. What the neuroscientific evidence suggests instead is that conscious properties cannot be instantiated outside a neural environment. Those wary of even this much optimism counter that subjective perspectivity, intentionality and qualitative character are irreducible to anything neural. While we may not know exactly what the nature of these conscious properties is, reducing them to properties or neural assembly properties is mistaken.

Since conscious properties are higher-order properties, they are implemented by mechanisms or processes of some sort. But what sorts of mechanisms are conscious properties implemented by? This chapter investigates two arguments against the claim that neural mechanisms and their properties implement conscious properties. According to the first, neural mechanisms are *too big* and their properties not sufficiently lower-order; according to the second, neural mechanisms are *not big enough* and their properties not sufficiently higher-order. Several counterarguments to microphysical reduction are presented. Developing some of them takes time and entails defending emergent causation against the charge of overdetermination. In the latter third of the chapter, vehicle externalism is picked back up, and its use in arguments for rejecting computational representationalism is examined in greater detail. This examination continues in Chapter 12.

MICROPHYSICAL REDUCTION

As argued in Chapter 2, reductive physicalism comes in a variety of forms. Those that are the target of non-reductionist ire have both microphysical and neural dimensions. Recall:

(RPC)   Physical events or parts thereof exhaust everything that is concrete, and there is a supervenience relation between all families of conscious properties and microphysical properties such that subvening microphysical properties are the only realizers of supervening conscious properties.

(NR)   Physical events or parts thereof exhaust everything that is concrete, and there is a supervenience relation between all families of conscious properties and microphysical properties of neural assembly activity such that subvening microphysical properties of neural assembly activity are the only realizers of supervening conscious properties.

Since all species of (NR) reductionism are species of (RPC) reductionism while some species of (RPC) reductionisms are not (NR) reductionisms, (RPC) is less restrictive than (NR). Hence, if (RPC) is false for conscious properties, then (NR) is false for conscious properties as well.

Non-reductionists opposed to (NR) find it incredible that the doings of consciousness are exhaustively inherited from the to-and-fro of microphysical neural properties. Some non-reductionists object to (NR)'s commitment to reducing conscious properties to microphysical properties; others object to (NR)'s commitment to reducing conscious properties to neural properties; still others object to both aspects. Note that even if conscious properties are not realized by microphysical properties or processes, they may be realized by non-microphysical properties or implemented by non-microphysical properties. If so, (NR) is false while some other kind of reduction may be true. Again, even if conscious properties are not realized by neural properties or processes, they may be realized by non-neural physical properties or implemented by non-neural physical processes. If so, then (NR) again fails, although some other form of reduction may not.

Microphysical and neural reduction

One kind of non-reductionist who argues against (NR) and (RPC) is opposed not to the neural dimension of reduction identified in them but to driving reduction to the microphysical properties of neural assemblies and neural assembly activity. Such an antimicrophysicalist might be perfectly happy to allow that conscious properties are realized by neural properties that are not microphysical properties. So, even if she rejects (NR) and (RPC), she might affirm the following:

(RPC)' Physical events or parts thereof exhaust everything that is concrete, and there is a supervenience relation between all families of conscious properties and physical properties such that subvening physical properties are the only realizers of supervening conscious properties.

An antimicrophysicalist of this sort argues only that subvening microphysical properties do not exhaust the realizers of conscious properties. She claims instead that there are realizers of conscious properties other than microphysical properties. She can argue either that these other realizers are not microphysical even if they are physical or that they are not physical at all, whether microphysical or not. That is, (RPC)' is consistent with the following:

(NR)' Physical events or parts thereof exhaust everything that is concrete, and there is a supervenience relation between all families of conscious properties and non-microphysical properties of neural assembly activity such that subvening non-microphysical properties of neural assembly activity are the only realizers of supervening conscious properties.

An antimicrophysicalist who thinks (NR)' is true can hold that realizers of conscious properties are physical properties of neural assembly activity, so long as those properties are not microphysical properties.

The second kind of non-reductionist targets the neural requirements of (NR)'. Whereas antimicrophysicalists argue that conscious properties are complex in some way that precludes their realization by microphysical properties, antineuralists argue that conscious properties are complex in a way that precludes their realization by neural properties. Note that antineuralists can claim that conscious properties reduce to microphysical non-neural properties, say, the microphysical properties of neural assemblies plus the microphysical properties of the extracranial world. Someone advocating this kind of position would be reductionist in so far as he advocates that the only realizers of conscious properties are microphysical properties, but he would not be a neural reductionist. After all, he denies that the realizers of conscious properties are exhausted by microphysical properties of neural assemblies.

Although this is an option, most antineuralists are, it has to be admitted, opposed both to microphysical and neural reduction, so their target is the thesis with which we started, that is, (NR). Such non-reductionists argue that conscious properties are not exhaustively realized by microphysical properties and that they are not exhaustively realized by neural properties either. For this kind of non-reductionist, conscious properties may be totally realized by physical properties, but they are not totally realized by what goes on in the head, whether microphysical or not. Whereas critics of microphysical reductionism focus on the alleged implausibility of conscious properties realized by microphysical properties, critics of neural reduction focus on the alleged implausibility of conscious properties realized entirely within the head. There are thus two dimensions – the large/small dimension and the inside/outside dimension – at play in arguments against neural reduction, and these dimensions provoke distinct and sometimes conflicting arguments. We discuss the first dimension in this chapter. In the following chapter, we focus on the second dimension.

Microphysical reduction, mechanism and organization

Some of the most pointed arguments against microphysical and neural reduction of conscious properties attack not *multiple* realization but microphysical *realization*. Both (RPC) and (NR) proponents assume that reduction to microphysics is unavoidable. Even if the subvening property that immediately satisfies a given conscious property's causal profile is not a microphysical property of some neural assembly, that neural property in turn is reducible to some biochemical property of (some of) the cells that compose the neural assembly, and that biochemical property in turn is reducible to some property of the molecules that compose the cell. For (RPC) and (NR) proponents, this process continues until microphysical entities and their microphysical properties are reached.

Non-reductionists opposed to (RPC) face the challenge of justifying the point below which further reduction is rejected. The first step in accomplishing this task is to establish that reduction need not extend to microphysical properties. One way to establish that reduction need not extend to microphysical properties is to argue that thinking that it does so leads to absurdity. An argument for that conclusion has been proposed by Block (2003). (RPC) and (NR) assume that every conscious property supervenes on and is causally realized by microphysical properties. That is, causation bottoms out with a family of microphysical properties. What if that is false, that is, what if microphysical properties are not bedrock? It has been claimed that it is an open empirical question whether microphysical properties are bedrock, indeed, whether there is any causal bedrock at all. Since, according to (RPC) and (NR), all causal powers must be inherited from the microphysical family of properties and microphysical properties may not be bedrock, then microphysical properties may not have any causal powers for conscious properties to inherit. All causal powers may simply "drain away" into the infinite divisibility of the physical. If so, there would be no causation anywhere, and causal realization would collapse. For the reductionist who argues from causal realization to reduction, the collapse of causation immediately entails the falsity of causal realization. Hence, if causal drainage is true, then (RPC) and (NR) are false; moreover, until causal drainage is shown to be false, neither (RPC) nor (NR) is demonstrably true. It is possible to respond to this criticism by trying to isolate conscious properties as the only family of properties subject to causal drainage, permitting other functional properties to retain causal powers *via* reduction (Kim 2003), but arguments on behalf of this claim have so far met with little support (Block 2003; Esfeld 2005; Marras 2007).

Suppose, however, that the causal drainage argument is put to the side as inconclusive and microphysical properties are allowed funds of causal powers. Non-reductionists may still argue that (NR) and (RPC) are false because reduction of conscious properties continues only to a certain point that occurs somewhere before reaching microphysical properties. If so, there is a property from some property family X that a particular conscious property is realized by and no property from a microphysical property family Y eligible to realize the conscious property in question. Of course, if so, properties from family X better not themselves reduce to properties from the microphysical property family, for if they do, reduction to the microphysical will be regained. There may well be such a family of properties that is a minimum threshold for realizers of conscious properties, and a handful of philosophers and neuroscientists have been brave enough to nominate particular families of properties to block the door against the microphysical barbarians. Nominations have been few and far between – properties of cellular and molecular biology appear to be the most popular candidates (among others, Boogerd *et al.* 2005; Revonsuo 2006; Searle 2004). But, given the amount and quality of empirical knowledge we currently have about conscious properties and candidate realizer properties, trying to establish a minimum threshold by philosophical means alone is not likely to produce much confidence. Another approach is probably better: use philosophical reflection to identify the difficulties that intentionality, subjective perspectivity and qualitative character pose for microphysicalist and neural reduction programmes and let the relevant sciences have at them, constrained by the knowledge that these properties are components of any adequate explanation of consciousness and are to be relinquished only if it is not possible to hammer them into a form consistent with the relevant sciences (Burge [1993] 2007 makes a related point using a distinct argument).

A similar conclusion can be reached from a different direction. Were there no more to the difference between a set of molecules and the cells they compose than spatiotemporal contiguity of the molecules, then there would be no cross-classification between property level and property order. Higher-order properties would be straightforward aggregations of lower-level microphysical properties, and in that case any reorganization of the microentities that have lower-level properties would be as good as the next. But for the antimicrophysicalist, a cell is more than aggregated molecules cobbled together in a particular region of space, and a cell's causal powers are more than the aggregated causal powers of the molecules that compose it. For the antimicrophysicalist, the molecules must be *organized* as a mechanism in order to be a cell that functions. A *mechanism* is an organized whole – a system – that does something (Armstrong 1981, [1968] 1993; Fodor [1974] 1980a; Putnam 1975; recall Chapter 8's discussion of re-entrant processing). Mechanisms are composed of simpler component parts that exhibit cooperative and prohibitory behaviour required to fulfil the function of the mechanism. Component parts of a mechanism or system, unlike parts of an aggregated whole, are not intersubstitutable, cannot be reaggregated without change in behaviour, and cannot be added or subtracted with only qualitative changes in behaviour (Craver & Bechtel 2006). It is a mechanism's increased organization and complexity that are relevant for determining property order, not only the size of the mechanism. A higher-order functional property is realized by or implemented in a particular mechanism when the mechanism's components and the causal relations between them fulfil the function. In the life sciences – biochemistry, biology, neurology, cognitive science and psychology – mechanistic reductions are ubiquitous. Indeed, they are much more common than deductive explanations that move from general laws plus evidence to what is to be explained (Craver & Bechtel 2006). This is one reason why the concerns about conscious property anomaly have all but disappeared from the consciousness literature (and why, in addition, Davidson's anomalous monism has become a curiosity).

Some mechanisms are spatial mechanisms organized according to shape, size, orientation, connections and boundaries. An example of spatial organization is provided by a desk. Were a desk simply an aggregated whole, any arrangement of 1″ cubes would suffice to constitute it, including the arrangement in which they are all simply thrown into a pile. But of course, a pile of desk part cubes is not a desk. The desktop, legs and drawers are component parts connected in various ways and spatially organized according to shape, size, orientation and boundaries in a particular configuration. Other mechanisms are *processes* organized spatially and temporally by sequential order, rate, duration and frequency of activity. An example of temporal organization is a radio rebuild. My cousin Paul and I used to take old radios and TVs apart to figure out how they work. I was never particularly good at it, but Paul was (predictably, he grew up to be a Silicon Valley guy). Sometimes I found that after taking a radio apart, I could not put it back together again even though all the parts were lying right there in front of me on the garage floor. At that point, Paul would come to the rescue and remind me of the particular order that reconstruction had to follow and the point in that order which I had forgotten. The lights would go on, and I would remember the rest of the rebuild.

Some processes are feedforward, some are parallel, and some are feedback. In a sequentially organized *feedforward* process, component parts perform operations on the spatially adjacent and temporally prior products of other components' operations. In *feedback* processes, the product of a process later in a sequence feeds back into a process earlier in the sequence. Negative feedback loops occur when a product of a process inhibits a component of an earlier process as occurs, for example, in a thermostat that tells the furnace both to fire and then to stop firing. Positive feedback loops occur when a product of a process increases the responsiveness of a component of an earlier process as occurs, for example, in living processes such as blood-clotting (Craver & Bechtel 2006).

Mechanisms and processes and their properties provide the resources for a less drastic species of realization and reduction than that found in microphysical reduction of the (RPC) and (NR) types. This alternative is *indexical* reductionism, a form of reduction indexed to decompositional cycle, where a *decompositional cycle* is a task-driven investigation into the constituent components and activities of a mechanism or process (Bechtel & Abrahamsen 2005). Since mechanistic reductions are the rule rather than the exception in the life sciences, and since mechanistic reductions are indexical reductions, the rule rather than the exception in the life sciences are indexical reductions.

In general, (RPC) and (NR) entail eliminating every feature of a higher-order property that is not captured by its microrealizing property. So, if there are features of the higher-order property we do not want to lose, then either the microrealizing property better have all of those features or (RPC) better be prepared to defend some pretty drastic eliminativist implications. Hence, in particular, if the alternatives for conscious properties are adhering to (RPC) and (NR) and losing features of conscious properties we do not want to lose or keeping those features and losing (RPC) or (NR), wariness towards (RPC) and (NR) reductions is preferable. And losing subjective perspectivity, intentionality and qualitative character, or writing them off as merely epiphrastic (that is, properties induced by but extending no further than a predicate), is unacceptable, at least pending convincing argument to the contrary. Moreover, the strongest arguments to the contrary, such as the supervenience argument, are just not that convincing, as will be argued below.

Those leery of (RPC) and (NR) but open to less drastic forms of reduction may find indexical reduction attractive. For example, an implication of indexical reductionism is that it is not possible to determine *a priori* what a mechanism's components and properties must be, so it is not possible to determine *a priori* what level or order its components and properties must occupy. Indexical reduction and the explanations offered under its name assume phenomena and go looking for the constituent elements whose interactive behaviour explains their occurrence. Hence, indexical reduction is consistent with and predicts the discovery of properties from different orders in a particular mechanism causally interacting with one another to get the job done. As Machamer *et al.* (2000) note, in the life sciences and in the sciences relevant for reducing conscious properties in particular, it is a regular finding that, entities and activities at multiple levels are required to make the explanation intelligible. The entities and activities in the mechanism must be understood in their important, vital, or otherwise significant context, and this requires an understanding of the working of the mechanism at multiple levels…. Higher-level entities and activities are thus essential to the intelligibility of those at lower levels, just as much as those at lower levels are essential for understanding those at higher levels. It is the integration of different levels into productive relations that renders the phenomenon intelligible and thereby explains it. (Machamer *et al.* 2000: 23)

A more flexible kind of reduction thus results: a higher-order functional property is indexically reduced whenever it is decomposed into a lower-order implementing mechanism or process, that is, whenever it is decomposed into an integrated organization of constituent parts working together to subserve or generate the functional property as a product. Since it is in virtue of the constituent parts' behaviour that the mechanism or process works, and since the constituent parts are less complex than the mechanism or process as a whole, the functional property is realized by or implemented in the properly functioning mechanism or process and so reduces to it (indexed of course to the decompositional cycle).

For the indexical reductionist, there is simply no reason to suppose, as microphysical reductionists suppose, that reduction must be driven to the microphysical level in order to be reduction at all. For the indexical reductionist, reduction stops once a realizing mechanism or process for some functional property has been successfully described. Nothing metaphysically committing hangs on the idea of a successful description: a description is successful when, for a particular decomposition cycle of some supervening functional property, researchers describe the organized performance of a mechanism's or a process's components such that those components in that organization engaging in their characteristic activity yield the functional property. Depending on the decompositional cycle and the functional property, some indexical reductions will require one realizing mechanism or process, some perhaps a second that realizes the first, some perhaps more. But some particular indexical reduction that successfully explains how something is implemented is not judged a failure simply because it does not continue to the microphysical level.

The microphysical reductionist will no doubt insist that the job is not done until the microphysical level is reached. Such complaints are likely to prompt a shrug of the shoulders from the indexical reductionist. She will point out that there is no reason to suppose that "detailed knowledge of how the component parts or subparts operate will already be available in lower-level disciplines since … these parts will be operating in specialized contexts not typically studied by practitioners of the lower-level science" (Bechtel & Hamilton 2007:

411). "Context" here covers an array of issues, the most important of which is that practitioners of more basic sciences typically do not study something's properties when that something is organized with other things of the same (and different) scales into a mechanism or process. Another specialized context, especially important for organic systems and typically ignored by more basic sciences, is the environment in which a mechanism operates. Organic mechanisms and processes evolve in response to the environment in which they are placed. A washing machine, even one with the latest "fuzzy logic" circuitry, does not evolve: once plugged in, the washing machine will, without any changes to its internal structure ever taking place, continue to run through its cycles until it wears out. Organic systems, on the other hand, do not need to evolve internal systems to provide something if the environment has plenty of it and evolve differently when they are placed in differentially endowed environments.

Some mechanisms and processes integrate components and properties of multiple orders of complexity, so such mechanisms and processes have emergent properties that downwardly cause changes in basal properties. Hence, if (RPC) proponents continue to insist that microphysical reductionism is preferable to indexical reductionism, they must either: (a) reject the existence of such mechanisms and processes; (b) reject the data from which such mechanisms and processes are inferred; or (c) charge the antimicrophysicalist with an erroneous interpretation of data. Antimicrophysicalists find none of these manoeuvres nearly as compelling as rejecting the philosophical arguments (such as the supervenience argument) that provoke the objection necessitating the manoeuvres (Burge [1993] 2007 makes a similar point).

EMERGENCE AND OVERDETERMINATION

As noted, indexical reduction is consistent with the existence of emergent properties. Still, (RPC) and (NR) advocates are within their rights to press the issue that even if all but one of the individual steps of the supervenience argument can be defused, the overdetermination problem still remains for any advocate of indexical reduction. If some mechanism entails emergent causation, there must be a way to provide those emergent properties with causal powers that are not exhaustively inherited from their subvenient basal properties. So long as such a model of emergent causation is unavailable, any emergent component of a mechanism or process will be threatened with epiphenomenality. Hence, a lot rides on the viability of thinking that emergent causal powers are distinct from the causal powers of their subvenient bases.

Qualifying higher-order properties as causes requires showing that higher-order properties have causal powers distinct from those of their lower-order realizers. Currently, the most popular way to satisfy this requirement is to argue that the causal powers of a realized higher-order property are a subset of its realizing lower-order property's causal powers. Consider, for instance, a case of microphysical reduction. A realized higher-order property has unique and novel causal powers distinct from those of its microrealizers because its causal powers are a subset of its microrealizers' causal powers. Suppose there is a group of three microphysical events, each one of which instantiates certain properties that have certain causal powers: the first element's causal powers constitute the set $\{C', C''\}$, the second element's causal powers constitute the set $\{C^*, C^{**}\}$, and the third element's causal powers constitute the set $\{C^\circ, C^{\circ\circ}\}$ (none of the member causal powers are identical or subsets of the others). Putting all the causal powers together yields the union set of that group's causal powers: $\{C', C'', C^*, C^{**}, C^\circ, C^{\circ\circ}\}$. Suppose also that that group instantiates a higher-order event of the instantiation of a higher-order property P that has causal powers $\{C', C^\circ, C^*\}$. Since $\{C', C^*, C^\circ\}$ is distinct from $\{C', C''\}$, distinct from $\{C^*, C^{**}\}$ and distinct from $\{C^\circ, C^{\circ\circ}\}$, the higher-order event has distinct causal powers from each of the events that realize it.

Some reductionists are unimpressed with this manoeuvre, for they point out that since higher-order causal powers $\{C', C^\circ, C^*\}$ are members of the union set of realizing causal powers $\{C', C'', C^*, C^{**}, C^\circ, C^{\circ\circ}\}$, they are found somewhere in that set and are not distinct after all. Kim, for instance, includes these subsets of causal powers in his formulation of the causal inheritance thesis (Kim 2003, 2005). As amended, causal inheritance states that if a functionalized supervening property is instantiated at some time in virtue of one of its subvening properties being instantiated at that time, the causal powers of the former are identical to, *or a subset of*, the causal powers of the latter. However, this amendment is not consistent with what most reductionists, including Kim, think reduction implies. Since, as will be presently shown, a higher-order property's causal powers form a distinct subset of realizer causal powers, Kim's accommodating amendment is consistent with the appearance of distinct higher-order causal powers. If so, then, contrary to what is claimed on its behalf, causal inheritance is *not* exhaustive: there are distinct causal powers that only supervening higher-order properties have and that no subvening lower-order property has.

The argument is by analogy. Where "n" is a natural number, the set of all squares between 1 and 100 is a proper subset of the set of all natural numbers between 1 and 100, but the two sets are distinct since, for example, 17 is a member of the latter but not the former set. Although none of the square numbers are new numbers in virtue of being in the set induced by the squaring function, the squaring function induces a unique and new subset – $\{1, 4, 9, 16, 25, 36, 49, 64, 81, 100\}$ – that no other function induces on the set of naturals between 1 and 100. If causal powers are functions from contexts to probabilities of subsequent events occurring, then, like the squaring function, a set of such causal powers is a set induced by a certain function on realizer causal powers that is distinct from all other subsets induced by other functions on realizer causal powers. So, while no causal power in a higher-order property's set of causal powers fails to appear somewhere in the union set of realizer causal powers, a higher-order property's causal power may yet be distinct from that of its realizers. That is enough to qualify higher-order properties as distinct causes.

In some cases of realization, the higher-order property and lower-order property are realized by the same thing. For example, a snowflake's pattern is realized by the chemical bonds between the water molecules that constitute the snowflake. In other cases, higher-order properties of big things are realized by lower-order properties of groups of little things such that no one of the members of the group of entities that has the realizing lower-order property individually has it. Rather, in such cases, it is the group of entities that has the lower-order property that realizes the higher-order property.

Suppose it granted that higher-order properties have some claim for having distinct causal powers from the lower-order properties on which they supervene. One might think that qualifying higher-order properties and events as causes still does not solve the overdetermination problem, for even if qualified they may still be causally redundant on lower-order properties and events. This is the most serious aspect of overdetermination. Overdetermination does not go away by shifting from big to little things, groups of little things, or by shifting from higher-order property realization to lower-order property realization. Even if a higher-order property of a macroentity is realized by a lower-order property of a macroentity, a lower-order property of a microentity, or a lower-order property of a group of microentities, so long as overdetermination threatens higher-order properties, their future as causes looks bleak. But the subset analysis of higher-order properties provides a plausible solution to the overdetermination challenge. Since the causal powers of a higher-order property are a subset of the causal powers had by a lower-order realizing property, the higher-order and lower-order properties do not overdetermine some effect or, if they do, that they do is not a problem. Shoemaker states the case for this latter alternative:

> This is not overdetermination of an objectionable sort; it can be compared with the case in which we say both that Smith's death was caused by the salvo of shots fired by the firing squad and that it was caused by the shot fired by Jones, where Jones's shot was the only member of that salvo that hit Smith. (Shoemaker 2007: 52–3)

Hence, the higher-order and the lower-order properties may both be causes of an effect without the higher-order property overdetermining that effect in an objectionable way.

This analysis of higher-order property causal powers applies, of course, to emergent properties as a special case. Supervenient emergents and subvenient basals are applications of the higher-order/lower-order distinction applied to a particular kind of higher-order property. Emergent properties are higher-order properties that appear only when realizing entities are organized in particular ways into mechanisms or processes. Emergent causal powers are *latent* in the realizing entities (microentities or macroentities) prior to their combining to form an organized mechanism or process and *manifest* only when the realizing group of entities or microentities is so organized (Shoemaker 2007). So, while entities in their pre- and post-system career have latent emergent causal powers by the truckload, it is only in the stage(s) of an entity's career during which it is a constituent of a mechanism or process that those latent emergent causal powers become manifest emergent causal powers. Of course, not all of an entity's causal powers are latent. Entities have funds of manifest basal causal powers even while not members of any mechanism or process. The point is that upon becoming constituents of a mechanism or process, manifest basal causal powers are supplemented with the now-manifest emergent causal powers of the organized mechanism or process that the entities help constitute. Membership has its privileges.

The difference between an entity's manifest basal and latent emergent causal powers and the manifest emergent causal powers of groups of entities or microentities can be illustrated by reconsidering the difference between decomposable and non-decomposable entities and systems. Recall, an entity or system is decomposable when it is composed of constituent entities whose behaviour over time is *not* a one-to-one function of the behaviour of the other constituents, and an entity or system is non-decomposable whenever it is not decomposable, that is, whenever it is composed of constituent entities whose behaviour *is* a one-to-one function ofn the behaviour of the other constituents. Take a non-decomposable system, say a day in your life, and consider one of the constituents of such a system – say, your friend Doug. Doug has certain causal powers. Some of Doug's causal powers are manifest causal powers, those that he has even if he is not a constituent of the non-decomposable system of a day in your life. Some of Doug's causal powers are latent system causal powers, those that he has when he remains not a constituent in the non-decomposable system of a day in your life. And some of Doug's causal powers are manifest system causal powers, those that he has when he is organized in the non-decomposable system of a day in your life. Emergent causal powers are paradigmatically non-decomposable, for emergent properties covary with basal properties in the unique manner required by supervenience.

Non-decomposability has a curious consequence. Since an emergent is non-decomposable, specifying its manifest emergent causal powers turns out to be alone sufficient for identifying its causal behaviour. Although manifest basal causal powers exist and ground the causal relations between basal entities, those basal causal powers and entities make no difference to emergent behaviour beyond a "certain fluctuation which, in the long run, disappears. In short, the complexity introduced by strong [basal]-level interaction simply drops out of the big picture ..." (Strevens 2005b: 539). So, identifying manifest emergent causal powers is alone sufficient for determining whether an emergent is a relatum of a high-level or downwards causal relation; citing in addition the manifest basal causal powers of the constituting entities is superfluous. Hence, emergent properties also do not overdetermine effects in an objectionable way, and since they are higher order, there is a sense in which they do not *over*determine effects at all. Were the basal entities not organized as they are, the mechanism's emergent causal powers would not be manifest, remaining instead latent in those basal entities. Of course, manifest emergent causal powers do not pop into existence *ex nihilo* when a set of basal entities organize together into a mechanism. Manifest emergent causal powers would not be as they are, were the manifest causal powers of, and causal relations between, basal entities not as they are.

Establishing the existence of emergents in a particular domain such as conscious properties is not vouchsafed by defending the overall coherence of emergence. Rather, one argument against conscious properties being emergent does not establish what it claims to establish, so one more *a priori* attempt to partition investigation of that domain into philosophically acceptable and unacceptable alternatives fails. All that is thus revealed is a playing field cleared of certain philosophical debris. Nor does non-decomposability provide an account of why or how emergence occurs, so it cannot pretend to explain emergence. The existence of emergents no more explains how they get that way than the existence of supervenients explains how they get to be supervenient. So, in much the same way that supervenience states the problem of non-reduction without solving it, emergence reveals the problem of non-reductionist causation without explaining it. One wants to know *how* a system generates emergent conscious events in the first place and *how* those emergent events carry out their causal work once established. That is a job for science and philosophy working together.

Emergent properties have sometimes been characterized as enigmatic emanations from another realm that magically appear on top of the physical. Not so – emergent properties are instead the distinct and sometimes unpredictable consequences of particular kinds of physical systems, some of them evolving biological organisms. Of course, it takes a lot of philosophical and empirical scientific work to determine whether any given mechanism or process has emergent properties rather than higher-order and supervenient but non-emergent properties. For many mechanisms and processes, the answer will surely be "no". For some, however, the answer may well be "yes", and for them the causal autonomy of their emergent properties can be defended against the clutches of the supervenience argument. Emergence advocates can therefore rest a little easier at night knowing that this particular threat is declawed.

General empirical and philosophical considerations thus suggest that both multiple realization and microphysical realization of conscious properties are mistaken. Moreover, neuroscientific and neuropsychological evidence suggests that conscious properties are probably not multiply realized across species, across individuals or across times. The empirical evidence also suggests that the most relevant kinds of conscious property reductions are more likely to be reductions to neural mechanisms, processes and neural activity, some of which have emergent properties that downwardly cause subvenient properties. Of course, allowing emergents back in reignites the worry that downwards emergent causes are superfluous epiphenomena. But the overdetermination concern is turned because emergent causal powers are latent in their realizers until those realizers are organized into a mechanism, upon which organization they become manifest causal powers of the mechanism.

Nothing in these general considerations immediately implies that conscious properties are realized by neural assembly activity, much less that they are realized by some particular kind of neural assembly activity. However, these general considerations do imply that the hunt for the realizing mechanisms, processes and activities of conscious properties does not require that it lead to microphysical properties. It may be that the realizing mechanisms and processes of conscious properties are discovered to be no more basic than, say, biochemistry. Again, at the current juncture, we do not know enough about the realizers of conscious properties to know the answer to such questions. But proposed non-microphysical realizers are not ruled out as candidate realizers of conscious properties, and some non-microphysical realizers need not inherit all their causal powers from microphysical properties.

It is one thing to clear away *a priori* arguments against conscious properties being emergent; it is another thing to argue that conscious properties actually are emergent; and it is still another thing to identify that from which they emerge if they are emergent. These latter projects are collaborative ones between science and philosophy and will take years to complete, with no guarantee of success – it might turn out that all conscious properties are emergent, that none of them are, or that some but not all of them are. We will not know until a good deal more is understood in general about the neurophysiology of the neural assemblies that correlate with conscious properties. Most of the needed answers are some distance away. Still, some preliminary points can be made. First, it appears likely that neural realizers of conscious properties are significantly more complex than individual neurons. With a few exceptions, such as is sometimes suggested by the work of, for example, Logothetis (1998) and Zeki and Bartels (1998), those researching the neural realizers of conscious properties are investigating functionally identified assemblies of neurons and their activity as the likely neural implementers of conscious properties. So too with philosophy: insisting that realization must be microphysical does not appear to be the best option. Since the overdetermination problem can be defused, there need be no prohibition against conscious properties being emergent higher-order properties realized by lower-order properties of entities no simpler than, say, neural assemblies or the processes into which such assemblies enter. It is, therefore, most unlikely that reduction of conscious properties will ever need to dip down far enough to explicitly enlist the low-order properties of the micro-entities studied by microphysics (Burge [1993] 2007).

That the implementing neural correlates of conscious properties are likely to turn out to be assemblies of neurons and their emergent activities rather than microphysical entities and their basal activities does not imply that those correlates are complex neural networks rather than simpler neural modules. But the likelihood that the neural correlates of conscious properties are something more complex than widespread modules does increase once other considerations are acknowledged. One of these considerations is the following. As we have seen, a characteristic feature of neuroimaging and neuropsychological research is that it attempts to discover the neural correlates of particular conscious processes, such as attention and working memory, particular conscious events, such as olfaction and vision, and particular dysfunctions in and compromises to conscious experience, such as agnosia, aphasia, achromatopsia, blindsight and hemispheric neglect. The great promise of this research is its increasing precision, for as precision increases, so too does the specificity of the neural correlates of particular conscious properties. But that increasing precision can betray the researcher's hopes when the studied phenomenon is an emergent phenomenon. If a phenomenon is emergent, its dissection past a certain point entails the loss of structure and organization requisite for a certain class of emergent causal powers to be manifest. If, then, conscious properties are members of this class of emergent properties, then their neural correlates can be no more basic than what is required to sustain their manifest emergent causal powers. The best bet on what those neural correlates are may well be that they are properties of widespread neural networks. But, again, this is a matter to be decided empirically.

A second consideration likewise suggests that the neural correlates of conscious properties are emergent properties of neural networks. Neuroimaging studies and neuropsychological research can with increasing fine-grain identify neural correlates for this or that conscious process, event or abnormality. Such research thus provides a set of interlocking differential correlates for specific conscious processes and events. But discovering, *via* a neuroimaging study, a differential correlate for the olfactory character of, say, a rose does not imply either that that neural correlate is a core correlate for that olfactory experience or that it is a total correlate for that olfactory experience. Even less does it imply that that neural correlate is a core or total correlate for all qualitatively endowed conscious experience. The problem here is that neuroimaging studies that identify correlates for this or that conscious process employ subjects who are *already* conscious (Searle 2000). Conscious properties are not likely to be instantiated piecemeal with each individually distinct conscious event, a dollop of intentionality for this conscious event of thinking of Negril, a dollop of subjective perspectivity apportioned to that conscious event of watching television, and one more of qualitative character for that taste event that accompanies eating Borriello Brothers' pizza. Thinking that this is how conscious properties are instantiated assumes that the unified field of intentional and qualitatively endowed conscious experience is built up out of a collection of conscious building blocks (Searle 2000), the individual cognitive, interoceptive, proprioceptive, perceptual and affective processes that correlate with the differentially active neural assemblies that animate an fMRI image. However, these differentially active parts of the brain are probably not the only parts of the brain implicated in the generation of conscious events.

Research that adopts an atomistic or building block approach to neural correlates contrasts with some of the *holistic* or *field* approaches investigated in earlier chapters. These field approaches are characterized by Searle as follows:

> Instead of thinking of my current state of consciousness as made up of the various bits – the perception of the computer screen, the sound of the brook outside, the shadows cast by the evening sun falling on the wall – we should think of all of these as modifications, forms that the underlying basal conscious field takes after my peripheral nerve endings have been assaulted by the various external stimuli. The research implication of this is that we should look for consciousness as a feature of the brain emerging from the activities of large masses of neurons, and which cannot be explained by the activities of individual neurons. (Searle 2000: 575)

On the field approach to neural realization of consciousness, the commitment to conscious properties as emergent properties is unavoidable. Episodes of conscious perception, interoception, proprioception, affection and cognition modify an already existing conscious state, and the candidate neural correlates of that already existing state are emergent properties of the activity of a relatively large and complex network of neural assemblies.

Field approaches to conscious property instantiation have increased in popularity. Consider, as just one example, how the field approach can be used to support Postle's model of endogenous attention. Activity in a particular neural network clustered in right DLPFC and VLPFC, anterior cingulate cortex and regions of parietal cortex is then a core correlate of phasic executive attention without being a total correlate of phasic attention. Only that entire complex is the total neural correlate of endogenous attention. Core neural correlates of endogenous attention are ephemeral, arising with and lapsing with particular attention episodes, but the non-core part of the total correlate attention is more stable and provides the background state against which such episodes occur. If so, endogenous attention is not something that introduces conscious events to a brain's activity at all, but something that *modifies* an already consciously active brain (Searle 2000). Generalizing, if the distinction between core and total correlates is applied systematically to neuroscientific research into the neural substrates of conscious properties, a fairly muted assessment of many of its claimed successes is implied. Since it is only the collective activity of a large number of neural assemblies that subserves any conscious property instantiation, it would be astonishing to discover that the differential activity of the assemblies subserving one dated conscious event held all of its correlate or substrate cards. If so, research that tries to identify neural correlates, neural substrates or neural realizers of conscious properties with the activity of neural assemblies dedicated to some particular perceptual, interoceptive, proprioceptive, affective or cognitive process is fundamentally misguided (Bayne & Chalmers 2003; Revonsuo 2006; Searle 2000; Shoemaker 2003; Von der Malsburg 2002).

ISOMORPHISM, REPRESENTATION AND COUPLING

The tacit assumption made by many neuroscientific researchers that the category of representation is understood well enough to play a foundational role has intermittently bubbled up as a problematic assumption (Burge [2006] 2007; Haselager *et al.* 2003b; Haugeland [1991] 1998). Even if at an abstract computational level a representation makes sense as the category of entity over which computations operate, it is a good deal less obvious what feature, if any, makes a neural vehicle or neural process a representation. One answer is that computational-functional properties and processes are isomorphic with neural properties and processes and that this isomorphism suffices to label neural properties and processes as representations.[1] Suppose, for example, that there are computationally understood representational processes, A and B, and "$A \rightarrow B$" is true for the computational system that contains A and B. Given isomorphism, there will then be neural vehicles or neural processes that A and B map to, and, just as "$A \rightarrow B$" is true in the computational system, so too in the isomorphic neural vehicles or processes, if one occurs, the other occurs. In such cases, the neural vehicles or processes are then also neural representations.

Appealing to isomorphism in this way obscures two serious issues. First, if neural vehicles or processes are identified as neural representations, attributing representational content properties to them becomes almost unavoidable. The assumption that this is acceptable forms part of the background of much of contemporary neuroscience (Noë & Thompson 2004a). However, if neural vehicles or processes have content and if neural content must match conscious content, then neural vehicles or processes must have properties that are either identical with or are the total realizers of conscious content properties, which entails that the properties of conscious content must find a match with some property or properties of neural vehicles or processes. A viable candidate for a neural property that can plausibly qualify as content has yet to be found. It would be a huge relief if it were possible to reject the matching content requirement before it had the opportunity to infect neural realization discussions, for otherwise epiphenomenalism and eliminativism not just about content properties but perhaps about the other conscious properties as well seem likely outcomes.

What, then, would it take to relieve the theoretical headaches that follow from assuming that neural vehicles or processes have content? The answer is disjunctive: either some neural vehicles or processes are discovered to have a kind of content that matches conscious content and thus realizes content, *or* neural vehicles and neural processes are not the kinds of things that have to have content in order to be implicated in the realization of content. The first disjunct is, as we have just seen, unlikely to be satisfied. The second disjunct is more promising. Although neural vehicles and processes may be constituents of complex states that instantiate content properties, they need not be the only components of those complexes that instantiate content properties. Such an alternative is consistent with thinking of neural vehicles and processes as core realizers of content properties without thereby also requiring that they be total realizers of content properties (Bayne 2004; Van Gulick 2004). On this way of thinking, neural assemblies and neural processes are not the kinds of thing that have content to begin with, even though the complex states of which they are constituents do have content. The matching content requirement is thus moot and quarantined as an irrelevant sideshow (McLaughlin & Bartlett 2004).

Most neuroscientists do not bother with trying to come to grips with the matching content requirement or with ways of avoiding it and, admittedly, insouciance towards such foundational matters is often appropriate. After all, even if a neuroimaging study or a neural model of consciousness quantifies over representations or contents, such quantification may be interpreted to imply only that a vehicle or a process is a substrate relatum or a core realizer in a representation relation, not the total realizer of a representational state. Unfortunately, many neuroimaging studies and neuroscientific proposals appear to intend much more than such non-committal quantification. Look in almost any number of any scientific journal reporting on neuroimaging and neuropsychological experiments, and you will find some author talking about neural mechanisms responsible for constructing phenomenal objects, or about a neural assembly's representational content, or about visual or auditory neural representations, or about representations of objects for perception. Towards such views, a dose of wariness is appropriate.

A second, parallel, argument addresses not content but the realization relation between representations and neural vehicles and processes. As argued in Chapter 3, supervenience is not strong enough to establish that computational-functional properties and processes are realized by neural properties and processes. Properties and processes individuated by their content and their transformational roles can be supervenient upon properties and processes individuated by their physical and causal roles in a neural system and yet the former need not be realized by the latter. Even if something more is added to the physical properties and their causal roles – for example, requiring that the causal relations between the physical states be lawlike and support counterfactuals – some physical system can always be found that is isomorphic to a computational system (Haselager *et al.* 2003b; Putnam 1988), including physical systems that appear not to host representations at all.[2]

A popular way of showing that isomorphism between a representation and a neural vehicle or process is insufficient for a neural vehicle or process to be a representation has been an argument from analogy with the Watt Governor, a mechanical device that controls engine speed. This argument, first described in Van Gelder (1995), marked the jumping-off point for dynamicism and the then-fledgling vehicle externalism movement. It is an intuitively appealing argument. A Watt Governor works by adjusting throttle speed so that an engine does not spin out of control. As the angle of the governor's arm increases, the throttle adjusts to decrease engine speed to the desired level. Now, it is undeniable that a computational algorithm that describes the behaviour of a Watt Governor *can* be provided. It would look something like this: (1) measure flywheel speed; (2) compare measured flywheel speed against desired speed; (3) if there is no discrepancy, return to (1); if there is a discrepancy, then (a) measure steam pressure; (b) calculate desired steam pressure change; (c) calculate necessary throttle adjustment; (4) adjust throttle; (5) return to (1). It is also undeniable that this algorithm correlates with and is, indeed, isomorphic with arm angle. However, it is doubtful that the arm angle of a Watt Governor *represents* anything, including engine speed. In order for the governor's arm angle to represent engine speed, it would have to be a state that carries information content used by the system to adjust the throttle. While the arm angle is certainly used by the system to adjust the throttle, there is no plausible candidate for the arm angle's state – whether it be internal or external – that carries information content used to adjust the throttle. Indeed, invoking some such internal or external informational state of the arm just looks superfluous in describing the behaviour of the governor. In this case, then, arm angle behaviour is isomorphic to engine speed even while it does not represent engine speed. Hence, isomorphism is insufficient for representation.

The soundness of this argument is still very much up in the air. It has been challenged by those, such as Bechtel (1998), who argue that arm angle does represent engine speed after all, despite not being an information-content-bearing vehicle. After all, the system uses that arm angle to adjust the throttle, and there is a one-to-one mapping – an isomorphism – between angle arm and throttle adjustment (see also Chemero 2009). But this move bleaches content right out of representation and makes representation indistinguishable from causation. Representations are used as a stand-in for something else, and the arm angle does not stand in for anything – it is caused by increasing engine speed, and when it reaches a particular angle it adjusts the valve that lowers engine speed. Haselager *et al.* (2003b) put the point as follows:

> all that seems to be happening in the Watt Governor is a transfor-
> mation of forces. If transformation of forces is enough to warrant a
> representational interpretation, it would follow that even a bike is a
> representational system. One could say, after all, that the force that a
> person exerts on the pedals is represented by the chain, which is used
> by the chain ring in order to determine the speed of the wheel.
>
> (Haselager *et al.* 2003b: 17)

In brief, if a device such as a Watt Governor does represent engine speed, then either there is a state of it that has information content and is used by the system to adjust engine speed or representation reduces to causation. The former horn seems hopeless – it is the angle of the arm that causes the throttle adjustment, not any information content. But the latter also appears false – representation is, as noted, something more than causation. Indeed, if representation were nothing more than causation, then *any* state, internal *or* external, could be a representa-tion, and any systemic process could be a computational system. And if that is true, then representationalism is unfalsifiable – everything represents. And if *that is* true, then representationalism loses all empirical force (Beer 2000).

Since the representationalist theory of consciousness is the dominant view of consciousness and it receives ongoing empirical support from cognitive neuro-science experiments that describe everything from single-cell measurements to widespread parallel network activity as representations, this alternative must be taken seriously. It is true that "representation" is regularly used so loosely that it compromises some of the evidence for the reduction of conscious properties – especially content and qualitative properties – to neural assembly activity, their properties, and the processes into which they enter. It must also be allowed that the Watt Governor argument just rehearsed raises knotty issues about the dif-ference between symbolic and non-symbolic representation, about the status of classical computationalism, about represented content, and about the relevance of the cranial boundary. Some of these matters are investigated in greater detail in the next chapter.

Here, note that a more dramatic inference from these arguments may also be derived. This inference is the vehicle externalist's inference: the computational representationalist view of consciousness is not just weakened by the careless way that representations are bandied about but, more damaging still, the compu-tational representationalist view of consciousness is irreparably flawed because the brain does not contain representations – computational or otherwise – *at all*. If so, the two problems with representation just discussed are immediately diagnosable as the inevitable result of trying to understand conscious content in terms of a category of entity that cannot but misdescribe what that conscious content is.

If conscious events are one and all representational, then the brain that sup-ports them is a representational system. That is, conscious events picked out by their representational-content properties and transformations (whether computationally understood or not) are isomorphic to the brain's neural assemblies and their properties and activities, or the processes into which those assemblies, properties and activities enter. And, in virtue of that isomorphism, those neural assemblies, properties and activities or the processes they are constituents of are neural representations. Van Gelder describes a representationalist brain thus:

> The sense organs convert physical stimulation into elementary symbolic representations of events in the body and in the environment, and the motor system converts symbolic specifications of actions into movements of the muscles. Cognitive episodes take place in a cyclic and sequential fashion: first there is sensory input to the cognitive system, then the cognitive system algorithmically manipulates symbols, coming up with an output which then causes movement in the body; then the whole cycle begins again. Internally, the cognitive system has a modular, hierarchical construction; at the highest level, there are modules corresponding to vision, language, planning, and so on, and each of these modules breaks down into simpler modules for more elementary tasks ... Note that because the cognitive system traffics only in symbolic representations, the human body and the physical environment can be dropped from consideration; it is possible to study the cognitive system as an autonomous, bodiless, and worldless system whose function is to transform input representations into output representations.   (Van Gelder 1995: 372)

On this representationalist view, representationalist processes are modular and sequentially ordered, and their description can be exhaustively supplied without recourse to other intra- or extra-organismic systems. Moreover, given their isomorphism to the brain's neural assemblies and processes, the neural counterparts to representationalist processes are themselves modular and sequentially ordered, and their description can likewise be given without recourse to other intra- or extra-organismic systems.

But the representationalist view is not the only game in town. There is, in addition, the vehicle externalist view, according to which the brain is a dynamic situated system. If so, then even if there are representational events picked out by their content properties and transformations and even if those representationalist events are isomorphic to the brain's neural assemblies and their properties and activities or the processes into which they enter, isomorphism is not sufficient to identify the brain's neural activities as representations. For, the brain's architecture does not contain the kinds of neural entities to which neural content can be attributed. Rather, the brain's architecture is, like the Watt Governor, dynamically coupled with the systems in which it is *embodied* and the environment in which it is *embedded*. Van Gelder describes this view as follows:

[T]he cognitive system is not just the encapsulated brain; rather since the nervous system, body, and environment are all constantly changing and simultaneously influencing each other, the true cognitive system is a single unified system embracing all three. The cognitive system does not interact with the body and the external world by means of the occasional static symbolic inputs and outputs; rather, interaction between the inner and outer is best thought of as a matter of coupling, such that both sets of processes continually influence each other's direction of change. At the level at which mechanisms are best described, cognitive processing is not sequential and cyclic, for all aspects of the cognitive system are undergoing change all the time. Any sequential character in cognitive performance is the high-level, overall trajectory of change in a system whose rules of evolution specify not sequential change but rather simultaneous mutual coevolution. (Van Gelder 1995: 373)

On this alternative, conscious processes are not modular and sequentially ordered but parallel and simultaneously interactive, and their description must make recourse to other intra- or extra-organismic systems. Moreover, the brain's neural assemblies and processes that are the neural counterparts to conscious processes are themselves parallel and simultaneously interactive, and their description must likewise make recourse to other intra- or extra-organismic systems.

Vehicle externalism is the subject of considerable contemporary debate in the philosophy of mind. Many of these disputes are tangential to our interests (for defences of various aspects, see, among others, Chemero 2009; Gallagher 2005; Noë & Thompson 2004a; Robbins & Aydede 2009; Rowlands 2003, 2009; Thompson 2007; for criticisms, see among others, Adams & Aizawa 2008, 2009; Grush 1997, 2003; Horgan & Kriegel 2008; Prinz 2009). However, its emphasis on the embodied embeddedness of the conscious subject is germane here. As already argued, the prospects for microphysical neural reduction are bleak. If vehicle externalism is correct, neural reductions of conscious properties, whether microphysical or not, whether representationalist or not, are also doomed. Reduction gets things wrong from the start by trying to reduce conscious property instantiation to neural assemblies, assembly properties and activities, or the intracranial processes into which they enter. On vehicle externalist accounts, there are no causal gaps between the neural network, the body of which that network is a component, and the larger environment in which that embodied neural network is embedded. Conscious properties extend beyond the boundary of the brain: they, like the brain, are coupled with the body and the environment, each continuously influencing the other two in a non-linear cycle of feedforward and feedback loops. Coupling precludes both the construction of static internal representational neural states and the realization of any conscious property by neural assemblies alone.

Just what the dust-ups over vehicle externalism will lead to is at this point a little unclear. What is clear is that it challenges every attempt to neurally reduce conscious properties, for it appears to pull the rug right out from under a category of entity – the representation – that in attempts to understand conscious properties and their neural implementation has been assumed to be central. And without representation, there appears be nothing on which to hang conscious intentionality, for representations are the kind of entities that are one of the relata of intentional relations. Even if that problem can be solved, a more remarkable consequence of vehicle externalism is that it renders the neural reduction of conscious properties impossible even if they are *not* understood along representationalist lines. Vehicle externalism implies that conscious properties are not implemented entirely by processes within the confines of the cranium but are instead implemented by an emergent complex spread between the brain, the body and the world. If so, the search for the neural correlates of conscious properties will, even if completed, never yield total realizers of conscious properties. After all, the total realizers of conscious properties are those neural correlates that are also the neural substrates of conscious properties and from which conscious properties inherit all their causal powers. But if the body and the environment are also constituents of any mechanism that implements conscious properties, then the causal powers of conscious properties must include those of the relevant systems of the body and environment.

The challenge vehicle externalism presents to the neural reduction programme is thus twofold, in part directed against the pervasiveness of representationalist understandings of conscious properties, in part directed against the internalism characteristic of contemporary neuroscience. So, if representation is to play a role in understanding the peculiarities of at least some of the conscious properties, it must occupy an irreplaceable place in our understanding of those peculiarities and, at the same time, both avoid collapsing into causation and yet also be something for which there are plausible neural correlates (cf. Burge [2006] 2007, who makes a similar point). And if conscious properties are to be implemented by neural assemblies, assembly properties, or assembly activity properties or the processes into which those assemblies, properties or activities enter, then it cannot be, as vehicle externalism claims, that conscious properties are implemented only by a system coupled with the extra-organismic environment.

This chapter has followed a trajectory from the intracranial and lower-order to the extracranial and emergent. We first argued against microphysical reductionism, concluding that it is extremely unlikely that conscious properties are ever going to reduce to microphysical properties, whether they be microphysical properties of neurons or neural assemblies. Moreover, the best philosophical argument for thinking that conscious properties *must* so reduce to microphysical properties – the argument for the conclusion that every kind of property other than microphysical properties is overdetermined by those microphysical properties – was shown to be unsound. Having cleared the ground of the overdetermination threat, the landscape opens up to countenance emergent properties as legitimate properties. So in the third section we unpacked in a little greater detail one such kind of an emergence view, vehicle externalism, according to which the intracranial world and the extracranial world are coupled in mutual feedback and feedforward loops of causal interaction. We now turn to another set of arguments against neural reduction, those that proceed directly from the nature of representation and content.

12. EMBODIED AND EMBEDDED CONSCIOUSNESS

Grant that intentional content, subjective perspectivity and qualitative character supervene on and covary with neural events and neural properties, and grant that the latter are core and even differential realizers of the former. Grant that nothing much less complex than widespread activity in the thalamocortical system is implicated as the neural realizer of any conscious property. Grant all of that – it's another question whether even this widespread field of neural activity is itself enough for conscious property instantiation. Perhaps the base relative to which all the conscious properties are higher-order or emergent is composed not only of neural assemblies and their activity, no matter how many of them there are or how sophisticated that activity is, but also of extracranial objects and events and their activity. If so, then not only would conscious properties and events not be realized by individual neurons, dedicated neural assemblies, or widely distributed networks of activity in numerous neural assemblies, they would not be realized only by the brain. In that case, consciousness would, in one way of thinking about it, no longer be in our heads.

In this chapter, arguments for the conclusion that the conscious properties of content, qualitative character and subjective perspectivity are in part extracranially constituted are detailed. If properly qualified, content and qualia externalism are true and have consequences for particular kinds of reduction. The case of externalism about subjective perspectivity is another matter – here there is little reason to think that externalist arguments gain traction. More radical forms of externalism, as advocated by vehicle externalists, are shown to be too strong.

INTERNALISM AND EXTERNALISM

If the argument against emergent overdetermination in the previous chapter is sound, the strongest philosophical argument on behalf of microphysical reduction of conscious properties collapses. Of course, not all reductive physicalisms are microphysical, so other reductive physicalisms are not thereby shown false. (RPC)′ and (NR)′ are ready examples of such options:

(RPC)′   Physical events or parts thereof exhaust everything that is concrete, and there is a supervenience relation between all families of conscious properties and physical properties such that subvening physical properties are the only realizers of supervening conscious properties.

(NR)′   Physical events or parts thereof exhaust everything that is concrete, and there is a supervenience relation between all families of conscious properties and properties of neural assembly activity such that subvening properties of neural assembly activity are the only realizers of supervening conscious properties.

Both (RPC)′ and (NR)′ are reductionist but not microphysical. And just as (RPC) is weaker than (NR), so too (RPC)′ is weaker than (NR)′. After all, (RPC)′ is, while (NR)′ is not, consistent with conscious properties being realized by non-neural physical properties. So, even if (NR)′ is false, some other kind of reductive physicalism about conscious properties consistent with (RPC)′ may be true. Of course, if (RPC)′ is false, then so too is (NR)′.

As we have already seen in Chapters 8 and 11, a considerable amount of philosophical smoke is currently swirling around both (NR)′ and (RPC)′. We begin with (NR)′. Criticisms of (NR)′ attach both to the claims it makes about the particulars of conscious events and to the properties that make psychological events conscious. Initially, then, there are four alternatives to consider:

(α)   The particular of a conscious event is a neural assembly, and its conscious property supervenes on a neural assembly activity property such that the latter is the only realizer of the former

This is a version of (NR)′. According to (α), the particulars of conscious events are neural assemblies, and their conscious properties supervene only upon neural properties. The next alternative rejects the supervenience of conscious properties solely on neural properties:

(β)   The particular of a conscious event is a neural assembly, and its conscious property does not supervene on a neural assembly activity property such that the latter is the only realizer of the former

According to (β), particulars of conscious events are neural assemblies, but their conscious properties do not supervene solely on neural properties. Hence, if (β) is true, then (NR)′ is false. A third alternative is this:

(γ)   The particular of a conscious event is not a neural assembly, and its conscious property does not supervene on a neural assembly activity property such that the latter is the only realizer of the former

According to (γ), particulars of conscious events are not neural assemblies, and their conscious properties do not supervene on neural properties either. So, again, if (γ) is true, then (NR)' is false. Finally:

(δ)   The particular of a conscious event is not a neural assembly, and its conscious property supervenes on a neural assembly activity property such that the latter is the only realizer of the former

If (δ) is true, particulars of conscious events are not neural assemblies, but their properties supervene only on neural properties. Still, since (δ) denies that the particulars of conscious events are neural assemblies, it too is inconsistent with (NR)'.

This last option – (δ) – has not found defenders, so we henceforth dispense with it. The live disagreements are between (α), (β) and (γ); (α) is a version of (NR)' and (β) and (γ) are claims inconsistent with (α) and, hence, inconsistent with (NR)'. It can be tempting, especially to representationalists, to think that a completely general argument attaches to all three conscious properties at once and will prove that either (α), (β) or (γ) is true. Suppose, for example, that all conscious properties are representational properties. If a general argument shows that all representational properties must be internal, then that general argument will apply equally to content, qualitative character and subjective perspectivity. However, one of the neuroscientific discoveries about qualitative character, content and subjective perspectivity is that they can and do dissociate. Moreover, as already argued, qualitative character and subjective perspectivity are not wholly representational properties. If so, there can be little reason to hope that a general representationalist argument for or against internalism or externalism will be forthcoming. Similar considerations may apply to each case, but separate argument must show that (β) and (γ) are true before (NR)' is shown to be mistaken for all conscious properties. So, versions of (β) and (γ) must be provided separately for content, qualitative character and subjective perspectivity.

Following others (e.g. Horgan & Kriegel 2008), the word "vehicle" may be substituted for "particular" when stating these alternatives. The first group of views are both vehicle and property *internalist*. These are:

VEHICLE INTERNALISM/PROPERTY INTERNALISM
  (a) conscious event vehicles are neural assemblies, and content is realized only by properties of neural assembly activity
  (b) conscious event vehicles are neural assemblies, and qualitative character is realized only by properties of neural assembly activity

   (c)   conscious event vehicles are neural assemblies, and subjective perspectivity is realized only by properties of neural assembly activity

Computational representationalism is a paradigmatic example of vehicle/property internalism. Views that reject vehicle and property internalism are vehicle and property *externalist*:

VEHICLE EXTERNALISM/PROPERTY EXTERNALISM
   (d)   conscious event vehicles are not neural assemblies, and content is realized by properties of neural assembly activity plus properties of events in the extracranial world
   (e)   conscious event vehicles are not neural assemblies, and qualitative character is realized by properties of neural assembly activity plus properties of events in the extracranial world
   (f)   conscious event vehicles are not neural assemblies, and subjective perspectivity is realized by properties of neural assembly activity plus properties of events in the extracranial world

Situated cognition views are paradigmatic vehicle and property externalisms. Views that reject only property internalism are vehicle internalist and property externalist. To wit:

VEHICLE INTERNALISM/PROPERTY EXTERNALISM
   (g)   conscious event vehicles are neural assemblies, and content is realized by properties of neural assembly activity plus properties of events in the extracranial world
   (h)   conscious event vehicles are neural assemblies, and qualitative character is realized by properties of neural assembly activity plus properties of events in the extracranial world
   (i)   conscious event vehicles are neural assemblies, and subjective perspectivity is realized by properties of neural assembly activity plus properties of events in the extracranial world.

Semantic externalism of the Burgean kind (Burge 2007) is the paradigmatic vehicle internalism/property externalism. Pretty obviously, (a), (b) and (c) are entirely internalist; (g), (h) and (i) are entirely externalist; and (d), (e) and (f) are somewhere between the extremes. If (a), (b) and (c) are all true, then (NR)' is true. If either (d) or (g) is true, then (a) and (NR)' are false; if either (e) or (h) is true, then (b) and (NR)' are false; and if either (f) or (i) is true, then (c) and (NR)' are false.

    The distinction between core and total realizers drawn in previous chapters helps make sense of the options. Each of (a), (b) and (c) is a way of stating that properties of neural assembly activity are the total realizers of conscious properties; all the other options are inconsistent with neural assembly activity being the total realizers of conscious event properties. Externalism about vehicles and properties – (d), (e) and (f) above – is inconsistent both with neural assembly activity being the vehicle of conscious events and with neural assembly activity being the total realizer of content, qualitative character or subjective perspectivity. Vehicle internalism/property externalism – (g), (h) and (i) above – states that neural assembly activities are the vehicles of conscious events but that neural assembly activities are not the total realizers of content, qualitative character or subjective perspectivity. Of course, although neural assembly activity may not be a total realizer of each kind of conscious property, it may still be a core realizer of conscious properties, for it may be that neural assembly activity is a salient part of a total realizer without which each kind of conscious property cannot be instantiated. It is just that, as core realizers, neural assembly activity can occur without a conscious property thereby being instantiated. Something else is needed.

CONTENT

One result of neuroscientifically informed philosophical discussions of conscious properties is a set of sharply drawn arguments that purport to show that qualitative character, subjective perspectivity and intentional content are not realized only by neural assembly activity, no matter how complex or multifaceted that assembly's activity may be. These arguments focus on the requirement that realization of one property by another is possible only if the former supervenes only on the latter. Since reduction obtains only if realization does, and realization obtains only if supervenience obtains, if qualitative character, intentional content and subjective perspectivity do not supervene only on neural activity, then the possibility of their neural realization and reduction is undercut. Whether this is true or not forms the core of the internalism/externalism debate. The internalism/externalism debate emerged first as a debate about belief content. As a result, the arguments for content externalism are better developed than those concerning qualitative character and subjective perspectivity. In some ways, this focus may appear to be unfortunate – after all, defending qualitative character externalism may seem straightforward in a way that defending content externalism does not. However, qualitative character externalism is not straightforward, as will be seen, and the argument that content is partially external shows why.

Vehicle internalism/content internalism

If both the vehicle and properties of conscious events supervene only on what happens in the brain, then *everything* relevant for realizing conscious events happens in the brain. Since for a neural reductionist *all* that happens in the brain is the sparking and whirring of neural assemblies, that activity is the only possible candidate for subvening conscious event vehicles and properties. Hence, it is only the internal properties of neural assembly activity that are candidates for being the substrates of, and realizers for, conscious events. Candidates for neural assembly internal properties that might be substrates for conscious properties include spiking rate, activation level, activation pattern, connection weights, non-random synchronous gamma activation, feedforward corollary discharge signals and re-entrant processing. Some neural versions of internalism identify the relevant boundary as the cranium, but it is more plausible to fix it as the central nervous system. Nothing in what follows will hang on this, but the careful may substitute "intrasystemic" and "extrasystemic" wherever "intracranial" and "extracranial" are encountered.

It is a caricature that the default position for philosophy of mind and consciousness is content internalism. Nevertheless, it is undeniable that content internalism is widespread in the discipline and is easily generated with straightforward examples. A stick in the water looks bent, so there is something that the stick looks like. But when we remove the stick from the water, we discover that it is not bent the way it looks. Similarly, a hallucination of a floating cow is not a part of the extracranial world. In both the case of illusion and the case of hallucination, it seems that something must be added to what is found in the world to account for their content. The way the stick looks must be distinct from the stick itself, so in addition to sticks, an intracranial look of the bent stick (or a perspectival taking of the bent stick or a sense-datum of the bent stick) must be added to the list of what exists. Likewise, the hallucinated cow must also be added to the list of what exists even if it exists only in consciousness. Generalizing, content internalists infer that for every kind of conscious experience, there is an internal something-or-other – a sense-datum or a look or a representation that is the direct object of conscious experience and from or through which the external world is on occasion indirectly experienced. So, if we hear a meadowlark singing, we *directly* experience an internal something-or-other that represents the meadowlark's song and use that something-or-other to *indirectly* hear the external song.

Such arguments and conclusions have had an astonishingly long shelf life in philosophy. Many of them are used as precursors to scepticism about the extracranial world. We need not walk down this particular garden path, for doing so conflates justification and explanation, taking occasional malfunctions of perceptual mechanisms to impose constraints on all perceptual knowledge (Evans 1985; Mackie 1976; Rorty 1979). But the obvious assumption is that in properly functioning perceptual experience we transparently perceive and gain the foundations for knowing external objects and events and their properties as they are presented to us without any internal intermediary. Sceptics replace this obvious assumption with the bizarre assumption that in properly functioning perceptual experience we perceive and gain the foundations for knowing only internal somethings *via* which we regain external objects and events by inference.

However, even if we are trying only to get clear about the role of neural correlates of perception, it can seem that dreams, illusions and hallucinations imply that all we ever consciously perceive are mind-internal objects. Consider the Müller-Lyer illusion (Figure 12.1). The two horizontal lines look to be of different length, the top line looking shorter than the bottom line. But they are the same length, as can be confirmed by dropping a vertical line from the top vertices to the bottom vertices (Figure 12.2). Since the lines in Figure 12.1 continue to look to be of different lengths even after confirming that they are the same length, as in Figure 12.2, there is something at least in visual experience that is its content and distinct in some way from the way the extracranial world is. Whatever that content may turn out to be, it has been thought to be sufficient to establish content internalism about visual experience. Supposing that all conscious perceptual experience is subject to similar modality-specific illusions, the content internalist infers that since all conscious perceptual events are intentionally structured, then they are all likewise related to a content that is intracranial and distinct in some way from the way the world is.

If sound, this argument shows both how to implicate illusions in any empirical account of conscious perceptual experience and how to use them to buttress content internalism. Having secured content internalism, identifying the neural correlates of that content will provide the first step in completing a neural reduction of content, and thus a vindication of (NR)' for content. But how strong is the argument? First, the generalization required to generate content internalism across perceptual modalities, much less across other psychological modalities, such as cognitive, interoceptive and affective modalities, is severely undermotivated by even a pocketful of illusion. For the generalization to hold, all the other perceptual, cognitive, interoceptive and affective modalities have to be subject to relevantly similar illusions. Second, using illusions to generate conclusions about normal perceptual experience is suspect, for illusions are instances in which our normal perceptual experience breaks down. But there would be no way even to identify an illusion as an illusion if our perceptual experience were

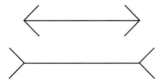

Figure 12.1 The Müller-Lyer illusion.

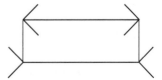

Figure 12.2 The Müller-Lyer lines are the same length.

not to function properly in the vast majority of cases (Burge [1986b] 2007). Put these concerns to the side. Note rather that if the content internalist's assessment of visual illusions is itself mistaken, then this argument for content internalism collapses. The content internalist's interpretation of visual illusions is mistaken if, among other reasons, the recalcitrant illusory content is not intracranial, as the internalist claims, but extracranial. And it is pretty clear that the illusory content is extracranial. Consider again the Müller-Lyer illusion. The content of the Müller-Lyer illusion is illusory because the bottom line's length continues to appear to be longer than the top line's length despite confirmation to the contrary. But it is the two lines that appear to differ in length, not the visual experience of them, and the two lines are printed on a page of this book, and this book is extracranial.[1]

The content internalist is confronted with problems other than a tenuous interpretation of visual illusions. Among them is that the view leads to bizarre results. The argument for this conclusion starts with an analogy. Compare two ways of thinking about a photograph's content. Suppose you have a photograph taken out of an airplane window of Kingston, Jamaica. On the first alternative, the content of the photograph is what is represented, i.e. Kingston itself, the city on the southern coast of Jamaica. The representational vehicle is then the paper that hosts the photographic image of Kingston, and the representational feature is the image of Kingston, that is, the pattern of colours and shapes impregnated in the paper. What makes the vehicle/feature pair represent Kingston is that the patterns of colours and shapes impregnated in the paper map appropriately to the buildings of Kingston, to the Blue Hills behind the buildings, and to the skyline, viewed from a certain spatial location (the perspective of the photographer). On the second alternative, the representational vehicle remains the photographic paper, the representational feature remains the pattern of colours and shapes, but the content of the photograph is the image constituted by that pattern of colours and shapes on the photographic paper. The actual city of Kingston, its buildings, and the Blue Hills behind them, all fall out of the content, replaced by the image of them.

Thinking of photographic content as a pattern of colours and shapes on photographic paper is relevantly similar to thinking of conscious content as supervening solely on internal neural features. In both cases, content is exhausted by properties of, and relations between, internal elements and whatever supervenes only on them. In the case of conscious content, this view has awkward consequences, for it readily leads to the view that conscious content is an internal *object*, an internal thingamajig that somehow recreates – re-presents – an external thingamabob. If so, then the consciously experienced external world is duplicated intracranially. This duplication immediately entails a degenerate view known as *Cartesian materialism*, according to which the brain is a neural machine that engages in unconscious perceptual, affective, interoceptive, proprioceptive and cognitive processing, whose results are projected forwards to a central executive somewhere in prefrontal cortex where everything comes together for the subject to experience as multimodal conscious content (Dennett 2006; Dennett & Kinsbourne 1995).

While Cartesian materialism rejects Descartes' immaterial soul-subject, it acquiesces to a subject that perceives and cognizes about internal representations. But, first, reifying content as an internal representation object merely moves the problem of representation from one place to another; it does not explain representation. Explaining our visual and olfactory experience of a bear is made no easier by moving the bear inside our brain, experienced as if we were watching an internal movie in Smell-o-Vision. Second, Cartesian materialism encourages the thought that there must be a neurofunctional centre in the brain where everything is bound together. But even if neither incoming sensory information itself nor the early stages of perceptual workup are sufficient for conscious experience, and even if we consciously perceive an external world, all neural processing need not come together at some particular location in the brain.

Third, where content is internally reified, the properties of what is represented are replicated by that which represents them. This is an example of *vehicle/content confusion* (Dennett & Kinsbourne 1995; Millikan 1991, 2008). As argued in Chapter 11 (recall the discussion of isomorphism), vehicle/content confusions grow easily on the soil of internalist proposals where a vehicle's properties need to resemble or match represented content properties. Given the symmetry of resemblance, it can easily seem that there must be something in the brain that bears some similarity to what is represented. But representation, unlike resemblance, is asymmetric, and there is no such requirement. Neither the representation vehicle, nor the representation feature, nor the representation vehicle/feature pair need replicate the properties of what is represented in order for them to successfully represent those properties. Hence, even trying to meet the expectation that vehicle/feature pairs either replicate or resemble represented content properties is an error, and views that do not try to meet the expectation are not failures despite not trying.

Fourth, if the events of the consciously experienced extracranial world are duplicated inside as a set of internal events that supervene solely on properties of neural assembly activity, and if these internal events are what we consciously experience when we consciously experience anything, then the extracranial world risks becoming irrelevant. If what is experienced is an internal representation that supervenes solely on neural assembly activity properties, then, as Fodor once suggested (1980b), invoking relations to extracranial events as pertinent considerations for determining content becomes superfluous. This view is known as *methodological solipsism*. According to it, content is supervenient upon and totally realized by internal neural assembly activity, and the objects and events of the extracranial world have nothing to do with individuating content, even if they cause it.

One generalization from methodological solipsism about belief content is methodological solipsism about consciousness, the view that all the properties of conscious experience are supervenient upon and totally realized by internal neural assembly activity. It is undeniable that methodological solipsism is a working assumption of a number of neuroscientists. Some neuroscientifically minded philosophers of consciousness also endorse just such a view. A recent advocate is Thomas Metzinger, who claims that, "conscious experience, as such, is an internal affair. Whatever else may or may not be true about consciousness, once all the internal properties of your nervous system are set, all the properties of your conscious experience – its subjective content and the way it *feels* to you – are fully determined" (Metzinger 2009a: 21). Here we get the complete view – content, subjective perspectivity *and* qualitative character are supervenient only upon and totally determined by the internal properties of the nervous system. This looks very much like Cartesian materialism.

The consensus in contemporary neuroscience and philosophy is that representationalist views of conscious content can avoid Cartesian materialism's unappetizing consequences and solipsism by claiming that representation vehicles are intracranial and their activity is caused by but not identical with what those vehicles represent, and then adding to that the further claim that we consciously perceive external objects and events by representing them (Maund 2003). If these views are adopted, then since inference to extracranial objects and events is not necessary and since representing is caused by the represented extracranial objects and events, Cartesian materialism and solipsism are both avoided. It all sounds good. However, many neuroscience studies are not nearly as free of Cartesian ghosts as proponents like to think, for wherever content is modelled as an internal representation, there relations between subject and internal content do nothing more than replicate relations between subject and represented content (Burge [2006] 2007). Since this tangled assumption is the source of Cartesian materialism and methodological solipsism, it must be actively guarded against.

Vehicle internalism/content externalism

In addition to negative arguments against content internalism, there are also positive arguments for the conclusion that while the vehicles of conscious content are neural assemblies, some content properties are realized only by properties of neural assembly activity plus objects, events and properties of events in the extracranial world. These positive arguments are frequently motivated by philosophical considerations concerning the content of so-called *de re* beliefs, beliefs about mind-external things and events ("*de re*" means "of the thing"). Other beliefs, so-called *de dicto* beliefs, are beliefs about propositions ("*de dicto*" means "of what is said"). The difference between *de re* and *de dicto* belief content is not simply that for *de re* belief content external objects, events and properties cause internal events that have them as their referent. It is the more contentious claim that external objects, events and properties are constituents of *de re* content. If *de re* content is constituted in part by objects and events in the external world, then it is not exhaustively subserved by neural assembly activity. Thus is this alternative *externalist* about conscious content.

Content externalism is philosophically motivated by variations on a thought experiment, due originally to Putnam (1975) and Burge ([1982] 2007), concerning beliefs of a pair of molecule-by-molecule twins. Here is a version. Suppose neurophysiological twins, Frick and Frack, the first of whom lives in Brazil and the second of whom lives in Suriname. What buildings and public spaces are built of in Brazil is regular concrete, while in Suriname what buildings and public spaces are built of is high-strength concrete. Regular concrete has a particular chemical formula, while high-strength concrete, which has silica added to it, has a different formula. Still, the two types of concrete look, taste, smell and work just like each other. Since Frick and Frack live in distinct environments and concrete is regular concrete in the one and high-strength concrete in the other, Frick and Frack differ in the content of their respective beliefs of the concrete they are looking at that it would be a good skateboarding surface. Since Frick's belief is about regular concrete and Frack's belief is about high-strength concrete, and since regular concrete and high-strength concrete are constituents of, respectively, Frick's and Frack's *de re* concrete beliefs, at least one constituent of their belief contents lies beyond the limits of their bodies and includes features of the environment external to them. However, by hypothesis, Frick and Frack are molecule-by-molecule duplicates of each other, so the internal properties of their neural assemblies are identical too. Since one of the constituents of the content of each of Frick's and Frack's *de re* beliefs differs and lies beyond the limit of their bodies, whatever the content of the internal activity that correlates with conscious beliefs may be, it will not be the same content as the content of their conscious *de re* beliefs of concrete. Hence, at least some conscious content does not have only internal properties as its sole substrate. If so, some conscious content is not realized only by internal neural assembly activity (cf. also Burge [1986a] 2007, [1995] 2007).

Content externalism attaches not just to *de re* beliefs but to many other kinds of contentful conscious events, including most obviously those of the various perceptual, interoceptive and proprioceptive modalities. These too have content that is in part constituted by objects and events in the extracranial world. Call perceptual, interoceptive and proprioceptive content individuated at least in part by objects and events in the extracranial world *world-involving* content (allowing that some world-involving content extends to only a very small part of the extracranial world, perhaps no farther than our skin, as in interoceptive and proprioceptive content). So, the argument goes, content externalism spells the doom not just for the prospects of providing total neural realizers for a class of conscious belief contents but also of providing total neural realizers for a much larger class of conscious events, namely all those that have world-involving content. Hence, even if a gazillion neural correlates for conscious events that have world-involving content are enumerated, they will remain forever only correlates and substrates. Since having total realizers is necessary for reduction, neurally reducing this large class of conscious events is undermined, and no conscious perceptual event is ever reduced to or identical with its neural substrates.

Grant that constituents of world-involving content are extracranial. The neural correlates of such content are then not candidates for either total neural substrates or total neural realizers of that content. However, this does not entail that such correlates cannot be core substrates or core realizers of world-involving content. Even if such content does not supervene solely on what goes on in intracranial neural assemblies, it does supervene on that neural assembly activity plus extracranial events that are its other constituent (Burge [1993] 2007). Note also that claiming that externalistically individuated content does not have a neural vehicle substrate because world-involving content has extracranial constituents is mistaken, akin to thinking that a penny in my pocket is not in my pocket because what makes it a penny – the social practice of money exchange – is not in my pocket (Yablo 1997). The activity of edge-detectors in visual cortex provides a ready example. Their activity is, pretty obviously, to detect edges and edges are in the environment outside the head. But their activity is still the neural substrate of the intentionally loaded perceptions of edges (Burge [1986a] 2007; Jack & Prinz 2004). The activity of edge-detectors is an obvious core realizer of the intentionality of edge detection in conscious visual experience, and the activity of edge-detectors plus the edges they detect are together the total realizer of edge-detection.

Generalizing, the core/total distinction can be applied to all the purported scientific laws that support the claim that neural assembly activity is a core substrate for and core realizer of world-involving content. The result is a set of scientific laws that govern the neural substrates that are core realizers of intentionality and that govern both the neural and non-neural core realizers of intentionality. Nothing insuperably difficult faces the generation of such laws: the supervenience of conscious content properties on physical properties guarantees that there will be neural properties with which content properties nomologically covary, and the neural correlate programme is on its way to filling in some of the details by specifying particular neural/content property pairs. There is still a long way to go and a lot of refinements and corrections to be made, but the project is far from hopeless, and were it to be completed, it would be a remarkable achievement. But generating all these scientific laws will yield less than the more ambitious neural reductionists have been hoping for – their hope has been that conscious content is totally realized by neural assembly activity. Since core realizers of conscious properties are not and never will be total realizers of conscious properties, identifying the core realizers of conscious properties is less thrilling than has been promised. Some of the more ambitious neural reduction claims are too strong and must be weakened.

Vehicle externalism/content externalism

A more provocative proposal is that the vehicles of conscious content are also external to the brain, that, in other words, conscious content vehicles supervene on neural assembly activity plus things and events in the extracranial world. Most vehicle externalist arguments are deployed against neural realizers of conscious content vehicles. Clark and Chalmers (1998) offer the prototypical argument for the view. It concerns the use of external cognitive processing aids, such as pen and paper, and external memory aids, such as notebooks. An instance of the argument goes as follows. I am somewhat forgetful, especially when I am busy. Suppose I promise to meet my wife for lunch at Monica's Taco Shop at one o'clock. She believes that Monica's is at the corner of Fillmore and Nevada, and she will remember to meet me there. If I am busy that morning, I know myself well enough to know that even if I remember where Monica's is, I may forget to leave my office in time to meet her there. On such days, I write things down on sticky notes and stick them to my computer screen in obtrusive places. In both her case and my case, we know where Monica's is, we know that we have agreed to meet there at one o'clock, and we remember to leave in time to arrive there at one o'clock. But whereas my wife consults her memory to prompt her to pick up her keys, I consult the sticky note. In my case, an element of the external world plays the same causal role as an element of the internal world plays in my wife's case. So, the argument goes, my conscious memory is in part external to my neural goings-on. Since something external to neural assembly activity is a constituent of my conscious belief, my conscious belief is not subserved solely by properties of neural assembly activity. Hence, it is not the case that my conscious belief is realized solely by that neural assembly activity. Hence, neural assembly activity is not a total realizer of some conscious vehicles.

As with content externalism, vehicle externalism is the result of a negative argument against the claim that the neural vehicles of content realize content and a positive argument for the claim that the vehicles of content are often external to the brain. The negative argument again zeroes in on the constitutional sufficiency of realization. Vehicle externalists claim that for some contentful events, neural substrates are not constitutionally sufficient and so do not totally realize them. Having gained the negative result that content vehicles do not have neural realizers, they offer analyses of content vehicles on which they are quite literally spread out beyond the internal neural milieu into the extracranial world. Content vehicles are thus emergent complexes constituted in part by neural assemblies and their activities and in part by extracranial objects and their activities. Different versions highlight distinct mechanisms by which spread content vehicles are realized, but they typically share commitments to three general ideas (Rowlands 2006, 2009). First, the extracranial world feeds information into an organism's conscious events and processes (perceptual, interoceptive and proprioceptive processes, affective processes such as emotion and qualitative character, and cognitive processes, such as memory, inference-making and higher-order reasoning). Second, many (though certainly not all) conscious events and processes straddle internal and external modalities of information processing. Third, the conscious events and processes that do straddle internal and external modalities of information processing are dynamic activities by which we manipulate and transform the features of the information-carrying mind-external environment (see Clark 1997, 2008; Clark & Chalmers 1998; Hurley 1998; Noë 2004; Thompson 2007; and Wilson & Clark 2009 for additional arguments on behalf of the hypothesis).

Vehicle externalism has provoked intense, often hostile, reaction from some philosophers. This critical assessment is grounded in part on the suspicion that its advocates conflate causal conditions required for conscious event vehicles to instantiate content properties with constituents of content property instantiations and in part by the worry that extending the mind into the external environment leaches subjective perspectivity out of consciousness (Adams & Aizawa 2008, 2009; Horgan & Kriegel 2008). The first concern parallels a concern already lodged against content externalism: just because what makes a neural assembly the assembly it is, is not intracranial does not mean the assembly is not intracranial. While edge detector neural assemblies are edge detector neural assemblies because they detect edges in the extracranial world, they are not themselves in the extracranial world. Generalizing, although the vehicles of conscious content represent extracranial content, that they so represent does not entail that they are themselves in the extracranial world.

A second worry is that just as higher-order theories of consciousness threaten to turn external things, events and properties in the surrounding environment into conscious things, events and properties, so vehicle externalism similarly threatens to turn external objects and events in the surrounding environment into conscious objects and events. Here is the argument. By hypothesis, a conscious event vehicle can be external to intracranial neural activity. So, like intracranial vehicles, that extracranial vehicle can host conscious content. Since conscious content is subjectively perspectival, it appears that an extracranial vehicle can also host subjectively perspectival conscious content. But that implies that the paper I use to help me solve a maths problem hosts conscious content from a subjective perspective. But then whose subjective perspective is it? Certainly not the paper's – even if I use pencil and paper and even if the paper hosts derived intentional content, neither pencil nor paper host conscious content from their subjective perspective. Perhaps, then, the paper hosts conscious content from my subjective perspective? But that seems false as well – my conscious experience of using the paper is from a subjective perspective, but subjective perspectivity does not thereby bleed outwards from my conscious experience into the paper. In brief, either subjective perspectivity is a property only of intracranial events and vehicle externalism must be rejected, or vehicle externalism is accepted and subjective perspectivity turns out not to be a property only of intracranial events. Pending more persuasive argument to the contrary, the former alternative is preferable to the latter (Adams & Aizawa 2008, 2009).

Construed as a denial of content internalism, vehicle externalism amounts to the negative claim that not all content is constituted entirely intracranially. However, inferring from this negative claim that all conscious content is constituted at least in part by extracranial elements is in turn too strong. Dreams, hallucinations, mental images, hearing music, reflection, monitoring, self-awareness and talking to oneself are all occurrent conscious events whose content is not constituted even in part by extracranial elements (Prinz 2009, among many others). Even if conscious content is hosted by vehicles that are entirely and always in the head, in perception and other world-involving conscious processes and events those neural vehicles host content properties whose substrates are in part extracranial things, events and properties, while in experiences of after-images, dreams, hallucinations and the like, content substrates are exhausted by neural activity. It is up to the relevant sciences to determine what intracranial neural resources and what extracranial resources are engaged in the two kinds and how the neural resources differ across the kinds. Thus, a challenge for contemporary neuroscience, to date almost entirely unmet, is to differentiate core from total realizers for the two kinds of content.

QUALITATIVE CHARACTER

It would be astonishing to discover that the qualitative properties of conscious experience have no neural correlates. It would be equally astonishing to discover that the qualitative properties of objects as consciously experienced are replicated in the conscious experience of disembodied spirits. There may be something that a fresh mango tastes like for a disembodied spirit or soul, but whatever it may be it is at best only remotely similar to what it tastes like for us embodied ones. Spirits lack the neural wherewithal of the gustatory, olfactory and associative cortices with which we come loaded and which play a role in producing the mango's taste.

Denying that neural processing plays a substantive role in generating qualitative features of conscious experience is silly. Chapters 6 and 7 reviewed a fraction of the neuropsychological and neuroimaging evidence about the perceptual, interoceptive, affective and cognitive pathways and a relatively small set of dysfunctional processes. As small as that set may be, it is large enough to give an idea of the strength of neuroscientific explanations of qualitative deficits and to be confident that similar explanations are available also for numb touching, deaf hearing, motion and change blindness, akinetopsia (visual motion blindness), achromatopsia (not seeing colour at all), chromatopsia (seeing everything tinged in a particular colour) and synaesthesia (Robertson & Sagiv 2005; Tonkonogy & Puente 2009). Of course, there is no reason to think that neuroscientific studies are limited to providing neural correlates of perceptual qualitative properties. Similar studies of a wide variety of interoceptive and proprioceptive qualitative properties are also available, each of them identifying with variable precision the neural assemblies and cortical regions whose activity correlates with and is caus-ally required for the associated qualitative property to be instantiated.

Does the scientific evidence show that activity in neural assemblies totally realizes qualitative property instantiation? Qualitative internalism affirms that it does; qualitative externalism affirms that it does not, that is, neural assembly activity is not alone constitutively sufficient for the instantiation of qualitative properties.

Vehicle internalism/qualitative character internalism

Were the qualitative properties of conscious experience to be totally realized by neural assembly activity, all their causal powers would be exhausted by the causal powers of the neural assembly activities that are their substrates, and qualita-tive character would reduce to those assemblies and their activity. Such a view is internalist both about the vehicles of qualitatively endowed conscious events and the qualitative properties those vehicles instantiate in conscious events. As noted in Chapter 4, qualitative character internalism is easily motivated by mundane observations. Visual experience of the world, not the world as visually experienced, becomes blurry when you take your glasses off; when you cross your eyes, you instantly create offset images of what you are looking at; if you suffer from tinnitus, the source of the persistent ringing is a property of the activ-ity of the internal mechanisms responsible for auditory experience; if you look at something that is bright red and then close your eyes, you experience a green after-image. At least some qualitative properties are revealed upon reflection to be properties only of conscious experience and not at all of the things and events present in conscious experience. Neuropsychological disorders such as agno-sia, synaesthesia, achromatopsia, chromatopsia, akinetopsia, blindsight, numb touching, deaf hearing, motion and change blindness strengthen the suspicion that all qualitative properties are properties only of conscious experience and not of the things and events present in conscious experience.

In one way of understanding it, this suspicion cannot but be true. Were we not neurally equipped as we are, we would not have the qualitatively endowed experience we do. We notice the constitutive role of all that unconscious and non-conscious neural activity only when it malfunctions and spits out some-thing weird. For example, all the neural activity responsible for spatial, location, feature, part and sequence binding requisite for visual experience to be as it is breaches consciousness only when conscious content or qualitative character becomes *un*bound in the peculiar ways associated with disorders such as agnosia, blindsight, akinetopsia, achromatopsia and chromatopsia. As we have seen in earlier chapters, isomorphic intramodal binding processes for auditory, gustatory, olfactory and tactile experience also go kaput on occasion and lead to still other species of modality-specific unbound conscious experience. Neural malfunctions that yield more complex disorders of inter- and supramodally bound content and character, such as retrograde amnesia, split-brain syndrome, executive dysfunction disorder and depersonalization syndrome all confirm the constitutive importance of our neural kit.

Focus on perceptual binding. In a general way of thinking about them, binding processes are nothing less than the set of neural processes by which the unified content and qualitative character of conscious experience are generated. On this way of thinking, there are *lots* of binding processes at many different levels of complexity. Even if considerable advances have been made in isolating some of their neuroanatomical locales and functioning, it should be obvious that plenty of empirical work remains. Most of the assemblies responsible for inter- and supramodal binding are, for example, currently undescribed. Moreover, many of the perceptual binding assemblies that occur downstream from early processes feed back into the upstream stages of perceptual binding, and these complicated feedback pathways are also currently undescribed and severely underdescribed (Ramachandran & Hubbard 2005). Again, downstream cognitive binding processes sometimes feed back into upstream perceptual binding processes. While such downstream and cognitive penetrability of perception is currently under cognitive neuroscience's investigative microscope, results to date are fragmentary and inconclusive (Raftopoulos 2005). Just as significant, cognitive penetrability of perception is an opening wedge for other research – most of which has not even begun – into cognitive penetrability of affection and affective penetrability of perception and cognition (Panksepp 2003, 2007, among others).

As interesting as the future of binding research may be, it must be noted that the causal and constitutive necessity of neural processing for generating qualitative character that such research maps is not at issue in the internalism/externalism debate. What separates qualitative character internalists from externalists is that the former affirm and the latter deny that the role that neural processing plays in generating the qualitative character of conscious experience is one of totally realizing that qualitative character. That is, internalists affirm and externalists deny that neural processing is constitutively sufficient for generating qualitative character.

On the face of it, qualitative character internalism seems patently false: how *could* neural processing be constitutively sufficient for the taste of a mango, the smell of a banana, the sound of the surf, or the vivid red colour of bougainvillea? When put this way, the idea can simply seem daft (Burge [1986b] 2007).

However, the internalist has arguments for the conclusion, and some of these arguments are far from silly. A recent argument against qualitative character externalism from Pautz is representative (Pautz 2006; we ignore some details of the version as it appears there). The argument assumes the causal necessity of neural processing for qualitative properties. Consider a case in which two individuals, Tex and Rex, both look at a hunk of jade that reflects light of, say, 500 nm wavelength. For most people, Rex included, an object that reflects light of that wavelength is consciously experienced as green. However, Tex is wired differently. Perhaps because he is a chromotopsiac or has some kind of spectrum shift, Tex consciously experiences objects that reflect light of 500 nm wavelength as yellow, not as green (Hardin 1988). Their receptor systems are the same – the rods and cones in Rex's eyes and Tex's eyes take in light of given wavelengths in the same way, and they output the same electrochemical information to pre-thalamic neural processes. We can even assume that that information remains the same as it emerges from the thalamus and transmits to primary visual cortex. However, somewhere in their subsequent colour binding processes, the information that eventually results in the hunk of jade being consciously experienced by Rex as green eventually results in the hunk of jade being consciously experienced by Tex as yellow. So, despite having the same causes, the difference in neural processing in Rex and Tex results in different colour experience. Perceptual qualitative properties of gustation, audition, touch and olfaction, and interoceptive qualitative features such as pain, can similarly be subjected to the same sort of analysis. Since perceptual neural processing thus *determines* the qualitative properties that we represent external objects as having, *all* qualitative features – even those presented in conscious experience as qualitative properties of world-involving content – turn out to be neurally determined properties of perceptual experience. Generalizing across perceptual, interoceptive, affective and cognitive modalities yields qualitative character internalism.

Vehicle internalism/qualitative character externalism

Some versions of qualitative character internalism take it to imply that the extra-cranial world is bereft of qualitative character and that our conscious experience of it as having qualitative character is a grand illusion. But the implication fails since even internalism can distinguish between the qualitative properties of things and events as consciously experienced and the qualitative properties of conscious experience (Armstrong [1968] 1993; 1981). With that distinction, the generalization required for the illusion collapses. Granted, the distinction complicates any account of qualitative character, and its implications are far from being fully mapped in neuroscience. Yet without it, empirically testable distinctions cannot be made. Sharply perceiving fuzzy edges, blurrily perceiving sharp edges, and blurrily perceiving fuzzy edges are different visual experiences, just as clearly hearing muted sounds, barely hearing loud sounds, and barely hearing muted sounds are different auditory experiences. Without the difference between qualitative properties of conscious experience and qualitative properties of things and events as consciously experienced, every qualitative property defaults to being a qualitative property of conscious experience (Dretske 1988). But then a blurry perception of a sharp edge and a fuzzy edge sharply perceived would both be qualitative properties of visual experience, and then they would be indistinguishable from each other. That is unacceptable. Moreover, the suspicion remains that even the neural resources differ across the two cases.

The qualitative character externalist's general challenge to internalism is rather that even if qualitative properties of conscious experience are totally realized by neural properties, qualitative properties of things and events as consciously experienced are not totally realized by neural activity, no matter how complex it or the assembly that has it may be. If so, the causal powers of neural assembly activity do not exhaust the causal powers of at least those qualitatively endowed conscious events whose content involves the extracranial world. Something else is needed to get a total realizer of qualitative character of what is consciously experienced if what is consciously experienced involves the extracranial world. So, again, since there is no reduction without total realizers and there are no total neural realizers of such qualitative properties, (NR)' fails for them.

Opposed to internalists who advocate a one-factor analysis of the constitution of all kinds of qualitative character, qualitative character externalists advocate what has been called a *two-factor* analysis of the constitution of qualitative properties of world-involving conscious content (Burge [2006] 2007; Byrne & Tye 2006; Pautz 2006). On such a view, the qualitative properties of conscious experience have as their substrates neural events that host only internal neural properties, whereas the qualitative properties of extracranial things and events as consciously experienced have as their substrates internal neural events that host both internal neural properties and relational properties whose instantiation entails extracranial properties. As a result of this additional factor, qualitative properties of extracranial things and events as consciously experienced must accommodate our status as embodied beings embedded in a qualitatively rich environment. Since we are embodied and embedded in an environment, our neural resources can never be enough for realizing the qualitative properties of experienced things and events external to the neural system and we must look in addition to our bodies and to the environment to supply the remaining resources required for having total realizers of this family of qualitative properties.

Vehicle externalism/qualitative character externalism

One might also argue that even the vehicles of qualitatively endowed conscious events supervene on emergent complexes constituted by neural assembly activity and a partial state of the extracranial world. Candidate examples come from the domains of flavour and olfaction. Consider first an example from Alva Noë, the flavour of sipped wine. Noë argues that "the only way – or the only biological way – to produce just the flavour sensations one enjoys when one sips wine is by rolling a liquid across one's tongue. In that case, the liquid, the tongue, and the rolling action would be part of the physical substrate for the experience's occurrence" (Noë 2004: 220). Again, consider experiencing a bear stripping blue-berries twenty feet away, and consider in particular its odour. A bear's musky odour imprints itself powerfully on to the human olfactory apparatus. Although not unpleasant, the odour is utterly distinctive, and once experienced, it will not be forgotten. For vehicle externalists, the vehicle of olfactory perception supervenes in part on behaviour of the constituent molecules that make up the volatilized chemical compound itself. Olfaction of the bear's odour supervenes not just on a neural event caused by extracranial environmental features; instead, those extracranial environmental features are constituent vehicles of qualitatively endowed olfactory experience.

Vehicle externalism about qualitative character thus results from two claims. First, the presumed neural vehicles of qualitative character – neural assemblies and neural assembly activity – do not, contrary to vehicle internalism, exhaust the vehicles of at least some qualitatively endowed conscious events; second, the vehicles of at least some qualitatively endowed conscious events are emergent complexes one of whose component vehicles is extracranial. Having shown the insufficiency of neural assembly activity, the vehicle externalist proposes that, in addition to neural assembly activity, the activity of rolling the wine over one's tongue and the volatized molecules exuding from the bear are additional con-stituent vehicles of conscious flavour and olfactory experience. As for flavour and olfaction, so for the rest of the sensory modalities – the extracranial world is literally a storehouse of pertinent information that feeds an organism's percep-tual, interoceptive and proprioceptive processes, its affective processes such as emotion and qualitative character, and its cognitive processes, such as memory, inference-making and higher-order reasoning.

Flavour and olfaction provide particularly suggestive cases for vehicle exter-nalism in part because the wine and the odour's volatized chemical molecules actually invade the skin's barrier. Yet the cases are really no more convincing for flavour and olfaction than they might be for the other sensory modalities. Take the case of the bear's odour. Even if the volatized molecules of the bear's odour activate nerve endings within the envelope of the nasal cavity, they are not *constituent vehicles* of olfactory neural processing, for, as with all perceptual processing, they are translated by neural assembly activity into electrochemical messages that are henceforth the vehicles for all subsequent olfactory process-ing. Since it is only downstream from that initial translation that the neural activity that correlates with conscious olfaction occurs, the volatized molecules are never in the position to become the vehicles of conscious olfaction. Hence, even if these volatized molecules are causal precursors to olfaction and thus participate in olfaction, they are not constituent vehicles of olfactory qualitative properties. Similar considerations apply to the flavour. Food and drink molecules that activate taste buds are not the vehicles of conscious flavour experience even if they precipitate such qualitatively loaded experience. Since olfaction and flavour are the most suggestive cases of vehicle externalism about qualitative properties and vehicle externalism fails for them, failure for vehicle externalism for touch, audition and vision is also implied.

This counterargument to vehicle externalism can be deployed against qualitative character externalism, but doing so will not be successful, and that this is so reveals some of the thorny issues at the centre of current philosophical debate about the prospects of neurally reducing qualitative character. Here is the candidate counterargument against qualitative character externalism: just as elements and properties of the extracranial world are causal precipitants but not constituents of the intracranial neural vehicle that hosts the qualitative properties of conscious experience, so by parallel reasoning, elements and properties of the extracranial world are causal precipitants but not constituents of the intracranial neural activity that goes into constituting the qualitative properties of conscious experience. The argument fails because what is true of the neural vehicle that hosts the qualitative properties thus constituted is not thereby true of the constitution of the qualitative properties of extracranial objects, events and properties as consciously experienced. If, for example, the vehicle externalist is correct that at least some perceptual, interoceptive, proprioceptive, affective and cognitive conscious events and processes are causally coupled with extracranial things, events and properties, then where that coupling fails to obtain, there the qualitative properties hosted by those intracranial events and processes would fail to be instantiated. Even if this view is incorrect, that is, even if all perceptual, interoceptive, proprioceptive, affective and cognitive conscious events and processes have uncoupled represented content, the qualitative properties of those content-bearing events is still world-involving if the content is, as it is with *de re* content.

While the qualitative properties of some conscious events are constituted in part by extracranial elements, some qualitatively endowed conscious events are not constituted even in part by extracranial elements. The qualitative properties of mental images, dream images, negative after-images and hallucinations are obvious examples. Unlike illusions, the qualitative properties of these conscious events are not constituted even in part by extracranial elements (Adams & Aizawa 2009; Prinz 2009). However, if inferring from causal coupling that all qualitative properties are constituted in part by extracranial vehicles is too strong, inferring from after-images, dreams and hallucinations that all qualitative properties are constituted entirely by intracranial vehicles is also too strong. True, qualitative properties are hosted by vehicles that are entirely and always in the head. True, the substrates of the qualitative properties of after-images, dreams, hallucinations and the like are exhausted by neural activity. But in perception and other world-involving conscious processes and events, neural vehicles host qualitative properties whose substrates are in part extracranial things, events and properties. Again, the relevant sciences have to determine what intracranial neural resources and what extracranial resources are engaged in the two kinds and how the neural resources differ across the kinds, thus differentiating core from total realizers for the two kinds.

SUBJECTIVE PERSPECTIVITY

Subjective perspectivity is often run together with qualitative character and content. Talk of the "what-it-is-likeness" of conscious experience exacerbates such conflations. After all, part of what conscious experience is like is that it is from a subjective perspective, part of what conscious experience is like is that it has qualitative character, and part of what it is like is that it is about something. All three go into composing the "what-it-is-likeness" of conscious experience. But the challenges posed by subjective perspectivity are not removed by disentangling it from other properties or by disavowing "what-it-is-likeness" talk.

The history of the self and subjectivity in philosophy and psychology is long and tortured. Anything anyone says about it has at least one historical precedent and dozens more critics. Philosophical understanding of subjective perspectivity starts with a prereflective sense of being a unified organism in space and time, where by "prereflective" we understand a conscious event or process that is not directed at itself (among others, Metzinger 2003; Nietzsche 1968, [1886] 1989; Sartre 1948, [1936] 1962; Zahavi 2008). Whether subjective perspectivity is exhausted by that prereflective starting point is the primary topic of the protracted philosophical debate. But pinning down the starting point of being a unified organism embedded in an environment is itself not straightforward, for subjective perspectivity is something more complex than the anodyne "geometrical feature" (Blanke & Metzinger 2009: 9) of there being an embodied point of projection in conscious experience, while at the same time it is something less complex than a property that entails possession of a self concept as a condition of its instantiation.

Consider each point in turn. Were subjective perspectivity nothing more than that geometric property, then it would be no more interesting than my smile being *my* smile (Sosa 2002). Since all that is required to understand why my smile is my smile is that it is caused by my facial muscles, my teeth and my lips, subjective perspectivity would amount to no more than my conscious experience being caused by my embodied neural activity. If that is all subjective perspectivity amounts to, then frog and lizard experience is also subjectively perspectival, for their sensations are likewise caused by their embodied neural activity. However, even if frogs and lizards are conscious, they are not conscious simply because their embodied neural activity is their embodied neural activity, since plenty of neural activity in them (and in us) is not conscious. Moreover, although all conscious perceptual, interoceptive, proprioceptive and affective experience is from a perspective because that is the way neural assembly activity delivers it, that kind of perspectivity is not therefore *subjective* perspectivity. Only some neural activity generates subjectively perspectival experience, either because it is alone constitutively sufficient for subjective perspectivity and is therefore its total realizer, or it is with other constituents a core part of what is constitutively sufficient for subjective perspectivity.

Whatever that something may be, however, it is not a self concept, for were subjective perspectivity to entail possession of a self concept as a condition of its instantiation, then, as argued earlier in Chapter 4 in a parallel context, our experience would be unconscious far more frequently than it actually is. As noted there with regards to higher-order awareness, conscious experience does not cease to be conscious when we are not aware that it is so from the higher-order perspective. Similarly, conscious experience does not cease to be conscious when a self concept is not a constituent. A self concept – arguably required for, and a constituent element of, monitoring, self-reflection and self-consciousness – is a sophisticated accomplishment that presupposes subjectively perspectival conscious events (Burge [2006] 2007 makes the same point in a comment on Kant), but it is not a prerequisite of subjective perspectivity.

Neuroscience and philosophy help fix the appropriate starting point for subjective perspectivity. A cohort of neuroscientific researchers have coalesced around the idea that there is a *minimal phenomenological sense of self* that is the weakest sense of self sufficiently strong to play a role in subjectively perspectival conscious experience (Blanke & Metzinger 2009; Blanke & Mohr 2005; Metzinger 2003; Vogeley & Fink 2003). Let us unpack this notion, substituting "minimal subjective perspectivity" for "minimal phenomenological sense of self". Call the anodyne geometric property *weak first-person perspective*. Then minimal subjective perspectivity is some augmentation of weak first-person perspective, intermediate between it and other more robust forms of subjectively perspectival conscious experience that presuppose a self concept and are explicitly cognitive. These more robust forms may be called *super-strong first-person perspectives*; they are what is implicated in monitoring, self-reflection and self-consciousness (Metzinger 2009b). Investigating them takes us beyond the scope of this book.

What is of interest is, then, stronger than weak first-person perspective and weaker than super-strong first-person perspectives – it is that first-person perspective minimally strong enough to support a subjective perspective. Consistent with the philosophers cited above, neuroscientific researchers identify minimal subjective perspectivity as the property of being an integrated and spatiotemporally located system that is interoceptively, proprioceptively, affectively and perceptually embedded in and engaged with an environment (Blanke

& Mohr 2005; Lopez & Blanke 2007; Vogeley & Fink 2003). As such, minimal subjective perspectivity is not obviously cognitive, for its instantiation is not mediated by concepts, and all cognitive properties are mediated by concepts. Nor, as Blanke and Metzinger note, is minimal subjective perspectivity "a static internal cop[y] of some mysterious thing or individual substance ('the' self);" it is rather the "ongoing processes of tracking and controlling global bodily properties" (Blanke & Metzinger 2009: 8). Here, global properties are properties of the perceptual–affective–interoceptive–proprioceptive system taken as a whole, not its subsystemic local properties. So, minimal subjective perspectivity is multidimensional as compared to each of those constituent subsystems and emergent from them.

The emergent complexity of minimal subjective perspectivity as described suggests that its neural correlates are probably relatively complex as well. Not surprisingly, the correlates typically nominated are heteromodal assemblies clustered in the temporoparietal junction region downstream from unimodal perceptual, interoceptive, affective and proprioceptive assemblies (Blanke & Metzinger 2009; Blanke & Mohr 2005; Mesulam 2000). Upstream unimodal assemblies are of course required for minimal subjective perspectivity to be instantiated – they are causally necessary, and their activity is constitutive of weak first-person perspective – yet it is only when those upstream assemblies feed information forwards to the heteromodal associative areas in temporoparietal cortex that transformations sufficient for generating global properties occur. Assuming that these correlates find a home in substantive scientific laws, they would be plausible candidates for neural substrates of subjective perspectivity as well. Since these are assemblies downstream from unimodal perceptual assemblies, and downstream too from unimodal interoceptive, affective and proprioceptive assemblies, it falls out that minimal subjective perspectivity is a relatively late neural accomplishment. If so, then although animals lacking the requisite neural complexity could enjoy certain kinds of qualitatively endowed, contentful experience, their experience would not for all that be subjectively perspectival.

The claim is sometimes made (Gazzaniga & Le Doux 1978; Marks 1981) that split-brain patients (those who have had the white matter tracts connecting the two hemispheres cut to prevent epileptic seizure) have two streams of consciousness and that even if each stream is internally unified, the two are not unified with one another. This way of describing split-brain phenomena appears to entail that the patient's ongoing sequence of conscious experiences is actually two such sequences that, at best, only partially communicate with one another. But a split-brain patient's dysfunctions may instead be described as a kind of content disunity (Bayne 2008). While a split-brain patient's conscious unity is compromised, the phenomenology of the compromise can be accounted for as consisting not in separate streams of consciousness but in a single stream of consciousness with disunified – unbound – content. For example, in some split-brain patients, visual content is unbound with that of the other perceptual modalities even though the content of each perceptual modality is bound intramodally. Other split-brain patients fail to bind one kind of intramodal content (e.g. shape or colour) with another kind of the same intramodal content (e.g. size or motion). For neither symptom must separate unbound sequences of conscious experiences be posited; each is explained by the content failing to be bound in conscious experience (Bayne 2008).

Were all the issues raised by split-brain symptoms to be resolved thus, the case for conscious disunity being entirely content-based would be strong, which in turn would imply that conscious unity is entirely content-based. But other neurological disorders result in kinds of disunity that are difficult to square with content-based disunity. For example, severe concussion can cause the fronto-polar region of DLPFC to collide with the cranium and cause the white matter tracts of the corpus callosum to twist, resulting in dysfunctional but not severed communication between hemispheres. Such individuals sometimes report that while their perceptual content is unified, what it is like to perceive that content is queer. They readily grant that the content is perceived but report that it is not they who perceive it. They further report that they realize upon reflection that they must be mistaken and that their experience is, after all, their experience (Filley 2001). In such cases, perceptual content is bound across the perceptual modalities but not subjectively unified prereflectively. That sort of unity failure is not obviously content based. Other disorders, such as dysexecutive syndrome and dissociative identity disorder, may provide additional evidence for non-content-based failures of unity (Brook & Raymont 2006; Gallagher 2000).

Philosophical reasons for doubting that the unity of minimal subjective perspectivity is entirely content based are every bit as suggestive. Minimal subjective perspectivity is, as described, prereflective. As such, it is consistent with, and in fact implies, those versions of self-representationalism on which a unified self is given as a constituent part of a conscious event's content and not as the content of a logically distinct event. But thinking of subjective perspectivity in this way has certain drawbacks, chief among them being that some qualitatively loaded and subjectively perspectival conscious experiences – blurred vision, tinnitus, hunger pangs, micturition, orgasm, and some olfactory, somatosensory and auditory hallucinations – have no apparent content. Having no content, such conscious experiences have nothing to which the self can attach as a constituent part. Were subjective perspectivity to be entirely content based, then where there is no content, there subjective perspectivity would lapse. That is contrary to fact. So, subjective perspectivity is not entirely content based.

A compromise allows that content unity standardly contributes to subjective perspectivity without thereby exhausting it. On this account, some other factor of its instantiation must be added as a second factor to what is supplied by content unity. Burge has recently proposed that qualitatively endowed conscious experience is constitutively reflexive, that is, the presentation of the self is a

291

constitutive feature or aspect of qualitatively endowed experience, a mode by which all qualitatively endowed conscious events are presented (Burge [2006] 2007). Take pain as an example. Pain is presented to each of us by itself. It is, as Burge puts the point, "present to and presented to the mind ... through itself. The pain is its own mode of presentation" (Burge [2006] 2007: 408). Even if some pains have represented content, their subjective perspectivity is not only a penumbral aspectual part of that content but also and more primordially a mode of its presentation. The point generalizes beyond interoceptive experience such as pain to proprioceptive, affective and perceptual experience – subjective perspectivity is a constitutive feature of the qualitatively loaded experience from each modality.

Assume that subjective perspectivity is in standard cases a constitutive feature of all qualitatively loaded conscious experience. An interesting consequence arguably follows. Unlike the content and qualitative properties of some conscious events, for which persuasive arguments for their externalist constitution exist, parallel arguments on behalf of externalism about subjective perspectivity, much less arguments on behalf of vehicle externalism, are not persuasive. Vehicle externalism for subjective perspectivity is false. If it were true, then the class of vehicles that host subjective perspectivity would expand to include not only intracranial events but extracranial objects and events such as pieces of paper, hard drives and computer calculations. However, a piece of paper on which I have written a mathematical equation hosts derived intentional content, not original intentional content, much less original content from its own or my subjective perspective. Thinking that paper hosts content from my subjective perspective entails subjective perspectivity seeping from my conscious experience into the paper, and thinking that it hosts content from its own subjective perspective entails panpsychism. Both alternatives are unacceptable. If so, vehicle externalism about subjective perspectivity is false.

Similarly, the subjective perspectivity of conscious events is constituted intracranially. Were subjective perspectivity constituted in part by extracranial events and objects, then dreams, hallucinations and after-images would not be conscious experiences, for there is neither extracranial content nor extracranial qualitative character instantiated by any of them. But as anyone who has dreamed, talked to themselves or been in a sensory deprivation tank knows, conscious experience not only does not lapse, it continues apace, and its subjective perspectivity remains fully intact (Prinz 2009). So, alone among the properties of consciousness, *none* of the neural substrates of subjective perspectivity are immediately disqualified by externalist considerations from being total realizers. There may be other reasons for thinking that subjective perspectivity is not totally realized by neural activity, but they are not externalist reasons.

The externalism and internalism debates are ongoing and are far from being resolved. This chapter has tried to steer a course through the debate's extremes by distinguishing between property and vehicle internalisms and externalisms and applying the distinction to conscious properties and vehicles. No compelling reason was found for accepting any form of vehicle externalism. This implies that some of the more extraordinary claims made on behalf of situated cognition and consciousness are false and that the only viable externalisms are property externalisms. Of the three conscious properties that form the core of this book's enquiries – intentionality, qualitative character and subjective perspectivity – the most persuasive externalist arguments focus on the content properties of *de re* beliefs and perceptions, interoceptions and proprioceptions. However, qualitative property externalism is also defensible if a further distinction between the qualitative properties of experience of things and the qualitative properties of things experienced is made. The one conscious property for which no plausible externalist story can be told is subjective perspectivity. Alone among conscious properties, it appears to be explained without appealing to extracranial elements.

CONCLUDING SEMI-SCIENTIFIC POSTSCRIPT

This book has focused on three general topics. Chapters 1–4 introduced the dominant philosophical accounts of conscious properties and reduction and some of the philosophical difficulties that conscious properties and reduction pose. In Chapters 5–8, we introduced some of the recent neuropsychological and other neuroscientific findings about conscious properties and suggested how those findings have been used to help understand some of the standard philosophical difficulties with reducing conscious properties to something physical. And in Chapters 9–12, we introduced some of the current philosophical thinking about conscious properties that promises to stir up trouble about both the dominant philosophical views and the findings from the neurosciences.

It can easily seem that the philosophers' debates about the neurosciences are examples of nothing more than their familiar scepticism that strips the tread from explanations just as they are beginning to gain traction. But neurally reducing consciousness is, as I hope by now is clear, actually quite an extraordinary proposal. It is, therefore, appropriate to point out how provocative the proposal is, to describe the ways in which it is so, and to urge wariness both against being intimidated by philosophical demands for metaphysical hygiene and against being swept up by the wave of momentum spawned by advances in neuroimaging and neuropsychological research. This is not to discount the importance of philosophical good health or to diminish the considerable advances that have been made in various arenas of neuropsychology and the other neurosciences. It is to point out that some philosophical questions concerning consciousness and its properties are not as pressing as may have been thought and that some philosophical questions are still no closer to answers than they have ever been.

Philosophical arguments have numerous iterations and spinoffs, and philosophers are often intent on responding to the latest, most refined iteration or spinoff. One result is that our vision is sometimes blinkered – we show that a particular philosophical argument is unsound or that its conclusion is invalidly inferred while ignoring the obvious. Some of the philosophical arguments about consciousness are of this sort. The alleged threat of conscious epiphenomenalism is a case in point. The supervenience argument takes what is obviously true – conscious events have other psychological and physical effects – and, on the basis of what are offered up as plausible intuitions and meta-physical principles, concludes that what is obviously true is so only if conscious events are nothing but microphysical events and properties. Parts of this book have been devoted to showing that this and other influential philosophical argu-ments about conscious properties – such as proreduction arguments from the definition of "is" and the functionalization argument, and antireduction argu-ments from multiple realizability, multiple realization and anomaly – rely on philosophical intuitions and metaphysical principles that are less persuasive than the claims they are invoked to undermine (Burge [1993] 2007 makes the same point).

For all the strange and sometimes epicyclical loops philosophers are prone to following, an equally serious risk is not recognizing the complexity of the issues to which the loops are responses. This kind of shortcoming is also found in the consciousness literature, best exemplified by the increasingly common practice of using neuroimaging and neuropsychological evidence that there are behav-ioural and neural correlates of conscious events and processes to fuel quick arguments for the conclusion that those conscious events and processes are identical with or reducible to those correlates. Such overreaching arguments are often plausible and provocative enough to goad someone into initiating a research programme. Scientific psychologists and neuroscientists have under-taken a number of research programmes about mentality and consciousness on the basis of such arguments that are best described as stabs in the dark – phre-nology, introspectionism, artificial intelligence, classical computationalism and the 40 Hz oscillation hypothesis are a few notable examples. Each of them fails when applied to consciousness and its properties, some more spectacularly than others. So, other parts of this book have been devoted to showing where some of the inferential gaps between neuropsychological and other neuroscientific evidence and conclusions about conscious properties are located and what those inferential gaps imply about the conclusions derived when they are ignored.

Conscious properties are first and foremost psychological phenomena, and the science that studies them – psychology – is a paradigmatic special science. Psychology is a special science just as chemistry, geology, biology, neuroanat-omy, neurophysiology and neurobiology are special sciences, which is to say that none are atomic physics. Being special implies, among other things, that the set of entities of which the science speaks – its quantification domain – is a set of entities that are, in specifiable ways, more complex than those studied by atomic physics and that its explanations fold that specified complexity into its ongoing investigations. In the case of psychology, the domain of quantification includes events such as conscious beliefs, perceptions, emotions and interocep-tions, and their properties, and processes such as working memory, attention, reflection and monitoring, and their properties. Neuropsychologists and other neuroscientists who study these events and processes are typically not interested in the nature of the atomic and subatomic behaviour of the molecules that compose the neurons that are organized into pathways whose emergent activity subserves conscious events and processes; they presuppose that subatomic and atomic behaviours are as they are whenever emergent molecular, neural and pathway activity is investigated. But that is as should be expected, for like all special sciences, psychology, neuropsychology and other neurosciences bracket investigation of certain phenomena so that they can focus on the phenomena that are of interest to them.

To the extent that the entities and properties quantified over in psychological explanations are individuated only by including extracranial elements, to that extent is psychology committed to certain externalist elements. Psychology is hardly alone in this: biology and geology, to name two other special sciences, also talk about externalistically individuated entities and properties (Burge [1989] 2007). Just as geology wants to know what is going on in a rock or a soil type and just as biology wants to know what's going on in a plant engaging in photosynthesis or in an organism engaging in digestion, psychology wants to know what is going on in the head of an organism engaging in cognition, affection, proprioception and perception. And just as geology's typing of granite as intrusive, felsic and igneous and its typing of land masses as plates are both constitutively externalistic, and just as biology's typing of organs such as a heart is constitutively externalistic, psychology's typing of at least some conscious events and processes entails commitment to extracranial elements and so is likewise constitutively externalistic. The content of world-involving conscious thoughts, perceptions, interoceptions and affections requires explanations of those conscious events and processes that acknowledge those extracranial elements. This set of explanations leads away from neural reduction and towards explanations that embody and embed consciousness and its properties in larger social and natural milieux.

What is true of psychology in general is true also of neuropsychology and the other neurosciences, both of which also regularly rely on externalist presuppositions. Even if neuropsychologists and other neuroscientists are not interested in determining the nature of the world's objects and events that neural events, states and processes hook up to, both kinds of scientists nevertheless presuppose that those objects and events are as they are whenever they investigate the neural mechanisms whose activities help constitute the connections. That this is so for the modalities of perception and for certain kinds of thinking is fairly obvious, but as noted in Chapter 12, even many interoceptive, affective and proprioceptive events and processes are routinely individuated externalistically.

Other conscious events and processes – such as those that occur during monitoring, reflection, dreaming, hallucinating and sensory deprivation experiences, and those that constitute the goings-on of the default mode – require explanations that appear to invoke only intracranial events and processes (even if the content of the thoughts monitored, reflected upon, and so forth are world-involving). The persistence of conscious continuity in the face of switches to surrounding environments strengthens the case for content internalism, and perforce for neural reductionism. The extent that such internalist explanations are complete measures the extent to which some conscious events and processes use only neural resources. These neuroscientific explanations do not, of course, support the generalized claim that no conscious events or processes have world-involving content, but, frankly, I do not understand either how the general claim can be supported or why anyone is still tempted by it.

The weaker claim that some conscious events and processes do not have world-involving content is still plenty interesting, for if true, then at least those conscious events and processes whose content is entirely intracranial are plausible candidates for neural reduction. Arguing against this claim by pointing out that even conscious content individuated intracranially can be composed of elements whose causal history includes conscious content externalistically individuated is not on point. Allow that one's hallucination of a pink elephant could not occur had one never perceived the colour pink and elephants or pictures of them. What is germane is that the content of the occurrent conscious event of hallucinating a pink elephant is not obviously composed of any externalistically individuated perceptual element. Thinking to oneself in language or monitoring one's cognitive processes provide ready additional examples of conscious events that may contain externalistically individuated elements at some point in their causal past. Even if the sentences used in episodes of internal reflection, monitoring and attention have the meanings they do in part because of the causal and other relations one bears to the extracranial environment and the linguistic community of which one is a member, an occurrent conscious event of, say, thinking about where to place a subordinate clause in a sentence by running the alternatives through one's endogenous attentive processes is not obviously composed of any element that occurrently discloses or requires acknowledging the extracranial environment and that linguistic community. And even if elements of the contents of some dreams are externalistically individuated – as, for instance, when a ringing alarm clock incorporates directly into a dream – the content of other dreams is not obviously composed of any externalistically individuated cognitive, perceptual, interoceptive or proprioceptive elements.

Considerations about differing kinds of conscious events, about how the world's goings-on factor into individuating the differing kinds, about how much of the world's goings-on is a component of each of the differing kinds, and about whether even asking these and related questions is justified have driven philosophers to distraction for as long as there have been philosophers. In Chapter 12, we considered some of the recent perturbations these questions have prompted and we offered up a distinction between core and total realizers as a way to avoid some of the more astonishing claims made on behalf of the philosophical positions currently in play. I am the first to admit that my application of the distinction between core and total realizers may get it wrong – some of these matters are taxing to think through clearly, and realization may not be the core issue. But we must also acknowledge that plausible answers to some of these philosophical issues cannot be resolved by using philosophical means alone. In such a setting, looking outside the philosophical hothouse to see what the latest neurosciences have to say about the ways the brain's neural networks actually process information and build it up into something recognizably representational might be helpful in limiting what philosophers can expect from representational events and processes. It will also point in new directions for resolving the long-standing disputes between internalists and externalists.

Of course, neuropsychology and the other neurosciences are all quite young special sciences, and that immaturity carries with it the caution that it is too early to be confident that the neural bases of conscious events and their properties have been properly fixed. There may yet be room for further downwards or outwards movement, and if so, then neural correlates of conscious properties will never amount to substrates or realizers. But, to be frank, I think a lot of movement in either direction is pretty unlikely. Too much common sense, psychological, philosophical and neurological evidence both that cortex is where most of the action is and that we are connected with the world without being spread out into it (except metaphorically) already exists. So in these ways at least, neural reductionism and conscious property externalism are more modest positions than either microphysical reductionism or vehicle externalism. Both neural reductionism and property externalism rely substantively, directly and narrowly on neuropsychological and other neuroscientific discoveries, and neither rely heavily on philosophical arguments. On the other hand, microphysical reductionism and vehicle externalism rely less on neuropsychological and other neuroscientific discoveries than on philosophical argument. Both hold neuropsychology and other neurosciences up to the bar of philosophical claims about overdetermination, pre-emption and causal exclusion (in the case of microphysical reduction) or about the constitution of things (in the case of vehicle externalism). Using these claims, it turns out that what gets bracketed from below and from outside so thoroughly permeates neural events and processes that what the neurosciences take to be their domain is not even the right place to look for informative answers to the questions they are asking.

Holding the neurosciences up to the demands of microphysical reductionism and vehicle externalism puts two heavily laden metaphysical carts before a lot of scientific horses. One can allow that scientists come to their disciplinary interests and even their disciplinary investigations with antecedent ontological commitments and assumptions and still argue that the philosophical assumptions and commitments on which microphysical reductionism and vehicle externalism rely are too contentious to bear as much weight as required. Most neuroscientists would be astonished to discover that, simply in virtue of being neuroscientists, they must therefore be committed to the view that the neural processes involved in, say, conscious perception are reducible to atomic or even subatomic behaviour. They would be equally astonished to discover either that, again simply in virtue of being neuroscientists, they must therefore be committed to the view that the neural processes involved in, say, conscious perception *totally* realize conscious perception or that notebooks have original, non-derived intentionality. Someone antecedently committed to a particular set of philosophical assumptions about causal powers and internal properties and overdetermination might well take neuropsychological and other neuro-scientific discoveries about conscious perception to imply the former; someone antecedently committed to certain philosophical views about object and complex constitution might well take certain claims about aided cognition to imply the latter. But were either proposition to be put to working neuroscientists, most would probably reply a little tensely that they are only interested in their research and beat a hasty retreat to the lab. And they would be right to do so most of the time, for loading up neuropsychological and other neuroscientific discoveries with philosophical commitments imputes to them something that is almost never and in most cases need not ever be in their scope.

Uncovering hidden assumptions and spelling out larger implications that others have yet to think of are not disreputable jobs; it is just that neuroscientists rarely have any reason to perform them. It is the job for the philosophically minded critic to root out hidden assumptions and the philosophically minded speculator to spell out larger implications. Earlier chapters have discussed some of the contentious assumptions in the neurosciences of consciousness and its properties, but since this book has as one of its other stated intentions some philosophically minded speculation, it is time to engage in a little of it.

Philosophy of mind, in general, and philosophy of consciousness and its properties, in particular, have both changed significantly in the past twenty years. This claim is hardly novel or controversial. But it bears repeating because we sometimes forget or ignore that the kind of *a priori* philosophizing that dominated the field only twenty years ago is, while still present, rapidly losing ground to philosophy informed by the neurosciences. With the exception of the work of Paul and Patricia Churchland, Daniel Dennett, Ned Block, Jerry Fodor and a few others, neuropsychological or other neuroscientific findings any more detailed than the obligatory hand waving at C-fibres were rarely encountered in philosophy journals as recently as ten years ago. Today, it is increasingly common to find philosophers using neuroscientific and cognitive scientific findings to support a philosophical point about consciousness and its properties. Examples have been provided in earlier chapters.

Changes to the landscape on the other side of the disciplinary fence line have been just as significant. I suspect that a majority of neuropsychologists and other neuroscientists in the early 1990s pretty comfortably thought (to the extent that they thought about it at all) that the neural mechanisms and processes they were discovering and describing would fit smoothly into some kind of classical computational model of cognition. The vast majority of them would not have ventured near intentionality, qualitative character or the subjective perspectivity of conscious experience. Today, however, a growing number of scientists are actively pursuing research programmes into the neural bases of intentionality, qualitative character, subjective perspectivity and affectivity. Not surprisingly, with all the new evidence, some early assumptions have had to be modified. Classical computationalism's ambitions have been tempered by well-focused criticism and hard experience, connectionism and neural network models have made significant inroads against classicism's pre-eminence, and externalist and situated cognition models have suggested the benefits of incorporating dynamic systems theory into neuroscience.

The category of representation in particular seems at this point a little harried. If representations are to continue to play the foundational role in neuroscientific accounts of consciousness and at least some of its properties, they must satisfy a threefold demand: first, representations must be irreplaceable; second, they must avoid collapsing into causal nodes; and, third, they must be something for which there actually are believable neural correlates and perhaps believable substrates or realizers. The best approach for satisfying the first demand is to show that representing is the only plausible candidate for "offline" cognition about things, events, processes and properties not present either through perception, interoception or affection (Grush 1997, 2004). Satisfying the second demand is accomplished only if representation is required to understand such offline cognition, and content is *not* reducible to some other, more mechanical, species of causal element (Haselager *et al.* 2003a, 2003b; Burge [1995] 2007). Satisfying the third demand is the most difficult, for it requires an enormous number of empirical and meta-analytic studies, an understanding of both the heterogeneity of conscious content and the variety of neural structures that are candidate correlates, and vigilance against being seduced by explanations that work only because that heterogeneity of content and structure are being ignored.

Despite advances in the neurosciences, nagging doubts will probably continue to dog them for some time. For all the pretty pictures that neuroimaging studies provide and for all the neural correlates that neuropsychological studies discover, one sometimes wonders (as noted earlier) whether the whole lot is not just Technicolor phrenology. That is a bit harsh, but some version of this judgement is supported directly by reflection on the nature of the neuroimaging and neuropsychological evidence, which, while persuasive that conscious events and processes occur in the brain, does not tell us enough about the workings of those events and processes or their properties to warrant the strong conclusions sometimes inferred. Of course, other neurosciences – neurochemistry, neurobiology, neurophysiology, and the various neural models of consciousness and its properties – step in to supply other evidence and other explanations. But every explanation of a conscious event, process or property that utilizes the theoretical resources of one scientific theory introduces slippage between it and explanations of the same event, process, or property utilizing the theoretical resources of other scientific theories. To date, little of the meta-analytic and cross-disciplinary work needed to tighten things up and straighten things out has been done, in part because the number of researchers working on conscious properties in each subfield of the neurosciences is small, in part because the nature of their work is for the most part preliminary, provisional and exploratory, and in part because so many researchers still shy away from consciousness altogether.

Larger issues also come into play. The explanatory gap argument (Levine 1983) uncovers a deeper reason to be sceptical about neuropsychological and other neuroscientific evidence about and explanations of consciousness and its properties. Any honest appraisal of contemporary neuroscientific accounts of conscious properties immediately leads to the conclusion that the number of explanatory gaps is *enormous*. The easiest family of explanatory gaps to expose is this: for *each and every* bit of correlational evidence and for *each and every* neural explanation of a conscious event, process or property, one can ask, *why* does this neural event or process instantiate the conscious property it does? Another kind of explanatory gap can be quickly exposed by asking, *how* does this neural event or process instantiate the conscious property it instantiates? The intensity of bewilderment that accompanies attempts to answer iterations of these questions is a measure of the width of the explanatory gap the candidate answer leaves. As stated, these explanatory gaps are diagnostic rather than explanatory or prescriptive: they reveal that we do not yet have answers to any of a whole family of questions and are not confident about how to get answers or even whether the questions we are posing are well formed. Granted, the diagnostic point needs to be made. When it comes to consciousness and its properties, our scientific understanding is dramatically incomplete, even inchoate, akin to a few puddles of light on the floor of an otherwise unlit ballroom. Identifying explanatory gaps induces the scientific investigations required to discover the findings that can close the gaps. These investigations have begun in earnest only recently.

Explanatory gaps can be categorized according to the following schema: the boringly recalcitrant; the misleadingly recalcitrant; and the disturbingly recalcitrant. Some explanatory gaps are intractable and not worth worrying about. A high school student knows less about calculus than a maths professor does, but the high school student's bewilderment does not reveal a significant explanatory gap in calculus. The gap between a pretheoretic understanding of conscious events, processes and properties and a scientific understanding of those conscious events, processes and properties is not much different.

Other gaps that appear to be intractable are not as intractable as they appear. One of these is the gap between our immediate, lived familiarity with the properties of conscious experience and the properties presented in conscious experience and the relative obscurity of the scientific descriptions of those properties. To the extent that this latter gap is distinct from that between a pretheoretic and post-theoretic understanding of consciousness, it can be closed by distinguishing between kinds of concepts and kinds of properties. Many of the intuition pumps used to buttress the irreducibility of qualitative properties, such as the arguments reviewed in Chapter 3, rely on the subjective immediacy of our knowledge about the qualitative character of conscious events and processes as compared with the lack of immediacy of our knowledge of the neural activity that correlates with them. But a single property can be picked out by any number of concepts. Some concepts are immediately known and subjective, others are mediately known and objective (Block [2002] 2007; Loar 1999). Applying the distinction to qualitative properties, the subjective immediacy of our knowledge about qualitative character need be no bar to identifying or reducing what is experienced to something neural, for the same neural activity properties can be picked out by both subjective and objective concepts. So the immediately known character of, say, experiencing the timbre of a soprano's voice singing an aria is not by itself a reason to think that the experience's qualitative properties are not identical with, or partially realized by, particular patterns of neural activity routing through posterior temporal cortex, unimodal rostral and anterolateral areas, superior temporal cortex, inferior parietal cortex and orbitofrontal prefrontal cortex.

All the discoveries and advances in the neurosciences, in classical and connectionist computationalism, and in various forms of externalism lead some to think that all the explanatory gaps we currently face fall into these two categories and so are either already easily ignored or will melt away over time. When they do eventually disappear, the difficult philosophical problems with consciousness will likewise simply dissolve. One reason for thinking that this kind of conclusion is true is that, as Dennett remarks somewhere, every successful explanation of any phenomenon leaves *something* out. Perhaps the explanatory gaps that the sciences of consciousness and its properties are alleged to leave and the hard problem they are alleged not to answer are nothing more than the inevitable dregs left in the bottom of the glass when one explanatory regime supplants another.

Given the nascent and unsettled state of the neurosciences of consciousness, both of these speculations strike me as premature attempts to rule out of court legitimate philosophical worries. Some explanatory gaps are recalcitrant and troublesome. The most alarming gesture at the suspicion that neuroscientific theorizing about consciousness and its properties is wrong-headed or a kind of category error. Most of these philosophical explanatory gaps are supported by arguments that move from certain philosophical claims thought to be true of conscious properties to the conclusion that a neuroscientific explanation of those properties cannot work. Some of these claims are, as has been argued in previous chapters, not as persuasive as has been thought. Moreover, there are now enough explanations of conscious properties originating from within the neurosciences to throw the suspicion itself into doubt. Neuroscientists certainly do not have good answers to some of the questions that trouble philosophers and perhaps they never will, but they are at least looking, and the answers they are coming up with are not obviously nonsensical. That is *prima facie* evidence that continuing with such investigations is not a category mistake. Pending conclusive reason for thinking that neuroscientific investigations are in general wrong-headed, we have to remain open-minded about their prospects even if specific shortcomings are diagnosable.

Other explanatory gaps, while too weak to drive the conclusion that neuroscience is a category mistake, are nevertheless disturbing. One such family of gaps is to be found in discussions of conscious causation. Understanding conscious causation is vexed. The most daunting challenge to conscious causation comes from the threats of overdetermination and epiphenomenalism. The best argument for displaying the threats – the supervenience argument – shows why the two almost invariably come packaged together. Overdetermination of supervening conscious causes by their subvening physical bases leads to epiphenomenality of conscious causes unless they are reduced to their subvening physical bases. Although this argument is, I think, unsound, having it cleared from the argumentative landscape leaves us in a peculiar no-man's-land. For, the views of conscious causation constrained by supervenience – functionalism and computationalism – have for the past thirty years been the most popular frameworks for understanding how the conscious and the mental relate to the neural if the conscious and the mental are not type identical to the neural (or something else physical). So long as supervenience was thought to provide the requisite philosophical machinery to sanction conscious causation, non-reductive physicalism seemed protected. However, since supervenience is a non-causal relation between different orders of properties that does not explain causation between properties of different orders, the unsoundness of the supervenience argument returns us to a state of large-scale ignorance. No one knows whether causation between kinds of conscious events or between conscious events and other kinds of events is unified, or, if it is, whether it is a kind of emergent causation, or, if it is, what its emergence base might be or how, if at all, it works (Burge [1989] 2007 and [1993] 2007 make related points). Given this state of affairs, it appears to me that philosophers and neuroscientists have no choice but to continue, and to develop new, collaborative efforts.

Another troubling explanatory gap problem is what Block has called the *harder problem* of consciousness (Block [2002] 2007). In order to understand the harder problem and why it is grouped here as a kind of explanatory gap, the hard problem has to be reintroduced. As with the explanatory gap argument, there are a number of distinct problems bandied about as *the* hard problem. In the Introduction, we identified one version of the hard problem by contrasting it with one version of the explanatory gap problem. One kind of explanatory gap problem asks: given that the brain's activity results in conscious properties being instantiated, how *does* it do it? In contrast, one version of the hard problem asks: given that none of the brain's neural activities are any different from the workings of any other physical mechanism, how *can* it do it? I think that this version of the hard problem overreaches its epistemological warrant. Given the antecedent, a negative answer is immediately implied, but the antecedent is probably false – it increasingly appears that the brain's activities are among the most complex in nature and are certainly *very* different from virtually all other physical mechanisms. It cannot be assumed that those differences are irrelevant for understanding the physical basis of consciousness and its properties. Even if we now know a lot more about the brain's neural activity than we have ever known, we do not know nearly enough to know that it cannot instantiate conscious properties.

A distinct version of the hard problem is this: why are the neural bases of a conscious property the neural bases of any conscious property rather than no conscious property at all? This version is related to the first version as follows: if the answer to the first version is that the brain's activity cannot instantiate conscious properties, then any answer to this second version will be inconsistent with microphysical or neural reductionism or, indeed, with any kind of physicalism, externalist physicalisms included. However, the converse implication does not hold: if there are answers to the second version that are consistent with neural reductionism or with content and character externalism (even if they are not consistent with microphysical reductionism or vehicle externalism), then a non-negative answer to the first version is available. For, any such answer would still be consistent with physicalism; it is just that it would not be consistent with microphysical or vehicle externalist species of physicalism. So the two versions of the hard problem are not equivalent. The second version is still plenty hard to answer – indeed, it may be as hard to answer as the first version – and the reasons it is so hard to answer may be the very reasons that make a negative answer to the first version seem overwhelmingly right. Still, the sliver of daylight between the two shows, first, that at least some versions of the hard problem may be hard to affirmatively answer because the way the question is asked precludes an affirmative answer and, second, that other versions of explanatory gap problems might lead to an unanswerable demand but need not immediately necessitate it.

The second version of the hard problem – why are the neural bases of a conscious property the neural bases of any conscious property rather than no conscious property at all? – can be used as warrant for the first version – given that none of the brain's neural activities are any different from the workings of any other physical mechanism, how can that activity be the basis of a conscious property? – if we add the premise that whatever substantive affirmative answers to the second version might be out there are cognitively inaccessible to us. Just as a chimp cannot speak like a human because its voice box does not permit fine distinctions in vowel formation and all the neural pathways sub-serving its vocalization route only through affective and motor cortices, there may be something about our brain or our way of thinking that in principle prevents us from ever gaining the required knowledge to fill in the explanatory gap exposed by the second version of the hard problem. This is the approach of the so-called new mysterians about consciousness, exemplified by the work of McGinn (1989, 1991). The premise that there may be something about our way of thinking or our brain that in principle prevents us from gaining the required knowledge to fill in the explanatory gap exposed by the second version of the hard problem is in part an epistemological claim about our way of thinking, in part an explanatory claim about the grounds for the epistemological claim. On the bare epistemological reading, mysterianism says only that there are inelimi-nable limits to our ways of thinking that prevent closing certain explanatory gaps about consciousness and its properties. I return to this presently. Note, however, that epistemological mysterianism is explained if the other part of mysterianism is true. If we are blocked from access to the explanations that would close the irritating explanatory gaps because our brains are not struc-tured to support such access, then our brains are responsible for our cognitive inability to understand how they are responsible for our conscious life. This might be true, but if so, it seems a last resort.

Like epistemological mysterianism, the harder problem is also an epistemo-logical problem that results in the inaccessibility of physicalism. Suppose we do not now know enough about brain activity to know that it cannot instantiate conscious properties. The obvious solution to these explanatory gaps, as already suggested, is to undertake more research. The harder problem suggests, as does epistemological mysterianism, that there are limits to what this research will yield. One way of putting the harder problem is this: we will never know enough about brain activity to know either that it does instantiate conscious properties or, if it does, how it instantiates the conscious properties it does. Echoes of epis-temological mysterianism are apparent: after all, if, as epistemological mysteri-anism claims, there is something about our way of thinking that blocks closing the explanatory gap between neuroscientific knowledge about brain activity and the instantiation of conscious properties, then, as the harder problem suggests, we will never know enough to know that or how brain activity instantiates the conscious properties it does. Again, however, the converse implication does not hold, which is to say that the harder problem may have bite even if epistemo-logical mysterianism is false. Since epistemological mysterianism is stronger than the harder problem, if the harder problem is strong enough to show that neuropsychological and other neuroscientific research cannot provide explana-tions that close the explanatory gaps we think need to be closed, then epistemo-logical mysterianism is stronger than needed to make the point. Correlatively, if the harder problem is *not* strong enough to show that neuropsychological and other neuroscientific research cannot provide explanations that close the explanatory gaps we think need to be closed, then either we are wrong that those explanatory gaps need to be closed or something akin to epistemological mysterianism will be required to show that we are not wrong.

The formulation of the harder problem found in the previous paragraph is, it must be acknowledged, not Block's own formulation, which relies instead on science fiction, a device we have consistently abjured. However, the points made with science fiction examples can also be made without them (Block [2002] 2007), so that brings the harder problem within our scope, and, since we are engaged in speculation, this is the place (if any place is the place) to take up the issues the argument raises. Block assumes, as we have assumed, that qualitative properties are real, that naturalism is correct, and that scepticism is false. The harder problem is that if these assumptions are true, then, (i) although physicalism is the default philosophical position to adopt for studying consciousness and its properties, it is inaccessible and meta-inaccessible to us, and (ii) although it is an open question whether an organism whose physical constitution is significantly different from ours but who appears on all counts to have qualitatively endowed consciousness is conscious, the subjective default position is that such a one is not conscious (Block [2002] 2007: 419–20).

As with all things that bear the Block copyright, the arguments for these conclusions are intricate, scholarly and dense. We make do with stripped-down versions. Begin by splitting the problem apart into its constituents. Assume that qualitative properties are real; assume that naturalism is true; and assume that scepticism is false (we henceforth ignore the last assumption). Then:

(a) physicalism is the default philosophical position to adopt for studying consciousness and its properties; and
(b) physicalism is inaccessible and meta-inaccessible to us; and
(c) it is an open question whether an organism whose physical constitution is significantly different from ours and who appears on all counts to have qualitatively endowed consciousness is conscious; and
(d) the subjective default position is that an organism whose physical constitution is significantly different from ours and who appears on all counts to have qualitatively endowed consciousness is not conscious.

The arguments for (a) and (c) are quick. By assumption, naturalism is true and qualitative properties are real; but all naturalisms adopt physicalism as the default philosophical position for studying consciousness and its qualitative properties; hence, (a) physicalism is the default position to adopt for studying consciousness and its qualitative properties. Again, by assumption, naturalism is true and qualitative properties are real; but all naturalisms adopt an agnostic attitude to whether an organism whose physical constitution is significantly different from ours and who appears on all counts to have qualitatively endowed consciousness is conscious; hence, (c) it is an open question whether an organism whose physical constitution is significantly different from ours but who appears on all counts to have qualitatively endowed consciousness is conscious.

Grant that these arguments are sound. The harder problem emerges when (a) is conjoined with (b) and when (c) is conjoined with (d). Both of these conjunctions – (a) + (b) and (c) + (d) – have a whiff of contradiction about them. Given that (a) and (c) are unproblematic, (b) and (d) are the source of the bad odour. Here is an argument for (b). By assumption, physicalism is the default philosophical position to adopt for studying consciousness and its properties. If so, then there is a physical property or a disjunction of physical properties shared by all conscious organisms. Suppose there is such a disjunction of physical properties shared by all conscious organisms. Still, we conscious ones have no conception of any reason for accepting any of the disjuncts other than the disjunct we conscious ones actually share with each other. So, for example, a silicon-based organism – such as Commander Data from the *Star Trek: Next Generation* television series – is portrayed as being at least a plausible candidate for being conscious. But even if the physical property that subserves consciousness in Commander Data is sanctioned by physicalism, it is so radically different from the physical property that subserves consciousness in our case that we conscious meatheads cannot at this point get our minds around the issues that might be relevant for determining whether that other physical property subserves Commander Data's consciousness or, if it does, how it does it. Hence, one of the constituent planks of physicalism is cognitively and epistemologically inaccessible to us. Moreover, not only is that plank inaccessible to us, it is meta-inaccessible as well, for not only do we not have any ground for believing that Commander Data's silicon-based psychology is conscious, we do not have a clue about how to acquire such a ground. Hence, (b) – physicalism is inaccessible and meta-inaccessible to us – is true.

Consider next an argument for (d). By assumption, (a), (b) and (c) are true. If (b) is true, then the truth of physicalism is cognitively and epistemologically inaccessible to we conscious ones. If the truth of physicalism is epistemologically inaccessible to us, then although we have no evidence against Commander Data's being conscious, all the evidence there is for Commander Data's being conscious is epistemologically inaccessible to us. So we have no rational grounds for believing any of the evidence that he is conscious; indeed, all of our rational grounds are inconsistent with believing that evidence. If so, then physicalism is the default philosophical position about consciousness *and* it is an open question whether Commander Data is conscious, *but* our only actual rational grounds concerning Commander Data's consciousness are for believing that he is not conscious. Hence, (d) – the subjective default position is that an organism whose physical constitution is significantly different from ours and who appears on all counts to have qualitatively endowed consciousness is not conscious – is true.

308

Supposing both (a) + (b) and (c) + (d) true leaves us in a serious bind about our knowledge about the physical basis of consciousness and its properties in aliens such as Commander Data. Although naturalism encourages an open-minded attitude about the consciousness of aliens whose physical structure is significantly distinct from our own, still, by (b), we currently do not have, and do not have a clue about how to acquire, any ideas about adjudicating claims made on behalf of Commander Data's consciousness, and, by (d), our subject-ive default position is that he is not conscious. That is a discouraging state of affairs. But *how* discouraging is it? Commander Data's consciousness puts us in a parallel bind about our consciousness only if the epistemological limitations that attach to our knowledge about Commander Data's consciousness attach also to our knowledge about ours. What makes the Commander Data thought experiment compelling is the prospect of coming into contact with an organ-ism that appears for all the world to be conscious but which is also so radically different from everything here on earth that we do not currently know what we might then say about it. But we are not in *this* epistemological position about *our* consciousness, for by hypothesis of the harder problem, we may some day discover the nature of human consciousness (Block [2002] 2007). Even if the harder problem is, as advertised, extremely hard to answer, we are not there-fore forced to accept either that it has to be answered before trying to fill in the already identified explanatory gaps with more and better neuropsychologi-cal and other neuroscientific explanations of human consciousness or that not answering it first weakens whatever neuropsychological and other neuroscien-tific explanations of human consciousness we discover. Given the perplexities that some of the explanatory gaps produce, it strikes me that they and not the hard problem or the harder problem are what require our immediate conscious attention and concerted conscious effort.

APPENDIX: FUNCTIONAL NEUROANATOMY

THE BRAIN'S COMPONENTS

The adult brain is a toaster-sized lump of cells enclosed by the cranium, 1,200–1,500 cubic centimetres (cm³) in volume and weighing between 1,100 and 1,700 grams. In a living body, it looks like a great big, squishy, red walnut with fissures and wrinkles across its surface. Some of the brain's cells are contained entirely within the cranium, and others spread down the spinal column and from there into the periphery of the body. The *central nervous system* is composed of the brain and spinal cord; its partner, the *peripheral nervous system*, is the highway of nerves that feeds neural messages to the central nervous system. The brain is the top of the central nervous system. Everything above the spinal column up to and including pons and cerebellum is *hindbrain*. The short structure immediately above the pons is *midbrain*. Everything above midbrain is *forebrain*. Figure A.1 provides a side view, slightly exploded to show the regions.

Hindbrain (rhombencephalon)

The hindbrain is the terminus of the spinal column and transition to the midbrain and forebrain. The hindbrain contains three major structures – the medulla oblongata, the pons and the cerebellum – and a number of smaller structures.

The *medulla oblongata* (Latin for "oblong marrow") is the lowest organ of the brain, below the pons and in front of the cerebellum. The medulla oblongata controls autonomic functions and serves as a relay station for a vast variety of signals going to and coming from the spinal cord, such as motor tracts, cardiac and respiratory signals, and signals directing muscular control of blood vessels. It is also the location of nerves that control coughing, gagging, swallowing, hiccupping and vomiting.

The *pons* (Latin for "bridge") is above the medulla oblongata and in front of the cerebellum. Like the medulla oblongata, the pons serves as a relay station,

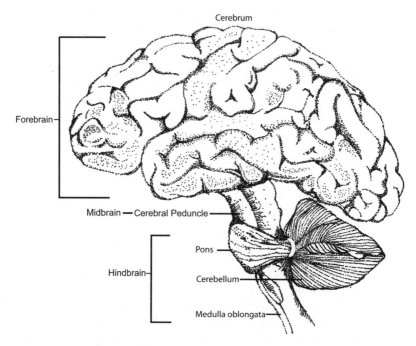

Cerebrum

Forebrain

Midbrain — Cerebral Peduncle

Pons

Hindbrain

Cerebellum

Medulla oblongata

Figure A.1 Hindbrain, midbrain and forebrain, side view.

not between the rest of the brain and spinal cord, but between the cerebellum and cerebrum of the brain, relaying messages about muscular control of respiration, facial muscles, tongue, teeth and eyeball movement. Two significant formations in the area of the pons are the *reticular formation* and the *locus coeruleus*. The reticular formation (Latin for "netlike") is a hugely complicated bundle of reciprocal neural connections upwards to the thalamus, hypothalamus and cortex, and downwards to the cerebellum and sensory nerves. The reticular formation is implicated in circadian rhythm maintenance, respiration, cardiac rhythms and consciousness. Psychoactive drugs target its neurons, and damage to the area induces immediate and irreversible coma.

The *locus coeruleus* (Latin for "blue spot") is one of the primary synthesis sites for the neurotransmitter norepinephrine. It receives messages from the hypothalamus, cingulate gyrus, raphe nuclei, amygdala and prefrontal cortex; is reciprocally connected to the hypothalamus and amygdala; and sends messages to a huge variety of cerebral and spinal areas, including various regions of cortex, basal ganglia, thalamus, cerebellum and spinal cord. The norepinephrine delivered by the locus coeruleus excites most of the rest of the brain, playing a regulatory role in everything from waking–sleeping cycles to preparing neurons for electrochemical input.

The *cerebellum* (Latin for "little brain") is immediately behind the pons and immediately below the occipital lobe cortex of the cerebrum. The cerebellum contains more than half of all the brain's neurons and has about 200 million input neurons from most of the other regions of the brain, 40 million of which come directly from the cerebral cortex. (In comparison, the entire visual tract is composed of about 1 million neurons.) For many years, it was thought that the cerebellum was responsible only for integrating activity of the motor regions. But its rapidity – the cerebellum contains the fastest myelinated neurons in all the brain's regions – and its extraordinary connectivity – all messages concerning motor activity leaving the brain go through the cerebellum – have led to a flurry of research in the past few years on its role in language and speech acquisition and production, cognitive skills, sensory acquisition, discrimination, tracking and prediction integration, and emotions.

Midbrain (mesencephalon)

The midbrain is an area of dense, closely packed neurons with high connectivity to both what is above – forebrain – and below – hindbrain – but few discrete structures of its own. The *cerebral peduncle* (Latin for "little brain stem") is a bundle of neurons emerging from the cerebellum on their way to the pons and thence to the cerebrum. These neurons are input and output pathways to and from the cerebellum. The cerebral peduncle is responsible for transmitting a wide range of motor behaviour information, including proprioceptive information, the sense of our body and its parts being interrelated. The second structure of interest is the *tectum* (Latin for "roof"), composed of the *superior colliculus* (Latin for "big hill") and *inferior colliculus* (Latin for "little hill"), the former of which relays visual information to the lateral geniculate of the thalamus, the latter of which relays auditory information to the medial geniculate of the thalamus. The third structure is the *tegmentum* (Latin for "covering"), composed of the *red nucleus*, the *substantia nigra* (Latin for "black substance") and the *ventral tegmentum* (often called "VTA" for "ventral tegmental area"). The red nucleus receives motor input from the cerebellum and sends output to the shoulders and arms. The substantia nigra is one of two dopamine synthesizing structures in the brain and is responsible for controlling certain kinds of eye movement. The ventral tegmentum is the other dopamine synthesizing structure and also produces serotonin. It is connected to, among other places, frontal lobes of cortex. Along with the nucleus accumbens, it is part of the pleasure-reward system. Cocaine and other psychoactive drugs target the activity of the ventral tegmentum.

Forebrain (prosencephalon)

The stem of hindbrain and midbrain supports the forebrain, which fits over it like an overgrown mushroom cap. The forebrain structures immediately above midbrain and inside cerebrum and the great efflorescence of cortex are the thalamus, hypothalamus, epithalamus and pituitary gland. Together, these are the *diencephalon*. Cerebrum and cortex, along with the linking corpus callosum, basal ganglia, olfactory bulb and limbic systems, are the *telencephalon*.

Subcerebral forebrain (diencephalon)

The subcerebral forebrain is a tangle of evolutionarily ancient structures that maintain and regulate bodily function. Figure A.2 is a view of the brain from the outside looking in to these central regions. The *thalamus* (Latin for "inner chamber") sits on top of midbrain structures right in front of the epithalamus. The thalamus has about ten million myelinated neurons arranged in fifty to sixty bundles. The thalamus translates significant portions of neural input into forms "readable" by cortex. For example, all sensory information except olfactory information passes through the thalamus. The thalamus also regulates the transition from sleep to wakeful states. The myelinated neural loops between thalamus and various cortical regions are abundant and reciprocal. Figure A.3 shows the thalamus, and Table A.1 shows select input/output thalamic pathways and functions.

The *epithalamus* ("epi" is Greek for "on" or "above") is famous more for historical reasons than anything else. The epithalamus is home to the *pineal gland*, which Descartes claimed was the brain structure in which non-extended thoughts initiated minute changes in the fluids that control muscular changes. The actual func-

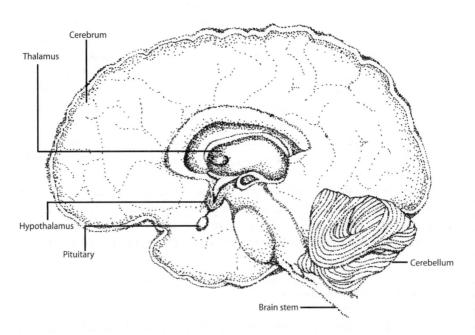

Figure A.2 Subcerebral forebrain structures.

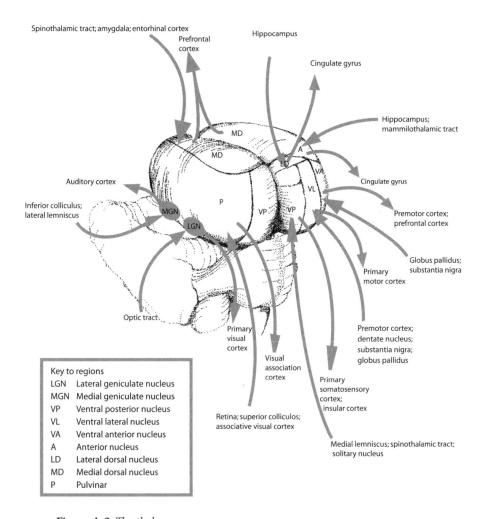

Figure A.3 The thalamus.

tion of the pineal gland is important but less glamorous: it produces melatonin, a hormone that controls circadian rhythm of sleeping and waking.

The *hypothalamus* ("hypo" is Greek for "under" or "below") is a mass of cells below the thalamus. The hypothalamus is one of the most complex and active regions of the brain: it regulates body temperature, appetite and thirst; it links the endocrine system to the nervous system at the pituitary gland; it produces and secretes many hormones, including dopamine; and through the secretion of gonadotropin-releasing hormone, it is linked to the limbic system and thus is involved in emotions such as aggression and fear, hunger and thirst, and sexual activity.

Table A.1 Select thalamic input/output pathways and functions (derived from Nolte 2002: Table 16-2, 401).

Name of nucleus	Major neural input	Major neural output	Psychological function
Lateral geniculate (LGN)	Optic tract	Primary visual cortex	Vision
Medial geniculate (MGN)	Inferior colliculus and lateral lemniscus	Primary auditory cortex	Audition
Ventral posterior (VPN)	Medial lemniscus, spinothalamic tract, trigeminothalamic tracts and solitary nucleus	Primary somato-sensory cortex and insular cortex	Touch; pain; temperature; taste; thirst (interoception, proprioception)
Ventral lateral (VLN)	Dentate nucleus, substantia nigra, globus pallidus	Primary motor cortex, premotor cortex	Initiation of movement
Ventral anterior (VAN)	Globus pallidus, substantia nigra	Premotor cortex and prefrontal cortex	Planning of movement
Interior (IN)	Hippocampus (fornix), mammillothalamic tract	Cingulate gyrus	Emotion and memory (limbic)
Pulvinar (PN)	Retina, superior colliculus, secondary visual cortex	Parietal-occipital-temporal association cortex	Vision
Lateral dorsal (LDN)	Hippocampus (fornix)	Cingulate gyrux	Memory (limbic)
Dorsomedial (DMN)	Spinothalamic tract, amygdala and entorhinal cortex	Prefrontal cortex	Emotional response to pain and memory; interoception
Centromedial (CMN)	Reticular formation, spinothalamic tract	Frontal and parietal lobes, caudate nucleus and putamen	Alertness and response to pain; interoception
Reticular (RN)	All thalamic nuclei and cortical regions	All thalamic nuclei	Attention

The *pituitary* (Latin for "mucous") lies adjacent to the hypothalamus. It is the primary or sole synthesis area for a large number of hormones, including antidiuretic hormone (ADH), growth hormone (GH), prolactin (PRL), follicle-stimulating hormone (FSH), luteinizing hormone (LH), thyroid-stimulating hormone (TSH) and adrenocorticotropic hormone (ACTH).

Subcortical cerebrum (telencephalon)

The *telencephalon* or *cerebrum* (Latin for "brain") is composed of cortex – the outer surfaces of convoluted tissue we think of when we think of the brain – and structures immediately interior to cortex. As with the structures of the diencephalon, the subcortical cerebral structures are compact and complex. Phylogenetically, these structures are among the oldest parts of the human brain. Figure A.4 shows many of them, in a cross section of the brain cut vertically, on a plane roughly from ear to ear.

The *amygdala* (Latin for "almond") is a small organ located deep within the temporal lobe but inside temporal cortex. The amygdala is associated with emotional reactions, especially fear, with formation of emotionally laden memories and with memory consolidation.

The *hippocampus* (Greek for "sea horse") is located deep within the temporal lobe and inside temporal cortex. Hippocampus is typically divided into the *dentate gyrus* and *subiculum*. The dentate gyrus receives messages from entorhinal cortex at the very front of the temporal lobe and sends messages to other

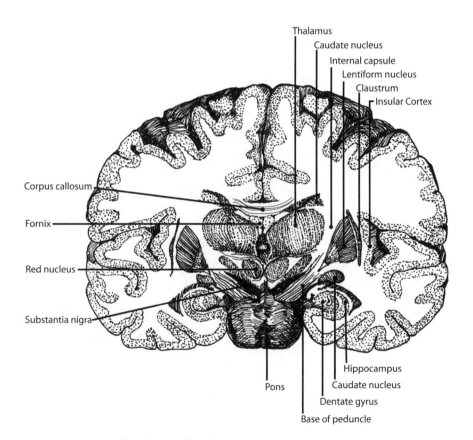

Figure A.4 The subcortical cerebrum.

317

hippocampal areas. It is one of only a handful of regions in the brain where neurons are generated throughout adult life. The subiculum receives messages from other hippocampal regions and sends messages to many other cranial regions, including the nucleus accumbens, prefrontal cortex, hypothalamus, amygdala and entorhinal cortex. The hippocampus is essential in the formation of new episodic, declarative and working memories, plays a role in navigation, and is implicated in addiction. Figure A.5 shows it, along with other subcortical structures.

The *basal ganglia* (Latin for "lowest cluster") are composed of two primary structures, the *caudate nucleus* (Latin for "tail nut") and the *lentiform nucleus* (Latin for "lens nut"). The outer part of the lentiform nucleus is the *putamen* (Latin for "shell"). The putamen receives messages from the thalamus and substantia nigra and sends messages to the premotor cortex and thalamus. Basal ganglia are associated with motor control, voluntary movement, emotions and learning.

The *nucleus accumbens* (Latin for "leaning nut") is located near the lentiform nucleus. Its inputs come from prefrontal cortex, the ventral tegmentum, amygdala and hippocampus. It sends messages to the *globus pallidus* (Latin for "pale globe"), a formation that in turn targets the thalamus and prefrontal cortex. The

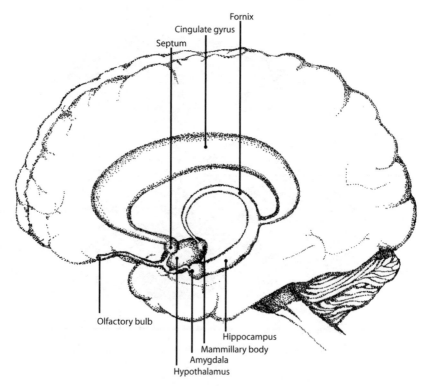

Figure A.5 Side view of certain subcortical structures.

neurons of the nucleus accumbens are specifically targeted by nicotine, cocaine, amphetamine and many other addictive drugs that increase dopamine levels. It has been identified as the pleasure centre of the brain.

The *claustrum* (Latin for "barrier") is a thin layer of unmyelinated neurons between the extreme and external capsules and is reciprocally connected with frontal cortex. Its function is not fully understood. The *extreme capsule* is a group of myelinated neurons reciprocally connecting the claustrum and insular cortex. The *external capsule* is a group of myelinated neurons reciprocally connecting the claustrum and lentiform nucleus. The *internal capsule* is a group of myelinated neurons reciprocally connecting cortex and medulla oblongata.

The left and right cortical hemispheres are connected by the *corpus callosum* (Latin for "hard body"), a mass of about 250 million myelinated neurons. The corpus callosum is widely connective between the hemispheres. Dysfunction in, inadequate development of, and lesions of the corpus callosum cause significant cognitive and affective alterations. (The real "Rain Man", Kim Peek, lacked a functioning corpus callosum.) Split-brain patients who have undergone a com-missurotomy have had their corpus callosum severed.

Cortex (telencephalon)

Finally, we arrive at *cortex* (Latin for "bark" or "shell"). Some cortical components are not visible from the outside. They are described first.

Insular cortex (Latin for "island cortex") is located deep within the Sylvian fissure separating the parietal lobe from the temporal lobe. Insular cortex is reciprocally connected to the thalamus, amygdala, orbitofrontal and primary sensory cortices. It has been implicated in emotions, particularly disgust, unease, fear, other visceral states and sensory perception of taste. Insular cortex is one of two regions in the brain known to be populated in part by *spindle neurons* (the other region is the anterior cingulate cortex, discussed next) and one of two regions in the brain known to be populated in part by *mirror neurons* (the other region is the pars opercularis of the frontal lobe, discussed below). Insular cortex has been the subject of intense recent research on emotion and empathy.

Cingulate cortex (Latin for "belt") surrounds the corpus callosum. It is routinely divided between *anterior cingulate cortex* and *posterior cingulate cortex*. Anterior cingulate cortex (ACC) is reciprocally connected to prefrontal and parietal cortex and the motor system. It hosts a population of spindle neurons and is thought to play a significant role in memory, attention, directed effort and error detection.

There are four cortical *lobes: occipital, parietal, temporal* and *frontal*. Frontal, temporal and parietal lobes each have *gyri*, ridges that are visible to the naked eye, each of which is named. Some lobes have other named subregions. The lobes and gyri can be identified as shown in Figure A.6.

Each of the lobes has various psychological functions associated with it. In general, the *occipital lobe* is associated with visual processing. The *parietal lobe*

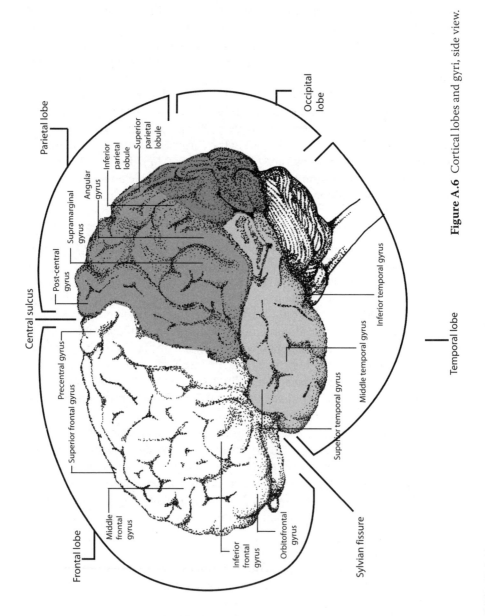

Figure A.6 Cortical lobes and gyri, side view.

is associated with the movement, orientation, recognition and perception of stimuli. The *temporal lobe* is associated with perception and recognition of auditory stimuli, memory and speech. The *frontal lobe* is associated with reasoning, planning, parts of speech, movement, emotions and problem-solving. As with the lobes, so too with the gyri: each has more specialized psychological functions associated with it. Figure A.7 shows some of those functions.

Occipital lobe The occipital lobe is the location of *primary and secondary visual cortex*, which receive neural input from the *lateral geniculate nucleus* in the thalamus, which in turn receives neural input from the retina of the eye. If we had X-ray vision that permitted us to look inside the brain at the neural pathways from the eyes to visual cortex, we would be able to see that they start in the eyes, traverse the optic chiasm where they switch to the contralateral (opposite) hemisphere of the brain, then travel to the thalamus, from which they project (at the lateral geniculate nucleus) to primary visual cortex. The occipital lobe is also home to the *lingual gyrus* (Latin for "tongue ridge"), which plays a role in dreaming and in printed word recognition.

Parietal lobe The parietal lobe is located in front of the occipital lobe, above the temporal lobe and behind the frontal lobe. The parietal lobe integrates sensory

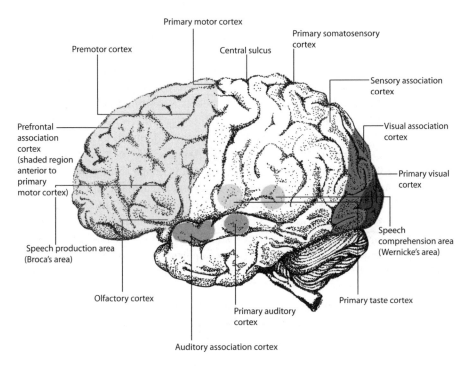

Figure A.7 Cortical functional areas, side view.

321

information – including kinesthesia (perception of body position), proprioception (perception of bodily states), temperature, vibration and vision – and integrates information that enables us to manipulate objects. At the front of the
parietal lobe, in the postcentral gyrus, is *primary somatosensory cortex*, the primary area for the senses of touch and taste. In the middle of the parietal lobe,
we find the *supramarginal* (or *superior marginal*) *gyrus*, which is implicated in
certain texture discrimination tasks, tactile learning and memory. Towards the
bottom of the parietal lobe is the *angular gyrus* (Latin for "ridge with corners"),
a region that some claim is unique to humans. The angular gyrus and parts of
the supramarginal gyrus, along with parts of superior temporal cortex, together
compose *Wernicke's area*, and are involved in speech processing, visual symbol
recognition and metaphor processing. It has also been implicated in explanations of phantom limb syndrome and out-of-body experiences. Finally, certain
parietal regions adjoining the *intraparietal sulcus*, the fissure that goes across
the parietal lobe, have been implicated in processing symbolic numerical information and in interpreting others' intentions.

Temporal lobe Below the frontal lobe and parietal lobe and in front of the occipital lobe is the *temporal lobe*. The temporal lobe may be broken down into three
areas. *Superior temporal cortex* (or *gyrus*) is a ridge immediately below the parietal lobe. It contains *primary*, *secondary* and *tertiary auditory cortex*. Auditory
cortex is functionally organized. Primary auditory cortex identifies pitch and
loudness information coming to it from the geniculate nucleus; secondary auditory cortex processes melodic and rhythmic patterns; and tertiary auditory cortex integrates the output of primary and secondary cortex. Superior temporal
cortex also contains a portion of Wernicke's area, which is involved in speech
integration. Wernicke's aphasia, in which speech is grammatical but meaningless, results from lesions in this area. Beneath the superior temporal gyrus is *middle temporal cortex*, which is involved, among other things, in face recognition.
Beneath middle temporal cortex is, not surprisingly, *inferior temporal cortex*,
which is involved in visual information concerning shape. The posterior middle part of inferior temporal cortex is *fusiform cortex* (Latin for "spindle ridge"),
which processes, among other things, colour information, face recognition, and
word and number recognition. Finally, on the inside of inferior temporal cortex,
we find *parahippocampal cortex*, which surrounds the hippocampus and is, as
is the hippocampus, involved with memory, in particular with episodic, declarative, topographical memory and emotion expression.

Frontal lobe The frontal lobe is separated from the parietal lobe by the central sulcus (a "sulcus" is a fissure). The most posterior part of the frontal lobe is *primary
motor cortex*, which is associated with initiation of nerve pathways that eventuate in voluntary physical movement. Moving forward, we find *premotor cortex*,
which stores motor patterns and plays a role in voluntary activities. Moving

forward again from premotor cortex, there is *prefrontal cortex*. Prefrontal cortex is crucial for higher cognitive functioning, such as judgement, decision-making, thought, elaboration, attention and other executive functions.

The frontal lobe has named gyri. The *superior frontal gyrus* is the very top of frontal cortex and contains part of *dorsolateral prefrontal cortex* and the *frontal eye fields*. The *middle frontal gyrus* is the large region between the superior and inferior gyri and contains the majority of *dorsolateral prefrontal cortex* and the very front of the brain, the *frontopolar* region. The *inferior frontal gyrus* contains *ventrolateral prefrontal cortex*, *orbitofrontal prefrontal cortex* and some of *Broca's area*. On the interior of prefrontal cortex, immediately adjacent to the fissure separating the brain's hemispheres, is *ventromedial prefrontal cortex*.

Putting much of the preceding information together, we have the architectural components of the brain shown in Figure A.8.

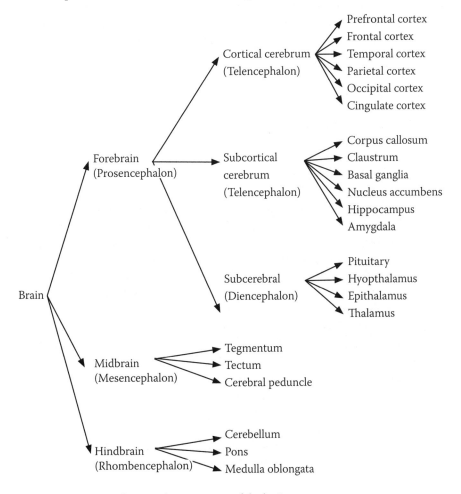

Figure A.8 Architectural components of the brain.

323

Functional lateralization

There is generalized lateralization to cognitive function and some lateralization to perceptual and affective (or emotional) processing. Language (written, heard and spoken), logic, mathematics, order, abstract cogitation, linguistic memory and pattern processing are typically, but not always, lateralized to the left hemisphere. The vast majority of the right-handers and three-quarters of the left-handers in the world have lateralization of speech, for example. Spatial, symbolic, image and some emotional processing, and auditory, visual and spatial memory are typically, but again not always, lateralized to the right hemisphere. Some attentional networks are thought to be lateralized to the right hemisphere. Some emotional dysfunctions, such as depression, are more strongly associated with left frontal pathways than any other pathways, while other emotional dysfunctions, such as lack of affect, are more strongly associated with right hemispheric pathways. Sensory processing, certain memory functions, learning, and certain executive and emotional processing are bilateral.

Allocortex, mesocortex, neocortex

A frequent practice among neuroscientists is to distinguish various regions and kinds of cortex along phylogenetic, structural and functional lines. Here is a way to make sense of this practice.

There is, to begin with, *allocortex*, composed of *archicortex* and *paleocortex*. These terms refer to phylogenetically old and structurally primitive kinds of cortex, typically with but two layers of neurons, each of a different type. The hippocampus is archicortex; the primary olfactory region or *pyriform* cortex is paleocortex. Next, there is *mesocortex*. This term refers to cortex that is phylogenetically newer and structurally more complex than allocortex. Having three rather than two layers of neurons, mesocortex is of intermediate structural complexity. Included in mesocortex are orbitofrontal cortex, insular cortex, parahippocampal cortex and cingulate cortex.

Finally, there is *neocortex* or, as it is also called, *isocortex*. These terms refer to the phylogenetically young and structurally complex cortex that constitutes 90 per cent of all human cortex. Neocortex is composed of six (or even seven, as in some visual areas) layers of neuron types. Going from outside to inside, we have the following layers. The *molecular layer* contains a few scattered neurons. The *external granular layer* contains a dense mixture of small granular neurons and small pyramidal neurons. The *external pyramidal layer* contains rows of pyramidal cells. The *internal granular layer* contains a mixture of granular and pyramidal neurons, but it is thinner than the external granular layer. The *internal pyramidal layer* contains large pyramidal neurons. The *fusiform* or *multiform* layer contains large pyramidal neurons and other, various, neurons. The top three layers engage in interhemispheric reciprocal connections. The internal granular level engages in intrahemispheric connections and is the main target of thalamocortical neurons. The internal pyramidal layer is the primary source of motor-related subcortical connections. And the fusiform layer is the primary source of corticothalamic connections.

Within the category of neocortex, functional subdivisions are usually introduced. First, we can subdivide between *idiotypic cortex* and *homotypic* or *association cortex*. Idiotypic areas include primary motor cortex, primary somatosensory cortex, primary visual cortex and primary auditory cortex. Association cortex

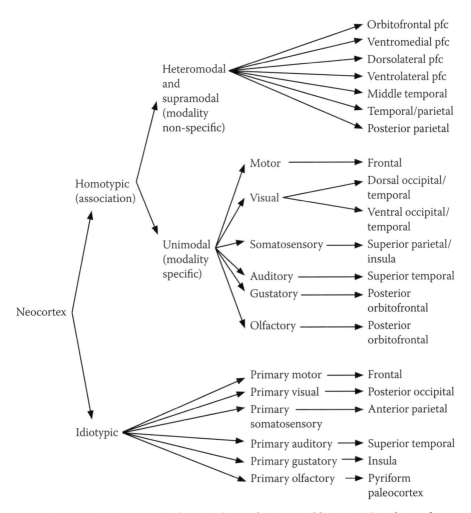

Figure A.9 Neocortex by functional type, function and location. Note that no functions are listed for heteromodal or supramodal cortex. The reason is simple: they are so numerous that they do not fit on the page.

constitutes the largest region of the human brain. Within association cortex, there are *unimodal* or *modality-specific* zones, *heteromodal* (sometimes "multimodal" or "polymodal" or "transmodal") *higher-order* zones and *supramodal higher-order zones* (Benson 1993). Unimodal association areas include auditory association in superior temporal cortex, motor association cortex in superior parietal cortex, somatosensory association in superior parietal cortex, and visual association areas in extrastriate occipital cortex. Each unimodal area borders its associated idiotypic sensory cortical area. Heteromodal areas include some regions of cortex at the fusion area between parietal and occipital and between parietal and temporal cortex, middle temporal cortex, inferior parietal cortex, and others. Heteromodal association areas are bidirectionally connected with unimodal association areas and with other heteromodal areas, but are often at some distance from those areas. Supramodal areas are restricted to prefrontal cortex. Supramodal prefrontal cortex is a highly heterogeneous area functionally and is the focus of intense ongoing research. Much of this research has established associations between regions of prefrontal cortex and complex psychological abilities. Prefrontal cortex is now typically subdivided into the following areas.

Orbitofrontal prefrontal cortex (OFPFC) (its interior portion abutting the wall separating the two hemispheres is sometimes called *ventromedial prefrontal cortex* (VMPFC)) is located immediately above the eyes, below dorsolateral cortex, behind the frontopolar region and in front of temporal cortex. OFPFC receives messages from somatosensory cortex, temporal cortex, olfactory cortex, primary taste cortex, insula, amygdala and thalamus. It sends output to temporal cortex, entorhinal cortex, cingulate cortex, hypothalamus, hippocampus, ventral tegmental area, caudate nucleus, globus pallidus, substantia nigra and nucleus accumbens. OFPFC contains secondary taste cortex, secondary and tertiary olfactory cortex, and associative cortex that combines taste and olfaction into flavour and gauges satisfaction. In addition, orbitofrontal cortex has been associated with the feelings of touch (painful and pleasurable), and with winning and losing. It has been repeatedly implicated in decision-making, reinforcement learning, rewards, socially appropriate behaviour, expectation and planning. Destruction or dysfunction of OFPFC and orbitofrontal-subcortical pathways leads to an inability to consider emotional and social consequences of actions, and thus to rash decisions, increased swearing, inappropriate sexuality, compulsive risk taking and poor management. Concussions and Lou Gehrig's disease (amyotrophic lateral sclerosis (ALS)) are known to damage or destroy OFPFC.

Dorsolateral prefrontal cortex (DLPFC) is located between the very front of the brain and Broca's area, above ventrolateral prefrontal cortex, and in front of premotor cortex. DLPFC receives input from thalamus, occipital cortex, temporal cortex, parietal cortex, visual association cortex, auditory association cortex, somatosensory association cortex and cingulate cortex. It sends output to supplementary motor and premotor cortex, temporal cortex, parietal cortex, cingulate cortex, caudate nucleus of the basal ganglia, globus pallidus, hippocampus, thalamus, cerebellum and superior colliculus. DLPFC has been closely associated with semantic fluency and verbal processing, monitoring, sustaining attention, inhibition and working memory, in particular with working memory of spatial location and with the monitoring and maintaining temporal order of events, narrative structure and autobiographical memories. Destruction or dysfunction of DLPFC and dorsolateral-subcortical pathways leads to attention disorders, inability to follow temporal sequences and compromised monitoring.

Ventrolateral prefrontal cortex (VLPFC) is located below the very front of the brain and dorsolateral cortex and above orbitofrontal cortex. VLPFC is usually thought to include Broca's area. VLPFC receives input from occipital cortex, temporal cortex, parietal cortex, visual association cortex, auditory association cortex and somatosensory association cortex. It sends output to temporal cortex, specifically to Wernicke's area. In the part of Broca's area known as the *pars triangularis*, neural signals from Wernicke's area that have come forward on the bundle of myelinated neurons called the *arcuate fasciculus* are interpreted and transmitted to the *pars opercularis*, where coordination and production of speech is initiated. The pars opercularis is home to groups of mirror neurons. Damage to this area can cause *Broca's aphasia*, which prevents formation of grammatically correct sentences. In addition to its role in speech production, VLPFC is associated with spatial planning and with working memory, in particular with working memory of object identification and the sense of ownership in autobiographical memories. Dysfunction of VLPFC leads to anxiety disorders and to cognitive disinhibition.

Both in absolute terms and proportional to other cortical types, the amount of association neocortex increases dramatically as the phylogenetic ladder is climbed. About 90 per cent of a rat's cortex is primary sensory cortex, less than 10 per cent is association cortex. In comparison, about 25 per cent of a human's cortex is primary sensory cortex and 75 per cent is unimodal, heteromodal and supramodal association cortex (Nolte 2002). About a third of all human cortex is prefrontal heteromodal and supramodal cortex alone.

NEURONS

The two most important occupants of these cortical regions are neurons and glial cells. *Neurons* (Greek for "nerve") are specialized signal transmitter cells. *Glial cells* (Greek for "glue cells") are specialized supporting cells. The number of neurons in the brain exceeds 100 billion, and the number of glial cells exceeds a trillion.

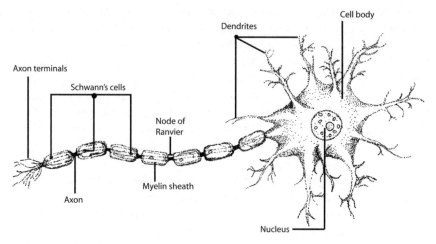

Figure A.10 Schematic neuron.

Neuron structure

Neurons are cells. As such, they contain structures responsible for enzyme, membrane, organelle and protein synthesis. But neurons are specialty agents, and their specialty is transmitting electrochemical signals. Figure A.10 is a schematic drawing of a neuron, showing major structures.

A *dendrite* (Greek for "tree") is a tapering extension of the cell body that receives electrochemical signals from other neurons and transmits them to the soma. The *soma* or *cell body* is the metabolic engine of the cell. Typically, one axon and multiple dendrites protrude from it. Its neural function is to synthesize electrochemical signals received from dendrites and send them to the axon. An *axon* (Greek for "axle") is a cylindrical tube protruding from the cell body that conducts electrochemical signals to the synaptic terminal. The *synaptic terminal* is a bulb at the end of an axon adjacent to dendrites of distinct neurons that transmits electrochemical signals to dendrites on other neurons.

Subcellular structures and microtubules

Structural features of a neuron's component parts can in turn be identified. Dendrites, cell bodies and axons, for example, are variously constructed of microtubules, neurofilaments, Nissl bodies, mitochondria and the Golgi apparatus, each of which has its own function. *Microtubules* are typically 25 nanometres (nm) in diameter and composed of thirteen strands of tubulin protein encircling a hollow core. They enable cell organelles (subcellular structures with specialized functions) to move through neurons.

Myelination and white matter tracts

Axons contain additional structures required for their function as signal propagation devices. Of interest to us will be the *myelin sheath* (Greek for "marrow"), a feature that enhances signal propagation. Myelinated axons are components of neurons that form the *white matter* of the brain. Non-myelinated axons are components of neurons that form the *grey matter* of the brain. Myelinated neurons are transmission neurons; non-myelinated neurons are processing neurons. In the average human brain, about half its volume is composed of myelinated neurons, the other half is composed of non-myelinated neurons, glial cells, blood vessels and the ventricles. White matter tracts are grouped under three kinds. First, *projection tracts* connect cortical with subcortical regions. Those that ascend from subcortex to cortex are *corticopetal*; those that descend from cortex to subcortex are *corticofugal*. An important corticopetal tract is the *thalamocortical* tract, which runs from various thalamic nuclei to various regions of cortex; an important corticofugal tract is the *corticothalamic* tract, which runs from various regions of cortex to the thalamic nuclei. Together, these two form the *cortico-thalamocortical loop*. One of the most beautiful structures of the brain, the *corona radiata*, is a corticofugal white matter motor tract that leads from cortex to the spinal cord.

In addition to projection tracts, there are, second, *commissural tracts*, which connect the hemispheres. The best known of these is the *corpus callosum*, a bundle of 300 million myelinated neurons connecting homologous regions in the left and right hemispheres. In addition, there is the *anterior commissure*, which connects olfactory and temporal cortex in the two hemispheres, and the *hippocampal commissure*, which connects the two sides of the fornix, a bundle of neurons running from the hippocampus to the mammillary bodies and septal nuclei.

Finally, there are, third, *association tracts*, which connect various regions of cortex within each hemisphere. Most adjacent regions of cortex have *short association fibres* connecting them one to another. In addition, five named *long association tracts* bidirectionally link distal regions of the brain. We have already noted interconnections between neocortical regions. Here, we identify the tracts that implement those interconnections. First, the *cingulum* bidirectionally connects frontal/prefrontal cortex with parietal and temporal cortex. Second, the *uncinate fasciculus* bidirectionally connects frontal and temporal cortex. Third, the *inferior longitudinal fasciculus* bidirectionally connects occipital cortex and temporal cortex. Fourth, the *superior occipitofrontal fasciculus* bidirectionally connects frontal/prefrontal cortex with parietal and occipital cortex. Fifth, there is the *superior longitudinal fasciculus* (SLF) and its component, the *arcuate fasciculus*. The superior longitudinal fasciculus in humans is composed of four bundles: (a) SLF I begins in superior and medial parietal cortex and projects to areas in the superior gyrus and dorsolateral prefrontal cortex and to supplementary motor cortex; (b) SLF II begins in inferior parietal

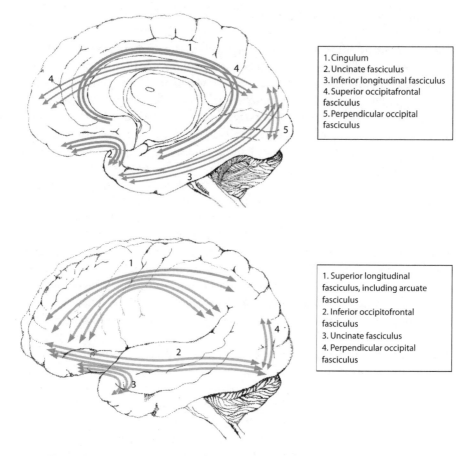

Figure A.11 Long association white matter tracts.

cortex and projects to dorsolateral prefrontal cortex; (c) SLF III begins in the supramarginal gyrus area of parietal cortex and projects to ventrolateral prefrontal cortex; (d) the arcuate fasciculus (AF) begins in superior temporal cortex and projects to dorsolateral prefrontal cortex. All four are bidirectional. Sixth, the *inferior occipitofrontal fasciculus* bidirectionally connects frontal/prefrontal cortex with temporal and occipital cortex. Finally, seventh, the *perpendicular occipital fasciculus* bidirectionally connects regions of occipital cortex. Figure A.11 shows first a view from inside, and second a view from the outside.

Signal propagation

Neurons work by propagating electrochemical signals down an axon to the synaptic terminal where neurotransmitters are released to cross the synaptic cleft to the postsynaptic neuron. Consider the signals from cell body to synaptic terminal. The propagation of electrochemical signals down axons is accomplished by changes in the electrical charge of the sheath that encloses the axon. This sheath or wall has a resting electrical charge of –65 millivolts (mv). Charged sodium and potassium molecules induce movement of an electrical charge down an axon by causing gates to selectively open and close in sequence. The resting potential of a neuron changes when a message is received from other neurons. If the message is *inhibitory*, the neuron's charge becomes more negative, thus decreasing its ability to send messages to other neurons. If the message is *excitatory*, the neuron's charge becomes more positive, thus increasing its ability to send messages to other neurons.

The cell membrane changes to permit sodium ions to enter. This influx of positively charged ions causes the cell's electrical potential to become positive, reaching its peak at +40 mv. The change from negative to positive charge is the neuron's *action potential*. When the charge of the cell reaches its positive peak, positively charged sodium ions are again forced out of the neuron. Their exit results in a negative potential that plunges deeper than –65 mv, and then it returns to resting potential. When the action potential within the neuron is sufficiently high, the neuron fires, sending an electrochemical message down an axon. Subsequent to firing, the neuron enters a *refractory* period during which it will not fire.

Some of the most devastating neurotoxins pervert action potential. Tetrodotoxin, for example, found in the livers of puffer fish, binds to voltage-gated sodium channels, preventing positively charged sodium ions from entering the axon. The result is immediate and systemic paralysis. In sufficiently large doses, it causes respiratory failure and death in minutes. There are also diseases associated with malfunctioning axonal transmission. Perhaps the best known is myotonia, a neural-muscular disorder that inhibits muscle relaxation following contraction. Although not common in humans, myotonic or "fainting" goats are relatively common. If startled, fainting goats go completely rigid and can be knocked over like bowling pins. Within seconds or minutes they are back up again grazing, without apparent awareness that anything has happened.

The synapse

Neurons are vastly interconnected with other neurons across the brain, through the brain stem, and out into the peripheral nervous system. Each neuron has, on average, 7,000 connections to other neurons (some neurons have as many as 100,000 connections). These connections are *synapses* (Greek for "connection"), which are shown in Figure A.12. The number of synapses in human brains is enormous: depending on which numbers are used, somewhere between 60 and 500 trillion in adults and approaching perhaps 1,000 trillion – a quadrillion – in prepubescent children.

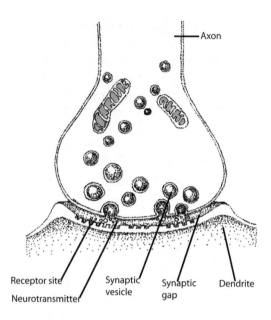

Receptor site   Synaptic   Synaptic   Dendrite
                vesicle   gap
Neurotransmitter

Figure A.12 Schematic synapse.

The *synaptic terminal* contains tiny membrane-enclosed packets called *synaptic vesicles*, each of which contains neurotransmitter molecules. Synaptic vesicles discharge *neurotransmitter* molecules in response to an electrical signal that has been propagated down the axon to the synaptic terminal. Upon release, neurotransmitter molecules migrate out of the synaptic terminal, cross the *synaptic cleft* between pre- and postsynaptic neurons, and bind themselves to other molecules in the postsynaptic neuron, thus initiating a subsequent electrochemical signal in the dendrite(s) of the postsynaptic neuron. If the signal is excitatory, the action potential then propagates down the line. Having accomplished their task, neurotransmitters are retrieved from the cleft and taken back into the presynaptic vesicles. This process is known as *reuptake.*

Neurotransmitter types and psychoactive neurochemicals

Including neuropeptides, more than five dozen neurotransmitter kinds exist. Some are unique to particular kinds of neurons, others are general purpose. Each has a characteristic function. Consider a handful of the more prevalent neurotransmitters, their functions, and perturbations in them induced by introducing other chemicals into the mix.

Dopamine is produced in the substantia nigra and the ventral tegmentum and plays a regulatory role in most cerebral neural activity. Neurons that use dopamine are *dopaminergic*. Dopaminergic neurons send messages upwardly to the amygdala, caudate nucleus, hypothalamus, hippocampus, putamen and cerebral cortex. Low levels of dopamine cause memory and attention disorders and are implicated in Attention Deficit/Hyperactivity Disorder (AD/HD). Just as importantly, dopamine levels increase when an unexpected reward occurs; thus, dopamine plays a role in the pleasure system. Recent work on the role of dopamine in prefrontal cortex activity suggests that it plays a role in maintaining ongoing cognitive activity and in determining when ongoing cognitive activity should be updated (Cohen 2005). Finally, a drop in dopamine levels is a characteristic symptom of individuals with Parkinson's disease. Cocaine blocks dopamine reuptake, leaving too much dopamine loitering in the synaptic cleft, inducing a state of euphoria. Haloperidol (Haldol) blocks dopamine receptors, thus relieving psychosis.

Norepinephrine is produced in the locus coeruleus and, like dopamine, plays a regulatory role in cerebral neural activity, especially in attention. Neurons using norepinephrine as their primary neurotransmitter are *noradrenergic*. Noradrenergic neurons deliver messages to virtually the entire central nervous system. Upwards, they connect to the tegmentum, thalamus, hypothalamus, limbic system and cerebral cortex. Downwards, they connect through the cerebral peduncle to the cerebellum, and through the brainstem down the spinal column. Norepinephrine has been specifically implicated in attention. Problems with regulating norepinephrine levels have been held to be responsible for AD/HD. Cocaine blocks norepinephrine reuptake, allowing norepinephrine to loiter in the synaptic cleft. Depression, panic attacks and post-traumatic stress disorder implicate the norepinephrine pathways of the brain.

Serotonin is produced in the raphe nuclei of the pons and by the medulla oblongata. Neurons using serotonin as their primary neurotransmitter are *serotonergic*. Serotonergic neurons send messages throughout the brain, both upwards and downwards. Serotonin plays a regulatory role in cerebral neural activity and is closely associated with general levels of wakefulness and sleepiness (as compared with noradrenergic neurons, which are implicated in changes in wakefulness induced by attention). Low serotonin levels have been implicated in depression, anorexia and various sleep disorders. Fluoxetine (Prozac) blocks serotonin reuptake.

Acetylcholine is produced in cells all over the body and plays a major role in motor behaviour and the peripheral nervous system, but a less important role in the central nervous system. In the central nervous system, acetylcholine is produced in the reticular formation, the putamen, and the caudate and basal nuclei. Neurons using acetylcholine as their primary neurotransmitters are *cholinergic* neurons, and they deliver signals upwards to the frontal, parietal and occipital lobes, and downwards to the amygdala and, through the midbrain and hindbrain, down the spinal column. Most cholinergic neurons are excitatory. The function of cholinergic neurons in the central nervous system appears to be general neural activity regulation and memory formation and retrieval.

Some research suggests that acetylcholine and norepinephrine work counter to one another in situations of uncertainty. Botulinum blocks acetylcholine release, inducing paralysis.

Glutamate is produced in neurons of the brain; GABA (the acronym for "γ-aminobutyric acid"), a derivative of glutamate, is likewise produced in brain neurons. Neurons using glutamate as their primary neurotransmitter are *glutamatergic* neurons; neurons using GABA as their primary neurotransmitter are *GABAergic* neurons. Glutamate is an excitatory neurotransmitter that enhances connections between neurons; GABA is an inhibitory neurotransmitter that degrades connections between neurons. Glutamate and GABA are the primary neurotransmitters in synapses between interneurons (neurons that connect only to other neurons). Since the human brain is composed almost entirely of interneurons, glutamate and GABA are the most abundant neurotransmitters in the brain. Excessive GABA levels induce excitotoxicity, which can kill or injure neurons, causing brain damage; low GABA levels have been implicated in anxiety disorder and post-traumatic stress disorder. Leaving GABA receptors open induces sedated states; increasing GABA-receptor frequency induces tranquility. Barbiturates promote GABA receptors being left open; Valium and Diazepam promote increasing GABA-receptor frequency. Morphine binds to GABA receptors, inducing euphoria. Phencyclidine (PCP, angel dust) blocks certain glutamate and GABA receptors called *NMDA* (for *N*-methyl-D-aspartate) receptors.

Psychoactive neurochemicals such as alcohol, marijuana, psilocybin, LSD, mescaline, caffeine, nicotine, morphine, opium and all of the rest of them affect the work of synapses. Consider just three: caffeine, nicotine and marijuana.

Caffeine mimics a neurotransmitter in the brain called adenosine. Adenosine slows neural activity down. When caffeine is introduced into the brain's chemistry, it binds to postsynaptic adenosine receptors. However, unlike adenosine, caffeine does not slow neural activity down and, hence, additional neural activity occurs. In response to the additional neural activity, the pituitary gland releases epinephrine (adrenaline), causing pupils to dilate, heartbeat to increase, bloodstream sugar levels to elevate, blood vesicles to constrict and muscles to tighten. Like heroin and amphetamine, caffeine also increases dopamine levels in the brain, thus inducing pleasure and addiction. Sudden withdrawal induces headaches, drowsiness and depression.

Nicotine mimics acetylcholine and causes significant receptor activity. But, unlike acetylcholine and like caffeine, nicotine is unregulated by the body. While neurons regularly release small amounts of acetylcholine, nicotine activates neurons using acetylcholine, and this causes significantly increased acetylcholine release rates, which in turn cause heightened activity in other neuronal pathways, especially in parietal cortex. By activating these pathways, nicotine improves reaction time and attention. As with caffeine, nicotine also promotes dopamine release in reward pathways. But it causes other physiological responses as well. First, nicotine releases glutamate, creating memories associating nicotine and pleasure, thus helping to cement the desire for more. Second, nicotine increases endorphin levels. *Endorphins* are small proteins, similar in structure to morphine, and are natural painkillers. Endorphins also induce feelings of euphoria – the endorphin rush. As a result, nicotine is highly addictive. Without a maintenance dose, the neurotransmitters that nicotine replaces are absent, and, when maintenance ceases, their absence causes irritability, anxiety and depression.

The active ingredient in *marijuana* is tetrahydrocannabinol or THC, a neurotransmitter that binds with cannabinoid receptors concentrated in the basal ganglia, cerebellum and hippocampus. THC mimics behaviour of a particular cannabinoid neurotransmitter, anandamide. THC replaces anandamide and binds with its receptors, causing subsequent changes in neural pathways that interfere with short-term memory (hippocampus), conscious and unconscious coordination (cerebellum and basal ganglia), and that cause hunger or "the munchies" (hypothalamus).

Neuron types

Neurons can be classified according to the neurotransmitter they release, to their architecture, to their excitatory or inhibitory roles, and to their function. There are four basic architectural types of neurons: unipolar, bipolar, multipolar and pyramidal. Figure A.13 diagrams the schematic types.

Especially within the multipolar neurons, further specification is usually encountered. Pyramidal cells, for example, are a kind of multipolar neuron. We here list those kinds of neurons relevant for our investigations. *Unipolar*

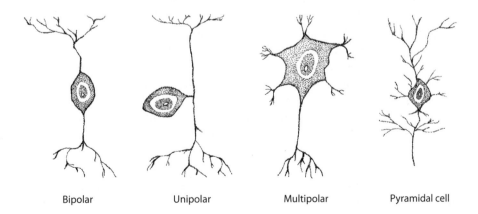

| Bipolar | Unipolar | Multipolar | Pyramidal cell |

Figure A.13 Basic neuron types.

neurons are the simplest kind of neuron. They have a single dendritic/axon and an associated cell body. *Bipolar* neurons have a single dendrite leading to the cell body and a single axon leading from the cell body. Many bipolar neurons are *interneurons,* that is, neurons that communicate only with other neurons. The human brain is composed entirely of interneurons, some of them bipolar, most of them multipolar. *Multipolar* neurons have multiple dendrites leading to the cell body and a single axon leading from the cell body. The human brain is composed primarily of multipolar cells.

There are various kinds of multipolar cells in the brain. Two of the most numerous are *pyramidal cells* and *Purkinje cells.* Pyramidal cells are identifiable by the shape of the cell body. Pyramidal cells are located primarily in the cortex and hippocampus. They are glutamatergic neurons and are the output neurons of cerebellar cortex, sending messages to the rest of the central nervous system. About 80 per cent of cortex neurons are pyramidal cells. Purkinje cells are located in the cerebellum and are identifiable by their treelike proliferating dendrites.

Granule cells are tiny neurons densely packed in the cerebellum beneath the Purkinje layer. They are also found in the granule layers of cortex, in the olfactory bulb, and in the hippocampus. Granule cells in the olfactory bulb and in the hippocampus are the only neuron type known to generate through adulthood.

Spindle neurons are a recent neuroanatomical discovery. Although they were identified by Von Economo in the early twentieth century (and are sometimes named after him), their physiology was not described in detail until 1999. Found only in humans, chimpanzees, orangutans, gorillas and some species of whales, spindle neurons are the focus of ongoing research. They are located in anterior cingulate and insular cortex and compose about 5–6 per cent of all neurons in the human brain. They are thought to play a unique role in error detection, self-control, intense emotional states (such as love, anger and lust), planning and self-awareness. Their appearance in insular cortex is thought to be especially noteworthy, since this area may have changed as recently as 200,000 years ago and so may provide a clue into the "great leap forward" of human evolution.

Mirror neurons are another recent neuroanatomical discovery, dating to the late 1980s. Mirror neurons are curious because they fire both when we engage in an action and when we observe someone else perform the same action (thus the name). Mirror neurons are found in the inferior parietal lobule and in Broca's area in humans and in some primates and birds. Although few in number even in humans and fewer still in other animals that have them at all, mirror neurons have been implicated in mimicry, imitation, social behaviour, language competence and consciousness.

Neurons that carry information from tissues and organs to the central nervous system are *afferent neurons.* Neurons that carry information from the central nervous system to tissues and organs are *efferent neurons.* Neurons that connect one neuron to another neuron in the central nervous system are *interneurons.* The terms "afferent" and "efferent" are also used to characterize connections between regions of the brain, incoming pathways from one region to another region being afferent pathways and pathways leading from one region to another region being efferent pathways.

Presynaptic neurons that cause a temporary increase in the resting potential of a postsynaptic neuron are *excitatory neurons* because the message from the presynaptic neuron to the postsynaptic neuron increases the latter's ability to send messages to other neurons. Presynaptic neurons that cause a temporary decrease in the resting potential of a postsynaptic neuron are *inhibitory neurons* because the message from the presynaptic neuron to the postsynaptic neuron decreases the latter's ability to send messages to other neurons. In addition, there are also *modulatory neurons*, presynaptic neurons whose impact on post-synaptic neurons is more complex than is captured by the excitatory-inhibitory distinction. Glutamatergic and cholinergic neurons are typically excitatory neurons; GABAergic neurons are typically inhibitory neurons; and dopaminergic and serotonergic neurons are typically modulatory neurons.

NOTES

1. CONSCIOUSNESS AND CONSCIOUS PROPERTIES

1. States are a way that a thing is: my being tired is a state of mine. Events are property exemplifications at a time by a particular: Caesar's death is an event that occurs to Caesar. Processes are organized sets of events: my dialing a telephone is a sequentially ordered set of events of pushing buttons and hence a process. For more on these matters, see Chapter 2.

2. Those who propose to explain them as non-natural phenomena initially have an easier time on this score, for those who try to account for them without appeal to mystery, magic or miracle are obliged to integrate what appear initially to be quite *un*natural properties into a naturalistic framework. However, although freeing ourselves from scientific scruple licences all sorts of speculative answers, appealing to miracles and magic are not much more than admitting that we have no explanation.

3. Idealism is sometimes the result of a sceptical philosophical argument. Given our inability to know anything about the external world, the only conclusion that can be drawn is that we know only the contents of consciousness (for a clear development and criticism of this argument, see Hanna 2006).

4. Hartley and La Mettrie were unable to offer much more than stabs in the dark when it came to trying to understand more about consciousness. Accurate cortical models of brain function were more than two hundred years away when they wrote; for that matter, even the neuroanatomical features of the brain were still almost completely undescribed. Both speculated about these matters, but Hartley's vibration theory of nerves was wrong from the start, and La Mettrie suggested, among many other bizarre things, that imagination is located in the *medulla oblongata*, a hindbrain structure.

5. The category mistake argument is equally telling against physicalism. Physicalists who affirm the identity of the mind and the brain or central nervous system hold that the mind is the brain, that is, that the mind is identical to a particular hunk of grey matter enclosed in the cranium. But that is as much a category error as the error the dualist makes. In both cases, "the mind" is assumed to be a singular term: in the one case, a singular term that refers to a non-spatial entity, in the other, a singular term that refers to a spatial entity. If the one use commits a category mistake, so too does the other. Many will start to feel a little uneasy at this point, and well they should, for thinking on the basis of semantic considerations that the mind cannot be the brain is not nearly as compelling as thinking on the basis of semantic considerations that the mind cannot be a non-spatial entity. If the category mistake argument does away with both dualism *and* physicalism, then it seems to prove too much.

2. IDENTITY, SUPERVENIENCE, REDUCTION AND EMERGENCE

1. As used in philosophy of neuroscience (Chalmers 2000; Haselager *et al.* 2003b; Noë & Thompson 2004a), "isomorphism" refers to a one-to-one mapping from conscious properties to neural properties. This use of "isomorphism" is similar to but looser than the way "isomorphism" is used in mathematics. In mathematics, "isomorphism" refers to a more stringent relation. To begin with, a mathematical isomorphism is both a one-to-one and an *onto* function (an *injective* function) from one set X to another set Y, where an injective function is a function f from one set X to another set Y such that, for each x in X, there is at most one y in Y to which x maps (alternatively, every element of the codomain Y is mapped to by at most one element of its domain X). But a mathematical isomorphism is also a *bijective* function, where a bijective function is an injective function such that for each y in Y, there is exactly one x in X such that $f(x) = y$ and no unmapped element exists in either X or Y. Moreover, a mathematical isomorphism is not only bijective but also has the additional property that the inverse mapping from Y to X is homomorphic, where a *homomorphic* mapping is a mapping that preserves structure. For this reason, mathematical isomorphism is sometimes called *bijective homomorphism*. It can be appreciated that the mathematical concept of isomorphism is narrower than the concept of isomorphism at use in philosophy of neuroscience. For example, supervenience is an isomorphism in the looser sense but not a mathematical isomorphism. Supervenience is injective but not bijective, much less bijective homomorphic. On the other hand, identity is a relation that satisfies both the looser and the more stringent concepts. For purposes of this book, the relevant concept of isomorphism is that which is at play in philosophy of neuroscience.

2. Not all consciousness investigators agree that the isomorphism constraint is true. Eliminativists, who recommend reducing as many conscious properties as can be and eliminating any residue as empty language, accept the isomorphism constraint as a methodological principle for engaging in scientific research on consciousness but do not commit themselves to anything more than that. Since accepting the isomorphism constraint as a methodological principle is consistent with its falsity, eliminativists do not feel bound to defend it if conscious properties that cannot be mapped one-to-one to physical properties are confirmed. About such conscious properties, eliminativists are dismissive. Instead of using the existence of such conscious properties to establish the bounds of scientific research, they use the bounds of scientific research to reject the existence of such properties.

3. One influential way of thinking of reduction that we will not pursue beyond mentioning it here considers reduction to be a relation between the laws of higher- and lower-level *theories*. According to this model, famously analysed by Ernest Nagel ([1961] 1979), a higher-level theory T_H reduces to a lower-level theory T_L whenever the properties mentioned in the laws of T_H are derivable from the laws of the lower-level theory T_L with the addition of bridge laws that assert the identity of the properties named in T_H and T_L. While influential, the requirement that the properties mentioned in the laws of T_H be identical to those mentioned in T_L entails that any multiply realizable type is then immediately deemed irreducible. If a property F from T_H is multiply realizable by properties G, H, I and J from T_L, then since F is not identical to any one of G, H, I or J but only to the disjunction of all of them, then F cannot be reduced to any of G, H, I or J. That sets the bar for reduction too high, for given the imaginary powers of philosophers, it is guaranteed that *every* functional type is multiply realizable, even if only by a logical or a conceptual possibility. We have already declined membership in this club, so we decline to discuss any further a form of reduction that requires joining. If multiple realizability figures in reduction, it must do so in some way other than what this version of reduction suggests.

3. REDUCTIVE AND NON-REDUCTIVE PHYSICALISMS

1. There is a second argument against type physicalism. The so-called *knowledge argument* purports to demonstrate that certain kinds of knowledge show that conscious events cannot be identical to any physical event. Jackson is credited with the argument (Jackson 1986). Here is a version:

    P1: There is someone who lives in a black and white environment and learns everything there is to know about the neurophysiology of colour
    P2: That person is moved from her environment to a colour environment
    P3: That person will learn something new, namely, what it is like to experience colour
    IC: It is not the case that knowing everything about the neurophysiology of colour is everything there is to know about what it is like to experience colour
    P4: If there is something to know about what it is like to experience colour, then there are properties of colour experience that are not identical to any neurophysiological property
    C: Colour experience is not neurophysiological

    The key premises are P3 and P4. Type physicalists claim against P3 that knowing all there is to know about the neurophysiology of colour entails knowing about the experience of colour. Likewise, type physicalists claim against P4 that while we learn something new, what we learn is consistent with it being something physical. So, while neurophysiology of colour is conceded not to explain everything there is to know about the experience of colour, the insistence that the residue is distinct from the physical is rejected. So, either what we learn upon experiencing colour is nothing new or, if it is something new, it is nothing that cannot be incorporated into physicalism. Although influential, the literature that flows from the knowledge argument would take us too far afield were it to be discussed further (for responses developing the one in this note, see Block [2002] 2007; Loar 1999).

2. The argument from functionalism to type physicalism, first presented by David Lewis (1966), is as follows. Begin by specifying some entity, that is, locating it in a functional network. Next, collect all the members of this group of functionally described entities and conjoin them in a long sentence. That sentence is our theory. Then go look for the physical entities that satisfy the theory. If there are such entities, they are the entities that *realize* the theory. These entities will come from some other theory that is already familiar. In the case of human consciousness, the relevant properties are subjective perspectivity and unity, intentionality and qualitative character. So long as these properties can be functionally described, the entities that realize them can then be discovered. The hunch is that these entities will be neurons or neural networks. Since neural events are electrochemical events, that is, events picked out in another theory by their chemical and electrical properties, all conscious properties are, as it turns out, identical to some chemical or electrical property. Since electrical and chemical properties are physical properties, conscious events are type identical to physical events.

3. The term "pre-emption" actually refers to two distinct phenomena. First, as discussed here, members from one family of properties may trump members from another family of properties. Pre-emption of one family by another then entails replacement of the former by the latter. Second, one event's occurrence at an earlier time than another's occurrence may make a mess of the latter's claim to cause anything because counterfactual dependency fails. We do not discuss the second sense. For those interested, consult Collins (2000); Lewis (1979, 1986a, 1986b, 2000); Paul (1998, 1999, 2000).

4. Huemer and Kovitz (2003), among others, argue that there are simultaneous causes. They cite examples such as a lead ball causing an indentation in a cushion on which it is placed,

lowering one end of a seesaw causing the other end of the seesaw to elevate, and the high temperature of an iron bar causing it to glow red. Each candidate can be reinterpreted as a case of diachronic causation or as not a case of causation at all.

4. REPRESENTATIONALIST THEORIES OF CONSCIOUS PROPERTIES

1. Some accounts are supplemented with *biofunctionalism* (see Dretske 1995, 2004; Millikan 1984, 1989). According to neural biofunctionalism, neural systems are representational vehicles whose representational content is what gets assigned to those systems by evolution. That in virtue of which a neural system represents – its representational feature – is then the entire evolutionary history of the system. If neurons and/or neural systems are representational vehicles and the brain is a product of evolution, then all of the resources of evolutionary theory can be brought to bear on explaining that about neural systems which makes them representations. Activity in a particular neural system represents or is about a particular kind of event whenever the neural system has evolved to detect that kind of event. Although I am sympathetic to biofunctionalism, the debates it has prompted are largely orthogonal to the concerns of this book.

5. CORTICAL EVOLUTION AND MODULARITY

1. I recently tried to killed a fly. I watched it, identified it, compared it to others (it was a big one), got irritated by its droning, swore at it, watched it some more, tried to ignore it, could not ignore it, decided to kill it, planned an attack, looked around for some newspaper, went to the kitchen, got the fly swatter, tripped over the dog on my return to the living room, swore again, found the fly with my eyes, muttered "You're dead meat!" followed it around with my eyes until it landed on the window, walked to the window, watched it take off at my approach, swore again, followed it around with the swatter in cocked-and-loaded position, thought about what a fool I looked like to the kid walking down the sidewalk, waited for the fly to land again, swatted it, missed it, swore again, tried again and finally injured it enough that it fell to the ground stunned. Then I scooped it up on the fly swatter, opened the door, and took it outside. The next time I will probably do something different – ignore it, be entertained, get enraged rather than irritated, roll up a newspaper instead of using the swatter, or open the screen door, invite the fly to savour the taste of freedom, and wait for it to leave on its own accord. Our fly-catching behaviour is *massively* more flexible than a frog's because our fly-catching behaviour is perceptual, cognitive and affective all at once and we have gobs of complex processing that, having started up, just keeps going. Frog fly-catching behaviour is completely unmediated by any cognitive or affective activity. As Mesulam (1998) notes, between sensory input and motor response output in reptiles and amphibians there are only one or two synaptic levels. For them, there is no associative processing, so the resulting behaviour is stereotypical, reflexive and monotonous. In primates, on the other hand, there are five or six synaptic levels between input and motor response. We are hard-wired to be flexible, predisposed not to be predisposed.

2. In the past ten years, some speculation that specific neuron types are responsible for the emergence of consciousness has occurred. One such contender is the *mirror neuron*. Mirror neurons appear in primates and a few other species fairly recently. Given their unique function – mirror neurons fire only when an organism is engaged in some activity or when it witnesses another organism engaged in that activity – the suggestion has been broached that they are responsible for human mimicry and, since mimicry is responsible for sociability, and sociability for consciousness, thus for consciousness as

well. Since, so the story goes, evidence of syntactically complex language first appears about 40,000 years ago, mirror neurons must have suddenly been triggered some time shortly before. It is hard to make much of such claims. First, other species, such as rhesus monkeys and chimps, also have mirror neurons and are not particularly good mimics. Second, what would have to be shown to implicate mirror neurons in the explanation of the appearance of consciousness is evidence that, compared to other primates, we have a disproportionately large number of mirror neuron synapses (we do), that consciousness is not possible without sociability, that sociability is not possible without mimicry, and that mimicry is not possible without mirror neurons. *Self*-consciousness is another matter: perhaps it does require sociability. If sociability requires mimicry and mimicry requires mirror neurons, then perhaps mirror neurons are required for self-consciousness (for overviews of work on mirror neurons, see Rizzolatti & Craighero 2004 and Rizzolatti & Sinigaglia 2008). A similar argument has been advanced about *spindle neurons* (Von Economo neurons). Like mirror neurons, spindle neurons are a relatively recent evolutionary development, found in insular cortex and anterior cingulate cortex in humans and homologous regions in chimps (numerous), gorillas (scattered) and orangutans (rare), certain whales (humpbacks and killers among them), and dolphins. Since they are found in no species more primitive than orangutans, it is thought that spindle neurons can be no older than 15 million years. Spindle neurons have been implicated in the emergence of consciousness through their attributed roles in empathy and other higher-order emotional responses and in communicating certain information about the ongoing physical state of the organism. Some have also speculated that, at least in humans, there may have been an evolutionary development in spindle neurons as recently as 100,000 years ago, which happily coincided with the great leap forwards in human cognitive development. However, until more evidence is in concerning the nature of that development, and the necessity of spindle neurons for empathy, it is too early to identify the role they played in the emergence of consciousness.

3. The advent of prefrontal control of speech in humans did not entail the end of emotional vocalization in humans. Plenty of our own vocalization remains limbic. Think of Glenn Gould and Thelonious Monk, whose piano playing was accompanied by ongoing humming. For that matter, think of crying, laughing, moaning, clicking, clucking, roaring, whistling, humming, screaming, wailing, yelling, screeching, growling, cooing, grunting and beeping. And think of semantically encoded limbic vocalizing, such as swearing, baby talk, shouting and singing. Even here, however, when the two forms commingle in an utterance, the semantically encoded and the emotional are correlated with distinct limbic and prefrontal pathways.

4. As impressive as bonobo symbol skills are they are still pretty poor, and except in captivity no bonobo has ever been known to learn symbol meaning or use symbols of any kind. Even those in captivity cannot put more than a couple of symbols together and cannot speak using those symbols. Savage-Rumbaugh reports ongoing vocal commentary when bonobos engage in their lexical activities, but these vocalizations are parsimoniously explained as indexical supplements or adjuncts to shared activity rather than as a vehicle for shared meaning (Savage-Rumbaugh *et al.* 2004). Still, unlike Hoover, the Boston Aquarium seal that used to utter "hey, how are ya?" and "get outta there", enculturated bonobos are more than mimics and appear to *mean* something by what they do with their lexically keyed computers.

5. If the above is correct, then symbol comprehension, symbol production and vocalization may be distinct processes, which raises the possibility that *H. neanderthalensis* or even *H. heidelbergensis* had the neural wherewithal – expanded working memory and other appropriately structured neuroanatomical areas – to segregate symbolic from other psychological activity, even if they could not or did not speak and even if they did not have full-blown semantic competence. No evidence yet discovered entails either this

supposition or its contrary, even if Neanderthal use of pigments and improved tool technologies suggest enhanced working memory.

6. A symptom of non-modularity is that some neural pathways and psychological processes are much more plastic than others. Early damage to modular subcortical regions typically results in devastating and irreversible dysfunction. However, damage done to many of these same modular subcortical regions later in life is usually much less devastating and sometimes completely correctable. In comparison, early damage to most non-modular associative regions is typically neither devastating nor irreversible, while later damage can be both devastating and irreversible. Virtually all associative cortical pathways are capable of at least a modicum of rewiring, and some are capable of complete rewiring. And the less than devastating functional loss associated with subcortical damage later in life suggests that the psychological processes these subcortical regions correlate with have had layers of neocortical redundancy added to them over the course of experience, available for backup, if and when needed. This pattern supports the idea that associative neocortex, and, to a lesser extent, allocortex and mesocortex, are plastic and not modular while subcortical pathways are modular and not plastic. We return to this difference in the discussion of multiple realization of conscious properties in Chapter 9.

6. AROUSAL, PERCEPTION AND AFFECT

1. There is general agreement that if any emotions are basic, fear and disgust are among them. But claiming that fear and disgust are basic emotions carries with it the suggestion that they are natural kinds, and at least some of the evidence cited in support of natural kind status is not ironclad. While there appears to be cross-cultural recognition of correlated facial expression and certain types of emotions, these correlational studies have been called into question (Barrett 2006). Moreover, the distinction between basic emotions and non-basic emotions is muddy – dogs and primates are capable of embarrassment and chagrin, and play may not be basic. Having entered these cautions, the disputes that prompt them will remain unresolved. Even if not natural kinds, fear and disgust are shared across humans and other primates, and there happens to be more neuroscientific work on them than, for example, on boredom, so their neural correlates are as firmly established as for any emotion. And, since our interest in this neuroscientific research is to reveal the neural substrates of qualitative properties, fear and disgust can serve as well as other emotions might.

7. ATTENTION, WORKING MEMORY, LANGUAGE AND EXECUTIVE FUNCTION

1. Despite widespread acceptance of this typology, it is a little awkward, for the endogenous/exogenous distinction does not map to the others. After all, endogenous interoceptive events such as thirst can impress themselves upon one's attention in a stimulus-driven, bottom-up manner just as readily as an exogenous event.

2. Think of Dr Seuss's Little Cats in *The Cat and the Hat Comes Back*, and you will have a pretty good idea of the problem. The Cat in the Hat has a smaller cat, Little Cat A, in his hat; Little Cat A has in his hat a still smaller cat, Little Cat B, who has in his hat a still smaller cat, Little Cat C ... and so on and so forth for every letter in the alphabet. Of course, Dr Seuss stops the iteration with Little Cat Z, the smallest of the little cats, who, although too small to see, nevertheless is the most powerful of all the little cats. We can see why – since he's the smallest, his causal powers underwrite those of all the other Little Cats.

3. The study of metacognition has its academic roots in developmental, social and

educational psychology. In these disciplines, metacognition is the set of cognitive processes constitutive of monitoring and controlling learning and memory strategies. But in the past decade the category of metacognition has changed disciplinary clothes, becoming interwoven with executive function.

8. NEURAL MODELS OF CONSCIOUS PROPERTIES

1. Morsella (2005) adds corroborating support for the global workspace by adding an explanation of the kinds of information that can and cannot be brought to the theatre of consciousness. Transmodal and supramodal processes implicated in the body's skeletomotor control are the only processes that rise to consciousness. Reflexes, vegetative functions, unconscious motor processing and lower levels of unimodal and (some) multimodal sensory processing are consciously impenetrable processes, while pain, micturition, air hunger, thirst, emotion, cognition and some perceptual processing are consciously penetrable.
2. This sense of "higher-order" is weaker than the philosophical sense discussed in Chapter 4, for it includes as higher-order processes those that are not higher-order in the philosophical sense of the term. While monitoring, reflexivity and self-consciousness are higher-order in the philosophical sense, not all symbolically encoded thought or affective regulation are.
3. Vehicle externalism is one way of defending direct realism about visual (and in general, all) conscious perceptual experience. For if all conscious perceptual experience is a dynamic system one of whose constituent elements is the perceived extracranial object, then perceptual experience is not a matter of intracranially reconstructing extracranial objects and events. So, perceptual experience of the world is not accomplished by representing it, contrary to representationalists. Indeed, Chemero (2009) takes this implication to be one of its chief virtues, for it receives empirical support from ecological theories of visual perception, such as those offered by Roger Gibson and his colleagues (see Gibson 1979; Shaw *et al.* 1982; Turvey *et al.* 1981).

9. MEASUREMENT, LOCALIZATION, MODELS AND DISSOCIATION

1. Brodmann areas are often used in neuroscience as a handy reference. They are named after Korbinian Brodmann, who used them to create an early and influential cortical map. We have instead used the equally popular method of naming cortical areas that correspond to Brodmann areas.
2. The "man in a gorilla suit" video does not establish the insufficiency of endogenous attention for conscious perception. In the video, there is a circle of basketball players passing the basketball to one another. The viewer is instructed to watch the ball, which of course initiates endogenous attention networks. When the video is over, the viewers are asked if anything unusual was observed. Most say "no" – they watched the ball pass from one person to another. They are then told that they missed something, something not easy to miss – a man in a gorilla suit who strolls right through the scene. Sure enough, upon rewatching, there is the man in the gorilla suit. Such cases demonstrate that despite the exogenous salience of a man in a gorilla suit walking right through one's visual field, endogenous attention on the ball can trump exogenous attention to the man in the gorilla suit. But it does not show that it is possible to be endogenously attentive to the basketball being passed around and not consciously perceive the basketball being passed around.
3. Although blindsighted individuals may correctly guess that a fork is in their blindfield, they never reach for it even if hungry. This has been taken to imply that the representation

of the fork is not available for subsequent reasoning and emotional response after all. Block uses this to argue that what is needed is a *super*-blindsighted individual, someone for whom contentful information from the blind contralateral field appears without prior qualitative consciousness of that information (Block 2005, [1995] 2007; see also Dennett 1991). Block is too grudging of the evidence. Cowey (2004) establishes access to something experienced without any qualitative features and qualitatively endowed experience of after-images caused by experience with no qualitative features. If blindsighters are aware of a fork they do not see and experience after-images of a fork they do not see, then some causally prior representation of the fork is available for subsequent reasoning.

10. CORRELATES, REALIZERS AND MULTIPLE REALIZATION

1. Recall (NR): Physical events or parts thereof exhaust everything that is concrete, and there is a supervenience relation between all families of conscious properties and microphysical properties of neural assembly activity such that subvening microphysical properties of neural assembly activity are the only realizers of supervening conscious properties.

11. MICROPHYSICAL REDUCTION, OVERDETERMINATION AND COUPLING

1. The relevant concept of isomorphism is, recall, a one-to-one mapping, such as supervenience, not a one-to-one onto homomorphic mapping (see Chapter 2, note 1, for the distinction).
2. This conclusion is parallel to and provides additional warrant for Kim's claim, introduced in Chapter 3, that if representational states and processes are constrained by the rationality requirement and the causal relations between neural states are nomologically constrained, then conscious belief attribution appears to be alone sufficient to infer a physical prediction about the neural properties of brain activity.

12. EMBODIED AND EMBEDDED CONSCIOUSNESS

1. The issues in play here are, admittedly, complicated. I assume but do not argue for the claim that explaining illusions does not require veridical perception. That assumption is, admittedly, contentious. It is premised on the claim that the phenomenal aspects of conscious experience are not subject to veridicality conditions (cf. Burge [2006] 2007: 406–8 for defence of this claim).

BIBLIOGRAPHY

Adams, F. & K. Aizawa 2008. *The Bounds of Cognition*. Oxford: Blackwell.

Adams, F. & K. Aizawa 2009. "Why the Mind Is Still in the Head". See Robbins & Aydede (2009), 78–95.

Allman, J., A. Hakeem & K. Watson 2002. "Two Phylogenetic Specializations in the Human Brain". *The Neuroscientist* **8**(4): 335–46.

Andersen, P. B., C. Emmeche, N. O. Finnemann & P. V. Christiansen (eds) 2000. *Downwards Causation*. Aarhus: Aarhus University Press.

Andersen, R. & C. Buneo 2002. "Intentional Maps in Posterior Parietal Cortex". *Annual Review of Neuroscience* **25**: 189–220.

Andersen, R., L. Snyder, D. Bradley & J. Xing 1997. "Multimodal Representation of Space in the Posterior Parietal Cortex and Its Use in Planning Movements". *Annual Review of Neuroscience* **20**: 303–30.

Anderson, J. 2007. *How Can the Human Mind Occur in the Physical Universe?* New York: Oxford University Press.

Arbib, M. 2001. "Co-evolution of Human Consciousness and Language". *Annals of the New York Academy of Sciences* **929** (April): 195–220.

Armstrong, D. 1981. *The Nature of Mind*. Brisbane: University of Queensland Press.

Armstrong, D. [1968] 1993. *A Materialist Theory of the Mind*, 2nd edn. New York: Routledge.

Atkinson, A., M. Thomas & A. Cleeremans 2000. "Consciousness: Mapping the Theoretical Landscape". *Trends in Cognitive Science* **4**(10): 372–82.

Atkinson, R. C. & R. M. Shiffrin 1971. "The Control of Short-term Memory". *Scientific American* **224** (August): 82–90.

Awh, E. & J. Jonides 2000. "Spatial Working Memory and Spatial Selective Attention". In *The Attentive Brain*, R. Parasuraman (ed.), 353–81. Cambridge, MA: MIT Press.

Awh, E. & J. Jonides 2001. "Overlapping Mechanisms of Attention and Spatial Working Memory". *Trends in Cognitive Science* **5**(3): 119–26.

Baars, B. 1988. *A Cognitive Theory of Consciousness*. Cambridge: Cambridge University Press.

Baars, B. 2005a. "Subjective Experience Is Probably Not Limited to Humans: The Evidence from Neurobiology and Behavior". *Consciousness and Cognition* **14**(1): 7–21.

Baars, B. 2005b. "Global Workspace of Consciousness: Towards a Cognitive Neuroscience of Human Experience". See Laureys (2005), 45–53.

Bacon, J. 1986. "Supervenience and Reducibility". *Philosophical Studies* **49**: 163–76.

Baddeley, A. 1986. *Working Memory*. New York: Oxford University Press.

Baddeley, A. 1996. "The Fractionation of Working Memory". *Proceedings of the National Academy of Sciences* **93**: 13,468–72.

Baddeley, A. 2000. "The Episodic Buffer: A New Component of Working Memory?" *Trends in Cognitive Science* **4**(11): 417–23.

Baddeley, A. 2002. "Is Working Memory Still Working?" *European Psychologist* **7**(2): 85–97.

Baddeley, A. 2003. "Working Memory: Looking Back and Looking Forward". *Nature Reviews Neuroscience* **4**: 829–39.

Badre, D. & A. Wagner 2007. "Left Ventrolateral Prefrontal Cortex and the Cognitive Control of Memory". *Neuropsychologia* **45**: 2883–901.

Ball, P. 1999. *The Self-Made Tapestry: Pattern Formation in Nature*. New York: Oxford University Press.

Banchetti-Robino, M. 2004. "Ibn Sīnā and Husserl on Intention and Intentionality". *Philosophy East and West* **54**(1): 71–82.

Barbas, H. 2005. "Organization of the Principal Pathways of Prefrontal Lateral, Medial, and Orbitofrontal Cortices in Primates and Implication for Their Collaborative Interaction in Executive Functions". In *The Frontal Lobes: Development, Function and Pathology*, J. Risberg & J. Grafman (eds), 21–68. Cambridge: Cambridge University Press.

Barkley, R. 2003. "Attention Deficit/Hyperactivity Disorder". In *Child Psychopathology*, 2nd edn, E. Mash & R. Barkley (eds), 75–143. New York: Guilford.

Barrett, L. 2006. "Are Emotions Natural Kinds?" *Perspectives on Psychological Science* **1**(1): 28–58.

Barrett, L., K. Lindquist, E. Bliss-Moreau *et al.* 2007. "Of Mice and Men: Natural Kinds of Emotions in the Mammalian Brain? A Response to Panksepp and Izard". *Perspectives on Psychological Science* **2**(3): 297–312.

Barrett, L., B. Mesquita, K. Ochsner & J. Gross 2007. "The Experience of Emotion". *Annual Review of Psychology* **58**: 373–403.

Bauer, R. 1984. "Autonomic Recognition of Names and Faces in Prosopagnosia: A Neuropsychological Application of the Guilty Knowledge Test". *Neuropsychologia* **22**: 457–69.

Bayne, T. 2004. "Self-consciousness and the Unity of Consciousness". *The Monist* **87**(2): 224–41.

Bayne, T. 2008. "The Unity of Consciousness and the Split-Brain Syndrome". *Journal of Philosophy* **105**(6): 277–300.

Bayne, T. & D. Chalmers 2003. "What is the Unity of Consciousness?" See Cleeremans (2003), 23–58.

Bechtel, W. 1998. "Representations and Cognitive Explanation: Assessing the Dynamicist's Challenge in Cognitive Science". *Cognitive Science* **22**: 295–318.

Bechtel, W. 2009. "Mechanism, Modularity, and Situated Cognition". See Robbins & Aydede (2009), 155–70.

Bechtel, W. & A. Abrahamsen 1991. *Connectionism and the Mind: An Introduction to Parallel Processing in Networks*. Oxford: Blackwell.

Bechtel, W. & A. Abrahamsen 2005. "Explanation: A Mechanist Alternative". *Studies in History and Philosophy of Biological and Biomedical Sciences* **36**: 421–41.

Bechtel, W. & A. Hamilton 2007. "Reduction, Integration, and the Unity of Science: Natural, Behavioral, and Social Sciences and the Humanities". In *Philosophy of Science: Focal Issues*, vol. I of the *Handbook of the Philosophy of Science*, T. Kuipers (ed.), 1–47. Amsterdam: Elsevier.

Bechtel, W. & R. Richardson 1993. *Discovering Complexity: Decomposition and Localization as Strategies in Scientific Research*. Princeton, NJ: Princeton University Press.

Beer, R. 2000. "Dynamical Approaches to Cognitive Science". *Trends in Cognitive Science* **4**: 91–9.

Beilock, S., B. Bertenthal, A. McCoy & T. Carr 2004. "Haste Does Not Always Make Waste: Expertise, Direction of Attention, and Speed versus Accuracy in Performing Sensorimotory Skills". *Psychonomic Bulletin & Review* **11**(2): 373–9.

Beilock, S., T. Carr, C. MacMahon & J. Starkes 2002. "When Paying Attention Becomes Counterproductive: Impact of Divided versus Skill-focused Attention on Novice and Experienced Performance of Sensorimotor Skills". *Journal of Experimental Psychology: Applied* **8**(1): 6–16.

Benson, D. 1993. "Prefrontal Abilities". *Behavioural Neurology* **6**(2): 75–81.

Berridge, K. 2003. "Pleasures of the Brain". *Brain and Cognition* **52**: 106–28.

Bickle, J. 1998. *Psychoneural Reduction: The New Wave*. Cambridge: Cambridge University Press.

Bisiach, E. 1993. "Mental Representation in Unilateral Neglect and Related Disorders". *The Quarterly Journal of Experimental Psychology* **46A**: 435–61.

Blanke, O. & T. Metzinger 2009. "Full-body Illusions and Minimal Phenomenal Selfhood". *Trends in Cognitive Sciences* **13**(1): 7–13.

Blanke, O. & C. Mohr 2005. "Out-of-body Experience, Heautoscopy, and Autoscopic Hallucination of Neurological Origin: Implications for Neurocognitive Mechanisms of Corporeal Awareness and Self-consciousness". *Brain Research News* **50**: 184–99.

Block, N. [1978] 2007. "Troubles with Functionalism". See Block (2007b), 63–102.

Block, N. [1995] 2007. "On a Confusion about a Function of Consciousness". See Block (2007b), 159–213.

Block, N. 2001. "Paradox and Cross Purposes in Recent Work on Consciousness". *Cognition* **79**(1–2): 197–220.

Block, N. [2002] 2007. "The Harder Problem of Consciousness". See Block (2007b), 397–433.

Block, N. 2003. "Do Causal Powers Drain Away?" *Philosophy and Phenomenological Research* **67**: 110–27.

Block, N. [2003] 2007. "Mental Paint". See Block (2007b), 533–70.

Block, N. 2005. "Two Neural Correlates of Consciousness". *Trends in Cognitive Science* **9**(2): 46–51.

Block, N. 2007a. "Consciousness, Accessibility, and the Mesh between Psychology and Neuroscience". *Behavioral and Brain Sciences* **30**: 481–548.

Block, N. 2007b. *Consciousness, Function, and Representation: Collected Papers*, vol. I. Cambridge, MA: MIT Press.

Block, N. & J. Fodor 1972. "What Psychological Properties Are Not". *The Philosophical Review* **89**(2): 159–81.

Boden, M. 1988. *Computer Models of Mind*. Cambridge: Cambridge University Press.

Boë, L., J. Heim, K. Honda & S. Maeda 2002. "The Potential Neandertal Vowel Space Was as Large as That of Modern Humans". *Journal of Phonetics* **30**: 465–84.

Bontly, T. 2002. "The Supervenience Argument Generalizes". *Philosophical Studies* **109**: 75–96.

Boogerd, F., R. Bruggerman, A. Richardson, A. Stephan & H. Westerhoff 2005. "Emergence and Its Place in Nature: A Case Study of Biochemical Networks". *Synthese* **145**: 131–64.

Bookheimer, S. 2002. "Functional MRI of Language: New Approaches to Understanding the Cortical Organization of Semantic Processing". *Annual Review of Neuroscience* **25**: 151–88.

Brentano, F. [1874] 1995. *Psychology from an Empirical Standpoint*, L. L. McAlister (ed.). London: Routledge.

Brook, A. 1996. *Kant and the Mind*, 2nd edn. Cambridge: Cambridge University Press.

Brook, A. 2005. "Kant, Cognitive Science, and Contemporary Neo-Kantianism". *Journal of Consciousness Studies* **11**(10–11): 1–25.

Brook, A. 2006. "Kant: A Unified Theory of the Representational Base of All Consciousness". In *Consciousness and Self-Reference*, U. Kriegel & K. Williford (eds), 89–110. Cambridge, MA: MIT Press.

Brook, A. & P. Raymont 2006. "Unity of Consciousness", http://plato.stanford.edu/entries/consciousness-unity/ (accessed November 2010).

Bruner, E. 2004. "Geometric Morphometrics and Paleoneurology: Brain Shape Evolution in the Genus *Homo*". *Journal of Human Evolution* **47**: 279–303.

Bruner, E., G. Manzi & J. Arsuaga 2003. "Encephalization and Allometric Trajectories in the Genus *Homo*: Evidence from the Neanderthal and Modern Lineages". *Proceedings of the National Academy of Sciences* **100**(26): 15,335–40.

Buckner, R., J. Andrews-Hanna & D. Schachter 2008. "The Brain's Default Network: Anatomy, Function, and Relevance to Disease". *Annals of the New York Academy of Sciences* **1124**: 1–38.

Bukach, C., I. Gauthier & M. Tarr 2006. "Beyond Faces and Modularity: The Power of an Expertise Network". *Trends in Cognitive Sciences* **10**(4): 159–66.

Buller, D. 2005a. *Adapting Minds: Evolutionary Psychology and the Persistent Quest for Human Nature*. Cambridge, MA: MIT Press.

Buller, D. 2005b. "Evolutionary Psychology: The Emperor's New Paradigm". *Trends in Cognitive Science* **9**(6): 277–83.

Bunge, S., K. Ochsner, J. Desmond, G. Glover & J. Gabrieli 2001. "Prefrontal Regions Involved in Keeping Information In and Out of Mind". *Brain* **124**: 2074–86.

Burge, T. [1982] 2007. "Other Bodies". See Burge (2007), 82–99.

Burge, T. [1986a] 2007. "Individualism and Psychology". See Burge (2007), 221–53.

Burge, T. [1986b] 2007. "Cartesian Error and the Objectivity of Perception". See Burge (2007), 192–207.

Burge, T. [1989] 2007. "Individuation and Causation in Psychology". See Burge (2007), 316–33.

Burge, T. [1993] 2007. "Mind–body Causation and Explanatory Practice". See Burge (2007), 344–62.

Burge, T. [1995] 2007. "Intentional Properties and Causation". See Burge (2007), 334–43.

Burge, T. [2006] 2007. "Reflections on Two Kinds of Consciousness". See Burge (2007), 392–419.

Burge, T. 2007. *Foundations of Mind: Philosophical Essays*, vol. 2. Oxford: Oxford University Press.

Bush, E. & J. Allman 2004. "The Scaling of Frontal Cortex in Humans and Carnivores". *Proceedings of the National Academy of Sciences* **101**(11): 3962–6.

Buss, D. & M. Haselton 2005. "The Evolution of Jealousy". *Trends in Cognitive Sciences* **9**(11): 506–7.

Buss, D., M. Haselton, T. Shackelford, A. Bleske & J. Wakefield 1998. "Adaptations, Exaptations, and Spandrels". *American Psychologist* **53**(5): 533–48.

Byrne, A. 1997. "Some Like It HOT: Consciousness and Higher-order Thoughts". *Philosophical Studies* **86**: 103–29.

Byrne, A. & M. Tye 2006. "Qualia Ain't in the Head". *Noûs* **40**(2): 241–55.

Byrne, R. & L. Bates 2007. "Sociality, Evolution, and Cognition". *Current Biology* **17**: R714–23.

Calder, A., A. Lawrence & A. Young 2001. "Neuropsychology of Fear and Loathing". *Nature Reviews Neuroscience* **2**: 352–63.

Carroll, S. 2003. "Genetics and the Making of *Homo sapiens*". *Nature* **422** (24 April): 840–56.

Carruthers, P. 2005. *Consciousness: Essays from a Higher-Order Perspective*. Oxford: Oxford University Press.

Caston, V. 2002. "Aristotle on Consciousness". *Mind* **111**: 751–815.

Cavana, A. & A. Nani 2008. "Do Consciousness and Attention Have Shared Neural Correlates?" *PSYCHE* 14, no page numbers.

Chalmers, D. 1995. "Facing Up to the Problem of Consciousness". *Journal of Consciousness Studies* **2**(3): 200–219.

Chalmers, D. 1996. *The Conscious Mind: In Search of a Fundamental Theory*. New York: Oxford University Press.

Chalmers, D. 2000. "What Is a Neural Correlate of Consciousness?" See Metzinger (2000), 17–40.

Chemero, A. 2009. *Radical Embodied Cognitive Science*. Cambridge, MA: MIT Press.

Chisholm, R. 1957a. *Perceiving*. Ithaca, NY: Cornell University Press.

Chisholm, R. 1957b. "The Sellars–Chisholm Correspondence on Intentionality". *Minnesota Studies in Philosophy of Science* II, 511–20. Minneapolis, MN: University of Minnesota Press.

Chomsky, N. [1959] 1967. "A Review of B. F. Skinner's *Verbal Behavior*". In *Readings in the Psychology of Language*, L. Jakobovits & M. Miron (eds), 142–71. New York: Prentice-Hall.

Chomsky, N. 2005a. "Universals of Human Nature". *Psychotherapy and Psychosomatics* **74**: 263–8.

Chomsky, N. 2005b. "Three Factors in Language Design". *Linguistic Inquiry* **36**(1): 1–22.

Churchland, P. 1979. *Scientific Realism and the Plasticity of Mind*. Cambridge: Cambridge University Press.

Churchland, P. 1988a. *Matter and Consciousness*, revised edn. Cambridge, MA: MIT Press.

Churchland, P. 1988b. *Neurophilosophy: Towards a Unified Science of the Mind-Brain*. Cambridge, MA: MIT Press.

Churchland, P. & T. Sejnowski 1989. "Neural Representation and Neural Computation". In *Neural Connections, Mental Computation*, N. Nadel, A. Cooper, P. Culicover & R. Harnish (eds), 69–103. Cambridge, MA: Bradford/MIT Press.

Clark, A. 1997. *Being There: Putting Brain, Body, and World Together Again*. Cambridge, MA: MIT Press.

Clark, A. 2008. *Supersizing the Mind: Embodiment, Action, and Cognitive Extension*. New York: Oxford University Press.

Clark, A. & D. Chalmers 1998. "The Extended Mind". *Analysis* **58**: 10–23.

Cleeremans, A. (ed.) 2003. *The Unity of Consciousness: Binding, Integration, and Dissociation* New York: Oxford University Press.

Cleeremans, A. 2005. "Computational Correlates of Consciousness". See Laureys (2005), 81–98.

Coady, D. 2004. "Preempting Preemption". In *Causation and Counterfactuals*, J. Collins, N. Hall & L. Paul (eds), 325–40. Cambridge, MA: MIT Press.

Cohen, J. 2005. "The Vulcanization of the Human Brain: A Neural Perspective on Interactions between Cognition and Emotion". *Journal of Economic Perspectives* **19**(4): 3–24.

Colby, C. & M. Goldberg 1999. "Space and Attention in Parietal Cortex". *Annual Review of Neuroscience* **22**: 319–49.

Cole, D. 2004. "The Chinese Room Argument", http://plato.stanford.edu/entries/chinese-room/ (accessed November 2010).

Collette, F., M. Van der Linden, S. Laureys *et al.* 2005. "Exploring the Unity and Diversity of the Neural Substrates of Executive Functioning". *Human Brain Mapping* **25**: 409–23.

Collins, J. 2000. "Preemptive Prevention". *Journal of Philosophy* **97**: 223–34.

Collins, J., N. Hall & L. Paul (eds) 2004. *Causation and Counterfactuals*. Cambridge, MA: MIT Press.

Coolidge, F. L. & T. Wynn 2001. "Executive Functions of the Frontal Lobes and the Evolutionary Ascendancy of *Homo sapiens*". *Cambridge Archaeological Journal* **11**: 255–60.

Coolidge, F. L. & T. Wynn 2005. "Working Memory, Its Executive Functions, and the Emergence of Modern Thinking". *Cambridge Archaeological Record* **15**(1): 5–22.

Corballis, M. 2004. "*FOXP2* and the Mirror System". *Trends in Cognitive Science* **8**(3): 95–6.

Corbetta, M., J. Kincade & G. Shulman 2002. "Neural Systems for Visual Orienting and Their Relationships to Spatial Working Memory". *Journal of Cognitive Neuroscience* **14**(3): 508–23.

Cosmides, L., J. Tooby, L. Fiddick & G. Bryant 2005. "Detecting Cheaters". *Trends in Cognitive Sciences* **9**(11): 505–6.

Courtney, S. 2004. "Attention and Cognitive Control as Emergent Properties of Representation in Working Memory". *Cognitive, Affective, and Behavioral Neuroscience* **4**(4): 501–16.

Cowey, A. 2004. "Fact, Artifact, and Myth about Blindsight". *The Quarterly Journal of Experimental Psychology* **57A**(4): 577–609.

Craig, A. 2002. "How Do You Feel? Interoception: The Sense of the Physiological Condition of the Body". *Nature Reviews Neuroscience* **3**: 655–66.

Craig, A. 2003. "Pain Mechanisms: Labeled Lines versus Convergence in Central Processing". *Annual Review of Neuroscience* **26**: 1–30.

Craig, A. 2004. "Human Feelings: Why Are Some More Aware Than Others?" *Trends in Cognitive Science* **8**(6): 239–41.

Crane, T. 2005. "The Problem of Perception", http://plato.stanford.edu/entries/perception-problem/ (accessed November 2010).

Craver, C. F. & W. Bechtel 2006. "Mechanism". In *Philosophy of Science: An Encyclopedia*, S. Sarkar & J. Pfeifer (eds), 469–78. New York: Routledge.

Crick, F. 1996. "Visual Perception: Rivalry and Consciousness". *Nature* **379**: 485–6.

Crick, F. & C. Koch 1990. "Towards a Neurobiological Theory of Consciousness". *Seminars in the Neurosciences* **2**: 263–75.

351

Crick, F. & C. Koch 2003. "A Framework for Consciousness". *Nature Neuroscience* **6**(2): 119–26.

Critchley, H., S. Wiens, P. Rothstein, A. Öhman & R. Dolan 2004. "Neural Systems Supporting Interoceptive Awareness". *Nature Neuroscience* **7**(2): 189–95.

Cummins, R. 1994. "Interpretational Semantics". See Stich & Warfield (1994), 278–301.

Curtis, C. & M. D'Esposito 2003. "Persistent Activity in the Prefrontal Cortex during Working Memory". *Trends in Cognitive Sciences* **7**(9): 415–23.

Curtis, V., R. Aunger & T. Rabie 2004. "Evidence That Disgust Evolved to Protect from Risk of Disease". *Proceedings of the Royal Society B* **271**: S131–3.

Dade, L., R. Zatorre, A. Evans & M. Jones-Gotman 2001. "Working Memory in Another Dimension: Functional Imaging of Human Olfactory Working Memory". *NeuroImage* **14**: 650–60.

Dainton, B. 2000. *Stream of Consciousness: Unity and Continuity in Conscious Experience*. New York: Routledge.

Damasio, A. 2000. *The Feeling of What Happens: Body and Emotion in the Making of Consciousness*. New York: Harcourt.

Damasio, A. 2003. "Feelings of Emotion and the Self". *Annals of the New York Academy of Sciences* **1001**: 253–61.

Dapretto, M. & S. Bookheimer 1999. "Form and Content: Dissociating Syntax and Semantics in Sentence Comprehension". *Neuron* **24**: 427–32.

Davidson, D. 1980a. "Psychology as Philosophy". In his *Essays on Actions and Events*, 229–38. New York: Oxford University Press.

Davidson, D. 1980b. "Mental Events". In his *Essays on Actions and Events*, 207–24. New York: Oxford University Press.

Davidson, D. 1993. "Thinking Causes". See Heil & Mele (1993), 3–17.

Davidson, T., J. Sedgh, D. Tran & C. Stepnowsky 2005. "The Anatomic Basis for the Acquisition of Speech and Obstructive Sleep Apnea: Evidence from Cephalometric Analysis Supports the Great Leap Forwards Hypothesis". *Sleep Medicine* **6**: 497–505.

Deacon, T. 1990. "Rethinking Mammalian Brain Evolution". *Integrative and Comparative Biology* **30**(3): 629–705.

Deacon, T. 2000. "Evolutionary Perspectives on Language and Brain Plasticity". *Journal of Communication Disorders* **33**(4): 273–91.

Dehaene, S. 2004. "Evolution of Human Cortical Circuits for Reading and Arithmetic: The 'Neuronal Recycling' Hypothesis". In *From Monkey Brain to Human Brain*, S. Dehaene, J. R. Duhamel, M. Hauser & G. Rizzolatti (eds), 1–33. Cambridge, MA: MIT Press.

Dehaene, S. & J.-P. Changeux 2004. "Neural Mechanisms for Access to Consciousness". In *The Cognitive Neurosciences*, 3rd edn, M. Gazzaniga (ed.), 1145–57. New York: Norton.

Dehaene, S. & J.-P. Changeux 2005. "Ongoing Spontaneous Activity Controls Access to Consciousness: A Neuronal Model for Inattentional Blindness". *PLOS Biology* **3**(5): 911–27.

Dehaene, S. & L. Naccache 2001. "Towards a Cognitive Neuroscience of Consciousness: Basic Evidence and a Workspace Framework". *Cognition* **79**: 1–37.

Dehaene, S., J.-P. Changeux, L. Naccache, J. Sackur & C. Sergent 2006. "Conscious, Preconscious, and Subliminal Processing: A Testable Taxonomy". *Trends in Cognitive Science* **10**(5): 204–11.

Dehaene, S., C. Sergent & J.-P. Changeux 2003. "A Neuronal Network Model Linking Subjective Reports and Objective Physiological Data during Conscious Perception". *Proceedings of the National Academy of Sciences* **100**: 8520–5.

Démonet, J.-F., G. Thierry & D. Cardebat 2005. "Renewal of the Neurophysiology of Language: Functional Neuroimaging". *Physiology Review* **85**: 49–95.

Dennett, D. 1988. "Quining Qualia". In *Consciousness in Contemporary Science*, A. Marcel & E. Bisiach (eds), 519–48. New York: Oxford University Press.

Dennett, D. 1991. *Consciousness Explained*. Boston, MA: Little, Brown.

Dennett, D. 2006. *Sweet Dreams: Philosophical Obstacles to a Science of Consciousness*. Cambridge, MA: MIT Press.

Dennett, D. & M. Kinsbourne 1995. "Time and the Observer: The Where and When of Consciousness in the Brain". *Behavioral and Brain Sciences* **15**(2): 183–247.

Denton, D. 2005. *The Primordial Emotions: The Dawning of Consciousness*. New York: Oxford University Press.

Denton, D., R. Shade, F. Zamarripa, G. Egan, J. Blair-West, M. McKinley, J. Lancaster & P. Fox 1999. "Neuroimaging of Genesis and Satiation of Thirst and an Interoceptor-driven Theory of Origins of Primary Consciousness". *Proceedings of the National Academy of Sciences* **96**: 5304–9.

Descartes, R. [1641] 1984–91. *Meditations on First Philosophy*. In *The Philosophical Writings of Descartes*, 3 vols, J. Cottingham, R. Stoothoff, D. Murdoch & A. Kenny (trans). Cambridge: Cambridge University Press.

Desimone, R. & J. Duncan 1995. "Neural Mechanisms of Visual Attention". *Annual Review of Neuroscience* **18**: 193–222.

D'Esposito, M. 2008. "Working Memory". In *Handbook of Clinical Neurology: Neuropsychology and Behavioral Neurology*, G. Goldenberg & B. Miller (eds), 237–47. Amsterdam: Elsevier.

Dretske, F. 1988. *Explaining Behavior: Reasons in a World of Causes*. Cambridge, MA: MIT Press.

Dretske, F. 1995. *Naturalizing the Mind*. Cambridge, MA: MIT Press.

Dretske, F. 1997. "What Good Is Consciousness?" *Canadian Journal of Philosophy* **27**(1): 1–15.

Dretske, F. 2004. "Psychological vs. Biological Explanation of Behavior". *Behavior and Philosophy* **32**: 167–77.

Dretske, F. 2006. "Perception without Awareness". In *Perceptual Experience*, T. Gendler & J. Hawthorne (eds), 147–80. New York: Oxford University Press.

Dronkers, N., D. Wilkins, R. Van Valin, B. Redfern & J. Jaeger 2004. "Lesion Analysis of the Brain Areas Involved in Language Comprehension". *Cognition* **92**(1–2): 145–77.

Duncan, J. 1998. "Converging Levels of Analysis in the Cognitive Neuroscience of Visual Attention". *Philosophical Transactions of the Royal Society B* **353**: 1307–17.

Duncan, J. & A. Owen 2000. "Common Regions of the Human Frontal Lobe Recruited by Diverse Cognitive Demands". *Trends in Neurosciences* **23**: 475–83.

Eccles, J. 1994. *How the Self Controls Its Brain*. New York: Springer.

Edelman, G. 1987. *Neural Darwinism: The Theory of Neuronal Group Selection*. New York: Basic Books.

Edelman, G. 1989. *The Remembered Present*. New York: Basic Books.

Edelman, G. 2003. "Naturalizing Consciousness: A Theoretical Framework". *Proceedings of the National Academy of Sciences* **100**: 5520–4.

Edelman, G. & G. Tononi 2000. *A Universe of Consciousness: How Matter Becomes Imagination*. New York: Basic Books.

Egan, G., T. Silk, F. Zamarripa *et al.* 2003. "Neural Correlates of the Emergence of Consciousness of Thirst". *Proceedings of the National Academy of Sciences* **100**(25): 15,241–6.

Eliasmith, C. 2003. "Moving beyond Metaphors: Understanding the Mind for What It Is". *Journal of Philosophy* **100**(10): 493–520.

Eliasmith, C. 2009. "Dynamics, Control, and Cognition". See Robbins & Aydede (2009), 134–54.

Elston, G. 2003. "Cortex, Cognition and the Cell: New Insights into the Pyramidal Neuron and Prefrontal Function". *Cerebral Cortex* **13**: 1124–38.

Emmeche, C., S. Køppe & F. Stjernfelt 2000. "Levels of Emergence, and Three Versions of Downwards Causation". See Andersen *et al.* (2000), 13–34.

Engel, A. K., P. Fries, P. König, M. Brecht & W. Singer 1999. "Temporal Binding, Binocular Rivalry, and Consciousness". *Consciousness and Cognition* **8**: 128–51.

Ermer, E., L. Cosmides & J. Tooby 2007. "Functional Specialization and the Adaptationist Program". See Gangestad & Simpson (2007), 153–60.

Esfeld, M. 2005. "Mental Causation and Mental Properties". *Dialectica* **59**: 5–18.

Evans, G. 1985. *Collected Papers*. New York: Oxford University Press.

Fan, J., B. D. McCandliss, J. Fossella, J. I. Flombaum & M. I. Posner 2005. "The Activation of Attention Networks". *NeuroImage* **26**: 471–9.

Farah, M. 2004. *Visual Agnosia*, 2nd edn. Cambridge, MA: MIT Press.

Farrell, M., G. Egan, F. Zamarripa *et al.* 2006. "Unique, Common, and Interacting Cortical Correlates of Thirst and Pain". *Proceedings of the National Academy of Sciences* **103**(7): 2416–21.

Federmeier, K. & M. Kutas 1999. "Right Words and Left Words: Electrophysiological Evidence for Hemispheric Differences in Meaning Processing". *Cognitive Brain Research* **8**: 373–92.

Feinberg, T., M. Venneri, A. Simone, Y. Fan & G. Northoff 2009. "The Neuroanatomy of Asomatognosia and Somatoparaphrenia". *Journal of Neurology, Neurosurgery, and Psychiatry*, published online 24 September 2009, doi:10.1136/jnnp.2009.188946.

Fellows, L. & M. Farah 2005. "Is Anterior Cingulated Cortex Necessary for Cognitive Control?" *Brain* **128**: 788–96.

Feredoes, E. & B. Postle 2007. "Localization of Load Sensitivity of Working Memory Storage: Quantitatively and Qualitatively Discrepant Results Yielded by Single-subject and Group-averaged Approaches to fMRI Group Analysis". *NeuroImage* **35**: 1–23.

Fernald, T. 1997. "The Evolution of Eyes". *Brain, Behavior, and Evolution* **50**: 253–9.

Fernandez-Duque, D., J. Baird & M. Posner 2000. "Executive Attention and Metacognitive Regulation". *Consciousness and Cognition* **9**: 288–307.

Ferro, J., L. Caeiro & A. Verdelho 2002. "Delirium in Acute Stroke". *Current Opinion in Neurology* **15**(1): 51–5.

Fetzer, J. (ed.) 2002. *Consciousness Evolving*. Amsterdam: John Benjamins.

Filley, C. M. 2001. *The Behavioral Neurology of White Matter*. New York: Oxford University Press.

Filley, C. M. 2002. "The Neuroanatomy of Attention". *Seminars in Speech and Language* **23**(2): 89–98.

Finlay, B. 2007. "*E pluribus unum:* Too Many Unique Human Capacities and Too Many Theories". See Gangestad & Simpson (2007), 294–303.

Finlay, B., R. Darlington & N. Nicastro 2001. "Developmental Structure in Brain Evolution". *Behavioral and Brain Sciences* **24**: 263–308.

Fitch, T. 2000. "The Evolution of Speech: A Comparative Review". *Trends in Cognitive Science* **4**(7): 258–67.

Fitch, T. & D. Reby 2001. "The Descended Larynx Is Not Uniquely Human". *Proceedings of the Royal Society B* **268**: 1669–73.

Fitch, T., M. Hauser & N. Chomsky 2005. "The Evolution of the Language Faculty: Clarifications and Implications". *Cognition* **97**: 179–210.

Flanagan, O. 1992. *Consciousness Reconsidered*. Cambridge, MA: MIT Press.

Flanagan, O. 1998. *The Nature of Consciousness*. Cambridge, MA: MIT Press.

Flor, H., T. Elbert, S. Knecht *et al.* 1995. "Phantom-limb Pain as a Perceptual Correlate of Cortical Reorganization Following Arm Amputation". *Nature* **375**: 482–4.

Fodor, J. 1975. *The Language of Thought*. Cambridge, MA: Harvard University Press.

Fodor, J. [1974] 1980a. "Special Sciences and the Disunity of Science as a Working Hypothesis". *Synthese* 28: 77–115; reprinted as "Special Sciences, or the Disunity of Science as a Working Hypothesis". In *Readings in Philosophy of Psychology*, vol. 1, N. Block (ed.), 120–33. Cambridge MA: Harvard University Press.

Fodor, J. 1980b. "Methodological Solipsism Considered as a Research Strategy in Cognitive Science". *Behavioral and Brain Sciences* **3**: 63–73.

Fodor, J. 1981. *Representations*. Cambridge, MA: MIT Press.

Fodor, J. 1983. *Modularity of Mind*. Cambridge, MA: MIT Press.

Fodor, J. 1987. *Psychosemantics*. Cambridge, MA: MIT Press.

Fodor, J. 1990. *A Theory of Content and Other Essays*. Cambridge, MA: MIT Press.

Fodor, J. 2008. *LOT 2: The Language of Thought Revisited*. New York: Oxford University Press.

Fodor, J. & Z. Pylyshyn 1988. "Connectionism and Cognitive Architecture: A Critical Analysis". *Cognition* **28**: 3–71.

Foucher, J. R., H. Otzenberger & D. Gounot 2004. "Where Arousal Meets Attention: A Simultaneous fMRI and EEG Recording Study". *NeuroImage* **22**: 688–97.

Freud, S. 1938. *An Outline of Psychoanalysis*. New York: Norton.

Friederici, A. & S. Kotz 2003. "The Brain Basis of Syntactic Processes: Functional Imaging and Lesion Studies". *NeuroImage* **20**: S8–17.

Fuster, J. 1973. "Unit Activity in Prefrontal Cortex during Delayed-response Performance: Neuronal Correlates of Transient Memory". *Journal of Neurophysiology* **63**: 814–31.

Fuster, J. 2000. "Prefrontal Neurons in Networks of Executive Memory". *Brain Research Bulletin* **52**(5): 331–6.

Fuster, J. 2001. "The Prefrontal Cortex – An Update: Time Is of the Essence". *Neuron* **30**: 319–33.

Gallagher, S. 2000. "Self-reference and Schizophrenia: A Cognitive Model of Immunity to Error through Misidentification". See Zahavi (2000b), 203–42.

Gallagher, S. 2005. *How the Body Shapes the Mind*. New York: Oxford University Press.

Gallagher, S. 2009. "Philosophical Antecedents of Situated Cognition". See Robbins & Aydede (2009), 35–51.

Gangestad, S. & J. Simpson (eds) 2007. *The Evolution of Mind: Fundamental Questions and Controversies*. New York: Guilford.

Garson, J. 1994. "Cognition without Classical Architecture". *Synthese* **100**: 291–305.

Garson, J. 2001. "(Dis)solving the Binding Problem." *Philosophical Psychology* **14**(4): 381–92.

Garson, J. 2002. "Evolution, Consciousness, and the Language of Thought". See Fetzer (2002), 89–110.

Gazzaniga, M. & J. Le Doux 1978. *The Integrated Mind*. New York: Plenum.

Gazzaniga, M., R. Ivry & G. Mangun 2002. *Cognitive Neuroscience: The Biology of the Mind*, 2nd edn. New York: Norton.

Gendler, T. & J. Hawthorne 2006. *Perceptual Experience*. New York: Oxford University Press.

Gibbons, J. 2006. "Mental Causation without Downwards Causation". *The Philosophical Review* **115**(1): 79–103.

Gibson, J. 1979. *The Ecological Approach to Visual Perception*. Boston, MA: Houghton-Mifflin.

Gibson, K. 2002. "Evolution of Human Intelligence: The Roles of Brain Size and Mental Construction". *Brain, Behavior and Evolution* **59**: 10–20.

Gödel, K. [1951] 1995. "Some Basic Theorems on the Foundations of Mathematics and Their Implications". In *Kurt Gödel: Collected Works, Vol. III: Unpublished Essays and Lectures*, S. Feferman, J. Dawson, W. Goldfarb, C. Parsons & R. Solovay (eds), 290–303. New York: Oxford University Press.

Goel, V. 2007. "Anatomy of Deductive Reasoning". *Trends in Cognitive Sciences* **11**(10): 435–41.

Goel, V. & R. Dolan 2004. "Differential Involvement of Left Prefrontal Cortex in Inductive and Deductive Reasoning". *Cognition* **93**: B109–B121.

Gold, B. & R. Buckner 2002. "Common Prefrontal Regions Coactivate with Dissociable Posterior Regions during Controlled Semantic and Phonological Tasks". *Neuron* **35**: 803–12.

Goldman-Rakic, P. 1987. "Circuitry of the Prefrontal Cortex and the Regulation of Behavior by Representational Memory". In *Handbook of Neurobiology*, V. Mountcastle, F. Plum & S. Geiger (eds), 373–417. Bethesda, MD: American Psychological Society.

Goldman-Rakic, P. 1990. "Cellular and Circuit Basis of Working Memory in Prefrontal Cortex of Nonhuman Primates". In *Progress in Brain Research*, H. Uylings, C. Eden, J. Debruin, M. Comer & M. Feenstra (eds), 325–36. Amsterdam: Elsevier.

Goldman-Rakic, P. 1996. "Regional and Cellular Fractionation of Working Memory". *Proceedings of the National Academy of Sciences* **93**: 13,473–80.

Gonzalez, J., A. Barros-Loscertales, F. Pulvermüller *et al.* 2006. "Reading *Cinnamon* Activates Olfactory Brain Regions". *NeuroImage* **32**: 906–12.

Gould, S. 1997a. "Darwinian Fundamentalism". *The New York Review of Books* **44**(10): 1–10.

Gould, S. 1997b. "The Exaptive Excellence of Spandrels as a Term and Prototype". *Proceedings of the National Academy of Sciences* **94**: 10,750–5.

Graham, G. & T. Horgan 2002. "Sensations and Grain Processes". See Fetzer (2002), 63–86.

Griecus, M., B. Krasnow, A. Reiss & V. Menon 2003. "Functional Connectivity in the Resting Brain: A Network Analysis of the Default Mode Hypothesis". *Proceedings of the National Academy of Sciences* **100**: 253–8.

Grodzinsky, Y. & A. Friederici 2006. "Neuroimaging of Syntax and Syntactic Processing". *Current Opinion in Neurobiology* **16**: 240–6.

Grush, R. 1997. "The Architecture of Representation". *Philosophical Psychology* **10**(1): 5–25.

Grush, R. 2003. "In Defense of Some 'Cartesian' Assumptions Concerning the Brain and Its Operation". *Biology and Philosophy* **18**: 53–93.

Grush, R. 2004. "The Emulation Theory of Representation: Motor Control, Imagery, and Perception". *Behavioral and Brain Sciences* **27**: 377–442.

Haldane, J. 1983. "Aquinas on Sense-perception". *The Philosophical Review* **92**(2): 233–9.

Hameroff, S. 2006. "The Entwined Mysteries of Anesthesia and Consciousness: Is There a Common Underlying Mechanism?" *Anesthesiology* **105**: 400–12.

Hameroff, S. & R. Penrose 1995. "Orchestrated Reduction of Quantum Coherence in Brain Microtubules: A Model for Consciousness?" *Neural Network World* **5**: 793–804.

Hanna, R. 2006. *Kant, Science, and Human Nature.* New York: Oxford University Press.

Hanna, R. & M. Maiese 2009. *Embodied Minds in Action.* New York: Oxford University Press.

Hannan, A. 2007. "Brain Phylogeny, Ontogeny and Dysfunction: Integrating Evolutionary, Developmental, and Clinical Perspectives in Cognitive Neuroscience". *Acta Neuropsychiatrica* **19**: 149–58.

Hardcastle, V. 1992. "Reduction, Explanatory Extension, and the Mind/Brain Sciences". *Philosophy of Science* **59**(3): 408–28.

Hardcastle, V. 1999. "How to Understand the N in NCC". See Metzinger (2000), 259–64.

Hardcastle, V. & C. Stewart 2002. "What Do Brain Data Really Show?" *Philosophy of Science* **69**: S72–S82.

Hardin, C. 1988. *Color for Philosophers: Unweaving the Rainbow.* Indianapolis, IN: Hackett.

Harman, G. 1990. "The Intrinsic Quality of Experience". In *Philosophical Perspectives*, vol. 4, J. Tomberlin (ed.), 31–52. Atascadero, CA: Ridgeview.

Harris, J., I. Harris & M. Diamond 2001. "The Topography of Tactile Working Memory". *The Journal of Neuroscience* **21**(2): 8262–9.

Hartley, D. [1749] 1970. "Observations on Man, his Frame, his Duty, and his Expectations". In *Between Hume and Mill: An Anthology of British Philosophy*, R. Brown (ed.). New York: The Modern Library.

Haselager, P., J. Van Dijk & I. Van Rooij 2008. "A Lazy Brain? Embodied Embedded Cognition and Cognitive Neuroscience". In *Handbook of Cognitive Science: An Embodied Approach*, P. Calvo & A. Gomila (eds), 273–90. Amsterdam: Elsevier.

Haselager, W., R. Bongers & I. Van Rooij 2003a. "Cognitive Science, Representations, and Dynamical Systems Theory". In *The Dynamical Systems Approach to Cognition: Concepts and Empirical Paradigms Based on Self-organization, Embodiment, and Coordination Dynamics. Studies of Nonlinear Phenomena in Life Science*, vol. 10, W. Tschacher & J.-P. Dauwalder (eds), 229–42. Singapore: World Scientific.

Haselager, W., A. De Groot & J. Van Rappard 2003b. "Representationalism versus Anti-representationalism: A Debate for the Sake of Appearance". *Philosophical Psychology* **16**(1): 5–23.

Haugeland, J. 1978. "The Nature and Plausibility of Cognitivism". *Behavioral and Brain Sciences* **I**: 215–26.

Haugeland, J. [1991] 1998. "Representational Genera". In his *Having Thought: Essays in the Metaphysics of Mind*, 171–208. Cambridge, MA: Harvard University Press.

Hauser, M., N. Chomsky & T. Fitch 2002. "The Faculty of Language: What Is It, Who Has It, and How Did It Evolve?" *Science* **298**: 1569–79.

Hayashi, M. 2006. "Spindle Neurons in the Anterior Cingulate Cortex of Humans and Great Apes". See Matsuzawa *et al.* (2006), 64–74.

Heil, J. & A. Mele (eds) 1993. *Mental Causation*. New York: Oxford University Press.

Hellman, G. & F. Thompson 1975. "Physicalism: Ontology, Determination, and Reduction". *Journal of Philosophy* **72**: 551–64.

Heylighen, F. 2003. "The Science of Self-organization and Adaptivity". *The Encyclopedia of Life Support Systems*, 1–26. Paris: Unesco-EOLSS.

Hickok, G. & D. Poeppel 2000. "Towards a Functional Neuroanatomy of Speech Perception". *Trends in Cognitive Science* **4**(4): 131–8.

Hickok, G. & D. Poeppel 2004. "Dorsal and Ventral Streams: A Framework for Understanding Aspects of the Functional Anatomy of Language". *Cognition* **92**: 67–99.

Hickok, G. & D. Poeppel 2007. "The Cortical Organization of Speech Processing". *Nature Reviews Neuroscience* **8**: 393–402.

Hirschfield, L. & S. Gelman (eds) 1994. *Mapping the Mind: Domain Specificity in Cognition and Culture*. Cambridge: Cambridge University Press.

Holt, J. 2003. *Blindsight and the Nature of Consciousness*. New York: Broadview.

Hooker, C. 1981. "Towards a General Theory of Reduction. Part I: Historical and Scientific Setting. Part II: Identity in Reduction. Part III: Cross-categorical Reduction". *Dialogue* **20**: 38–59, 201–36, 496–529.

Hopfinger, J., M. Buonocore & G. R. Mangun 2000. "The Neural Mechanisms of Top-down Attentional Control". *Nature Neuroscience* **3**(3): 284–91.

Horgan, T. 1993. "From Supervenience to Superdupervenience: Meeting the Demands of a Material World". *Mind* **102**: 555–86.

Horgan, T. 1994. "Computation and Mental Representation". See Stich & Warfield (1994), 302–11.

Horgan, T. & U. Kriegel 2008. "Phenomenal Intentionality Meets the Extended Mind". *The Monist* **91**: 353–80.

Houdé, O. & N. Tzourio-Mazoyer 2003. "Neural Foundations of Logical and Mathematical Cognition". *Nature Reviews Neuroscience* **4**: 507–14.

Houdé, O., L. Zago, E. Mellet *et al.* 2000. "Shifting from the Perceptual Brain to the Logical Brain: The Neural Impact of Cognitive Inhibition Training". *Journal of Cognitive Neuroscience* **12**: 721–8.

Huemer, M. & B. Kovitz 2003. "Causation as Simultaneous and Continuous". *Philosophical Quarterly* **53**: 556–65.

Hughes, J. 1991. *Thomas Willis 1621–1675: His Life and Works*. London: RSM Press.

Humphreys, P. 1997. "Emergence, Not Supervenience". *PSA 1996: Proceedings of the 1996 Biennial Meetings of the Philosophy of Science Association, Part II, Symposia Papers*, Suppl. to Vol. **4**(4): S337–45.

Hurley, S. 1998. *Consciousness in Action*. Cambridge, MA: Harvard University Press.

Izard, C. 2007. "Basic Emotions, Natural Kinds, Emotion Schemas, and a New Paradigm". *Perspectives on Psychological Science* **2**(3): 260–80.

Jack, A. & J. Prinz 2004. "Searching for Scientific Experience". *Journal of Consciousness Studies* **11**(1): 51–6.

Jackson, F. 1986. "What Mary Didn't Know". *Journal of Philosophy* **83**: 291–5.

James, W. 1890. *Principles of Psychology*. New York: Henry Holt.

John, E. R. 2001. "A Field Theory of Consciousness". *Consciousness and Cognition* **10**: 184–213.

John, E. R. 2003. "A Theory of Consciousness". *Current Directions in Psychological Science* **12**(6): 244–50.

John, E. R. 2005. "From Synchronous Discharges to Subjective Awareness?" See Laureys (2005), 143–71.

John, E. R. & L. Prichep 2005. "The Anesthetic Cascade: A Theory of How Anesthesia Suppresses Consciousness". *Anesthesiology* **102**: 447–71.

Jonides, J., R. Lewis, D. Nee, C. Lustig, M. Berman & K. Moore 2007. "The Mind and Brain of Short-term Memory". *Annual Review of Psychology* **59**: 15.1–15.32.

Jung-Beeman, M. 2005. "Bilateral Brain Processes for Comprehending Natural Language". *Trends in Cognitive Science* **9**(11): 512–8.

Jurado, M. & M. Rosselli 2007. "The Elusive Nature of Executive Functions: A Review of Our Current Understanding". *Neuropsychological Review* **17**: 213–33.

Kaan, E. & T. Swaab 2002. "The Brain Circuitry of Syntactic Comprehension". *Trends in Cognitive Sciences* **6**(8): 350–56.

Kaas, J. 2000. "Why Is Brain Size So Important: Design Problems and Solutions as Neocortex Gets Bigger or Smaller". *Brain and Mind* **1**: 7–23.

Kant, I. [1797] 1958. *The Critique of Pure Reason*, N. Kemp Smith (trans.). New York: Macmillan.

Kanwisher, N. 2001. "Neural Events and Perceptual Awareness". *Cognition* **79**: 89–113.

Kanwisher, N. & E. Wojciulik 2000. "Visual Attention: Insights from Brain Imaging". *Nature Reviews Neuroscience* **1**: 91–100.

Karl, A., N. Birbaumer, W. Lutzenberger, L. Cohen & H. Flor 2001. "Reorganization of Motor and Somatosensory Cortex in Upper Extremity Amputees with Phantom Limb Pain". *The Journal of Neuroscience* **21**(10): 3609–18.

Kastner, S. & L. Ungerleider 2000. "Mechanisms of Visual Attention in the Human Cortex". *Annual Review of Neuroscience* **23**: 315–41.

Kastner, S., M. Prisk, P. De Weerd, R. Desimone & L. Ungerleider 1999. "Increased Activity in Human Visual Cortex during Directed Attention in the Absence of Visual Stimulation". *Neuron* **22**: 751–61.

Kim, J. 1985. "Psychophysical Laws". In *Actions and Events: Perspectives on the Philosophy of Donald Davidson*, E. Le Pore & B. McLaughlin (eds), 369–86. Oxford: Blackwell.

Kim, J. 1988. "Supervenience for Multiple Domains". *Philosophical Topics* **16**: 129–50.

Kim, J. 1989. "The Myth of Nonreductive Materialism". *Proceedings of the American Philosophical Association* **63**: 31–47.

Kim, J. 1992a. "Multiple Realization and the Metaphysics of Reduction". *Philosophy and Phenomenological Research* **52**: 1–26.

Kim, J. 1992b. "'Downwards Causation' in Emergentism and Nonreductive Physicalism". In *Emergence or Reduction*, A. Beckermann, H. Flohr & J. Kim (eds), 119–38. Berlin: De Gruyter.

Kim, J. 1993. *Supervenience and Mind*. Cambridge: Cambridge University Press.

Kim, J. 1997. "Supervenience, Emergence, and Realization in the Philosophy of Mind". In *Mindscapes: Philosophy, Science, and the Mind*, M. Carrier & P. Machamer (eds), 271–93. Pittsburgh, PA: Pittsburgh University Press.

Kim, J. 1998. *Mind in a Physical World*. Cambridge, MA: MIT Press.

Kim, J. 1999. "Making Sense of Emergence". *Philosophical Studies* **95**: 3–36.

Kim, J. 2000. "Making Sense of Downward Causation". See Andersen *et al.* (2000), 305–21.

Kim, J. 2003. "Blocking Causal Drainage and Other Maintenance Chores with Mental Causation". *Philosophy and Phenomenological Research* **67**: 128–53.

Kim, J. 2005. *Physicalism, Or Something Near Enough*. Princeton, NJ: Princeton University Press.

King, P. 2005. "Why Isn't the Mind–Body Problem Medieval?" In *Forming the Mind: Essays on the Internal Senses and the Mind/Body Problem from Avicenna to the Medical Enlightenment*, H. Lagerlund (ed.), 1–20. Dordrecht: Springer.

Kirkcaldie, M. & P. Kitchener 2007. "When Brains Expand: Mind and the Evolution of Cortex". *Acta Neuropsychiatrica* **19**: 139–48.

Klein, C. 2009. "Images Are Not the Evidence in Neuroimaging". *British Journal for the Philosophy of Science*, advance access published on 7 August 2009, doi: 10.1093/bjps/axp035.

Klinger, E. 1971. *Structure and Function of Fantasy*. New York: Wiley.

Knudsen, E. 2007. "Fundamental Components of Attention". *Annual Review of Neuroscience* **30**: 57–78.

Koboyakawa, T., M. Wakita, S. Saito, N. Gotow, N. Sakai & H. Ogawa 2005. "Location of the

Primary Gustatory Area in Humans and Its Properties, Studied by Magnetoencephalography". *Chemical Senses* **30** (Suppl. 1): i226–7.

Koch, C. 2004. *The Quest for Consciousness: A Neurobiological Approach*. Denver, CO: Roberts.

Koch, C. & F. Crick 2001. "On the Zombie Within". *Nature* **411** (21 June): 893.

Koch, C. & K. Hepp 2006. "Quantum Mechanics in the Brain". *Nature* **440**: 611–2.

Koch, C. & K. Hepp 2007. "The Relation between Quantum Mechanics and Higher Brain Functions: Lessons from Quantum Computation and Neurobiology", http://papers.klab.caltech.edu/306/1/561.pdf (accessed November 2010).

Koch, C. & N. Tsuchiya 2007. "Attention and Consciousness: Two Distinct Brain Processes". *Trends in Cognitive Science* **11**(1): 16–21.

Kosslyn, S. & G. Hatfield 1984. "Representation without Symbol Systems". *Social Research* **51**: 1019–45.

Kriegel, U. 2006. "The Same-order Monitoring Theory of Consciousness". See Kriegel & Williford (2006), 143–70.

Kriegel, U. 2007. "Intentional Inexistence and Phenomenal Intentionality". *Philosophical Perspectives, Vol. 21: Philosophy of Mind*: 307–40.

Kriegel, U. 2009. "Self-representationalism and Phenomenology". *Philosophical Studies* **143**: 357–81.

Kriegel, U. & K. Williford (eds) 2006. *Self-representational Approaches to Consciousness*. Cambridge, MA: MIT Press.

Kriegeskorte, N., W. Simmons, P. Bellgowan & C. Baker 2009. "Circular Analysis in Systems Neuroscience: The Dangers of Double Dipping". *Nature Neuroscience* **12**(5): 535–40.

Kringelbach, M. 2004. "Food for Thought: Hedonic Experience beyond Homeostasis in the Human Brain". *Neuroscience* **126**: 807–19.

Kringelbach, M. 2005. "The Human Orbitofrontal Cortex: Linking Rewards to Hedonic Experience". *Nature Reviews Neuroscience* **6**: 691–702.

Kringelbach, M. & E. Rolls 2004. "The Functional Neuroanatomy of the Human Orbitofrontal Cortex: Evidence from Neuroimaging and Neuropsychology". *Progress in Neurobiology* **72**: 341–72.

Kringelbach, M., J. O'Doherty, E. T. Rolls & C. Andrews 2003. "Activation of the Human Orbitofrontal Cortex to a Liquid Food Stimulus Is Correlated with Its Subjective Pleasantness". *Cerebral Cortex* **13**: 1064–71.

Kripke, S. 1980. *Naming and Necessity*. Cambridge, MA: Harvard University Press.

Krubitzer, L. & K. Huffman 2000. "Arealization of the Neocortex in Mammals: Genetic and Epigenetic Contributions to the Phenotype". *Brain, Behavior and Evolution* **55**: 322–35.

Kurthen, M. 1995. "On the Prospect of a Naturalistic Theory of Phenomenal Consciousness". In *Conscious Experience*, T. Metzinger (ed.), 107–22. Exeter: Imprint Academic.

Lamme, V. 2003. "Why Visual Attention and Awareness Are Different". *Trends in Cognitive Sciences* **7**: 12–8.

Lamme, V. 2004. "Separate Neural Definitions of Visual Consciousness and Visual Attention; A Case for Phenomenal Awareness". *Neural Networks* **17**: 861–72.

Lamme, V. 2005. "Can Neuroscience Reveal the True Nature of Consciousness?" www.nyu.edu/gsas/dept/philo/courses/consciousness05/LammeNeuroscience.pdf (accessed November 2010).

Lamme, V. 2006. "Towards a True Neural Stance on Consciousness". *Trends in Cognitive Science* **10**(11): 494–501.

Laureys, S. (ed.) 2005. *The Boundaries of Consciousness: Neurobiology and Neuropathology, Progress in Brain Research*, vol. 150. Amsterdam: Elsevier.

Laureys, S., F. Perrin & S. Brédart 2007. "Self-consciousness in Non-communicative Patients". *Consciousness and Cognition* **16**: 722–41.

Leeds, S. 2002. "Perception, Transparency, and the Language of Thought". *Noûs* **36**(1): 104–29.

Leibniz, G. [1764] 1996. *New Essays on Human Understanding*. Cambridge: Cambridge University Press.

Leibniz, G. [1714] 2005. *Discourse on Metaphysics and the Monadology*. New York: Dover.

Levine, J. 1983. "Materialism and Qualia: The Explanatory Gap". *Pacific Philosophical Quarterly* **64**: 354–61.

Levine, J. 2001. *Purple Haze: The Puzzle of Consciousness*. New York: Oxford University Press.

Levy, H. M., R. I. Henkin, A. Hutter, C. S. Lin & D. Schellinger 1999. "Mapping Brain Activation to Odorants in Patients with Smell Loss by Functional MRI". *Journal of Computer Assisted Tomography* **22**: 96–103.

Lewis, D. 1966. "An Argument for the Identity Theory". *Journal of Philosophy* **63**: 17–25.

Lewis, D. 1979. "Counterfactual Dependence and Time's Arrow". *Noûs* **13**: 455–76.

Lewis, D. 1980. "Psychophysical and Theoretical Identifications". In *Readings in the Philosophy of Psychology*, vols 1 & 2, N. Block (ed.), 207–15. Cambridge, MA: Harvard University Press.

Lewis, D. 1986a. "Events". In his *Philosophical Papers*, vol. 2, 241–69. Oxford: Oxford University Press.

Lewis, D. 1986b. "Causation". In his *Philosophical Papers*, vol. 2, 159–213. Oxford: Oxford University Press.

Lewis, D. 2000. "Causation as Influence". *Journal of Philosophy* **97**: 182–97.

Lieberman, D., B. McBratney & G. Krovitz 2002. "The Evolution and Development of Cranial Form in *Homo sapiens*". *Proceedings of the National Academy of Sciences* **99**(3): 1134–9.

Lieberman, M., E. Berkman & T. Wager 2009. "Correlations in Social Neuroscience Aren't Voodoo". *Perspectives on Psychological Science* **4**(3): 299–307.

Lloyd, D. 2007. "What Do Brodmann Areas Do? Or: Scanning the Neurocracy", draft manuscript of 13 January 2007, www.trincoll.edu/~dlloyd/brodmann.html (accessed November 2010).

Loar, B. 1999. "Phenomenal States". In *The Nature of Consciousness: Philosophical Debates*, N. Block, O. Flanagan & G. Güzeldare (eds), 597–616. Cambridge, MA: MIT Press.

Locke, J. [1689] 1979. *An Essay Concerning Human Understanding*. New York: Oxford University Press.

Logothetis, N. K. 1998. "Single Units and Conscious Vision". *Proceedings of the Royal Society B* **353**: 1801–18.

Lopez, C. & O. Blanke 2007. "Neuropsychology and Neurophysiology of Self-consciousness: Multisensory and Vestibular Mechanisms". In *Hirnforschung und menschenbild: Beiträge zur interdiszinplinären verständigung*, A. Holderegger, B. Sitter-Lever & C. Hess (eds), http://espra.risc.cnrs.fr/Lopez_Blanke_2007_PROOFS2.pdf (accessed October 2009).

Lopez, C., P. Halje & O. Blanke 2008. "Body Ownership and Embodiment: Vestibular and Multisensory Mechanisms". *Clinical Neurophysiology* **38**: 149–61.

Lorenz, J., S. Minoshima & K. Casey 2003. "Keeping Pain Out of Mind: The Role of the Dorsolateral Prefrontal Cortex in Pain Modulation". *Brain* **126**: 1079–91.

Lotze, M., H. Flor, W. Grodd, W. Larbig & N. Birbaumer 2001. "Phantom Movements and Pain: An fMRI Study in Upper Limb Amputees". *Brain* **124**(11): 2268–77.

Lycan, W. 2001. "A Simple Argument for a Higher-order Representation Theory of Consciousness". *Analysis* **61**: 3–4.

Lyketos, C., A. Rosenblatt & P. Rabins 2004. "Forgotten Frontal Lobe Syndrome or 'Executive Dysfunction Syndrome.'" *Psychosomatics* **45**(3): 247–55.

Macaluso, E. 2006. "Multisensory Processing in Sensory-specific Cortical Areas". *The Neuroscientist* **12**(4): 327–37.

Macaluso, E. & J. Driver 2004. "Functional Imaging of Crossmodal Spatial Representations and Crossmodal Spatial Attention". In *Crossmodal Space and Crossmodal Attention*, C. Spence & J. Driver (eds), 247–76. New York: Oxford University Press.

Macaluso, E. & J. Driver 2005. "Multisensory Spatial Interaction: A Window onto Functional Integration in the Human Brain". *Trends in Neurosciences* **28**(5): 264–71.

Machamer, P., L. Darden & C. Craver 2000. "Thinking about Mechanisms". *Philosophy of Science* **67**: 1–25.

Mackie, J. 1976. *Problems from Locke*. New York: Oxford University Press.

Maia, T. & A. Cleeremans 2005. "Consciousness: Converging Insights from Connectionist Modeling and Neuroscience". *Trends in Cognitive Science* **9**(8): 397–404.

Malach, R. 2007. "The Measurement Problem in Consciousness Research". *Behavioral and Brain Sciences* **30**(5/6): 516–7.

Mandik, P. 2006. "The Neurophilosophy of Consciousness". In *The Blackwell Companion to Consciousness*, M. Velmans & S. Schneider (eds), 418–30. Oxford: Blackwell.

Marcus, G. & S. Fisher 2003. "*FOXP2* in Focus: What Can Genes Tell Us about Speech and Language?" *Trends in Cognitive Science* **7**(6): 257–62.

Marks, C. 1981. *Commissurotomy, Consciousness and Unity of Mind*. Cambridge, MA: MIT Press.

Marras, A. 2000. "Critical Notice of *Mind in a Physical World* by Jaegwon Kim". *Canadian Journal of Philosophy* **30**: 137–40.

Marras, A. 2007. "Kim's Supervenience Argument and Nonreductive Physicalism". *Erkenntnis* **66**: 305–27.

Mashour, G. 2004. "Consciousness Unbound: Towards a Paradigm of General Anesthesia". *Anesthesiology* **100**: 428–33.

Mashour, G. 2006. "Integrating the Science of Consciousness and Anesthesia". *Anesthesia and Analgesia* **103**(4): 975–82.

Massey, D. 2002. "A Brief History of Human Society: The Origin and Role of Emotion in Social Life". *American Sociological Review* **67**: 1–29.

Matsuzawa, T., M. Tomonaga & M. Tanaka (eds) 2006. *Cognitive Development in Chimpanzees*. Hong Kong: Springer.

Maund, B. 2003. *Perception*. Chesham: Acumen.

McClelland, J. & A. Cleeremans 2009. "Connectionism and Consciousness". In *The Oxford Companion to Consciousness*, T. Bayne, A. Cleeremans & P. Wilken (eds), 180–1. New York: Oxford University Press.

McCrone, J. 1994. "Inner Voices, Distant Memories". *New Scientist* **29**: 28–31.

McFadden, J. 2002. "Synchronous Firing and Its Influence on the Brain's Magnetic Field". *Journal of Consciousness Studies* **9**: 23–50.

McFadden, J. 2006. "The CEMI Field Theory: Seven Clues to the Nature of Consciousness". In *The Emerging Physics of Consciousness*, J. Tuszynski (ed.), 385–404. Berlin: Springer.

McGinn, C. 1989. "Can We Solve the Mind–Body Problem?" *Mind* **98**(391): 349–66.

McGinn, C. 1991. *The Problem of Consciousness*. Oxford: Blackwell.

McLaughlin, B. 1989. "Type Epiphenomenalism, Type Dualism, and the Causal Priority of the Physical". *Philosophical Perspectives* **3**: 109–35.

McLaughlin, B. 1993. "On Davidson's Response to the Charge of Epiphenomenalism". See Heil & Mele (1993), 27–40.

McLaughlin, B. 1995. "Varieties of Supervenience". In *Supervenience: New Essays*, E. Savellos & Ü. Yalcin (eds), 16–59. Cambridge: Cambridge University Press.

McLaughlin, B. & G. Bartlett 2004. "Have Noë and Thompson Cast Doubt on the Neural Correlates of Consciousness Program?" *Journal of Consciousness Studies* **11**(1): 56–67.

Melnyk, A. 2003. *A Physicalist Manifesto*. Cambridge: Cambridge University Press.

Mesulam, M. 1981. "A Cortical Network for Directed Attention and Unilateral Neglect". *Annals of Neurology* **10**: 309–25.

Mesulam, M. 1990. "Large-scale Neurocognitive Networks and Distributed Processing for Attention, Language, and Memory". *Annals of Neurology* **28**: 597–613.

Mesulam, M. 1998. "From Sensation to Cognition". *Brain* **121**: 1013–52.

Mesulam, M. 1999. "Spatial Attention and Neglect: Parietal, Frontal, and Cingulated Contributions to the Mental Representation and Attentional Targeting of Salient Extrapersonal Events".

Philosophical Transactions of the Royal Society B **354**: 1325–46.

Mesulam, M. 2000. "Behavioral Neuroanatomy: Large-scale Networks, Association Cortex, Frontal Syndromes, the Limbic System, and Hemispheric Specializations". In *Principles of Behavioral and Cognitive Neurology*, M. Mesulam (ed.), 1–120. New York: Oxford University Press.

Mesulam, M. 2002. "The Human Frontal Lobes: Transcending the Default Mode through Contingent Encoding". In *Principles of Frontal Lobe Function*, D. Stuss & R. Knight (eds), 8–30. New York: Oxford University Press.

Mesulam, M., A. Nobre, Y. Kim, T. Parrish & D. Gitelman 2001. "Heterogeneity of Cingulate Contributions to Spatial Attention". *NeuroImage* **13**: 1065–72.

Mettrie, J. O. de la. [1750] 1999. *L'Homme machine*. Paris: Flammarion.

Metzinger, T. (ed.) 2000. *Neural Correlates of Consciousness: Empirical and Conceptual Questions*. Cambridge, MA: MIT Press.

Metzinger, T. 2003. *Being No-One*. Cambridge, MA: MIT Press.

Metzinger, T. 2004. "Appearance Is Not Knowledge: The Incoherent Straw Man, Content-content Confusions, and Mindless Conscious Subjects". *Journal of Consciousness Studies* **11**(1): 67–71.

Metzinger, T. 2008. "Empirical Perspectives from the Self-model Theory of Subjectivity: A Brief Summary with Examples". *Progress in Brain Research* **168**: 215–45.

Metzinger, T. 2009a. *The Ego Tunnel: The Science of the Mind and the Myth of the Self*. New York: Basic Books.

Metzinger, T. 2009b. "Why Are Out-of-Body Experiences Interesting for Philosophers? The Theoretical Relevance of OBE Research". *Cortex* **45**: 256–8.

Miller, E. & J. Cohen 2001. "An Integrative Theory of Prefrontal Cortex Function". *Annual Review of Neuroscience* **24**: 167–202.

Miller, G. 2007. "Brain Evolution". See Gangestad & Simpson (2007), 287–93.

Millikan, R. 1984. *Language, Thought, and Other Biological Categories*. Cambridge, MA: MIT Press.

Millikan, R. 1989. "Biosemantics". *Journal of Philosophy* **86**(6): 281–97.

Millikan, R. 1991. "Perceptual Content and Fregean Myth". *Mind* **100**(4): 439–59.

Millikan, R. 2008. *On Clear and Confused Ideas: An Essay about Substance Concepts*. Cambridge: Cambridge University Press.

Milner, D. & M. Goodale 1995. *The Visual Brain in Action*. New York: Oxford University Press.

Mithen, S. 2007. "Key Changes in the Evolution of Human Psychology". See Gangestad & Simpson (2007), 256–66.

Montagnini, A. & A. Treves 2003. "The Evolution of Mammalian Cortex, from Lamination to Arealization". *Brain Research Bulletin* **60**: 387–93.

Monti, M., D. Osherson, M. Martinez & L. Parsons 2007. "Functional Neuroanatomy of Deductive Inference". *NeuroImage* **37**: 1005–16.

Morrison, J. 1970. "Husserl and Brentano on Intentionality". *Philosophy and Phenomenological Research* **31**(1): 27–46.

Morsella, E. 2005. "The Function of Phenomenal States". *Psychological Review* **112**(4): 1000–21.

Mulligan, K. & B. Smith 1985. "Franz Brentano and the Ontology of Mind". *Philosophy and Phenomenological Research* **45**: 627–44.

Nagel, T. 1974. "What Is It Like To Be a Bat?" *The Philosophical Review* **83**: 435–50.

Nagel, E. [1961] 1979. *The Structure of Science*, 2nd edn. Indianapolis, IN: Hackett.

Neill, D. 2007. "Cortical Evolution and Human Behavior". *Brain Research Bulletin* **74**: 191–205.

Nietzsche, F. 1968. *The Will to Power*, W. Kaufmann (trans.). New York: Vintage.

Nietzsche, F. [1886] 1989. *Beyond Good and Evil: Prelude to a Philosophy of the Future*, W. Kaufmann (trans.). New York: Vintage.

Nimchinsky, E., E. Gilissen, J. Allman, D. Perl, J. Erwin & P. Hof 1999. "A Neuronal Morophologic Type Unique to Humans and Great Apes". *Proceedings of the National Academy of Sciences* **96**: 5268–73.

Nishimura, T. 2006. "Descent of the Larynx in Chimpanzees: Mosaic and Multiple-step Evolution of the Foundations of Human Speech". See Matsuzawa *et al.* (2006), 75–95.

Noë, A. 2004. *Action in Perception (Representation and Mind)*. Cambridge, MA: MIT Press.

Noë, A. & E. Thompson 2004a. "Are There Neural Correlates of Consciousness?" *Journal of Consciousness Studies* **11**(1): 3–28.

Noë, A. & E. Thompson 2004b. "Sorting Out the Neural Basis of Consciousness". *Journal of Consciousness Studies* **11**(1): 87–98.

Nolte, J. 2002. *The Human Brain*, 5th edn. St Louis, MO: Mosby.

Obleser, J., R. Wise, M. Dresner & S. Scott 2007. "Functional Integration across Brain Regions Improves Speech Perception under Adverse Listening Conditions". *The Journal of Neuroscience* **27**(9): 2283–9.

O'Brien, G. & J. Opie 1999a. "A Connectionist Theory of Phenomenal Experience". *Behavioral and Brain Research* **22**(1): 127–48.

O'Brien, G. & J. Opie 1999b. "Putting Content into a Vehicle Theory of Consciousness". *Behavioral and Brain Sciences* **22**(1): 175–96.

O'Brien, G. & J. Opie 2001. "Connectionist Vehicles, Structural Resemblance, and the Phenomenal Mind". *Communication and Cognition* **34**: 13–38.

O'Dea, J. 2008. "Transparency and the Unity of Experience". In *The Case for Qualia*, E. Wright (ed.), 299–308. Cambridge, MA: MIT Press.

Okanoya, K. 2007. "Language Evolution and an Emergent Property". *Current Opinion in Neurobiology* **17**: 271–6.

Oken, B. S., M. C. Salinsky & S. M. Elsas 2006. "Vigilance, Alertness, or Sustained Attention: Physiological Basis and Measurement". *Clinical Neurophysiology* **117**: 1885–901.

Oppenheim, P. & H. Putnam 1958. "The Unity of Science as a Working Hypothesis". In *Minnesota Studies in the Philosophy of Science*, vol. 2, H. Feigl, M. Scriven & G. Maxwell (eds), 3–36. Minneapolis, MN: Minnesota University Press.

O'Regan, J. K. & A. Noë 2001. "A Sensorimotor Account of Vision and Visual Consciousness". *Behavioral and Brain Sciences* **24**: 939–73.

Owen, A. 2008. "Disorders of Consciousness". *Annals of the New York Academy of Sciences* **1124**: 225–38.

Oxnard, C. 2004. "Brain Evolution: Mammals, Primates, Chimpanzees, and Humans". *International Journal of Primatology* **25**(5): 1127–58.

Panksepp, J. 2003. "At the Interface of the Affective, Behavioral, and Cognitive Neurosciences: Decoding the Emotional Feelings of the Brain". *Brain and Cognition* **52**: 4–14.

Panksepp, J. 2005. "Affective Consciousness: Core Emotional Feelings in Animals and Humans". *Consciousness and Cognition* **14**: 30–80.

Panksepp, J. 2007. "Neurologizing the Psychology of Affects: How Appraisal-based Constructivism and Basic Emotion Theory Can Coexist". *Perspectives on Psychological Science* **2**(3): 281–96.

Panksepp, J. & J. B. Panksepp 2000. "The Seven Sins of Evolutionary Psychology". *Evolution and Cognition* **6**(2): 108–31.

Panksepp, J., J. Moskal, J. B. Panksepp & R. Kroes 2002. "Comparative Approaches in Evolutionary Psychology: Molecular Neuroscience Meets the Mind". *Neuroendocrinology Letters Special Issue* **23** (Suppl. 4, December): 105–15.

Passingham, D. & K. Sakai 2004. "The Prefrontal Cortex and Working Memory: Physiology and Brain Imaging". *Current Opinion in Neurobiology* **14**: 163–8.

Paul, L. 1998. "Problems with Late Preemption". *Analysis* **58**: 48–53.

Paul, L. 1999. "Keeping Track of the Time: Emending the Counterfactual Analysis of Causation". *Analysis* **59**: 191–8.

Paul, L. 2000. "Aspect Causation". *Journal of Philosophy* **97**: 223–34.

Pautz, A. 2006. "Sensory Awareness Is Not a Wide Physical Relation: An Empirical Argument against Externalist Intentionalism". *Noûs* **40**(2): 205–40.

Peelen, M., D. Heslenfeld & J. Theeuwes 2004. "Endogenous and Exogenous Attention Shifts Are Mediated by the Same Large-scale Neural Network". *NeuroImage* **22**: 822–30.

Peirce, C. S. 1976. *The New Elements of Mathematics by Charles S. Peirce*, 4 vols in 5, vol. 4, C. Eisele (ed.), 20–1. The Hague: Mouton.

Peissig, J. & M. Tarr 2007. "Visual Object Recognition: Do We Know More Now than We Did 20 Years Ago?" *Annual Review of Psychology* **58**: 75–96.

Penrose, R. 1990. *The Emperor's New Mind*. New York: Oxford University Press.

Penrose, R. 1994. *Shadows of the Mind*. New York: Oxford University Press.

Pessoa, L. & L. Ungerleider 2004. "Top-down Mechanisms for Working Memory and Attentional Processes". In *The New Cognitive Neurosciences*, 3rd edn, M. Gazzaniga (ed.), 919–30. Cambridge, MA: MIT Press.

Pessoa, L., S. Kastner & L. Ungerleider 2003. "Neuroimaging Studies of Attention: From Modulation of Sensory Processing to Top-down Control". *The Journal of Neuroscience* **23**(10): 3990–8.

Petrides, M. 2000. "The Role of the Mid-dorsolateral Prefrontal Cortex in Working Memory". *Experimental Brain Research* **133**: 44–54.

Petrides, M., B. Alivisatos & S. Frey 2002. "Differential Activation of the Human Orbital, Mid-ventrolateral, and Mid-dorsolateral Prefrontal Cortex during the Processing of Visual Stimuli". *Proceedings of the National Academy of Sciences* **99**(8): 5649–54.

Phillips, M., W. Drevets, S. Rauch & R. Lane 2003. "Neurobiology of Emotion Perception I: The Neural Basis of Normal Emotion Perception". *Biological Psychiatry* **54**: 504–14.

Pinker, S. & R. Jackendoff 2005. "The Faculty of Language: What's Special About It?" *Cognition* **95**: 201–36.

Pitt, D. 2004. "The Phenomenology of Cognition or What Is It Like to Think that P?" *Philosophy and Phenomenological Research* **69**: 1–36.

Pockett, S. 2002. "Difficulties with the Electromagnetic Field Theory of Consciousness". *Journal of Consciousness Studies* **9**(4): 51–6.

Poeppel, D. 2006. "Language: Specifying the Site of Modality-independent Meaning". *Current Biology* **16**(21): R930–2.

Poeppel, D. & M. Hackl 2008. "The Functional Architecture of Speech Perception". In *Topics in Integrative Neuroscience: From Cells to Cognition*, J. Pomerantz (ed.), 154–80. Cambridge: Cambridge University Press.

Poeppel, D. & G. Hickok 2004. "Towards a New Functional Anatomy of Language". *Cognition* **92**: 1–12.

Polger, T. & O. Flanagan 2002. "Consciousness, Adaptation, and Epiphenomenalism". See Fetzer (2002), 21–41.

Posner, M. 1994. "Attention: The Mechanism of Consciousness". *Proceedings of the National Academy of Sciences USA* **91**(16): 7398–402.

Posner, M. (ed.) 2004. *Cognitive Neuroscience of Attention*. New York: Guilford.

Posner, M. & S. Petersen 1993. "The Attention System of the Human Brain". *Annual Review of Neuroscience* **13**: 25–42.

Postle, B. 2006. "Working Memory as an Emergent Property of the Mind and Brain". *Neuroscience* **139**: 23–38.

Postle, B., T. Druzgal & M. D'Esposito 2003. "Seeking the Neural Substrates of Visual Working Memory Storage". *Cortex* **39**: 927–46.

Prinz, J. 2000. "A Neurofunctional Theory of Visual Consciousness". *Consciousness and Cognition* **9**: 243–59.

Prinz, J. 2009. "Is Consciousness Embodied?" See Robbins & Aydede (2009), 419–36.

Putnam, H. 1975. "The Nature of Mental States". In his *Mind, Language, and Reality: Philosophical Papers*, vol. 2, 429–40. Cambridge: Cambridge University Press.

Putnam, H. 1988. *Representation and Reality*. Cambridge, MA: MIT Press.

Quine, W. V. O. 1981. "On the Individuation of Attributes". In his *Theories and Things*, 100–113. Cambridge, MA: Harvard University Press.

Raftopoulos, A. (ed.) 2005. *Cognitive Penetrability of Perception: Attention, Action, Strategies, and Bottom-up Constraints*. New York: Nova Science.

Raichle, M. & A. Snyder 2007. "A Default Mode of Brain Function: A Brief History of an Evolving Idea". *NeuroImage* **37**: 1083–90.

Raichle, M., A. MacLeod, A. Snyder, W. Powers & D. Gusnard 2001. "A Default Mode of Brain Function". *Proceedings of the National Academy of Sciences USA* **98**: 676–82.

Ramachandran, V. & W. Hirstein 1998. "The Perception of Phantom Limbs". *Brain* **121**: 1603–30.

Ramachandran, V. & E. Hubbard 2005. "The Emergence of the Human Mind: Some Clues from Synesthesia". In *Synesthesia: Perspectives from Cognitive Neuroscience*, L. Robertson & N. Sagiv (eds), 147–92. New York: Oxford University Press.

Rappaport, S. 1999. "How Did the Human Brain Evolve? A Proposal Based on New Evidence from *in vivo* Brain Imaging during Attention and Ideation". *Brain Research Bulletin* **50**(3): 149–65.

Ravenscroft, I. 2004. "*Where Angels Fear to Tread* – The Evolution of Language". *Biology and Philosophy* **19**: 145–58.

Rauschecker, J. & B. Tian 2000. "Mechanisms and Streams for Processing of 'What' and 'Where' in Auditory Cortex". *Proceedings of the National Academy of Sciences* **97**(22): 11,800–806.

Raz, A. 2004. "Anatomy of Attentional Networks". *The Anatomical Record Part B: The New Anatomist)* **281B**: 21–36.

Raz, A. & J. Buhle 2006. "Typologies of Attentional Networks". *Nature Reviews Neuroscience* **7**: 367–79.

Rees, G., G. Krieman & C. Koch 2002. "Neural Correlates of Consciousness in Humans". *Nature Reviews Neuroscience* **3**: 261–70.

Reid, T. [1785] 2002. *Essays on the Intellectual Powers of Man*, D. Brookes (ed.). University Park, PA: Pennsylvania State University Press.

Revonsuo, A. 1999. "Binding and the Phenomenal Unity of Consciousness". *Consciousness and Cognition* **8**: 173–85.

Revonsuo, A. 2000. "Prospects for a Scientific Research Program on Consciousness". See Metzinger (2000), 57–76.

Revonsuo, A. 2006. *Inner Presence: Consciousness as a Biological Phenomenon*. Cambridge, MA: MIT Press.

Rey, G. 2002. "Searle's Misunderstanding of Functionalism and Strong AI". In *Views into the Chinese Room: New Essays on Searle and Artificial Intelligence*, J. Preston & M. Bishop (eds), 201–26. New York: Oxford University Press.

Ridderinkhof, K., W. Van den Wildenberg, S. Segalowitz & C. Carter 2004. "Neurocognitive Mechanisms of Cognitive Control: The Role of Prefrontal Cortex in Action Selection, Response Inhibition, Performance Monitoring, and Reward-based Learning". *Brain and Cognition* **56**: 129–40.

Rizzolatti, G. & L. Craighero 2004. "The Mirror-Neuron System". *Annual Review Neuroscience* **27**: 169–92.

Rizzolatti, G. & M. Gentilucci 1988. "Motor and Visual-motor Functions of the Pre-motor Cortex". In *Neurobiology of Neocortex*, P. Rakic & W. Singer (eds), 269–84. New York: Wiley.

Rizzolatti, G. & C. Sinigaglia 2008. *Mirrors in the Brain: How Our Minds Share Actions and Emotions*. Oxford: Oxford University Press.

Rizzolatti, G., M. Fabbri-Destro & L. Cattaneo 2009. "Mirror Neurons and Their Clinical Relevance". *Nature Clinical Practice: Neurology* **5**(1): 24–34.

Robbins, P. & M. Aydede (eds) 2009. *The Cambridge Handbook of Situated Cognition*. Cambridge: Cambridge University Press.

Robertson, L. 2003. "Binding, Spatial Attention, and Perceptual Awareness". *Nature Reviews Neuroscience* **4**: 93–102.

Robertson, L. & N. Sagiv (eds) 2005. *Synesthesia: Perspectives from Cognitive Neuroscience*. New York: Oxford University Press.

Rodd, J., M. Davis & I. Johnsrude 2005. "The Neural Mechanisms of Speech Comprehension: fMRI Studies of Semantic Ambiguity". *Cerebral Cortex* **14**: 1261–9.

Rogers, T. & J. McClelland 2004. *Semantic Cognition: A Parallel Distributed Processing Approach*. Cambridge, MA: MIT Press.

Rolls, E. 2000. "Orbitofrontal Cortex and Reward". *Cerebral Cortex* **10**: 284–94.

Rolls, E. 2004. "Convergence of Sensory Systems in the Obitofrontal Cortex in Primates and Brain Design for Emotion". *The Anatomical Record Part A, Discoveries in Molecular, Cellular, and Evolutionary Biology* **281A**: 1212–25.

Rolls, E. 2005. "Taste, Olfactory, and Food Texture Processing in the Brain, and the Control of Food Intake". *Physiology and Behavior* **85**: 45–56.

Rolls, E. 2007. "A Computational Neuroscience Approach to Consciousness". *Neural Networks* **20**: 962–82.

Rolls, E. & L. L. Baylis 1994. "Gustatory, Olfactory, and Visual Convergence within the Primate Orbitofrontal Cortex". *The Journal of Neuroscience* **14**: 5437–52.

Rolls, E. T., M. L. Kringelbach & I. E. T. De Araujo 2003. "Different Representations of Pleasant and Unpleasant Odours in the Human Brain". *European Journal of Neuroscience* **18**: 695–703.

Romanski, L. 2004. "Domain Specificity in the Primate Prefrontal Cortex". *Cognitive, Affective and Behavioral Neuroscience* **4**(4): 421–9.

Rorty, R. 1979. *Philosophy and the Mirror of Nature*. Princeton, NJ: Princeton University Press.

Rosenfeld, R. & D. Touretsky 1988. "Coarse-coded Symbol Memories and Their Properties". *Complex Systems* **2**: 463–84.

Rosenthal, D. 2002. "Explaining Consciousness". In *Philosophy of Mind: Classical and Contemporary Readings*, D. Chalmers (ed.), 406–21. New York: Oxford University Press.

Roth, G. & U. Dicke 2005. "Evolution of Brain and Intelligence". *Trends in Cognitive Science* **9**(5): 250–57.

Rowlands, M. 2003. *Externalism: Putting Mind and World Back Together Again*. Chesham: Acumen.

Rowlands, M. 2006. *Body Language: Representation in Action*. Cambridge, MA: MIT Press.

Rowlands, M. 2009. "Situated Representation". See Robbins & Aydede (2009), 117–33.

Royet, J. & J. Plailly 2004. "Lateralization of Olfactory Processes". *Chemical Senses* **29**(8): 731–45.

Royet, J., J. Hudry, D. Zald *et al.* 2001. "Functional Neuroanatomy of Different Olfactory Judgments". *NeuroImage* **13**: 506–19.

Ryle, G. 1949. *The Concept of Mind*. Chicago, IL: University of Chicago Press.

Sahin, N., S. Pinker & E. Halgren 2006. "Abstract Grammatical Processing of Nouns and Verbs in Broca's Area: Evidence from fMRI". *Cortex* **42**: 540–62.

Samuels, R. 1998. "Evolutionary Psychology and the Massive Modularity Hypothesis". *British Journal for the Philosophy of Science* **49**: 575–602.

Saper, C. 2002. "The Central Autonomic Nervous System: Conscious Visceral Perception and Autonomic Pattern Generation". *Annual Review of Neurosciences* **25**: 433–69.

Sarter, M., W. Gehring & R. Kozak 2006. "More Attention Must Be Paid: The Neurobiology of Attentional Effort". *Brain Research Reviews* **51**: 145–60.

Sartre, J.-P. 1948. *Being and Nothingness*, H. E. Barnes (trans.). New York: Philosophical Library.

Sartre, J.-P. [1936] 1962. *The Transcendence of the Ego*, F. Williams & R. Kirkpatrick (trans). New York: Noonday Press.

Savage-Rumbaugh, S., W. Fields & T. Spircu 2004. "The Emergence of Knapping and Vocal Expression Embedded in *Pan/Homo* Culture". *Biology and Philosophy* **19**: 541–75.

Schiffer, S. 1987. *Remnants of Meaning*. Cambridge, MA: MIT Press.

Schwabe, L. & O. Blanke 2007. "Cognitive Neuroscience and Agency". *Consciousness and Cognition* **16**: 661–6.

Schwartz, S., F. Assal, N. Valenza, M. Seghier & P. Vuilleumier 2005. "Illusory Persistence of Touch after Right Parietal Damage: Neural Correlates of Tactile Awareness". *Brain* **128**: 277–90.

Searle, J. 1980. "Minds, Brains and Programs [with Peer Commentaries]". *Behavioral and Brain Sciences* **3**: 417–57.

Searle, J. 1983. *Intentionality*. Cambridge: Cambridge University Press.

Searle, J. 1992. *The Rediscovery of the Mind*. Cambridge, MA: MIT Press.

Searle, J. 2000. "Consciousness". *Annual Review of Neuroscience* **23**: 557–78.

Searle, J. 2004. *Mind: A Brief Introduction*. New York: Oxford University Press.

Searle, J. 2007. "Dualism Revisited". *Journal of Physiology Paris* **101**: 169–78.

Semendeferi, K., A. Lu, N. Schenker & H. Damasio 2002. "Humans and Great Apes Share a Large Frontal Cortex". *Nature Neuroscience* **5**(3): 272–6.

Sergent, C., S. Baillet & S. Dehaene 2005. "Timing of the Brain Events Underlying Access to Consciousness during the Attentional Blink". *Nature Neuroscience* **8**: 1391–400.

Seth, A. & B. Baars 2005. "Neural Darwinism and Consciousness". *Consciousness and Cognition* **14**: 140–68.

Seth, A., B. Baars & D. Edelman 2005. "Criteria for Consciousness in Humans and Other Mammals". *Consciousness and Cognition* **14**: 119–39.

Seth, A., E. Izhikevich, G. Reeke & G. M. Edelman 2006. "Theories and Measures of Consciousness: An Extended Framework". *Proceedings of the National Academy of Sciences* **103**: 10,799–804.

Shapiro, S. 2004. *The Mind Incarnate*. Cambridge, MA: MIT Press.

Shaw, R., M. Turvey & W. Mace 1982. "Ecology Psychology: The Consequences of a Commitment to Realism". In *Cognition and the Symbolic Processes II*, W. Weiner & D. Palermo (eds), 159–226. Hillsdale, NJ: Erlbaum.

Shields, C. 2003. *Order in Multiplicity: Homonymy in the Thought of Aristotle*. New York: Oxford University Press.

Shimamura, A. 2000. "Towards a Cognitive Neuroscience of Metacognition". *Consciousness and Cognition* **9**: 313–23.

Shipp, S. 2004. "Brain Circuitry of Attention". *Trends in Cognitive Science* **8**(5): 223–30.

Shoemaker, S. 1996a. "First-Person Access". In his *The First-Person Perspective and Other Essays*, 74–96. Cambridge: Cambridge University Press.

Shoemaker, S. 1996b. "Unity of Consciousness and Consciousness of Unity". In his *The First-Person Perspective and Other Essays*, 176–200. Cambridge: Cambridge University Press.

Shoemaker, S. 2003. "Consciousness and Co-consciousness". See Cleeremans (2003), 59–71.

Shoemaker, S. 2007. *Physical Realization*. New York: Oxford University Press.

Sider, T. 2003. "What's So Bad about Overdetermination?" *Philosophy and Phenomenological Research* **67**: 719–26.

Siewert, C. 1998. *The Significance of Consciousness*. Princeton, NJ: Princeton University Press.

Siewert, C. 2004. "Is Experience Transparent?" *Philosophical Studies* **117**: 15–41.

Simmons, W., A. Martin & L. Barsalou 2005. "Pictures of Appetizing Foods Activate Gustatory Cortices for Taste and Reward". *Cerebral Cortex* **14**: 1602–8.

Singer, W. 1999. "Neuronal Synchrony: A Versatile Code for the Definition of Relations?" *Neuron* **24**: 49–65.

Singer, W. 2001. "Consciousness and the Binding Problem". *Annals of the New York Academy of Sciences* **929** (April): 123–46.

Singer, W. 2004. "Synchrony, Oscillations, and Relational Codes". In *The Visual Neurosciences*, L. M. Chalupa & J. S. Werner (eds), 1665–81. Cambridge, MA: MIT Press.

Sklar, L. 1967. "Types of Intertheoretic Reduction". *British Journal for the Philosophy of Science* **18**: 109–24.

Skokowski, P. 2009. "Networks with Attitudes". *AI and Society* **23**: 461–70.

Smith, A. 2008. "Translucent Experiences". *Philosophical Studies* **140**: 197–212.

Solé, R. & J. Bascompte 2006. *Self-Organization in Complex Ecosystems*. Princeton, NJ: Princeton University Press.

Solé, R. & S. Valverde 2008. "Spontaneous Emergence of Modularity in Cellular Networks". *Journal of the Royal Society Interface* **5**: 129–33.

Solé, R., R. Ferrer-Cancho, J. Montoya & S. Valverde 2003. "Selection, Tinkering, and Emergence in Complex Networks: Crossing the Land of Tinkering". *Complexity* **8**(1): 20–33.

Sosa, E. 1984. "Mind–Body Interaction and Supervenient Causation". *Midwest Studies in Philosophy* **9**: 271–81.

Sosa, E. 1993. "Davidson's Thinking Causes". See Heil & Mele (1993), 3–17.

Sosa, E. 2002. "Privileged Access". In *Consciousness: New Philosophical Perspectives*, Q. Smith & A. Jokic (eds), 273–94. New York: Oxford University Press.

Spitsyna, G., J. Warren, S. Scott, F. Turkheimer & R. Wise 2006. "Converging Language Streams in the Human Temporal Lobe". *The Journal of Neuroscience* **26**(28): 7328–36.

Sporns, O., G. Tononi & G. M. Edelman 2000. "Theoretical Neuroanatomy: Relating Anatomical and Functional Connectivity in Graphs and Cortical Connection Matrices". *Cerebral Cortex* **10**: 127–41.

Squire, L., C. Stark & R. Clark 2004. "The Medial Temporal Lobe". *Annual Review of Neuroscience* **27**: 279–306.

Stapp, H. 2004. *Mind, Matter, and Quantum Mechanics*, 2nd edn. Berlin: Springer.

Stepanyants, A. & D. Chklovskii 2005. "Neurogeometry and Potential Plasticity of Synaptic Connectivity". *Neuron* **34**: 275–88.

Stephan, A. 1999. "Varieties of Emergentism". *Evolution and Cognition* **5**: 49–59.

Stich, S. 1983. *From Folk Psychology to Cognitive Science: The Case Against Belief*. Cambridge, MA: MIT Press.

Stich, S. 1994. "What Is a Theory of Representation?" See Stich & Warfield (1994), 347–64.

Stich, S. & T. Warfield (eds) 1994. *Mental Representation: A Reader*. Oxford: Blackwell.

Strawson, G. 1997. "The Self". *Journal of Consciousness Studies* **4**: 405–28.

Strawson, G. 2000. "The Phenomenology and Ontology of the Self". See Zahavi (2000b), 39–54.

Strevens, M. 2005a. *Bigger than Chaos: Understanding Complexity through Probability*. Cambridge, MA: Harvard University Press.

Strevens, M. 2005b. "How Are the Sciences of Complex Systems Possible?" *Philosophy of Science* **72**(4): 531–56.

Striedter, G. 2005. *Principles of Brain Evolution*. Sunderland, MA: Sinauer.

Sturm, W. & K. Willmes 2001. "On the Functional Neuroanatomy of Intrinsic and Phasic Alertness". *NeuroImage* **14**: S76–84.

Taglialatela, J., S. Savage-Rumbaugh & L. Baker 2003. "Vocal Production by a Language-competent *Pan paniscus*". *International Journal of Primatology* **24**(1): 1–16.

Taylor, J. G. 2003. "Paying Attention to Consciousness". *Progress in Neurobiology* **71**: 305–35.

Taylor, J. G. 2005. "Mind and Consciousness: Towards a Final Answer?" *Physics of Life Reviews* **2**: 1–45.

Taylor, J. G. 2006. "On the Neurodynamics of the Creation of Consciousness". *Cognitive Neurodynamics* **I**: 97–118.

Taylor, J. G. 2007. "CODAM: A Neural Network Model of Consciousness". *Neural Networks* **20**(9): 983–92.

Thompson, E. 2007. *Mind in Life: Biology, Phenomenology, and the Sciences of the Mind*. Cambridge, MA: Harvard University Press.

Thompson-Schill, S., M. Bedny & R. Goldberg 2005. "The Frontal Lobes and the Regulation of Mental Activity". *Current Opinion in Neurobiology* **15**: 219–24.

Tomasello, M., J. Call & B. Hare 2003. "Chimpanzees Understand Psychological States: The Question Is Which Ones and to What Extent". *Trends in Cognitive Science* **7**(4): 153–6.

Tomasello, M., M. Carpenter, J. Call, T. Behne & H. Moll 2005. "Understanding and Sharing Intentions: The Origins of Cultural Cognition". *Behavioral and Brain Sciences* **28**: 675–735.

Tonkonogy, J. & A. Puente 2009. *Localization of Clinical Syndromes in Neuropsychology and Neuroscience*. New York: Springer.

Tononi, G. 2004. "An Information Integration Theory of Consciousness". *BMC Neuroscience* **5**(42): 1–22.

Tononi, G. 2005. "Consciousness, Information Integration, and the Brain". See Laureys (2005), 109–26.

Tononi, G. & G. Edelman 1998. "Consciousness and Complexity". *Science* **282**: 1846–51.

Tononi, G. & O. Sporns 2003. "Measuring Information Integration". *BMC Neuroscience* **4**(31): 1–20.

Tononi, G., O. Sporns & G. Edelman 1994. "A Measure for Brain Complexity: Relating Functional Segregation and Integration in the Nervous System". *Proceedings of the National Academy of Sciences* **91**: 5033–7.

Torey, Z. 2009. *The Crucible of Consciousness: An Integrated Theory of Mind and Brain*. Cambridge, MA: MIT Press.

Torunchuk, J. & G. F. R. Ellis 2007. "Affective Neuronal Darwinism: The Nature of the Primary Emotional Systems", www.mth.uct.ac.za/~ellis/ToronchuK%20&%20Ellis,%202010.pdf (accessed November 2010).

Treisman, A. 1996. "The Binding Problem". *Current Opinion in Neurobiology* **6**: 171–8.

Treisman, A. 1998. "Feature Binding, Attention, and Object Perception". *Philosophical Transactions of the Royal Society B* **353**: 1295–306.

Treisman, A. 1999. "Solutions to the Binding Problem: Progress through Controversy and Convergence". *Neuron* **24**: 105–11.

Tschacher, W. & J.-P. Dauwalder (eds) 2003. *The Dynamical Systems Approach to Cognition: Concepts and Empirical Paradigms Based on Self-Organization, Embodiment, and Coordination Dynamics*. Singapore: World Scientific.

Turing, A. 1937. "On Computable Numbers, with an Application to the *Entscheidungsproblem*", *Proceedings of the London Mathematical Society*, 2nd series **42**: 230–65.

Turing, A. 1950. "Computing Machinery and Intelligence". *Mind* **59**: 433–60.

Turvey, M., R. Shaw, E. Reed & W. Mace 1981. "Ecological Laws of Perceiving and Acting: In Reply to Fodor and Pylyshyn". *Cognition* **9**: 237–304.

Tye, M. 1995. *Ten Problems of Consciousness*. Cambridge, MA: MIT Press.

Tye, M. 2000. *Consciousness, Color, and Content*. Cambridge, MA: MIT Press.

Tye, M. 2002. "Representationalism and the Transparency of Experience". *Noûs* **36**(1): 137–51.

Tye, M. 2003. *Consciousness and Persons*. Cambridge, MA: MIT Press.

Tye, M. 2009. *Consciousness Revisited*. Cambridge, MA: MIT Press.

Ullman, M. 2004. "Contributions of Memory Circuits to Language: The Declarative/Procedural Model". *Cognition* **92**: 231–70.

Uttal, W. 2001. *The New Phrenology*. Cambridge, MA: MIT Press.

Van Cleve, J. 1999. *Problems from Kant*. New York: Oxford University Press.

Van Gelder, T. 1991. "What is the D in PDP?" In *Philosophy and Connectionist Theory*, W. Ramsey, S. Stich & D. Rumelhart (eds), 39–59. Hillsdale, NJ: Erlbaum.

Van Gelder, T. 1995. "What Might Cognition Be, If Not Computation?" *Journal of Philosophy* **91** (July): 345–82.

Van Gelder, T. 1998. "The Dynamical Hypothesis in Cognitive Science". *Behavioral and Brain Sciences* **21**: 615–65.

Van Gulick, R. 2004. "Neural Correlates and the Diversity of Content". *Journal of Consciousness Studies* **11**(1): 82–6.

Van Gulick, R. 2006. "Mirror, Mirror – Is That All?" See Kriegel & Williford (2006), 11–40.

Verhagen, D. M., E. T. Rolls & M. Kadohisa 2003. "Neurons in the Primate Orbitofrontal Cortex Respond to Fat Texture Independently of Viscosity". *Journal of Neurophysiology* **90**: 1514–25.

Vogeley, K. & G. Fink 2003. "Neural Correlates of the First-person Perspective". *Trends in Cognitive Science* **7**(1): 38–42.

Von der Malsburg, C. 1995. "Network Self-organization in the Ontogenesis of the Mammalian

Visual System". In *An Introduction to Neural and Electronic Networks*, 2nd edn, S. F. Zornetzer, J. Davis & C. Lau (eds), 447–63. New York: Academic Press.

Von der Malsburg, C. 1999. "The What and Why of Binding: The Modeler's Perspective". *Neuron* **24**: 95–104.

Von der Malsburg, C. 2002. "Self-organization and the Brain". In *The Handbook of Brain Theory and Neural Networks*, M. Arbib (ed.), 840–43. Cambridge, MA: MIT Press.

Von der Malsburg, C. 2004. "Vision as an Exercise in Organic Computing". In *Informatik 2004 (Gesellschaft fur informatik)*, vol. 2, P. Dadam & M. Reichert (eds), 631–5.

Vul, E. & N. Kanwisher, in press. "Begging the Question: The Non-independence Error in fMRI Data Analysis". In *Foundations and Philosophy for Neuroimaging*, S. Hanson & M. Bunzl (eds). Cambridge, MA: MIT Press.

Vul, E., C. Harris, P. Winkielman & H. Pashler 2009. "Puzzlingly High Correlations in fMRI Studies of Emotion, Personality, and Social Cognition". *Perspective on Psychological Science* **4**(3): 274–90.

Wager, T. & E. Smith 2003. "Neuroimaging Studies of Working Memory: A Meta-analysis". *Cognitive, Affective and Behavioral Neuroscience* **3**: 255–74.

Wager, T., L. Barrett, E. Bliss-Moreau, K. Lundquist, S. Duncan & H. Kober 2008. "The Neuroimaging of Emotion". In *Handbook of Emotions*, 3rd edn, M. Lewis, J. Haviland-Jones & L. Barrett (eds), 249–71. New York: Guilford.

Wallace, R. 2005. *Consciousness: A Mathematical Treatment of the Neuronal Global Workspace Model*. New York: Springer.

Welshon, R. 1999. "Anomalous Monism and Epiphenomenalism". *Pacific Philosophical Quarterly* **80**(1): 103–20.

Welshon, R. 2010. "Working Memory, Neuroanatomy, and Archaeology". *Current Anthropology* **51**: S1–9.

White, I. & S. Wise 1999. "Rule-dependent Neuronal Activity in the Prefrontal Cortex". *Experimental Brain Research* **126**: 315–35.

Wiens, S. 2005. "Interoception in Emotional Experience". *Current Opinion in Neurology* **18**: 442–7.

Wilkins, W. & J. Wakefield 1995. "Brain Evolution and Neurolinguistic Preconditions". *Behavioral and Brain Sciences* **18**(1): 161–226.

Wilson, R. 2004. *Boundaries of the Mind: The Individual in the Fragile Sciences: Cognition*. Cambridge: Cambridge University Press.

Wilson, R. & A. Clark 2009. "How to Situate Cognition: Letting Nature Take Its Course". See Robbins & Aydede (2009), 55–77.

Wiseman, H. & J. Eisert 2007. "Nontrivial Quantum Effects in Biology: A Skeptical Physicist's View," http://arxiv.org/PS_cache/arxiv/pdf/0705/0705.1232v2.pdf (accessed November 2010).

Wynn, T. 1998. "Did *Homo erectus* Speak?" *Cambridge Archaeological Journal* **8**: 78–81.

Wynn, T. 2002. "Archaeology and Cognitive Evolution". *Behavioral and Brain Sciences* **25**: 389–402.

Wynn, T. & F. L. Coolidge 2004. "The Expert Neanderthal Mind". *Journal of Human Evolution* **46**: 467–87.

Wynn, T. & F. L. Coolidge 2006. "The Effect of Enhanced Working Memory on Language". *Journal of Human Evolution* **50**: 230–31.

Yablo, S. 1997. "Wide Causation". *Philosophical Perspectives* **11**: 251–81.

Zahavi, D. 2000a. "Self and Consciousness". See Zahavi (2000b), 55–74.

Zahavi, D. (ed.) 2000b. *Exploring the Self*. Amsterdam: John Benjamins.

Zahavi, D. 2008. *Subjectivity and Selfhood: Investigating the First-Person Perspective*. Cambridge, MA: MIT Press.

Zeki, S. & A. Bartels 1998. "The Autonomy of the Visual Systems and the Modularity of Conscious Vision". *Philosophical Transactions of the Royal Society B* **353**(1377): 1911–2.

INDEX